Reactive Systems

A reactive system comprises networks of computing components, achieving their goals through interaction among themselves and their environment. Thus even relatively small systems may exhibit unexpectedly complex behaviours. As, moreover, reactive systems are often used in safety critical systems, the need for mathematically based formal methodology is increasingly important. There are many books that look at particular methodologies for such systems. This book offers a more balanced introduction for graduate students and describes the various approaches, their strengths and weaknesses and when they are best used. Milner's CCS and its operational semantics are introduced, together with the notions of behavioural equivalences based on bisimulation techniques and with recursive extensions of Hennessy-Milner logic. In the second part of the book the presented theories are extended to take timing issues into account. The book has arisen from various courses taught in Denmark and Iceland and is designed to give students a broad introduction to the area, with exercises throughout.

LUCA ACETO is Professor of Computer Science at Reykjavík University, Iceland, and Aalborg University, Denmark.

ANNA INGÓLFSDÓTTIR is Professor of Computer Science at Reykjavík University, Iceland, and Aalborg University, Denmark.

KIM G. LARSEN is Professor of Computer Science at Aalborg University, Denmark, and Twente University, The Netherlands.

JIŘÍ SRBA is Associate Professor in Computer Science at Aalborg University, Denmark.

'Many modern-day computing systems are reactive in nature; they persist indefinitely, responding to the interactions of users, and updating their internal structures accordingly. Over the last two decades, an elegant theory of these reactive systems has emerged, and is being increasingly applied in industrial settings.

And at last we have an accessible textbook for this area, written by a team who have played a central role in the development of the underlying theory, and the software tools which are essential to its successful application. It treats both timed and untimed systems and, although the underlying theory is carefully and methodically explained, the main trust of the book is to engage students with the material via a wealth of thought-provoking examples.

The clarity of the exposition is exceptional; it presents the essential ideas clearly, avoiding unnecessary detail, but at the same time has well-chosen pointers to more advanced concepts. The book is destined to become the standard textbook for reactive systems.'

Matthew Hennessy, Sussex University

'A must for anybody interested in formal analysis techniques for computing systems.'

Wan Fokkink, Vrije Universiteit Amsterdam

'This book is a gentle introduction to the basics of theories of interactive systems that starts with an introduction to CCS and its semantic theory and then moves to introducing modal logics and timed models of concurrency. By means of a number of small but intriguing examples and by using software tools based on sound theoretical principles, it leads the reader to appreciating and mastering a number of process algebra-based techniques that are also having a great impact outside academic circles.

The authors have managed to concentrate their expertise, enthusiasm and pedagogical ability in less than 300 pages. The presentation is very clear and conveys sufficient intuition to make the book appropriate also for students with limited mathematical background. An excellent advanced undergraduate text.'

Rocco De Nicola, Universitá di Firenze

'This book offers an introduction to model-based verification of reactive systems, a technology that is essential to all IT-developers of the future, given the global trend in information technology towards ubiquitous computing.

The book is unique in its pedagogical style, introducing the required theory (of models and specification formalisms for reactive systems) motivated carefully with its applications (in the development and use of automated verification tools in practice), and written as a textbook that can be used readily at many different levels of IT-related curricula.'

Mogens Nielsen, Aarhus University

Reactive Systems

Modelling, Specification and Verification

Luca Aceto[1,2] Anna Ingólfsdóttir[1,2]
Kim G. Larsen[1] Jiří Srba[1]

1 Department of Computer Science, Aalborg University, 9220 Aalborg Ø, Denmark
2 Department of Computer Science, School of Science and Engineering, Reykjavík University, Iceland

CAMBRIDGE
UNIVERSITY PRESS

CAMBRIDGE UNIVERSITY PRESS
Cambridge, New York, Melbourne, Madrid, Cape Town, Singapore, São Paulo

Cambridge University Press
The Edinburgh Building, Cambridge CB2 8RU, UK

Published in the United States of America by Cambridge University Press, New York

www.cambridge.org
Information on this title: www.cambridge.org/9780521875462

First published 2007

Printed in the United Kingdom at the University Press, Cambridge

A catalogue record for this publication is available from the British Library

ISBN 978-0-521-87546-2 hardback

Contents

v

Figures and tables

Figures

Tables

Preface

This book is based on courses that have been held at Aalborg University and at Reykjavík University over the last six years or so. The aim of these semester-long courses has been to introduce computer science students, at an early stage of their M.Sc. degrees or late in their B.Sc. degree studies, to the theory of concurrency and to its applications in the modelling and analysis of reactive systems. This is an area of formal-methods study that is finding increasing application outside academic circles and allows students to appreciate how techniques and software tools based on sound theoretical principles are very useful in the design and analysis of non-trivial reactive computing systems.

In order to carry this message across to students in the most effective way, the courses on which the material in this book is based have presented:

- some prime models used in the theory of concurrency (with special emphasis on state-transition models of computation such as labelled transition systems and timed automata);
- languages for describing actual systems and their specifications (with a focus on classic algebraic process calculi such as Milner's calculus of communicating systems and logics such modal and temporal logics); and
- the embodiment of these models and languages in tools for the automatic verification of computing systems.

The use of the theory and the associated software tools in the modelling and analysis of computing systems is a very important component in our courses, since it gives the students hands-on experience in the application of what they have learned and reinforces their belief that the theory they are studying is indeed useful and worth mastering. Once we succeed in awakening an interest in the theory of concurrency and its applications amongst students, it will be more likely that at least some will decide to pursue an in-depth study of the more advanced, and mathematically sophisticated, aspects of our field – perhaps, during M.Sc. thesis work or at a doctoral level.

It has been very satisfying for us to witness a change in attitude in the students taking our courses over the years. Indeed, we have gone from a state in which most students saw very little point in taking the course on which this material is based to one in which the relevance of the material we cover is uncontroversial to many of them! At the time when an early version of our course was elective at Aalborg University, and taken only by a few mathematically inclined individuals, one student remarked in his course evaluation form 'This course ought to be mandatory for computer science students.' Now the course is indeed mandatory; it is attended by all M.Sc. students in computer science at Aalborg University, and most of them happily play with the theory and tools we introduce in the course.

How did this change in attitude come about? And why do we believe that this is an important change? In order to answer these questions, it might be best to describe first the general area of computer science to which this textbook aims at contributing.

The correctness problem and its importance   Computer scientists build artifacts (implemented in hardware, or software or, as is the case in the fast growing area of embedded and interactive systems, a combination of both) that are supposed to offer some well-defined services to their users. Since these computing systems are deployed in very large numbers, and often control crucial and even safety-critical industrial processes, it is vital that they implement the specification of their intended behaviour correctly. The problem of ascertaining whether a computing system does indeed offer the behaviour described by its specification is called the *correctness problem* and is one of the most fundamental problems in computer science. The field of computer science that studies languages for the description of (models of) computer systems and their specifications and (possibly automated) methods for establishing the correctness of systems with respect to their specifications is called *algorithmic verification*.

Despite its fundamental scientific and practical importance, however, twentieth-century computer and communication technology did not pay sufficient attention to the correctness and dependability of systems in its drive toward faster and cheaper products. (See the editorial Patterson (2005) by a former president of the ACM for forceful arguments to this effect.) As a result, system crashes are commonplace, sometimes leading to very costly and even disastrous system failures, such as Intel's Pentium-II bug in the floating-point division unit Pratt (1995) and the crash of the Ariane-5 rocket due to the conversion of a 64-bit real number to a 16-bit integer (Lions, 1996).

Classic engineering disciplines have a time-honoured and effective approach to building artifacts that meet their intended specifications: before actually constructing the artifacts, engineers develop models of the design to be built and subject them to a thorough analysis. Surprisingly, such an approach has only recently been used extensively in the development of computing systems.

This textbook, and the courses we have given over the years based on the material it presents, stem from our deep conviction that every well-educated twenty-first-century computer scientist should be well versed in the technology of algorithmic model-based verification. Indeed, as recent advances in algorithmic verification and applications of model checking (Clarke, Gruemberg and Peled, 1999) have shown, the tools and ideas developed within these fields can be used to analyse designs of considerable complexity that, until a few years ago, were thought to be intractable using formal analysis and modelling tools. (Companies such as AT&T, Cadence, Fujitsu, HP, IBM, Intel, Motorola, NEC, Siemens and Sun – to mention but a few – are using these tools increasingly in their own designs to reduce the time to market and to ensure product quality.)

We believe that the availability of automatic software tools for the model-based analysis of systems is one of the two main factors behind the increasing interest amongst students and practitioners alike in model-based verification technology. Another is the realization that even small reactive systems – for instance, relatively short concurrent algorithms – exhibit very complex behaviours, owing to their interactive nature. Unlike in the setting of sequential software, it is therefore not hard for students to realize that systematic and formal analysis techniques *are useful*, even when not altogether necessary, in obtaining some level of confidence in the correctness of designs. The tool support that is now available to explore the behaviour of models of systems expressed as collections of interacting state machines of some sort should make the theory presented in this textbook very appealing for many students at several levels of their studies.

It is our firmly held belief that only by teaching the beautiful theory of concurrent systems, together with its applications and associated verification tools, to our students shall we be able to transfer the available technology to industry and improve the reliability of embedded software and other reactive systems. We hope that this textbook will offer a small contribution to this pedagogical endeavour.

Why this book? This book is by no means the first devoted to aspects of the theory of reactive systems. Some books that have been published in this area over the last 20 years or so are Baeten and Weijland (1990), Fokkink (2000), Hennessy (1988), Hoare (1985), Magee and Kramer (1999), Milner (1989), Roscoe (1999), Schneider (1999) and Stirling (2001), to mention but a few. However, unlike all the aforementioned books except Fokkink (2000), Magee and Kramer (1999) and Schneider (1999), the present book was written explicitly to serve as a *textbook*, and it offers a distinctive pedagogical approach to its subject matter that derives from our extensive use in the classroom of the material presented here in book form. In writing this textbook we have striven to transfer to paper the spirit of the lectures on which this text is based. Our readers will find that the style is often colloquial and attempts to mimic the Socratic dialogue with which we try to entice our student audience to take an active part in the lectures and associated exercise sessions. Explanations of the material presented in this textbook are interspersed with questions to our readers and exercises that invite the readers to check straight away whether they understand the material, as it is being presented. We believe that this makes the book suitable for self-study, as well as for use as the main reference text in courses ranging from advanced B.Sc. courses to M.Sc. courses in computer science and related subjects.

Of course, it is not up to us to say whether we have succeeded in conveying the spirit of the lectures in the book you now hold in your hands, but we sincerely hope that our readers will experience some of the excitement that we still have in teaching this material and seeing our students appreciate it and we hope that readers will enjoy working with concurrency theory and the tools it offers for the analysis of reactive systems.

For the instructor   We have used much of the material presented in this textbook in several one-semester courses at Aalborg University and at Reykjavík University, amongst others. These courses usually consist of about 30 hours of lectures and a similar number of hours of exercise sessions, where the students solve exercises and work on projects related to the material in the course. As stated above, we believe strongly that these practical sessions play a very important role in enabling students to appreciate the importance of the theory they are learning and to understand it in depth. Examples of recent courses based on this book may be found at the URL

www.cs.aau.dk/rsbook/.

There the instructor will find suggested schedules for his or her courses, exercises that can be used to supplement those in the textbook, links to other useful teaching resources available on the web, further suggestions for student projects and electronic slides that can be used for the lectures. (As an example, we usually supplement lectures covering the material in this textbook with from four to six 45-minute lectures on binary decision diagrams (Bryant, 1992), and their use in verification; these are based on Henrik Reif Andersen's excellent lecture notes (Andersen, 1998), which are freely available on the web, and on Randel Bryant's survey paper (Bryant, 1992).)

We recommend that the teaching of the material covered in this book be accompanied by the use of software tools for verification and validation. In our courses, we usually employ the Edinburgh Concurrency Workbench (Cleaveland, Parrow and Steffen, 1993) for the part of the course devoted to classic reactive systems and, not surprisingly, UPPAAL (Behrmann, David and Larsen, 2004) for lectures on real-time systems. Both these tools are freely available and their use makes the theoretical material covered during the lectures come alive for the students. Using these tools the students will be able to analyse systems of considerable complexity, and we suggest that courses based upon this book be accompanied by a couple of practical projects involving the use of these, or similar, tools for verification and validation.

We shall maintain a page with all the supporting material and other useful resources for students and instructors alike at the URL

www.cs.aau.dk/rsbook/.

In writing this book, we have tried to be at once pedagogical, careful and precise. However, despite our efforts, we are sure that there is still room for improvement in this text and for the correction of any mistake that may have escaped our attention. We shall use the above web page to inform the reader about additions and modifications to this book.

We welcome corrections (typographical or otherwise), comments and suggestions from our readers. You can contact us by sending an email to the address

rsbook@cs.aau.dk

with subject line 'RS Book'.

Historical remarks and acknowledgments   As already stated we have used this material in its present form for courses given at several institutions during the last few years. However, the story of its development is much older and goes back at least to 1986. During that year, the third author (Kim G. Larsen, then a freshly minted Ph.D. graduate from Edinburgh University) took up an academic position at Aalborg University. He immediately began designing a course on the theory of concurrency – the branch of theoretical computer science that he had worked on during his doctoral studies, under the supervision of Robin Milner. His aim was to use the course, and the accompanying set of notes and slides, to attract students to his research area by conveying his enthusiasm for it as well as his belief that the theory of concurrency is important in applications. That material has stood the 'lecture-room test' well and forms the basis for the first part of the book.

The development of those early courses was strongly influenced by the teaching and supervision of Robin Milner that Kim G. Larsen enjoyed during his doctoral studies in Edinburgh and would not have been possible without them. Even though the other three authors were not Milner's students themselves, the strong intellectual influence of his work and writings on their view of concurrency theory will probably be evident to the readers of this book. Indeed, the 'Edinburgh concurrency-theory school' features prominently in the academic genealogy of each of the authors. For example, Rocco De Nicola and Matthew Hennessy had a strong influence on the view of concurrency theory and/or the work of Luca Aceto and Anna Ingólfsdóttir, and Jiří Srba enjoyed the liberal supervision of Mogens Nielsen.

The material upon which the courses we have held at Aalborg University and elsewhere since the late 1980s were based has undergone gradual change before reaching the present form. Over the years, the part of the course devoted to Milner's calculus of communicating systems and its underlying theory has decreased, and so has the emphasis on some topics of mostly theoretical interest. At the same time, the course material has grown to include models and specification languages for real-time systems. The present material aims at offering a good balance between classic and real-time systems, and between the theory and its applications.

Overall, as already stated, the students' appreciation of the theoretical material covered here has been greatly increased by the availability of software tools based on it. We thank all the developers of the tools we use in our teaching; their work has made our subject matter come alive for our students and has been instrumental in achieving whatever level of success we might have had in our teaching based on this textbook.

This book was partly written while Luca Aceto was on leave from Aalborg University at Reykjavík University, Anna Ingólfsdóttir was working at deCODE Genetics and Jiří Srba was visiting the University of Stuttgart, sponsored by a grant from the Alexander von Humboldt Foundation. They thank these institutions for their hospitality and excellent working conditions. Luca Aceto and Anna Ingólfsdóttir were partly supported by the project 'The Equational Logic of Parallel Processes' (No. 060013021) of The Icelandic Research Fund. Jiří Srba received partial support from a grant of the Ministry of Education of the Czech Republic, project No. 1M0545.

We thank Silvio Capobianco, Pierre-Louis Curien, Gudmundur Hreidarson, Rocco De Nicola, Ralph Leibmann, MohammadReza Mousavi, Guy Vidal-Naquet and the students of the Concurrency Course (Concurrence) (number 2-3) 2004–5,

Master Parisien de Recherche en Informatique, for useful comments on and corrections of drafts of this text.

The authors used drafts of the book in courses taught in the spring terms of 2004, 2005 and 2006 and in the autumn term of 2006 at Aalborg University, Reykjavík University and the University of Iceland. The students who took those courses offered valuable feedback on the text and gave us detailed lists of errata. We thank Claus Brabrand for using a draft of the first part of this book in his course 'Semantics' (Q1, 2005 and 2006) at Aarhus University. The suggestions from Claus and his students helped us improve the text further. Moreover, Claus and Martin Mosegaard designed and implemented an excellent simulator for Milner's calculus of communicating systems and the 'bisimulation-game' game, which our students can use to experiment with the behaviour of processes written in this language and to play the bisimulation game described in the textbook.

Last, but not least, we thank David Tranah at Cambridge University Press for his enthusiasm for our project and also the three anonymous reviewers, who provided useful comments on a draft of this book.

Any remaining infelicity is solely our responsibility.

Luca Aceto and Anna Ingólfsdóttir dedicate this book to their son Róbert, to Anna's sons Logi and Kári and to Luca's mother, Imelde Diomede Aceto. Kim Larsen dedicates the book to his wife Merete and to his two daughters Mia and Trine. Finally, Jiří Srba dedicates the book to his parents, Jaroslava and Jiří and to his wife, Vanda.

Part I

A Classic Theory of Reactive Systems

1

Introduction

Aims of this book

The aim of the first part of this book is to introduce three basic notions that we shall use to describe, specify and analyse reactive systems, namely

- Milner's calculus of communicating systems (CCS) (Milner, 1989),
- the model known as labelled transition systems (LTSs) (Keller, 1976), and
- Hennessy–Milner logic (HML) (Hennessy and Milner, 1985) and its extension with recursive definitions of formulae (Larsen, 1990).

We shall present a general theory of reactive systems and its applications. In particular, we intend to show the following:

1. how to describe actual systems using terms in our chosen models (i.e. either as terms in the process description language CCS or as labelled transition systems);
2. how to offer specifications of the desired behaviour of systems either as terms of our models or as formulae in HML; and
3. how to manipulate these descriptions, possibly (semi-)automatically, in order to analyse the behaviour of the model of the system under consideration.

In the second part of the book, we shall introduce a similar trinity of basic notions that will allow us to describe, specify and analyse real-time systems – that is, systems whose behaviour depends crucially on timing constraints. There we shall present the formalisms of timed automata (Alur and Dill, 1994) and timed CCS (Yi, 1990, 1991a, b) to describe real-time systems, the model of timed

1

labelled transition systems (TLTSs) and a real-time version of Hennessy–Milner logic (Laroussinie, Larsen and Weise, 1995).

After having worked through the material in this book, you should be able to describe non-trivial reactive systems and their specifications using the aforementioned models and verify the correctness of a model of a system with respect to given specifications either manually or by using automatic verification tools such as the Edinburgh Concurrency Workbench (Cleaveland, Parrow and Steffen, 1993) and the model checker for real-time systems UPPAAL (Behrmann, David and Larsen, 2004).

Our, somewhat ambitious, aim is therefore to present a model of reactive systems that supports their design, specification and verification. Moreover, since many real-life systems are hard to analyse manually, we should like to have computer support for our verification tasks. This means that all the models and languages that we shall use in this book need to have a *formal* syntax and semantics. (The *syntax* of a language consists of the rules governing the formation of statements, whereas its *semantics* assigns meaning to each of the syntactically correct statements in the language.) These requirements of formality are not only necessary in order to be able to build computer tools for the analysis of system descriptions but are also fundamental in agreeing upon what the terms in our models are actually intended to describe in the first place. Moreover, as Donald Knuth once wrote:

> A person does not really understand something until after teaching it to a computer, i.e. expressing it as an algorithm.... An attempt to formalize things as algorithms leads to a much deeper understanding than if we simply try to comprehend things in the traditional way.

The pay-off from using formal models with an explicit formal semantics to describe our systems will therefore be the possibility of devising algorithms for the animation, simulation and verification of system models. These would be impossible to obtain if our models were specified only in an informal notation.

Now that, it is hoped, you know what to expect from this book, it is time to get to work. We shall begin our journey through the beautiful land of concurrency theory by introducing a prototype description language for reactive systems and its semantics. However, before setting off on such an enterprise, we should describe in more detail what we actually mean by the term 'reactive system'.

1.1   What are reactive systems?

The 'standard' view of computing systems is that, at a high level of abstraction, these may be considered as black boxes that take inputs and provide appropriate outputs. This view agrees with the description of algorithmic problems. An *algorithmic problem* is specified by a collection of legal inputs, and, for each legal input, its expected output. In an imperative setting, an abstract view of a computing system may therefore be given by describing how it transforms an initial *state* – i.e. a function from variables to their values – to a final state. This function will, in general, be *partial*, i.e. it may be undefined for some initial states, in order to capture that the behaviour of a computing system may be non-terminating for some input states. For example, the effect of the program

$$S = z \leftarrow x; x \leftarrow y; y \leftarrow z$$

is described by the function $[\![S]\!]$ from states to states, defined thus:

$$[\![S]\!] = \lambda s.\ s[x \mapsto s(y), y \mapsto s(x), z \mapsto s(x)],$$

where the new state $s[x \mapsto s(y), y \mapsto s(x), z \mapsto s(x)]$ is that in which the value of variable x is the value of y in state s and that of variables y and z is the value of x in state s. The values of all the other variables are those they had in state s. This state transformation is a way of describing formally that the intended effect of S is essentially to swap the values of the variables x and y.

However, the effect of the program

$$U = \textbf{while true do skip},$$

where we use **skip** to stand for 'no operation', is described by the *partial* function from states to states given by

$$[\![U]\!] = \lambda s.\ \text{undefined},$$

i.e. the always undefined function. This captures the fact that the computation of U never produces a result (final state), irrespective of the initial state.

In this view of computing systems, non-termination is a highly undesirable phenomenon. An algorithm that fails to terminate on some inputs is not one the users of a computing system would expect to have to use. A moment of reflection, however, should make us realize that we already use many computing systems whose behaviour cannot be readily described as a function from inputs to outputs – not least because, at some level of abstraction, these systems are inherently meant to be non-terminating. Examples of such computing systems are

- operating systems,
- communication protocols,
- control programs, and
- software running in embedded system devices such as mobile telephones.

At a high level of abstraction, the behaviour of a control program can be seen to be governed by the following pseudocode algorithm skeleton:

loop
    read the sensors' values at regular intervals
    depending on the sensors' values trigger the relevant actuators
forever

These and many others are examples of computing systems that interact with their environment by exchanging information with it. Like the neurons in a human brain, these systems react to stimuli from their computing environment (in the example control program above, these are variations in the values of the sensors) by possibly changing their state or mode of computation and, in turn, influence their environment by sending back some signals to it or initiating some operations that affect the computing environment (this is the role played by the actuators in the example control program). David Harel and Amir Pnueli coined the term *reactive system* in Harel and Pnueli (1985) to describe a system that, like those mentioned above, computes by reacting to stimuli from its environment.

As the above examples and discussion indicate, reactive systems are inherently parallel systems and a key role in their behaviour is played by communication and interaction with their computing environment. A 'standard' computing system can also be viewed as a reactive system in which interaction with the environment takes place only at the beginning of the computation (when inputs are fed to the computing device) and at the end (when the output is received). However, all the example systems given before maintain a continuous interaction with their environment, and we may think of the computing system and its environment as parallel processes that communicate with each other. In addition, as again nicely exemplified by the skeleton of a control program given above, non-termination is a *desirable* feature of some reactive systems. In contrast to the setting of 'standard' computing systems, we certainly do *not* expect the operating systems running on our computers or the control program monitoring a nuclear reactor to terminate!

Now that we have an idea of what reactive systems are, and of the key aspects of their behaviour, we can begin to consider what an appropriate abstract model for this class of systems should offer. In particular, such a model should allow us to describe the behaviour of collections of (possibly non-terminating) parallel processes that may compute independently or interact with one another. It should provide us with facilities for the description of well-known phenomena that appear in the presence of concurrency and are familiar to us from the world of operating systems and parallel computation in general (e.g., deadlock, livelock, starvation and so on). Finally, in order to abstract from implementation-dependent issues having to do with, say, scheduling policies, the chosen model should permit a clean description of *non-determinism* – a most useful modelling tool in computer science.

Our aim in the remainder of this book will be to present a general-purpose theory that can be used to describe, and reason about, *any* collection of interacting processes. The approach that we shall present will make use of a collection of models and formal techniques that is often referred to as *process theory*. The key ingredients in this approach are

- (process) algebra,
- automata or labelled transition systems,
- structural operational semantics, and
- logic.

These ingredients give the foundations for the development of (semi-)automatic verification tools for reactive systems that support various formal methods for validation and verification, which can be applied to the analysis of highly non-trivial computing systems. The development of these tools requires in turn advances in algorithmics and via the increasing complexity of the analysed designs feeds back to the theory-development phase by suggesting the invention of new languages and models for the description of reactive systems.

Unlike in the setting of sequential programs, where we would often prefer to believe that the development of correct programs can be done without any recourse to 'formalism', it is a well-recognized fact of life that the behaviour of even very short parallel programs may be very hard to analyse and understand. Indeed, analyzing these programs requires a careful consideration of issues related to the interactions amongst their components, and even imagining these is often a mind-boggling task. As a result, the techniques and tools that we shall present in this book are becoming widely accepted in the academic and industrial communities that develop reactive systems.

1.2 Process algebras

The first ingredient in the approach to the theory of reactive systems presented in this book is a prototypical example of a *process algebra*. Process algebras are prototype specification languages for reactive systems. They have evolved from the insights of many outstanding researchers over the last 30 years, and a brief history of the ideas that led to their development may be found in Baeten (2005). (For an accessible, but more advanced, discussion of the role that algebra plays in process theory, the reader could consult the survey paper Luttik (2006).) A crucial initial observation at the heart of the notion of process algebra is due to Milner, who noticed that concurrent processes have an algebraic structure. For example, once we have built two separate processes P and Q, we can form a new process by combining P and Q sequentially or in parallel. The results of these combinations will be new processes whose behaviour depends on that of P and Q and on the *operation* that we have used to compose them. This is the first sense in which these description languages are algebraic: they consist of a collection of operations for building new process descriptions from existing ones.

Since these languages aim at specifying parallel processes that may interact with one another, a key issue that needs to be addressed is how to describe communication or interaction between processes running at the same time. Communication amounts to information exchange between a process that produces the information (the *sender*) and a process that consumes it (the *receiver*). We often think of this communication of information as taking place via a *medium* that connects the sender and the receiver. If we are to develop a theory of communicating systems based on this view, we have to decide upon the communication medium used in inter-process communication. Several possible choices immediately come to mind. Processes may communicate via, for example, (un)bounded buffers, shared variables, some unspecified ether or the tuple spaces used by Linda-like languages (Gelernter, 1985). Which one do we choose? The answer is not at all clear, and each specific choice may in fact reduce the applicability of our language and the models that support it. A language that can properly describe processes that communicate via, say, FIFO buffers may not readily allow us to specify situations in which processes interact via, say, shared variables.

The solution to this riddle is both conceptually simple and general. A crucial original insight of figures such as Hoare and Milner was that we need not distinguish between active components, such as senders and receivers, and passive ones such as the communication media mentioned above. They may all be viewed as processes – i.e. as systems that exhibit behaviour. All these processes can interact via message-passing modelled as *synchronized communication*, which is the only basic mode of interaction. This is the key idea underlying Hoare's Communicating Sequential Processes (CSP) (Hoare, 1978, 1985), a highly influential proposal for a programming language for parallel programs, and Milner's Calculus of Communicating Systems (CCS) (Milner, 1989), the paradigmatic process algebra.

2

The language CCS

We shall now introduce Milner's Calculus of Communicating Systems (CCS). We begin by informally presenting the process constructions allowed in this language, and their semantics, in Section 2.1. Then, in Section 2.2, we proceed to put our developments on a more formal footing.

2.1 Some CCS process constructions

It is useful to begin by thinking of a CCS process as a black box. This black box may have a name that identifies it, and it has a *process interface*. This interface describes the collection of *communication ports*, also referred to as *channels*, that the process may use to interact with other processes that reside in its environment, together with an indication of whether it uses these ports for inputting or outputting information. For example, the drawing in Figure 2.1 pictures the interface for a process whose name is CS (for computer scientist). This process may interact with its environment via three ports, or communication channels, namely 'coffee', '$\overline{\text{coin}}$' and '$\overline{\text{pub}}$'. The port 'coffee' is used by process CS for input, whereas the ports '$\overline{\text{coin}}$' and '$\overline{\text{pub}}$' are used for output. In general, given a port name a we use $\bar{a}$ for the output on port a. We shall often refer to labels such as coffee or $\overline{\text{coin}}$ as *actions*.

A description like the one given in Figure 2.1 only gives static information about a process. What we are most interested in is the *behaviour* of the process being specified. The behaviour of a process is described by giving a 'CCS program'. The idea is that, as we shall soon see, the process constructions that are used in building the program allow us to describe both the structure of the process and its behaviour.

7

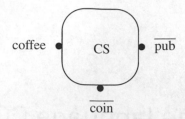

Figure 2.1 The interface for the process CS.

Inaction, prefixing and recursive definitions   Let us begin by introducing the constructs of the language CCS, by means of examples. The most basic process of all is the process **0** (read 'nil'). This performs no action whatsoever. The process **0** offers the prototypical example of a deadlocked behaviour – one that cannot proceed any further in its computation.

The most basic process constructor in CCS is *action prefixing*. Two example processes built using **0** and action prefixing are a match and a complex match, described by the expressions

$$\text{strike.0} \quad \text{and} \quad \text{take.strike.0},$$

respectively. Intuitively, a match is a process that dies after it has been performed (i.e. that becomes the process **0** after executing the *action* strike), and a complex match is one that needs to be taken hold of before it can behave like a match. More generally, the formation rule for action prefixing says that

if P is a process and a is a label then $a.P$ is also a process.

The idea is that a label such as strike or $\overline{\text{pub}}$ will denote an input or output action on a communication port and that the process $a.P$ is one that begins by performing action a and behaves like P thereafter.

We have already mentioned that processes can be given names, very much as procedures can. This means that we can introduce names for (complex) processes and that we can use these names in defining other process descriptions. For instance, we can give the name Match to the complex match defined thus:

$$\text{Match} \stackrel{\text{def}}{=} \text{take.strike.0}.$$

The introduction of names for processes allows us to give recursive definitions of process behaviours – compare with the recursive definition of procedures or methods in your favourite programming language. For instance, we may define the behaviour of an everlasting clock thus:

$$\text{Clock} \stackrel{\text{def}}{=} \text{tick.Clock}.$$

Note that, since the process name Clock is a short-hand for the term on the right-hand side of the above equation, we may repeatedly replace the name Clock with its definition to obtain that

$$
\begin{aligned}
\text{Clock} &\stackrel{\text{def}}{=} \text{tick.Clock} \\
&= \text{tick.tick.Clock} \\
&= \text{tick.tick.tick.Clock} \\
&\;\;\vdots \\
&= \underbrace{\text{tick.\ldots.tick}}_{n \text{ times}}.\text{Clock},
\end{aligned}
$$

for each positive integer n.

As another recursive process specification, consider that of a simple coffee vending machine:

$$
\text{CM} \stackrel{\text{def}}{=} \text{coin}.\overline{\text{coffee}}.\text{CM}. \tag{2.1}
$$

This is a machine that is willing to accept a coin as input, deliver coffee to its customer and thereafter return to its initial state.

Choice The CCS constructs that we have presented so far would not allow us to describe the behaviour of a vending machine that allows its paying customer to choose between tea and coffee, say. In order to allow for the description of processes whose behaviour may follow different patterns of interaction with their environment, CCS offers the *choice operator*, which is written '$+$'. For example, a vending machine offering either tea or coffee may be described thus:

$$
\text{CTM} \stackrel{\text{def}}{=} \text{coin}.(\overline{\text{coffee}}.\text{CTM} + \overline{\text{tea}}.\text{CTM}). \tag{2.2}
$$

The idea here is that, after having received a coin as input, the process CTM is willing to deliver either coffee or tea, depending on its customer's choice. In general, the formation rule for choice states that

if P and Q are processes then so is $P + Q$.

The process $P + Q$ is one that has the initial capabilities of both P and Q. However, choosing to perform initially an action from P will pre-empt the further execution of actions from Q, and vice versa.

Exercise 2.1 *Give a CCS process which describes a clock that ticks at least once and may stop ticking after each clock tick.* ◆

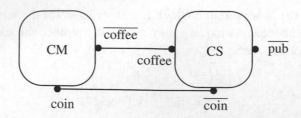

Figure 2.2 The interface for the process CM | CS.

Exercise 2.2 *Give a CCS process which describes a coffee machine that may behave like that given by (2.1) but may also steal the money it receives and fail at any time.*   ◆

Exercise 2.3 *A finite process graph T is a quadruple* (Q, A, δ, q_0)*, where*

- Q *is a finite set of states,*
- A *is a finite set of labels,*
- $q_0 \in Q$ *is the start state, and*
- $\delta : Q \times A \to 2^Q$ *is the transition function.*

Using the operators introduced so far, give a CCS process that describes T*.*   ◆

Parallel composition   It is well known that a computer scientist working in a research university is a machine for turning coffee into publications. The behaviour of such an academic may be described by the CCS process

$$CS \stackrel{\text{def}}{=} \overline{\text{pub}}.\overline{\text{coin}}.\text{coffee}.CS. \tag{2.3}$$

As made explicit by the above description, a computer scientist is initially keen to produce a publication – possibly straight from her doctoral dissertation – but she needs coffee to produce her next publication. Coffee is only available through interaction with the departmental coffee machine CM. In order to describe systems consisting of two or more processes running in parallel, and possibly interacting with each other, CCS offers the *parallel composition operation*, which is written '|'. For example, the CCS expression CM | CS describes a system consisting of two processes – the coffee machine CM and the computer scientist CS – that run in parallel one with the other. These two processes may communicate via the communication ports they share and use in complementary fashion, namely 'coffee' and 'coin'. By complementary, we mean that one process uses the port for input and the other for output. Potential communications are represented in Figure 2.2 by the solid lines linking complementary ports. The port 'pub', however, is used by the computer scientist to communicate with her research environment or, more

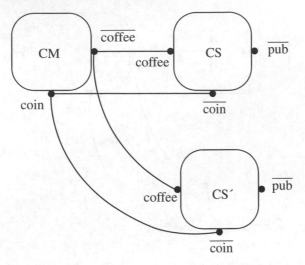

Figure 2.3 The interface for the process CM | CS | CS'.

prosaically, with other processes that may be present in her environment and that are willing to accept input along that port. One important thing to note is that the link between complementary ports in Figure 2.2 denotes that it is *possible* for the computer scientist and the coffee machine to communicate in the parallel composition CM | CS. However, we do *not* require that they must communicate with one another. Both the computer scientist and the coffee machine could use their complementary ports to communicate with other reactive systems in their environment. For example, another computer scientist CS' could use the coffee machine CM and, in so doing, make sure that he can produce publications to enhance his curriculum vitae and thus be a worthy competitor for CS in the next competition for a tenured position. (See Figure 2.3.) Alternatively, the computer scientist may have access to another coffee machine in her environment, as pictured in Figure 2.4.

In general, given two CCS expressions P and Q, the process $P | Q$ describes a system in which P and Q

- may proceed independently, or
- may communicate via complementary ports.

Restriction and relabelling Since academics such as our computer scientist often live in a highly competitive 'publish or perish' environment, it may be fruitful for her to make the coffee machine CM private to her and therefore inaccessible to her competitors. To make this possible, the language CCS offers an operation

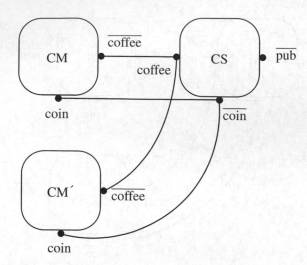

Figure 2.4 The interface for the process CM | CS | CM'.

called *restriction*, whose aim is to delimit the scope of channel names in much the same way as variables have a delimited scope in block-structured programming languages. For instance, using the operations \coin and \coffee, we may hide the coin and coffee ports from the environment of the processes CM and CS. Define the process SmUni (for 'small university') thus:

$$\text{SmUni} \stackrel{\text{def}}{=} (\text{CM} \mid \text{CS}) \setminus \text{coin} \setminus \text{coffee}. \tag{2.4}$$

As pictured in Figure 2.5, the restricted 'coin' and 'coffee' ports may now be used only for communication between the computer scientist and the coffee machine and are not available for interaction with their environment. Their scope is restricted to the process SmUni. The only port of SmUni that is visible to its environment, e.g., to the competing computer scientist CS', is the one via which the computer scientist CS outputs her publications. In general, the formation rule for restriction is as follows:

if P is a process and L is a set of port names then $P \setminus L$ is also a process.

In $P \setminus L$, the scope of the port names in L is restricted to P; these port names can only be used for communication within P.

Since a computer scientist cannot live on coffee alone, it is beneficial for her to have access to other types of vending machines offering, say, chocolate, dried figs and crisps. The behaviour of these machines may be easily specified by means of

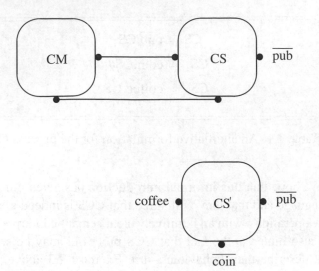

Figure 2.5 The interface for the process SmUni | CS'.

minor variations on equation (2.1). For instance, we may define the processes

$$\text{CHM} \overset{\text{def}}{=} \text{coin}.\overline{\text{choc}}.\text{CHM},$$
$$\text{DFM} \overset{\text{def}}{=} \text{coin}.\overline{\text{figs}}.\text{DFM},$$
$$\text{CRM} \overset{\text{def}}{=} \text{coin}.\overline{\text{crisps}}.\text{CRM}.$$

Note, however, that all these vending machines follow a common behavioural pattern and may be seen as specific instances of a *generic* vending machine that receives a coin as input, dispenses an item and restarts, namely the process

$$\text{VM} \overset{\text{def}}{=} \text{coin}.\overline{\text{item}}.\text{VM}.$$

All these specific vending machines may be obtained as appropriate 'renamings' of VM. For example,

$$\text{CHM} \overset{\text{def}}{=} \text{VM}[\text{choc}/\text{item}],$$

where VM[choc/item] is a process that behaves like VM but outputs chocolate whenever VM dispenses the generic item. In general,

if P is a process and f is a function from labels to labels satisfying certain requirements that will be made precise in Section 2.2 then $P[f]$ is a process.

By introducing the relabelling operation, we have completed our informal tour of the operations offered by the language CCS for the description of process

$$CS \stackrel{\text{def}}{=} \overline{\text{pub}}.CS_1$$
$$CS_1 \stackrel{\text{def}}{=} \overline{\text{coin}}.CS_2$$
$$CS_2 \stackrel{\text{def}}{=} \text{coffee}.CS$$

Table 2.1 An alternative formulation for the process CS

behaviours. We hope that this informal introduction has given our readers a feeling for the language and that they will agree that CCS is indeed a language based upon very few operations, with an intuitively clear semantic interpretation. In passing, we have also hinted at the fact that CCS processes may be seen as defining automata that describe their behaviour – see Exercise 2.3 above. We shall now expand a little on the connection between CCS expressions and the automata describing their behaviour. The presentation will again be informal, as we plan to highlight the main ideas underlying this connection rather than to focus immediately on the technicalities. The formal connection between CCS expressions and labelled transition labelled transition systems will be presented in Section 2.2, using the tools of structural operational semantics (Plotkin, 1981, 2004b).

2.1.1 The behaviour of processes

The key ideas underlying the semantics of CCS are that a process passes through *states* during its execution and that processes change their state by performing actions. For instance, for the purpose of notational convenience in what follows, let us redefine the process CS, see (2.3), as in Table 2.1. (*This is the definition of the process* CS *that we shall use from now on, both when discussing its behaviour in isolation and in the context of other processes – for instance, as a component of the process* SmUni.) Process CS can perform the action '$\overline{\text{pub}}$' and evolve into a process whose behaviour is described by the CCS expression CS_1 in doing so. Process CS_1 can then output a coin, thereby evolving into a process whose behaviour is described by the CCS expression CS_2. Finally, this process can receive coffee as input and behave like our good old CS all over again. Thus the processes CS, CS_1 and CS_2 are the only possible states of the computation in process CS. Note, furthermore, that there is really no conceptual difference between processes and their states! By performing an action, a process evolves to another process that describes what remains to be executed of the original process.

In CCS, processes change state by performing transitions, and these transitions are labelled by the action that caused them. An example of a state transition is

$$CS \xrightarrow{\overline{pub}} CS_1,$$

which says that CS can perform action $\overline{pub}$ and will become CS_1 in doing so. The operational behaviour of our computer scientist CS is therefore completely described by the following labelled transition system:

$$CS \xrightarrow{\overline{pub}} CS_1 \xrightarrow{\overline{coin}} CS_2$$

with a *coffee* transition arcing back from CS_2 to CS.

In much the same way, we can make explicit the set of states of the coffee machine described in (2.1) by rewriting that equation thus:

$$CM \overset{\text{def}}{=} coin.CM_1,$$
$$CM_1 \overset{\text{def}}{=} \overline{coffee}.CM.$$

Note that in state CS_1 the computer scientist is willing to output a coin, as witnessed by the transition

$$CS_1 \xrightarrow{\overline{coin}} CS_2,$$

and in its initial state the coffee machine is willing to accept that coin, because of the transition

$$CM \xrightarrow{coin} CM_1.$$

Therefore, when put in parallel with one another these two processes may communicate and change state simultaneously. The result of the communication should be described as a state transition of the form

$$CM \mid CS_1 \xrightarrow{?} CM_1 \mid CS_2.$$

However, we are now faced with an important design decision: what label should we use in place of the question mark labelling the above transition? Should we decide to use a standard label denoting input or output on some port, then a third process might be able to synchronize further with the coffee machine and the computer scientist, leading to multiway synchronization. The choice made by Milner in designing CCS was different. In CCS, communication is via *handshake* and leads to a state transition that is unobservable, in the sense that it cannot synchronize further. This state transition is labelled by a *new* label τ. So the above transition is indicated by

$$CM \mid CS_1 \xrightarrow{\tau} CM_1 \mid CS_2.$$

In this way, the behaviour of the process SmUni defined by equation 2.4 can be described by the following labelled transition system:

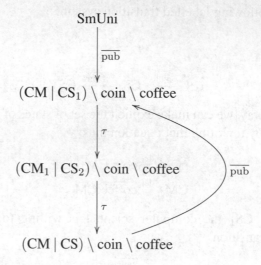

Since it is supposed that τ-actions are unobservable, the following process would seem to be an appropriate high-level specification of the behaviour exhibited by process SmUni:

$$Spec \stackrel{\text{def}}{=} \overline{pub}.Spec.$$

Indeed, we expect that SmUni and Spec describe the same observable behaviour, albeit at different levels of abstraction. We shall see in the remainder of this book that an important task in process theory is to come up with notions of 'behavioural equivalence' between processes which will allow us to establish formally that, for instance, SmUni and Spec do offer the same behaviour. But this is getting ahead of our story.

2.2   CCS, formally

Having introduced CCS by example, we now proceed to present formal definitions for its syntax and semantics.

2.2.1 The model of labelled transition systems

We have already indicated in our examples how the operational semantics for CCS can be given in terms of automata – which we have called labelled transition systems (LTSs), as is customary in concurrency theory. These we now proceed to define, for the sake of clarity. We first introduce the ingredients of the model of labelled transition systems informally and then provide its formal definition.

In this model, processes are represented by the vertices of certain edge-labelled directed graphs (the labelled transition systems themselves) and a change in process state caused by performing an action is understood as moving along an edge, labelled by the action name, that goes out of that state.

A labelled transition system consists therefore of a set of *states* (also referred to as *processes* or *configurations*), a set of *labels* (or *actions*) and a transition relation $\rightarrow$ describing changes in process states; if a process p can perform an action a and become a process p', we write $p \stackrel{a}{\rightarrow} p'$. Sometimes a state is singled out as the *start state* in the LTS under consideration. In that case, we say that the labelled transition system is *rooted*.

Example 2.1 Let us start with a variation on the classic example of a tea and coffee vending machine. The very simplified behaviour of the process determining the interaction of the machine with a customer can be described as follows. From the initial state, say, p, representing the situation 'waiting for a request', two possible actions are enabled. Either the tea button or the coffee button can be pressed (the corresponding action 'tea' or 'coffee' is executed) and the internal state of the machine changes accordingly to p_1 or p_2. Formally, this can be described by the transitions

$$p \stackrel{tea}{\rightarrow} p_1 \quad \text{and} \quad p \stackrel{coffee}{\rightarrow} p_2.$$

The target state p_1 records that the customer has requested tea, whereas p_2 describes the situation in which coffee has been selected.

Now the customer is asked to insert the corresponding amount of money, let us say one euro for a cup of tea and two euros for a cup of coffee. This is reflected by corresponding changes in the control state of the vending machine. These state changes can be modelled by the transitions

$$p_1 \stackrel{1€}{\rightarrow} p_3 \quad \text{and} \quad p_2 \stackrel{2€}{\rightarrow} p_3,$$

whose target state p_3 records that the machine has received payment for the chosen drink.

Finally, the drink is collected and the machine returns to its initial state p, ready to accept the request of another customer. This corresponds to the transition

$$p_3 \overset{\text{collect}}{\to} p.$$

♦

It is often convenient and suggestive to use a graphical representation for labelled transition systems. The following diagram represents the tea and coffee machine described above:

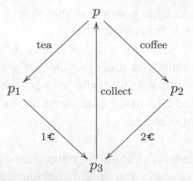

Sometimes, when referring only to the process p, we do not have to give names to the other process states (in our example p_1, p_2 and p_3) and it is sufficient to provide the following labelled transition system for the process p:

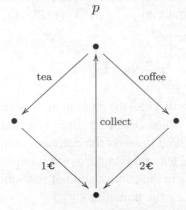

Remark 2.1 The definition of a labelled transition system permits situations like that in Figure 2.6 (where p is the initial state). In this labelled transition system the state p_2, where the action c can be performed in a loop, is irrelevant for the behaviour of the process p since, as you can easily check, p_2 can never be reached from p. This motivates us to introduce the notion of reachable states. We say that

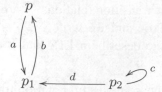

Figure 2.6 Labelled transition system with initial state p.

a state p' in the transition system representing a process p is *reachable* from p iff there exists a directed path from p to p'. The set of all such states is called the *set of reachable states*. In our example this set contains exactly two states, namely p and p_1.   ◆

Definition 2.1 (Labelled transition system) A *labelled transition system* (LTS) (at times also called a *transition graph*) is a triple $(\mathsf{Proc}, \mathsf{Act}, \{\xrightarrow{\alpha} \mid \alpha \in \mathsf{Act}\})$, where:

- Proc is a set of *states* (or *processes*);
- Act is a set of *actions* (or *labels*); and
- $\xrightarrow{\alpha} \subseteq \mathsf{Proc} \times \mathsf{Proc}$ is a *transition relation*, for every $\alpha \in \mathsf{Act}$. As usual, we shall use the more suggestive notation $s \xrightarrow{\alpha} s'$ in lieu of $(s, s') \in \xrightarrow{\alpha}$ and write $s \xnrightarrow{\alpha}$ (read 's refuses α') iff $s \xrightarrow{\alpha} s'$ for no state s'.

A labelled transition system is *finite* if its sets of states and actions are both finite.   ◆

For example, the LTS for the process SmUni defined by (2.4) (see the end of Section 2.1) is formally specified thus:

$$\mathsf{Proc} = \big\{\text{SmUni}, (\text{CM} \mid \text{CS}_1) \setminus \text{coin} \setminus \text{coffee}, (\text{CM}_1 \mid \text{CS}_2) \setminus \text{coin} \setminus \text{coffee},$$
$$(\text{CM} \mid \text{CS}) \setminus \text{coin} \setminus \text{coffee}\big\},$$

$$\mathsf{Act} = \{\overline{\text{pub}}, \tau\},$$

$$\xrightarrow{\overline{\text{pub}}} = \big\{\big(\text{SmUni}, (\text{CM} \mid \text{CS}_1) \setminus \text{coin} \setminus \text{coffee}\big),$$
$$\big((\text{CM} \mid \text{CS}) \setminus \text{coin} \setminus \text{coffee}, (\text{CM} \mid \text{CS}_1) \setminus \text{coin} \setminus \text{coffee}\big)\big\},$$

$$\xrightarrow{\tau} = \big\{\big((\text{CM} \mid \text{CS}_1) \setminus \text{coin} \setminus \text{coffee}, (\text{CM}_1 \mid \text{CS}_2) \setminus \text{coin} \setminus \text{coffee}\big),$$
$$\big((\text{CM}_1 \mid \text{CS}_2) \setminus \text{coin} \setminus \text{coffee}, (\text{CM} \mid \text{CS}) \setminus \text{coin} \setminus \text{coffee}\big)\big\}.$$

As mentioned above, we shall often distinguish a so-called *start state* (or *initial state*), which is one selected state in which the system initially starts. For example, the start state for the process SmUni presented above is, not surprisingly, the process SmUni itself.

Remark 2.2 Sometimes the transition relations $\xrightarrow{\alpha}$ are presented as a ternary relation $\rightarrow \subseteq$ Proc $\times$ Act $\times$ Proc and we write $s \xrightarrow{\alpha} s'$ whenever $(s, \alpha, s') \in \rightarrow$. This is an alternative way to describe a LTS and it defines the same notion as Definition 2.1.   ◆

Notation 2.1 Let us now give some useful notation for LTSs.

- We can extend the transition relation to the elements of Act* (the set of all finite strings over Act including the empty string ε). The definition is as follows:

  $s \xrightarrow{\varepsilon} s$ for every $s \in$ Proc, and
  $s \xrightarrow{\alpha w} s'$ iff there is a state $t \in$ Proc such that $s \xrightarrow{\alpha} t$ and $t \xrightarrow{w} s'$, for every $s, s' \in$ Proc, $\alpha \in$ Act and $w \in$ Act*.

  In other words, if $w = \alpha_1 \alpha_2 \cdots \alpha_n$ for $\alpha_1, \alpha_2, \ldots, \alpha_n \in$ Act then we write $s \xrightarrow{w} s'$ whenever there exist states $s_0, s_1, \ldots, s_{n-1}, s_n \in$ Proc such that

  $$s = s_0 \xrightarrow{\alpha_1} s_1 \xrightarrow{\alpha_2} s_2 \xrightarrow{\alpha_3} s_3 \xrightarrow{\alpha_4} \cdots \xrightarrow{\alpha_{n-1}} s_{n-1} \xrightarrow{\alpha_n} s_n = s'.$$

  For the transition system in Figure 2.6 we have, for example, that $p \xrightarrow{\varepsilon} p$, $p \xrightarrow{ab} p$ and $p_1 \xrightarrow{bab} p$.
- We write $s \rightarrow s'$ whenever there is an action $\alpha \in$ Act such that $s \xrightarrow{\alpha} s'$.
  For the transition system in Figure 2.6 we have, for example, that $p \rightarrow p_1$, $p_1 \rightarrow p$, $p_2 \rightarrow p_1$ and $p_2 \rightarrow p_2$.
- We use the notation $s \xrightarrow{\alpha}$ to mean that there is some $s' \in$ Proc such that $s \xrightarrow{\alpha} s'$.
  For the transition system in Figure 2.6 we have, for example, that $p \xrightarrow{a}$ and $p_1 \xrightarrow{b}$.
- We write $s \rightarrow^* s'$ iff $s \xrightarrow{w} s'$ for some $w \in$ Act*. In other words, $\rightarrow^*$ is the reflexive and transitive closure of the relation $\rightarrow$.
  For the transition system in Figure 2.6 we have, for example, that $p \rightarrow^* p$, $p \rightarrow^* p_1$ and $p_2 \rightarrow^* p$.   ◆

Exercise 2.4 *Consider the following LTS:*

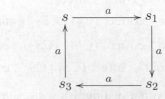

Define the LTS as a triple (Proc, Act, $\{\xrightarrow{\alpha} | \ \alpha \in$ Act$\}$). *Use sketches to illustrate the reflexive closure, symmetric closure and transitive closure of the binary relation $\xrightarrow{a}$?*   ◆

Definition 2.2 (Reachable states) Let $T = (\mathsf{Proc}, \mathsf{Act}, \{\overset{\alpha}{\to} \mid \alpha \in \mathsf{Act}\})$ be an LTS, and let $s \in \mathsf{Proc}$ be its initial state. We say that $s' \in \mathsf{Proc}$ is *reachable* in the transition system T iff $s \to^* s'$. The set of *reachable states* contains all states reachable in T. ◆

In the transition system from Figure 2.6, where p is the initial state, the set of reachable states is equal to $\{p, p_1\}$.

Exercise 2.5 *Find the set of reachable states in the labelled transition system in Figure 2.6 if its start state is p_2.* ◆

The step from a process denoted by a CCS expression to the LTS describing its operational behaviour is taken using the framework of structural operational semantics (SOS) pioneered by Plotkin (2004b). (The history of the ideas that led to SOS is recounted by Plotkin himself in Plotkin (2004).) The key idea underlying this approach is that the collection of CCS process expressions constitutes the set of states of a (large) LTS, whose actions will be either input or output actions on communication ports or τ-actions and whose transitions will be exactly those that can be proved to hold using a collection of syntax-driven rules. These rules will be seen to capture the informal semantics of the CCS operators presented above in a very simple and elegant way. The operational semantics of a CCS expression is then obtained by selecting that expression as the start state in the LTS for the whole language and restricting ourselves to the collection of CCS expressions that are reachable from it by transitions.

2.2.2 The formal syntax and semantics of CCS

The next step in our formal development is to offer the formal syntax for the language CCS. Since the set of ports plays a crucial role in the definition of CCS processes, we begin by assuming a countably infinite collection $\mathcal{A}$ of *(channel) names*. ('Countably infinite' means that we have as many names as there are natural numbers.) The set

$$\bar{\mathcal{A}} = \{\bar{a} \mid a \in \mathcal{A}\}$$

is the set of *complementary names* (or co-names for short). In our informal introduction to the language, we interpreted names as input actions and co-names as output actions. We let

$$\mathcal{L} = \mathcal{A} \cup \bar{\mathcal{A}}$$

be the set of *labels* and

$$\mathsf{Act} = \mathcal{L} \cup \{\tau\}$$

be the set of *actions*. In our formal developments, we shall use a, b to range over $\mathcal{L}$ and α as a typical member of Act, but, as in the previous section, we shall often use more suggestive names for channels in applications and examples. By convention, we assume that $\bar{\bar{a}} = a$ for each label a. (This also makes sense intuitively because the complement of output is input.) We also assume a given countably infinite collection $\mathcal{K}$ of *process names* or *process constants*. This ensures that we never run out of names for processes.

Definition 2.3 The collection $\mathcal{P}$ of *CCS expressions* is given by the following grammar

$$P, Q ::= K \,\Big|\, \alpha.P \,\Big|\, \sum_{i \in I} P_i \,\Big|\, P \mid Q \,\Big|\, P[f] \,\Big|\, P \setminus L,$$

where

- K is a process name in $\mathcal{K}$,
- α is an action in Act,
- I is a possibly infinite index set,
- $f :$ Act $\to$ Act is a *relabelling function* satisfying the constraints

$$f(\tau) = \tau,$$
$$f(\bar{a}) = \overline{f(a)} \text{ for each label } a,$$

and
- L is a set of labels from $\mathcal{L}$.

We write $\mathbf{0}$ for an empty sum of processes, i.e.

$$\mathbf{0} = \sum_{i \in \emptyset} P_i,$$

and $P_1 + P_2$ for a sum of two processes, i.e.

$$P_1 + P_2 = \sum_{i \in \{1,2\}} P_i.$$

Moreover, we assume that the behaviour of each process name $K \in \mathcal{K}$ is given by a defining equation

$$K \stackrel{\text{def}}{=} P,$$

where $P \in \mathcal{P}$. As made clear by the previous informal discussion, the constant K may appear in P.   ◆

We sometimes write $[b_1/a_1, \ldots, b_n/a_n]$, where $n \geq 1$, $a_i, b_i \in \mathcal{A}$ for each $i \in \{1, \ldots, n\}$ and the a_i are distinct channel names, for the relabelling $[f]$; here f is the relabelling function mapping each a_i to b_i, each $\overline{a_i}$ to $\overline{b_i}$, $i \in \{1, \ldots, n\}$, and acting as the identity function on all the other actions. For each label a, we often write $\backslash a$ in lieu of $\backslash \{a\}$.

To avoid the use of too many parentheses in writing CCS expressions, we use the convention that the operators have decreasing binding strength in the following order: restriction and relabelling (the tightest binding), action prefixing, parallel composition and summation. For example, the expression $a.\mathbf{0} \mid b.P \setminus L + c.\mathbf{0}$ stands for

$$((a.\mathbf{0}) \mid (b.(P \setminus L))) + (c.\mathbf{0}).$$

Exercise 2.6 *Which of the following expressions are syntactically correct CCS expressions? Why? Assume that A, B are process constants and a, b are channel names.*

$$a.b.A + B,$$
$$(a.\mathbf{0} + \overline{a}.A) \setminus \{a, b\},$$
$$(a.\mathbf{0} \mid \overline{a}.A) \setminus \{a, \tau\},$$
$$a.B + [a/b],$$
$$\tau.\tau.B + \mathbf{0},$$
$$(a.B + b.B)[a/b, b/a],$$
$$(a.B + \tau.B)[a/\tau, b/a],$$
$$(a.b.A + \overline{a}.\mathbf{0}) \mid B,$$
$$(a.b.A + \overline{a}.\mathbf{0}).B,$$
$$(a.b.A + \overline{a}.\mathbf{0}) + B,$$
$$(\mathbf{0} \mid \mathbf{0}) + \mathbf{0}.$$

$\blacklozenge$

Readers can easily check that all the processes presented in the previous section are indeed CCS expressions. Another example of a CCS expression is given by a counter, which is defined thus:

$$\text{Counter}_0 \stackrel{\text{def}}{=} \text{up.Counter}_1, \tag{2.5}$$

$$\text{Counter}_n \stackrel{\text{def}}{=} \text{up.Counter}_{n+1} + \text{down.Counter}_{n-1} \quad (n > 0). \tag{2.6}$$

The behaviour of such a process is intuitively clear. For each non-negative integer n, the process Counter_n behaves like a counter whose value is n; the 'up' actions increase the value of the counter by one and the 'down' actions decrease it by one. It would also be easy to construct the (infinite-state) LTS for this process on

$$\text{ACT} \quad \frac{}{\alpha.P \xrightarrow{\alpha} P}$$

$$\text{SUM}_j \quad \frac{P_j \xrightarrow{\alpha} P_j'}{\sum_{i \in I} P_i \xrightarrow{\alpha} P_j'} \quad \text{where } j \in I$$

$$\text{COM1} \quad \frac{P \xrightarrow{\alpha} P'}{P \mid Q \xrightarrow{\alpha} P' \mid Q}$$

$$\text{COM2} \quad \frac{Q \xrightarrow{\alpha} Q'}{P \mid Q \xrightarrow{\alpha} P \mid Q'}$$

$$\text{COM3} \quad \frac{P \xrightarrow{a} P' \quad Q \xrightarrow{\bar{a}} Q'}{P \mid Q \xrightarrow{\tau} P' \mid Q'}$$

$$\text{RES} \quad \frac{P \xrightarrow{\alpha} P'}{P \setminus L \xrightarrow{\alpha} P' \setminus L} \quad \text{where } \alpha, \bar{\alpha} \notin L$$

$$\text{REL} \quad \frac{P \xrightarrow{\alpha} P'}{P[f] \xrightarrow{f(\alpha)} P'[f]}$$

$$\text{CON} \quad \frac{P \xrightarrow{\alpha} P'}{K \xrightarrow{\alpha} P'} \quad \text{where } K \stackrel{\text{def}}{=} P$$

Table 2.2 SOS rules for CCS ($\alpha \in$ Act, $a \in \mathcal{L}$)

the basis of its syntactic description and on the intuitive understanding of process behaviour that we have so far developed. However, intuition alone can lead us to wrong conclusions and, most importantly, cannot be fed into a computer! To capture formally our understanding of the semantics of the language CCS, we therefore introduce the collection of SOS rules given in Table 2.2. These rules are used to generate an LTS whose states are CCS expressions. In that LTS, a transition $P \xrightarrow{\alpha} Q$ holds for CCS expressions P, Q and action α iff it can be proved using the rules in Table 2.2.

A rule such as

$$\frac{}{\alpha.P \xrightarrow{\alpha} P}$$

is an *axiom*, as it has no *premises*, i.e. it has no transition above the horizontal line. This means that proving that a process of the form $\alpha.P$ affords the transition $\alpha.P \xrightarrow{\alpha} P$ (the *conclusion* of the rule) can be done without establishing any further subgoal. Therefore each process of the form $\alpha.P$ affords the transition $\alpha.P \xrightarrow{\alpha} P$. As an example, we have that the transition

$$\overline{\text{pub}}.\text{CS}_1 \xrightarrow{\overline{\text{pub}}} \text{CS}_1 \tag{2.7}$$

is provable using the above rule for action prefixing.

However, a rule like

$$\frac{P \xrightarrow{\alpha} P'}{K \xrightarrow{\alpha} P'} \quad \text{where} \quad K \stackrel{\text{def}}{=} P$$

has a non-empty set of premises. This rule says that, to establish that constant K affords the transition mentioned in the conclusion of the rule, we have to prove first that the *body* of the defining equation for K, namely the process P, affords the transition $P \xrightarrow{\alpha} P'$. Using this rule, pattern-matching and the transition (2.7), we can prove the transition

$$\text{CS} \xrightarrow{\overline{\text{pub}}} \text{CS}_1,$$

which we derived informally for the version of process CS given in Table 2.1.

The aforementioned rule for constants has a *side condition*, namely $K \stackrel{\text{def}}{=} P$, which describes a constraint that must be met in order for the rule to be applicable. In this specific example, the side condition states intuitively that the rule may be used to derive an initial transition for constant K if 'K is declared to have body P'.

Another example of a rule with a side condition is that for restriction,

$$\frac{P \xrightarrow{\alpha} P'}{P \setminus L \xrightarrow{\alpha} P' \setminus L} \quad \text{where} \quad \alpha, \bar{\alpha} \notin L.$$

This rule states that every transition of a term P determines a transition of the expression $P \setminus L$, provided that neither the action producing the transition nor its complement are in L. For example, as you can check, this side condition prevents us from proving the existence of the transition

$$(\text{coffee}.\text{CS}) \setminus \text{coffee} \xrightarrow{\text{coffee}} \text{CS} \setminus \text{coffee}.$$

Finally, note that, when considering the binary version of the summation operator, the family of rules SUM_j reduces to the following two rules:

$$\mathrm{SUM}_1 \quad \frac{P_1 \overset{\alpha}{\to} P_1'}{P_1 + P_2 \overset{\alpha}{\to} P_1'}; \qquad \mathrm{SUM}_2 \quad \frac{P_2 \overset{\alpha}{\to} P_2'}{P_1 + P_2 \overset{\alpha}{\to} P_2'}.$$

To get a feeling for the power of recursive definitions of process behaviours, consider the process C defined thus:

$$C \overset{\text{def}}{=} \text{up}.(C \mid \text{down}.\mathbf{0}). \tag{2.8}$$

What are the transitions that this process affords? Using the rules for constants and action prefixing, you should have little trouble in arguing that the only initial transition for C is

$$C \overset{\text{up}}{\to} C \mid \text{down}.\mathbf{0}. \tag{2.9}$$

What next? Observing that $\text{down}.\mathbf{0} \overset{\text{down}}{\to} \mathbf{0}$ and using rule COM2 in Table 2.2 we can infer that

$$C \mid \text{down}.\mathbf{0} \overset{\text{down}}{\to} C \mid \mathbf{0}.$$

Since it is reasonable to expect that the process $C \mid \mathbf{0}$ exhibits the same behaviour as C – and we shall see later on that this does hold true –, the above transition effectively brings our process back to its initial state, at least up to behavioural equivalence. However, this is not all because, as we have already proved transition (2.9), using rule COM1 in Table 2.2 we have that the transition

$$C \mid \text{down}.\mathbf{0} \overset{\text{up}}{\to} (C \mid \text{down}.\mathbf{0}) \mid \text{down}.\mathbf{0}$$

is also possible. You might find it instructive to continue building a little more of the transition graph for process C. As you may begin to notice, the LTS giving the operational semantics of the process expression C looks very similar to that for Counter_0, as given in (2.5). Indeed, we shall prove later on that these two processes exhibit the same behaviour in a very strong sense.

Exercise 2.7 *Use the rules of the SOS semantics for CCS to derive the LTS for the process* SmUni *defined by (2.4). (Use the definition of* CS *in Table 2.1.)* ◆

Exercise 2.8 *Assume that* $A \overset{\text{def}}{=} b.a.B$. *By using the SOS rules for CCS prove the existence of the following transitions:*

$$(A \mid \overline{b}.\mathbf{0}) \setminus \{b\} \overset{\tau}{\to} (a.B \mid \mathbf{0}) \setminus \{b\},$$

$$(A \mid \overline{b}.a.B) + (\overline{b}.A)[a/b] \overset{\overline{b}}{\to} (A \mid a.B),$$

$$(A \mid \overline{b}.a.B) + (\overline{b}.A)[a/b] \overset{\overline{a}}{\to} A[a/b].$$

◆

Exercise 2.9 *Draw (part of) the transition graph for a process* A *whose behaviour is given by the defining equation*

$$A \stackrel{\text{def}}{=} (a.A) \setminus b.$$

The resulting transition graph should have infinitely many states. Can you think of a CCS term that generates a finite LTS that should intuitively have the same behaviour as A? ♦

Exercise 2.10 *Draw (part of) the transition graph for a process* A *whose behaviour is given by the defining equation*

$$A \stackrel{\text{def}}{=} (a_0.A)[f],$$

where we assume that the set of channel names is $\{a_0, a_1, a_2, \dots\}$ *and that* $f(a_i) = a_{i+1}$ *for each* i.

The resulting transition graph should (again!) have infinitely many states. Can you give an argument showing that there is no finite-state LTS that could intuitively have the same behaviour as A? ♦

Exercise 2.11

1. Draw the transition graph for a process Mutex_1, *whose behaviour is given by*

$$\text{Mutex}_1 \stackrel{\text{def}}{=} (\text{User} \mid \text{Sem}) \setminus \{p, v\},$$
$$\text{User} \stackrel{\text{def}}{=} \bar{p}.\text{enter}.\text{exit}.\bar{v}.\text{User},$$
$$\text{Sem} \stackrel{\text{def}}{=} p.v.\text{Sem}.$$

2. Draw the transition graph for the process Mutex_2, *whose behaviour is given by the defining equation*

$$\text{Mutex}_2 \stackrel{\text{def}}{=} ((\text{User} \mid \text{Sem}) \mid \text{User}) \setminus \{p, v\},$$

where User *and* Sem *are defined as before.*
Would the behaviour of the process change if User *were defined as*

$$\text{User} \stackrel{\text{def}}{=} \bar{p}.\text{enter}.\bar{v}.\text{exit}.\text{User}?$$

3. Draw the transition graph for the process FMutex, *whose behaviour is given by the defining equation*

$$\text{FMutex} \stackrel{\text{def}}{=} ((\text{User} \mid \text{Sem}) \mid \text{FUser}) \setminus \{p, v\},$$

where User *and* Sem *are defined as before, and the behaviour of* FUser *is given by the defining equation*

$$\text{FUser} \stackrel{\text{def}}{=} \bar{p}.\text{enter}.(\text{exit}.\bar{v}.\text{FUser} + \text{exit}.\bar{v}.\mathbf{0}).$$

Do you think that Mutex$_2$ *and* FMutex *offer the same behaviour? Can you argue informally for your answer?*

♦

2.2.3 Value-passing CCS

This section may be skipped on first reading as it is meant mainly as a pointer for further reading and self-study.

So far, we have introduced only so-called *pure CCS*, in which communication is pure synchronization and involves no exchange of data. In many applications, however, processes do exchange data when they communicate. To allow for a natural modelling of these examples it is convenient, although theoretically unnecessary, as argued in Milner (1989, Section 2.8), to extend our language to what is usually called *value-passing CCS*. We shall now introduce the new features in this language, and their operational semantics, by means of examples. In what follows, we will assume for simplicity that the only data type is the set of non-negative integers.

Assume that we wish to define a one-place buffer B which has the following behaviour:

- If B is empty then it is only able to accept one datum as input, along a channel called 'in'. The received datum is stored for further output.
- If B is full then it is only able to output the successor of the value it stores, and empties itself in doing so.

This behaviour of B can be modelled in value-passing CCS thus:

$$\text{B} \overset{\text{def}}{=} \text{in}(x).\text{B}(x),$$

$$\text{B}(x) \overset{\text{def}}{=} \overline{\text{out}}(x+1).\text{B}.$$

Note that the input prefix 'in' now carries a parameter that is a variable, in this case x, whose scope is the process that is prefixed by the input action. In this example the process is $\text{B}(x)$. The intuitive idea is that process B is willing to accept a non-negative integer n as input, bind the received value to x and thereafter behave like $\text{B}(n)$, i.e. like a full one-place buffer storing the value n. The behaviour of the process $\text{B}(n)$ is then described by the second equation above, where the scope of the formal parameter x is the whole right-hand side of the equation. Note that output prefixes such as '$\overline{\text{out}}(x+1)$' above may carry expressions, the idea being that the value being output is the one that results from evaluation of the expression.

The general SOS rule for input prefixing now becomes

$$\frac{}{a(x).P \stackrel{a(n)}{\to} P[n/x]} \quad \text{for } n \geq 0,$$

where we write $P[n/x]$ for the expression that results from replacing each free occurrence of the variable x in P by n. The general SOS rule for output prefixing is

$$\frac{}{\bar{a}(e).P \stackrel{\bar{a}(n)}{\to} P} \quad n \text{ is the result of evaluating } e.$$

In value-passing CCS, as we have already seen in our definition of the one-place buffer B, process names may be parameterized by value variables. The general form that these parameterized constants may take is $A(x_1, \ldots, x_n)$, where A is a process name, $n \geq 0$ and $x_1, \ldots, x_n$ are distinct value variables. The operational semantics for these constants is given by the following rule:

$$\frac{P[v_1/x_1, \ldots, v_n/x_n] \stackrel{\alpha}{\to} P'}{A(e_1, \ldots, e_n) \stackrel{\alpha}{\to} P'} \quad A(x_1, \ldots, x_n) \stackrel{\text{def}}{=} P \text{ and each } e_i \text{ has value } v_i.$$

To become familiar with these rules, you should apply them to the one-place buffer B and derive its possible transitions.

In what follows, we shall restrict ourselves to CCS expressions that have no free occurrences of value variables, i.e. those in which each occurrence of a value variable, say y, is within the scope of an input prefix of the form $a(y)$ or of a parameterized constant $A(x_1, \ldots, x_n)$, with $y = x_i$ for some $1 \leq i \leq n$. For instance, the expression

$$a(x).\bar{b}(y+1).\mathbf{0}$$

is disallowed because the single occurrence of the value variable y is bound neither by an input prefixing nor by a parameterized constant.

Since processes in value-passing CCS may manipulate data, it is natural to add an 'if bexp then P else Q' construct to the language, where bexp is a boolean expression. Assume, by way of example, that we wish to define a one-place buffer Pred that computes the predecessor function on the non-negative integers. This may be defined thus:

$$\text{Pred} \stackrel{\text{def}}{=} \text{in}(x).\text{Pred}(x),$$

$$\text{Pred}(x) \stackrel{\text{def}}{=} \text{if } x = 0 \text{ then } \overline{\text{out}}(0).\text{Pred else } \overline{\text{out}}(x-1).\text{Pred}.$$

We expect $\text{Pred}(0)$ to output the value 0 on channel 'out' and $\text{Pred}(n+1)$ to output n on the same channel for each non-negative integer n. The SOS rules for

if bexp **then** P **else** Q will allow us to prove this formally. They are the expected ones, namely

$$\frac{P \xrightarrow{\alpha} P'}{\textbf{if } bexp \textbf{ then } P \textbf{ else } Q \xrightarrow{\alpha} P'} \quad bexp \text{ is true}$$

and

$$\frac{Q \xrightarrow{\alpha} Q'}{\textbf{if } bexp \textbf{ then } P \textbf{ else } Q \xrightarrow{\alpha} Q'} \quad bexp \text{ is false.}$$

Exercise 2.12 *Consider a one-place buffer defined by*

$$\text{Cell} \stackrel{\text{def}}{=} in(x).\text{Cell}(x),$$

$$\text{Cell}(x) \stackrel{\text{def}}{=} \overline{out}(x).\text{Cell}.$$

Use Cell *to define a two-place 'bag' and a two-place FIFO queue. (Recall that a bag, also known as a multiset, is a set whose elements have multiplicity.) Give specifications of the expected behaviour of these processes, and use the operational rules given above to convince yourself that your implementations are correct.* ◆

Exercise 2.13 *Consider the process* B *defined thus:*

$$\text{B} \stackrel{\text{def}}{=} push(x).(\text{C}(x)^\frown\text{B}) + empty.\text{B},$$

$$\text{C}(x) \stackrel{\text{def}}{=} push(y).(\text{C}(y)^\frown\text{C}(x)) + \overline{pop}(x).\text{D},$$

$$\text{D} \stackrel{\text{def}}{=} o(x).\text{C}(x) + \bar{e}.\text{B},$$

where the linking combinator $P^\frown Q$ *is given by*

$$P^\frown Q = (P[\,p'/p, e'/e, o'/o] \mid Q[\,p'/push, e'/empty, o'/pop]) \setminus \{p', o', e'\}.$$

Draw the initial part of the transition graph for this process. What behaviour do you think B *implements?* ◆

Exercise 2.14 (For the theoretically minded) *Prove that the operational semantics for value-passing CCS that we have given above is in complete agreement with the semantics for this language given via translation into the pure calculus by Milner (1989, Section 2.8).* ◆

3

Behavioural equivalences

We have previously remarked that CCS, like all other process algebras, can be used to describe both implementations of processes and specifications of their expected behaviours. A language like CCS therefore supports the so-called *single-language approach* to process theory – that is, the approach in which a single language is used to describe both actual processes and their specifications. An important ingredient of these languages is therefore a notion of behavioural equivalence or behavioural approximation between processes. One process description, say SYS, may describe an implementation and another, say SPEC, may describe a specification of the expected behaviour. To say that SYS and SPEC are equivalent is taken to indicate that these two processes describe essentially the same behaviour, albeit possibly at different levels of abstraction or refinement. To say that, in some formal sense, SYS is an approximation of SPEC means roughly that every aspect of the behaviour of this process is allowed by the specification SPEC and thus that nothing unexpected can happen in the behaviour of SYS. This approach to program verification is also sometimes called *implementation verification* or *equivalence checking*.

3.1   Criteria for good behavioural equivalence

We have already argued informally that some processes that we have met so far ought to be considered as behaviourally equivalent. For instance, we claimed at the end of Section 2.1 that the behaviour of the process SmUni defined in (2.4) should be considered equivalent to that of the specification

$$\text{Spec} \stackrel{\text{def}}{=} \overline{\text{pub}}.\text{Spec},$$

31

and that the process C in (2.8) behaves like a counter. Our order of business now will be to introduce a notion of behavioural equivalence that will allow us to establish these expected equalities and many others.

Before doing so, however, it is instructive to consider the criteria that we expect a suitable notion of behavioural equivalence for processes to meet. First of all, we have already used the term 'equivalence' several times and, since this is a mathematical notion that some readers may not have met before, it is time to define it precisely.

Definition 3.1 Let X be a set. A *binary relation* over X is a subset of $X \times X$, the set of pairs of elements of X. If R is a binary relation over X, we often write $x \, R \, y$ instead of $(x, y) \in R$.

An *equivalence relation* over X is a binary relation R that satisfies the following constraints:

R is *reflexive*, i.e. $x \, R \, x$ for each $x \in X$;
R is *symmetric*, i.e. $x \, R \, y$ implies $y \, R \, x$ for all $x, y \in X$; and
R is *transitive*, i.e. $x \, R \, y$ and $y \, R \, z$ imply $x \, R \, z$ for all $x, y, z \in X$.

A reflexive and transitive relation is a *preorder*.   ♦

An equivalence relation is therefore a more abstract version of the elementary notion of equality.

Exercise 3.1 *Which of the following relations over the set of non-negative integers* $\mathbb{N}$ *is an equivalence relation?*

- *The identity relation* $I = \{(n, n) \mid n \in \mathbb{N}\}$.
- *The universal relation* $U = \{(n, m) \mid n, m \in \mathbb{N}\}$.
- *The standard* $\leq$ *relation.*
- *The parity relation* $M_2 = \{(n, m) \mid n, m \in \mathbb{N}, \, n \bmod 2 = m \bmod 2\}$.

Can you give an example of a preorder over the set $\mathbb{N}$ *that is not an equivalence relation?*   ♦

Since we expect that each process is a correct implementation of itself, a relation used to support implementation verification should certainly be reflexive. Moreover, as we shall now argue, it should also be transitive – at least if it is to support the stepwise derivation of implementations from specifications. In fact, assume that we wish to derive a correct implementation from a specification via a sequence of refinement steps that are known to preserve some behavioural relation R. In this approach, we might begin from our specification Spec and transform it into an

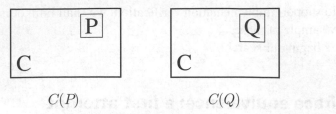

$$C(P) \qquad\qquad C(Q)$$

Figure 3.1 $P\ R\ Q$ implies that $C[P]\ R\ C[Q]$.

implementation Imp via a sequence of intermediate stages Spec_i, $0 \le i \le n$, thus:

$$\mathrm{Spec} = \mathrm{Spec}_0\ R\ \mathrm{Spec}_1\ R\ \mathrm{Spec}_2\ R \cdots R\ \mathrm{Spec}_n = \mathrm{Imp}.$$

Since each stage preserves the relation R, we would like to conclude that Imp is a correct implementation of Spec with respect to R, i.e. that

$$\mathrm{Spec}\ R\ \mathrm{Imp}$$

holds. This is guaranteed to be true if the relation R is transitive.

From the above discussion, it follows that a relation supporting implementation verification should at least be a preorder. The relations considered in the classic theory of CCS, and in the main body of this book, are also symmetric and are therefore equivalence relations.

Another intuitively desirable property for an equivalence relation R that supports implementation verification is that it is a *congruence*. This means that process descriptions that are related by R can be used interchangeably as parts of a larger process description without affecting the overall behaviour of the later. More precisely, if $P\ R\ Q$ and if $C[\ ]$ is a program fragment with a 'hole' then

$$C[P]\ R\ C[Q].$$

This is represented pictorially in Figure 3.1.

Finally, we expect our notion of relation supporting implementation verification to be based on the observable behaviour of processes, rather than on their structure, the actual name of their states or the number of transitions they afford. Ideally, we should like to identify two processes unless there is some sequence of 'interactions' that an 'observer' may have with them leading to different 'outcomes'. The lack of consensus on what constitutes an appropriate notion of observable behaviour for reactive systems has led to a large number of proposals for behavioural equivalences for concurrent processes. (See the study Glabbeek (2001), where van Glabbeek presents the linear time-branching time spectrum – a lattice of known behavioural equivalences and preorders over labelled transition systems, ordered by inclusion.) In our search for a reasonable notion of behavioural relation to support implementation verification, we shall limit ourselves to presenting a tiny sample of these.

So let's begin our search!

3.2   Trace equivalence: a first attempt

Labelled transition systems (LTSs) (Keller, 1976) are a fundamental model of concurrent computation, which is widely used in the light of its flexibility and applicability. In particular, they are the prime model underlying Plotkin's structural operational semantics (Plotkin, 2004b) and, following Milner's pioneering work on CCS (Milner, 1989), are now the standard semantic model for various process-description languages.

As we have already seen, LTSs model processes by explicitly describing their states and their transitions from state to state, together with the actions that produced these transitions. Since this view of process behaviours is very detailed, several notions of behavioural equivalence and preorder have been proposed for LTSs. The aim of such behavioural semantics is to identify those (states of) LTSs that afford the same 'observations', in some appropriate technical sense.

Now, LTSs are essentially (possibly infinite-state) automata, and the classic theory of automata suggests a ready-made notion of equivalence for them and thus for the CCS processes that denote them.

Let us say that a *trace* of a process P is a sequence $\alpha_1 \cdots \alpha_k \in \mathsf{Act}^*$, $k \geq 0$, such that there exists a sequence of transitions

$$P = P_0 \xrightarrow{\alpha_1} P_1 \xrightarrow{\alpha_2} \cdots \xrightarrow{\alpha_{k-1}} P_{k-1} \xrightarrow{\alpha_k} P_k,$$

for some $P_1, \ldots, P_k$. We write $Traces(P)$ for the collection of all traces of P. Since $Traces(P)$ describes all possible finite sequences of interactions that may take place with process P, it is reasonable to require that our notion of behavioural equivalence relates only processes that afford the same traces. Otherwise we would have a very good way of telling them apart – namely that there would be a sequence of actions that can be performed with one but not the other. This means that, for all processes P and Q, we require that

if P and Q are behaviourally equivalent then $Traces(P) = Traces(Q)$.   (3.1)

Taking the point of view of standard automata theory and abstracting from the notion of 'accept state', which is missing altogether in our treatment, an automaton may be completely identified by its set of traces, and thus two processes are equivalent iff they afford the same traces.

This point of view is totally justified and natural if we view our LTSs as non-deterministic devices that may generate or accept sequences of actions. However, is it still reasonable if we view our automata as reactive machines, which interact with their environment?

To answer these questions, consider the coffee and tea machine CTM defined in (2.2) and compare it with the following machine:

$$\text{CTM}' \overset{\text{def}}{=} \text{coin}.\overline{\text{coffee}}.\text{CTM}' + \text{coin}.\overline{\text{tea}}.\text{CTM}'. \qquad (3.2)$$

You should be able to convince yourself that CTM and CTM$'$ afford the same traces. (Do so!) However, if you were a user of the coffee and tea machine who loves coffee and hates tea, which machine would you like to interact with? It would certainly be preferable to interact with CTM, as that machine will give us coffee after receiving a coin whereas CTM$'$ may enter a state in which it will deliver only tea, having accepted our coin!

This informal discussion may be directly formalized within CCS by assuming that the behaviour of the coffee-starved user is described by the process

$$\text{CA} \overset{\text{def}}{=} \overline{\text{coin}}.\text{coffee}.\text{CA}.$$

Consider now the terms

$$(\text{CA} \mid \text{CTM}) \setminus \{\text{coin}, \text{coffee}, \text{tea}\}$$

and

$$(\text{CA} \mid \text{CTM}') \setminus \{\text{coin}, \text{coffee}, \text{tea}\}$$

that we obtain by forcing interaction between the coffee addict CA and the two vending machines. Using the SOS rules for CCS, you should convince yourself that the former term can only perform an infinite computation consisting of τ-labelled transitions, whereas the second term can deadlock thus:

$$(\text{CA} \mid \text{CTM}') \setminus \{\text{coin}, \text{coffee}, \text{tea}\} \overset{\tau}{\rightarrow} (\text{coffee}.\text{CA} \mid \overline{\text{tea}}.\text{CTM}') \setminus \{\text{coin}, \text{coffee}, \text{tea}\}.$$

Note that the target term of this transition captures precisely the deadlock situation that we intuitively expect, namely that the user only wants coffee but the machine is only willing to deliver tea. So trace-equivalent terms may exhibit different deadlock behaviour when made to interact with other parallel processes – a highly undesirable state of affairs.

In the light of the above example, we are forced to reject the law

$$\alpha.(P + Q) = \alpha.P + \alpha.Q,$$

which is familiar from the standard theory of regular languages, for our desired notion of behavioural equivalence. (Can you see why?) Therefore we need to refine our notion of equivalence in order to differentiate processes that, like the two vending machines above, exhibit different reactive behaviour while still having the same traces.

Exercise 3.2 (Recommended) *A completed trace of a process P is a sequence $\alpha_1 \cdots \alpha_k \in \mathsf{Act}^*$ $(k \geq 0)$ such that there exists a sequence of transitions*

$$P = P_0 \xrightarrow{\alpha_1} P_1 \xrightarrow{\alpha_2} \cdots \xrightarrow{\alpha_{k-1}} P_{k-1} \xrightarrow{\alpha_k} P_k \nrightarrow,$$

for some $P_1, \ldots, P_k$. The completed traces of a process may be seen as capturing its deadlock behaviour, as they are precisely the sequences of actions that could lead the process into a state from which no further action is possible.

1. Do the processes

$$(\mathsf{CA} \mid \mathsf{CTM}) \setminus \{\text{coin}, \text{coffee}, \text{tea}\}$$

and

$$(\mathsf{CA} \mid \mathsf{CTM}') \setminus \{\text{coin}, \text{coffee}, \text{tea}\}$$

defined above have the same completed traces?

2. Is it true that if P and Q are two CCS processes affording the same completed traces and L is a set of labels then $P \setminus L$ and $Q \setminus L$ also have the same completed traces?

You should, of course, argue for your answers.   ◆

3.3   Strong bisimilarity

Our aim in this section will be to present a key notion in the theory of processes, namely *strong bisimulation*. In order to motivate this notion intuitively, let us reconsider once more the two processes CTM and CTM$'$ that we used above in arguing that trace equivalence is not a suitable notion of behavioural equivalence for reactive systems. The problem was that, as fully formalized in Exercise 3.2, the trace-equivalent processes CTM and CTM$'$ exhibited different deadlock behaviour when made to interact with a third parallel process, namely CA. In hindsight, this is not overly surprising. In fact, if we look simply at the (completed) traces of a process, we are focusing only on the sequences of actions that the process may perform and are not taking into account the communication capabilities of the intermediate states traversed by the process as it computes. As the above example shows, the communication potential of the intermediate states *does matter* when interaction with the process is allowed at all times. In particular, there is a crucial difference in the capabilities of the states reached by CTM and CTM' after these processes have received a coin as input. Indeed, after accepting a coin the machine CTM always enters a state in which it is able to output both coffee and tea, depending on what its user wants, whereas the machine CTM' can only enter a state in which it is able to deliver either coffee or tea, but not both.

The lesson that we may learn from the above discussion is that a suitable notion of behavioural relation between reactive systems should allow us to distinguish processes that may have different deadlock potentials when made to interact with other processes. Such a notion of behavioural relation must take into account the communication capabilities of the intermediate states that processes may reach as they compute. One way to ensure that this holds is to require that, in order for two processes to be equivalent, not only should they afford the same traces but, in some formal sense, the states that they reach should still be equivalent. You can easily convince yourself that trace equivalence does not meet this latter requirement, as the states that CTM and CTM' may reach after receiving a coin as input are *not* trace equivalent.

The classic notion of strong bisimulation equivalence, introduced by David Park (1981) and widely popularized by Robin Milner (1989), formalizes the informal requirements introduced above in a very elegant way.

Definition 3.2 (Strong bisimulation) A binary relation $\mathcal{R}$ over the set of states of an LTS is a *bisimulation* iff whenever $s_1 \mathcal{R} s_2$ and α is an action:

if $s_1 \xrightarrow{\alpha} s_1'$ then there is a transition $s_2 \xrightarrow{\alpha} s_2'$ such that $s_1' \mathcal{R} s_2'$;
if $s_2 \xrightarrow{\alpha} s_2'$ then there is a transition $s_1 \xrightarrow{\alpha} s_1'$ such that $s_1' \mathcal{R} s_2'$.

Two states s and s' are *bisimilar*, written $s \sim s'$, iff there is a bisimulation that relates them. Henceforth the relation $\sim$ will be referred to as *strong bisimulation equivalence* or *strong bisimilarity*. ♦

Since the operational semantics of CCS is given in terms of an LTS whose states are CCS process expressions, the above definition applies equally well to CCS processes. Intuitively, a strong bisimulation is a kind of invariant relation between processes that is preserved by transitions in the sense of Definition 3.2.

Before beginning to explore the properties of strong bisimilarity, let us note one of its most appealing features, namely a proof technique for showing that two processes are strongly bisimilar that it supports. Since two processes are strongly bisimilar if there is a strong bisimulation that relates them, to prove that they are related by $\sim$ it suffices only to exhibit a strong bisimulation that relates them.

Example 3.1 Consider the LTS

$$(\mathsf{Proc}, \mathsf{Act}, \{\xrightarrow{\alpha} \mid \alpha \in \mathsf{Act}\}),$$

where

$$\mathsf{Proc} = \{s, s_1, s_2, t, t_1\},$$
$$\mathsf{Act} = \{a, b\},$$
$$\xrightarrow{a} = \{(s, s_1), (s, s_2), (t, t_1)\},$$
$$\xrightarrow{b} = \{(s_1, s_2), (s_2, s_2), (t_1, t_1)\}.$$

Here is a graphical representation of this LTS:

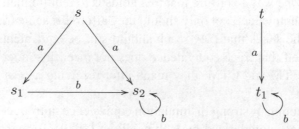

We will show that $s \sim t$. In order to do so, we have to define a strong bisimulation $\mathcal{R}$ such that $(s, t) \in \mathcal{R}$. Let us define it as

$$\mathcal{R} = \{(s, t), (s_1, t_1), (s_2, t_1)\}.$$

The binary relation $\mathcal{R}$ can be depicted graphically by dotted lines, as follows:

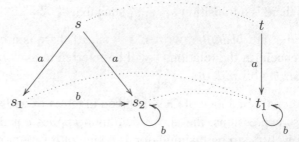

Obviously, $(s, t) \in \mathcal{R}$. We have to show that $\mathcal{R}$ is a strong bisimulation, i.e. that it meets the requirements stated in Definition 3.2. To this end, for each pair of states from $\mathcal{R}$ we have to investigate all possible transitions from one state and see whether they can be matched by corresponding transitions from the other state. Note that a transition from one process under some label can be matched only by a transition from the other process under the same label. We will now present a complete analysis of all the steps needed to show that $\mathcal{R}$ is a strong bisimulation, even though they are very simple and tedious.

- Let us consider first the pair (s, t).

  Transitions from s:
    $s \xrightarrow{a} s_1$ can be matched by $t \xrightarrow{a} t_1$ and $(s_1, t_1) \in \mathcal{R}$;
    $s \xrightarrow{a} s_2$ can be matched by $t \xrightarrow{a} t_1$ and $(s_2, t_1) \in \mathcal{R}$; and
    these are all the transitions from s.
  Transitions from t:
    $t \xrightarrow{a} t_1$ can be matched, e.g. by $s \xrightarrow{a} s_2$ and $(s_2, t_1) \in \mathcal{R}$ (another possibility
      would be to match it by $s \xrightarrow{a} s_1$ but finding one matching transition is
      enough); and
    this is the only transition from t.

- Next we consider the pair (s_1, t_1).

  Transitions from s_1:
    $s_1 \xrightarrow{b} s_2$ can be matched by $t_1 \xrightarrow{b} t_1$ and $(s_2, t_1) \in \mathcal{R}$; and
    this is the only transition from s_1.
  Transitions from t_1:
    $t_1 \xrightarrow{b} t_1$ can be matched by $s_1 \xrightarrow{b} s_2$ and $(s_2, t_1) \in \mathcal{R}$; and
    this is the only transition from t_1.

- Finally we consider the pair (s_2, t_1).

  Transitions from s_2:
    $s_2 \xrightarrow{b} s_2$ can be matched by $t_1 \xrightarrow{b} t_1$ and $(s_2, t_1) \in \mathcal{R}$; and
    this is the only transition from s_2.
  Transitions from t_1:
    $t_1 \xrightarrow{b} t_1$ can be matched by $s_2 \xrightarrow{b} s_2$ and $(s_2, t_1) \in \mathcal{R}$; and
    this is the only transition from t_1.

This completes the proof that $\mathcal{R}$ is a strong bisimulation and, since $(s, t) \in \mathcal{R}$, we
obtain $s \sim t$.

In order to prove that, for example, $s_1 \sim s_2$ we can use the following relation:

$$\mathcal{R} = \{(s_1, s_2), (s_2, s_2)\}.$$

The reader is invited to verify that $\mathcal{R}$ is indeed a strong bisimulation. ◆

Example 3.2 In this example we shall demonstrate that it is possible for the initial state of an LTS with infinitely many reachable states to be strongly bisimilar to a state from which only finitely many states are reachable. Consider the LTS

$(\mathsf{Proc}, \mathsf{Act}, \{\xrightarrow{\alpha} \mid \alpha \in \mathsf{Act}\})$, where

$$\mathsf{Proc} = \{s_i \mid i \geq 1\} \cup \{t\},$$
$$\mathsf{Act} = \{a\},$$
$$\xrightarrow{a} = \{(s_i, s_{i+1}) \mid i \geq 1\} \cup \{(t,t)\}.$$

Here is a graphical representation of this LTS:

$$s_1 \xrightarrow{\ a\ } s_2 \xrightarrow{\ a\ } s_3 \xrightarrow{\ a\ } s_4 \xrightarrow{\ a\ } \cdots$$

We can now observe that $s_1 \sim t$ because the relation

$$\mathcal{R} = \{(s_i, t) \mid i \geq 1\}$$

is a strong bisimulation and contains the pair (s_1, t). The reader is invited to verify this simple fact. ♦

Consider now the two coffee and tea machines in our running example. We can argue that CTM and CTM$'$ are *not* strongly bisimilar, thus. Assume, towards a contradiction, that CTM and CTM$'$ are strongly bisimilar. This means that there is a strong bisimulation $\mathcal{R}$ such that

$$\mathrm{CTM} \; \mathcal{R} \; \mathrm{CTM}'.$$

Recall that

$$\mathrm{CTM}' \xrightarrow{\mathrm{coin}} \overline{\mathrm{tea}}.\mathrm{CTM}'.$$

So, by the second requirement in Definition 3.2, there must be a transition

$$\mathrm{CTM} \xrightarrow{\mathrm{coin}} P$$

for some process P such that $P \; \mathcal{R} \; \overline{\mathrm{tea}}.\mathrm{CTM}'$. A moment of thought should be enough to convince the reader that the only process that CTM can reach by receiving a coin as input is $\overline{\mathrm{coffee}}.\mathrm{CTM} + \overline{\mathrm{tea}}.\mathrm{CTM}$. So we are requiring that

$$(\overline{\mathrm{coffee}}.\mathrm{CTM} + \overline{\mathrm{tea}}.\mathrm{CTM}) \; \mathcal{R} \; \overline{\mathrm{tea}}.\mathrm{CTM}'.$$

However, now a contradiction is immediately reached. In fact,

$$\overline{\mathrm{coffee}}.\mathrm{CTM} + \overline{\mathrm{tea}}.\mathrm{CTM} \xrightarrow{\overline{\mathrm{coffee}}} \mathrm{CTM},$$

but $\overline{\mathrm{tea}}.\mathrm{CTM}'$ cannot output coffee. Thus the first requirement in Definition 3.2 cannot be met. It follows that our assumption that the two machines were strongly bisimilar leads to a contradiction. We may therefore conclude that, as claimed, the processes CTM and CTM$'$ are *not* strongly bisimilar.

Example 3.3 Consider the processes P and Q defined thus:

$$P \stackrel{\text{def}}{=} a.P_1 + b.P_2,$$
$$P_1 \stackrel{\text{def}}{=} c.P,$$
$$P_2 \stackrel{\text{def}}{=} c.P$$

and

$$Q \stackrel{\text{def}}{=} a.Q_1 + b.Q_2,$$
$$Q_1 \stackrel{\text{def}}{=} c.Q_3,$$
$$Q_2 \stackrel{\text{def}}{=} c.Q_3,$$
$$Q_3 \stackrel{\text{def}}{=} a.Q_1 + b.Q_2.$$

We claim that $P \sim Q$. To prove that this holds, it suffices to argue that the following relation is a strong bisimulation:

$$\mathcal{R} = \{(P, Q), (P, Q_3), (P_1, Q_1), (P_2, Q_2)\}.$$

You are encouraged to check that this is indeed the case. ◆

Exercise 3.3 *Consider the processes P and Q defined thus:*

$$P \stackrel{\text{def}}{=} a.P_1,$$
$$P_1 \stackrel{\text{def}}{=} b.P + c.P$$

and

$$Q \stackrel{\text{def}}{=} a.Q_1,$$
$$Q_1 \stackrel{\text{def}}{=} b.Q_2 + c.Q,$$
$$Q_2 \stackrel{\text{def}}{=} a.Q_3,$$
$$Q_3 \stackrel{\text{def}}{=} b.Q + c.Q_2.$$

Show that $P \sim Q$ holds by exhibiting an appropriate strong bisimulation. ◆

Exercise 3.4 *Consider the processes*

$$P \stackrel{\text{def}}{=} a.(b.\mathbf{0} + c.\mathbf{0}),$$
$$Q \stackrel{\text{def}}{=} a.b.\mathbf{0} + a.c.\mathbf{0}.$$

Show that P and Q are not strongly bisimilar. ◆

Exercise 3.5 *Consider the following LTS.*

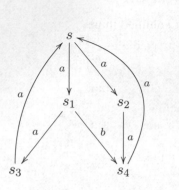
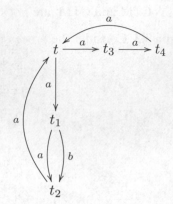

Show that $s \sim t$ *by finding a strong bisimulation* R *containing the pair* (s,t). ◆

Before looking at a few more examples, we now present some general properties of strong bisimilarity. In particular, we shall see that $\sim$ is an equivalence relation and that it is preserved by all the constructs in the CCS language.

The following result states the most basic properties of strong bisimilarity; it is our first theorem in this book.

Theorem 3.1 For all LTSs, the relation $\sim$

1. is an equivalence relation,
2. is the largest strong bisimulation, and
3. satisfies the following property:

$s_1 \sim s_2$ iff, for each action α,
   if $s_1 \xrightarrow{\alpha} s_1'$ then there is a transition $s_2 \xrightarrow{\alpha} s_2'$ such that $s_1' \sim s_2'$;
   if $s_2 \xrightarrow{\alpha} s_2'$ then there is a transition $s_1 \xrightarrow{\alpha} s_1'$ such that $s_1' \sim s_2'$.

Proof. Consider an LTS $(\mathsf{Proc}, \mathsf{Act}, \{\xrightarrow{\alpha} \mid \alpha \in \mathsf{Act}\})$. We will prove each of the above statements in turn.

Proof of 1. In order to show that $\sim$ is an equivalence relation over the set of states Proc, we need to argue that it is reflexive, symmetric and transitive. (See Definition 3.1.)

To prove that $\sim$ is reflexive, it suffices to provide a bisimulation that contains the pair (s, s) for each state $s \in \mathsf{Proc}$. It is not hard to see that the *identity relation*

$$\mathcal{I} = \{(s,s) \mid s \in \mathsf{Proc}\}$$

is such a relation.

We now show that $\sim$ is symmetric. Assume, to this end, that $s_1 \sim s_2$ for some states s_1 and s_2 contained in Proc. We claim that $s_2 \sim s_1$ also holds. To prove this claim, recall that since $s_1 \sim s_2$ there is a bisimulation $\mathcal{R}$ that contains the pair of states (s_1, s_2). Consider now the relation

$$\mathcal{R}^{-1} = \{(s', s) \mid (s, s') \in \mathcal{R}\}.$$

You should now be able to convince yourself that the pair (s_2, s_1) is contained in $\mathcal{R}^{-1}$ and that this relation is indeed a bisimulation. Therefore $s_2 \sim s_1$, as claimed.

We are therefore left to argue that $\sim$ is transitive. Assume, to this end, that $s_1 \sim s_2$ and $s_2 \sim s_3$ for some states s_1, s_2 and s_3 contained in Proc. We claim that $s_1 \sim s_3$ also holds. To prove this, recall that since $s_1 \sim s_2$ and $s_2 \sim s_3$ there are two bisimulations $\mathcal{R}$ and $\mathcal{R}'$ that contain the pairs of states (s_1, s_2) and (s_2, s_3) respectively. Consider now the relation

$$\mathcal{S} = \{(s_1', s_3') \mid (s_1', s_2') \in \mathcal{R} \text{ and } (s_2', s_3') \in \mathcal{R}', \text{ for some } s_2'\}.$$

The pair (s_1, s_3) is contained in $\mathcal{S}$. (Why?) Moreover, using the fact that $\mathcal{R}$ and $\mathcal{R}'$ are bisimulations, you should be able to show that $\mathcal{S}$ is also a bisimulation. Therefore $s_1 \sim s_3$, as claimed.

Proof of 2. We aim at showing that $\sim$ is the largest strong bisimulation over the set of states Proc. To this end observe, first of all, that the definition of $\sim$ states that

$$\sim = \bigcup \{\mathcal{R} \mid \mathcal{R} \text{ is a bisimulation}\}.$$

This yields immediately that each bisimulation is included in $\sim$. We are therefore left to show that the right-hand side of the above equation is itself a bisimulation. This we now proceed to do.

Since we have already shown that $\sim$ is symmetric, it is sufficient to prove that if

$$(s_1, s_2) \in \bigcup \{\mathcal{R} \mid \mathcal{R} \text{ is a bisimulation}\} \text{ and } s_1 \xrightarrow{\alpha} s_1' \qquad (3.3)$$

then there is a state s_2' such that $s_2 \xrightarrow{\alpha} s_2'$ and

$$(s_1', s_2') \in \bigcup \{\mathcal{R} \mid \mathcal{R} \text{ is a bisimulation}\}.$$

Assume, therefore, that (3.3) holds. Since

$$(s_1, s_2) \in \bigcup \{\mathcal{R} \mid \mathcal{R} \text{ is a bisimulation}\},$$

there is a bisimulation $\mathcal{R}$ that contains the pair (s_1, s_2). As $\mathcal{R}$ is a bisimulation and $s_1 \xrightarrow{\alpha} s_1'$, we have that there is a state s_2' such that $s_2 \xrightarrow{\alpha} s_2'$ and $(s_1', s_2') \in \mathcal{R}$.

Observe now that the pair (s'_1, s'_2) is also contained in

$$\bigcup \{\mathcal{R} \mid \mathcal{R} \text{ is a bisimulation}\}.$$

Hence, we have successfully argued that there is a state s'_2 such that $s_2 \xrightarrow{\alpha} s'_2$ and

$$(s'_1, s'_2) \in \bigcup \{\mathcal{R} \mid \mathcal{R} \text{ is a bisimulation}\},$$

which was to be shown.

Proof of 3. We now aim at proving that $\sim$ satisfies the following property:
$s_1 \sim s_2$ iff, for each action α,

if $s_1 \xrightarrow{\alpha} s'_1$ then there is a transition $s_2 \xrightarrow{\alpha} s'_2$ such that $s'_1 \sim s'_2$;
if $s_2 \xrightarrow{\alpha} s'_2$ then there is a transition $s_1 \xrightarrow{\alpha} s'_1$ such that $s'_1 \sim s'_2$.

The implication from left to right is an immediate consequence of the fact that, as we have just shown, $\sim$ is itself a bisimulation. We are therefore left to prove the implication from right to left. To this end, assume that s_1 and s_2 are two states in Proc having the following property:

($*$) for each action α,
   if $s_1 \xrightarrow{\alpha} s'_1$ then there is a transition $s_2 \xrightarrow{\alpha} s'_2$ such that $s'_1 \sim s'_2$;
   if $s_2 \xrightarrow{\alpha} s'_2$ then there is a transition $s_1 \xrightarrow{\alpha} s'_1$ such that $s'_1 \sim s'_2$.

We shall now prove that $s_1 \sim s_2$ holds by constructing a bisimulation that contains the pair (s_1, s_2).

How can we build the desired bisimulation $\mathcal{R}$? First of all, we must add the pair (s_1, s_2) to $\mathcal{R}$ because we wish to use that relation to prove $s_1 \sim s_2$. Since $\mathcal{R}$ is to be a bisimulation, each transition $s_1 \xrightarrow{\alpha} s'_1$ from s_1 must be matched by a transition $s_2 \xrightarrow{\alpha} s'_2$ from s_2, for some state s'_2 such that $(s'_1, s'_2) \in \mathcal{R}$. In the light of the property ($*$), this can be easily achieved by adding to the relation $\mathcal{R}$ all the pairs of states contained in $\sim$! However, since we have already shown that $\sim$ is itself a bisimulation, no more pairs of states need be added to $\mathcal{R}$.

The above discussion suggests that we consider the relation

$$\mathcal{R} = \{(s_1, s_2)\} \cup \sim .$$

Indeed, by construction, the pair (s_1, s_2) is contained in $\mathcal{R}$. Moreover, using property ($*$) and statement 2 of the theorem, it is not hard to prove that $\mathcal{R}$ is a bisimulation. This shows that $s_1 \sim s_2$, as claimed.

The proof is now complete.   □

Exercise 3.6 *Prove that the relations we built in the proof of Theorem 3.1 are indeed bisimulations.*   ♦

Exercise 3.7 *In the proof of Theorem 3.1(2), we argued that the union of all the bisimulation relations over an LTS is itself a bisimulation. Use the argument we adopted in the proof of that statement to show that the union of an arbitrary family of bisimulations is always a bisimulation.* ♦

Exercise 3.8 *Is it true that any strong bisimulation must be reflexive, transitive and symmetric? If yes then prove it. If not then give counter-examples, that is:*

- *define an LTS and a binary relation over states that is not reflexive but is a strong bisimulation;*
- *define an LTS and a binary relation over states that is not symmetric but is a strong bisimulation; and*
- *define an LTS and a binary relation over states that is not transitive but is a strong bisimulation.*

Are the relations that you have constructed the largest strong bisimulations over your LTSs? ♦

Exercise 3.9 (Recommended) *A binary relation $\mathcal{R}$ over the set of states of an LTS is a string bisimulation iff, whenever $s_1 \mathcal{R} s_2$ and σ is a sequence of actions in* Act,

if $s_1 \xrightarrow{\sigma} s_1'$ then there is a transition $s_2 \xrightarrow{\sigma} s_2'$ such that $s_1' \mathcal{R} s_2'$;
if $s_2 \xrightarrow{\sigma} s_2'$ then there is a transition $s_1 \xrightarrow{\sigma} s_1'$ such that $s_1' \mathcal{R} s_2'$.

Two states s and s' are string bisimilar *iff there is a string bisimulation that relates them.*

Prove that string bisimilarity and strong bisimilarity coincide. That is, show that two states s and s' are string bisimilar iff they are strongly bisimilar. ♦

Exercise 3.10 *Assume that the defining equation for a constant K is $K \stackrel{\text{def}}{=} P$. Show that $K \sim P$ holds.* ♦

Exercise 3.11 *Prove that two strongly bisimilar processes afford the same traces, and thus that strong bisimulation equivalence satisfies the requirement for behavioural equivalence that we set out in statement (3.1). Hint: Use your solution to Exercise 3.9 to show that, for each trace $\alpha_1 \cdots \alpha_k$ ($k \geq 0$),*

$$P \sim Q \text{ and } \alpha_1 \cdots \alpha_k \in \text{Traces}(P) \text{ imply that } \alpha_1 \cdots \alpha_k \in \text{Traces}(Q).$$

Is it true that strongly bisimilar processes have the same completed traces? (See Exercise 3.2 for the definition of a completed trace.) ♦

Exercise 3.12 (Recommended) *Show that the relations listed below are strong bisimulations:*

$$\{(P \mid Q, Q \mid P) \mid \text{where } P, Q \text{ are CCS processes}\},$$
$$\{(P \mid \mathbf{0}, P) \mid \text{where } P \text{ is a CCS process}\},$$
$$\{((P \mid Q) \mid R, P \mid (Q \mid R)) \mid \text{where } P, Q, R \text{ are CCS processes}\}.$$

Conclude that, for all P, Q, R,

$$P \mid Q \sim Q \mid P, \tag{3.4}$$
$$P \mid \mathbf{0} \sim P, \tag{3.5}$$
$$(P \mid Q) \mid R \sim P \mid (Q \mid R). \tag{3.6}$$

Find three CCS processes P, Q, R such that $(P + Q) \mid R \not\sim (P \mid R) + (Q \mid R)$. ◆

Exercise 3.13 *Is it true that, for all CCS processes P and Q,*

$$(P \mid Q) \setminus a \sim (P \setminus a) \mid (Q \setminus a)?$$

Does the following equivalence hold for all CCS processes P and Q and relabelling function f?

$$(P \mid Q)[f] \sim (P[f]) \mid (Q[f]).$$

If your answer to the above questions is positive then construct appropriate bisimulations. Otherwise provide a counter-example to the claim. ◆

As we saw in Exercise 3.12, parallel composition is associative and commutative modulo strong bisimilarity. Therefore, since the precise bracketing of terms in a parallel composition does not matter, we can use the notation $\Pi_{i=1}^{k} P_i$, where $k \geq 0$ and the P_i are CCS processes, to stand for

$$P_1 \mid P_2 \mid \cdots \mid P_k.$$

If $k = 0$ then by convention, the above term is just $\mathbf{0}$.

As mentioned before, one of the desirable properties for a notion of behavioural equivalence is that it should allow us to 'replace equivalent processes by equivalent processes' in any larger process expression without affecting its behaviour. The following theorem states that this is indeed possible for strong bisimilarity.

Theorem 3.2 Let P, Q, R be CCS processes. Assume that $P \sim Q$. Then:

- $\alpha.P \sim \alpha.Q$ for each action α;
- $P + R \sim Q + R$ and $R + P \sim R + Q$ for each process R;
- $P \mid R \sim Q \mid R$ and $R \mid P \sim R \mid Q$ for each process R;
- $P[f] \sim Q[f]$ for each relabelling f; and
- $P \setminus L \sim Q \setminus L$ for each set of labels L.

Proof. We limit ourselves to showing that $\sim$ is preserved by parallel composition and restriction. We consider these two operations in turn. In both cases, we assume that $P \sim Q$.

- Let R be a CCS process. We aim at showing that $P \mid R \sim Q \mid R$. To this end, we shall build a bisimulation $\mathcal{R}$ that contains the pair of processes $(P \mid R, Q \mid R)$. Consider the relation

$$\mathcal{R} = \{(P' \mid R', Q' \mid R') \mid P' \sim Q' \text{ where } P', Q', R' \text{ are CCS processes}\}.$$

You should readily be able to convince yourself that the pair of processes $(P \mid R, Q \mid R)$ is indeed contained in $\mathcal{R}$ and thus that all we are left to do to complete our argument is to show that $\mathcal{R}$ is a bisimulation. The proof of this fact will, hopefully, also highlight that the above relation $\mathcal{R}$ is not 'built out of thin air' and epitomizes the creative process that underlies the building of bisimulation relations.

First of all observe that, by symmetry, to prove that $\mathcal{R}$ is a bisimulation it is sufficient to argue that if $(P' \mid R', Q' \mid R')$ is contained in $\mathcal{R}$ and $P' \mid R' \xrightarrow{\alpha} S$ for some action α and CCS process S then $Q' \mid R' \xrightarrow{\alpha} T$ for some CCS process T such that $(S, T) \in \mathcal{R}$. This we now proceed to do.

Assume that $(P' \mid R', Q' \mid R')$ is contained in $\mathcal{R}$ and $P' \mid R' \xrightarrow{\alpha} S$ for some action α and CCS process S. We now proceed with the proof by a case analysis on the possible origins of the transition $P' \mid R' \xrightarrow{\alpha} S$. Recall that the transition that we are considering must be provable using the SOS rules for parallel composition given in Table 2.2. Therefore there are three possible forms that the transition $P' \mid R' \xrightarrow{\alpha} S$ may take, namely:

1. P' is responsible for the transition and R' 'stands still', i.e.

$$P' \mid R' \xrightarrow{\alpha} S,$$

   because, by rule COM1 for parallel composition in Table 2.2, $P' \xrightarrow{\alpha} P''$ and $S = P'' \mid R'$, for some P'';

2. R' is responsible for the transition and P' 'stands still', i.e.

$$P' \mid R' \xrightarrow{\alpha} S,$$

   because, by rule COM2 for parallel composition in Table 2.2, $R' \xrightarrow{\alpha} R''$ and $S = P' \mid R''$ for some R''; or

3. the transition under consideration is the result of a synchronization between a transition of P' and one of R', i.e.

$$P' \mid R' \xrightarrow{\alpha} S,$$

because, by rule COM3 for parallel composition in Table 2.2, $\alpha = \tau$, and there are a label a and processes P'' and R'' such that $P' \xrightarrow{a} P''$, $R' \xrightarrow{\bar{a}} R''$ and $S = P'' \mid R''$.

We now proceed by examining each of these cases in turn.

Case 1. Since $P' \xrightarrow{\alpha} P''$ and $P' \sim Q'$, we have that $Q' \xrightarrow{\alpha} Q''$ and $P'' \sim Q''$ for some Q''. Using the transition $Q' \xrightarrow{\alpha} Q''$ as the premise in rule COM1 for parallel composition in Table 2.2, we infer that

$$Q' \mid R' \xrightarrow{\alpha} Q'' \mid R'.$$

By the definition of the relation $\mathcal{R}$, we have that

$$(P'' \mid R', Q'' \mid R') \in \mathcal{R}.$$

We can therefore take $T = Q'' \mid R'$, and we are done.

Case 2. In this case, we have that $R' \xrightarrow{\alpha} R''$. Using this transition as the premise in rule COM2 for parallel composition in Table 2.2, we infer that

$$Q' \mid R' \xrightarrow{\alpha} Q' \mid R''.$$

By the definition of the relation $\mathcal{R}$, we have that

$$(P' \mid R'', Q' \mid R'') \in \mathcal{R}.$$

We can therefore take $T = Q' \mid R''$, and we are done.

Case 3. Since $P' \xrightarrow{a} P''$ and $P' \sim Q'$, we have that $Q' \xrightarrow{a} Q''$ and $P'' \sim Q''$ for some Q''. Using the transitions $Q' \xrightarrow{a} Q''$ and $R' \xrightarrow{\bar{a}} R''$ as the premises in rule COM3 for parallel composition in Table 2.2, we infer that

$$Q' \mid R' \xrightarrow{\tau} Q'' \mid R''.$$

By the definition of the relation $\mathcal{R}$, we have that

$$(P'' \mid R'', Q'' \mid R'') \in \mathcal{R}.$$

We can therefore take $T = Q'' \mid R''$, and we are done.

Therefore the relation $\mathcal{R}$ is a bisimulation, as claimed.

• Let L be a set of labels. We aim at showing that $P \setminus L \sim Q \setminus L$. To this end, we shall build a bisimulation $\mathcal{R}$ that contains the pair of processes $(P \setminus L, Q \setminus L)$. Consider the relation

$$\mathcal{R} = \{(P' \setminus L, Q' \setminus L) \mid P' \sim Q' \text{ where } P', Q' \text{ are CCS processes}\}.$$

You should readily be able to convince yourself that the pair of processes $(P \setminus L, Q \setminus L)$ is indeed contained in $\mathcal{R}$. Moreover, following the lines of the proof we have just gone through for parallel composition, it is an instructive exercise to show that

the relation $\mathcal{R}$ is symmetric, and

if $(P' \setminus L, Q' \setminus L)$ is contained in $\mathcal{R}$ and $P' \setminus L \xrightarrow{\alpha} S$ for some action α and CCS process S, then $Q' \setminus L \xrightarrow{\alpha} T$ for some CCS process T such that $(S, T) \in \mathcal{R}$.

You are strongly encouraged to fill in the missing details in the proof. □

Exercise 3.14 *Prove that $\sim$ is preserved by action prefixing, summation and relabelling.* ♦

Exercise 3.15 (For the theoretically minded) *For each set of labels L and process P, we may wish to build a process $\tau_L(P)$ that is obtained by turning into a τ-action each action α performed by P, with $\alpha \in L$ or $\bar{\alpha} \in L$. Operationally, the behaviour of the construct $\tau_L(\ )$ can be described by the following two rules:*

$$\frac{P \xrightarrow{\alpha} P'}{\tau_L(P) \xrightarrow{\tau} \tau_L(P')} \quad \text{if } \alpha \in L \text{ or } \bar{\alpha} \in L,$$

$$\frac{P \xrightarrow{\alpha} P'}{\tau_L(P) \xrightarrow{\alpha} \tau_L(P')} \quad \text{if } \alpha = \tau \text{ or } \alpha, \bar{\alpha} \notin L.$$

Prove that $\tau_L(P) \sim \tau_L(Q)$ whenever $P \sim Q$.

Consider the question whether the operation $\tau_L(\ )$ can be defined in CCS modulo $\sim$. That is, can we find a CCS expression $C_L[\ ]$ with a 'hole' (a place holder into which another process can be plugged) such that, for each process P,

$$\tau_L(P) \sim C_L[P]?$$

Argue for your answer. ♦

Now recall that we defined the specification of a counter thus:

$$\text{Counter}_0 \overset{\text{def}}{=} \text{up.Counter}_1,$$

$$\text{Counter}_n \overset{\text{def}}{=} \text{up.Counter}_{n+1} + \text{down.Counter}_{n-1} \quad (n > 0).$$

Moreover, we stated that we expect this process to be 'behaviourally equivalent' to the process C defined by

$$\text{C} \overset{\text{def}}{=} \text{up.(C} \mid \text{down.0)}.$$

We can now show that, in fact, C and Counter_0 are strongly bisimilar. To this end, note that this follows if we can show that the relation $\mathcal{R}$ defined by

$$\{(C \mid \Pi_{i=1}^k P_i, \text{Counter}_n) \mid (1)\ k \geq 0,\ (2)\ P_i = \mathbf{0} \text{ or } P_i = \text{down.0 for each } i,$$
$$(3) \text{ the number of } is \text{ with } P_i = \text{down.0 is } n\}$$

is a strong bisimulation. (Can you see why?) The following result states that this does hold true.

Proposition 3.1 The relation $\mathcal{R}$ defined above is a strong bisimulation.

Proof. Assume that

$$(C \mid \Pi_{i=1}^{k} P_i) \, \mathcal{R} \, \text{Counter}_n.$$

By the definition of the relation $\mathcal{R}$, each P_i is either $\mathbf{0}$ or down.$\mathbf{0}$, and the number of $P_i = \text{down}.\mathbf{0}$ is n. We shall now show that

1. if $C \mid \Pi_{i=1}^{k} P_i \xrightarrow{\alpha} P$ for some action α and process P then there is some process Q such that $\text{Counter}_n \xrightarrow{\alpha} Q$ and $P \, \mathcal{R} \, Q$, and
2. if $\text{Counter}_n \xrightarrow{\alpha} Q$ for some some action α and process Q then there is some process P such that $C \mid \Pi_{i=1}^{k} P_i \xrightarrow{\alpha} P$ and $P \, \mathcal{R} \, Q$.

We will establish these two claims separately.

Claim 1. Assume that $C \mid \Pi_{i=1}^{k} P_i \xrightarrow{\alpha} P$ for some some action α and process P. Then

> *either* $\alpha = \text{up}$ and $P = C \mid \text{down}.\mathbf{0} \mid \Pi_{i=1}^{k} P_i$
> *or* $n > 0$, $\alpha = \text{down}$ and $P = C \mid \Pi_{i=1}^{k} P_i'$, where the sequences of the processes $P_1, \dots, P_k$ and $P_1', \dots, P_k'$ differ in exactly one position ℓ and, at that position, $P_\ell = \text{down}.\mathbf{0}$ and $P_\ell' = \mathbf{0}$.

In the former case, argue that the matching transition is

$$\text{Counter}_n \xrightarrow{\text{up}} \text{Counter}_{n+1}.$$

In the latter, argue that the matching transition is

$$\text{Counter}_n \xrightarrow{\text{down}} \text{Counter}_{n-1}.$$

Claim 2. Assume that $\text{Counter}_n \xrightarrow{\alpha} Q$ for some some action α and process Q. Then

> *either* $\alpha = \text{up}$ and $Q = \text{Counter}_{n+1}$
> *or* $n > 0$, $\alpha = \text{down}$ and $Q = \text{Counter}_{n-1}$.

Finding matching transitions from $C \mid \Pi_{i=1}^{k} P_i$ is left as an exercise for the reader.

We can therefore conclude that $\mathcal{R}$ is a strong bisimulation, which was to be shown. $\qquad\square$

Exercise 3.16 *Fill in the missing details in the above proof.* ◆

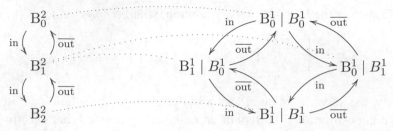

Figure 3.2 A bisimulation showing that $B_0^2 \sim B_0^1 \mid B_0^1$.

Using CCS, we may specify the desired behaviour of a buffer with capacity one thus:

$$B_0^1 \overset{\text{def}}{=} \text{in}.B_1^1,$$

$$B_1^1 \overset{\text{def}}{=} \overline{\text{out}}.B_0^1.$$

The constant B_0^1 stands for an empty buffer with capacity one, that is, a buffer with capacity one holding zero items, and B_1^1 stands for a full buffer with capacity one, that is, a buffer with capacity one holding one item.

By analogy with the above definition, in general we may specify a buffer of capacity $n \geq 1$ as follows, where the superscript stands for the maximal capacity of the buffer and the subscript for the number of elements the buffer currently holds:

$$B_0^n \overset{\text{def}}{=} \text{in}.B_1^n,$$

$$B_i^n \overset{\text{def}}{=} \text{in}.B_{i+1}^n + \overline{\text{out}}.B_{i-1}^n \quad (0 < i < n),$$

$$B_n^n \overset{\text{def}}{=} \overline{\text{out}}.B_{n-1}^n.$$

It seems natural to expect that we may implement a buffer of capacity $n \geq 1$ by means of the parallel composition of n buffers of capacity one. This expectation is certainly met when $n = 2$ because, as you can readily check, the relation depicted in Figure 3.2 is a bisimulation showing that

$$B_0^2 \sim B_0^1 \mid B_0^1.$$

That this holds regardless of the size of the buffer to be implemented is the import of the following result.

Proposition 3.2 For each natural number $n \geq 1$,

$$B_0^n \sim \underbrace{B_0^1 \mid B_0^1 \mid \cdots \mid B_0^1}_{n \text{ times}}.$$

Proof. Construct the following binary relation, where $i_1, i_2, \ldots, i_n \in \{0, 1\}$:

$$\mathcal{R} = \left\{ \left(B_i^n, \ B_{i_1}^1 \mid B_{i_2}^1 \mid \cdots \mid B_{i_n}^1 \right) \ \middle| \ \sum_{j=1}^n i_j = i \right\}.$$

Intuitively, the above relation relates a buffer of capacity n holding i items to a parallel composition of n buffers of capacity one, provided that exactly i of the latter are full.

It is not hard to see that

- $\left(B_0^n, \ B_0^1 \mid B_0^1 \mid \cdots \mid B_0^1 \right) \in \mathcal{R}$, and
- $\mathcal{R}$ is a strong bisimulation.

It follows that

$$B_0^n \sim \underbrace{B_0^1 \mid B_0^1 \mid \cdots \mid B_0^1}_{n \text{ times}}.$$

as required. We encourage you to fill in the details of this proof.   □

Exercise 3.17 (Simulation) *Let us say that a binary relation $\mathcal{R}$ over the set of states of an LTS is a simulation iff whenever $s_1 \ \mathcal{R} \ s_2$ and α is an action:*

if $s_1 \xrightarrow{\alpha} s_1'$ then there is a transition $s_2 \xrightarrow{\alpha} s_2'$ such that $s_1' \ \mathcal{R} \ s_2'$.

We say that s' simulates s, written $s \lesssim s'$, iff there is a simulation $\mathcal{R}$ for which $s \ \mathcal{R} \ s'$. Two states s and s' are simulation equivalent, written $s \simeq s'$, iff $s \lesssim s'$ and $s' \lesssim s$ both hold.

1. *Prove that $\lesssim$ is a preorder and that $\simeq$ is an equivalence relation.*
2. *Build simulations showing that*

$$a.0 \lesssim a.a.0,$$
$$a.b.0 + a.c.0 \lesssim a.(b.0 + c.0).$$

   Do the converse relations hold?
3. *Show that strong bisimilarity is included in simulation equivalence, that is, for any two strongly bisimilar states s and s' it holds that s' simulates s. Does the converse inclusion also hold?*

Is there a CCS process that can simulate any other CCS process?   ♦

Exercise 3.18 (Ready simulation) *Let us say that a binary relation $\mathcal{R}$ over the set of states of an LTS is a ready simulation iff, whenever $s_1 \ \mathcal{R} \ s_2$ and α is an action:*

if $s_1 \xrightarrow{\alpha} s_1'$ then there is a transition $s_2 \xrightarrow{\alpha} s_2'$ such that $s_1' \ \mathcal{R} \ s_2'$,
if $s_2 \xrightarrow{\alpha}$ then $s_1 \xrightarrow{\alpha}$.

We say that s' ready simulates s, written $s \sqsubseteq_{RS} s'$, iff there is a ready simulation $\mathcal{R}$ for which $s \mathcal{R} s'$. Two states s and s' are ready-simulation equivalent, written $s \simeq_{RS} s'$, iff $s \sqsubseteq_{RS} s'$ and that $s' \sqsubseteq_{RS} s$ both hold.

1. *Prove that $\sqsubseteq_{RS}$ is a preorder and that $\simeq_{RS}$ is an equivalence relation.*
2. *Do the following relations hold?*

$$a.0 \sqsubseteq_{RS} a.a.0,$$
$$a.b.0 + a.c.0 \sqsubseteq_{RS} a.(b.0 + c.0).$$

3. *Show that strong bisimilarity is included in ready-simulation equivalence, that is, for any two strongly bisimilar states s and s' it holds that s' ready simulates s. Does the converse inclusion also hold?*

Is there a CCS process that can ready simulate any other CCS process? ◆

Exercise 3.19 (For the theoretically minded) *Consider the processes*

$$P \stackrel{\text{def}}{=} a.b.c.0 + a.b.d.0,$$
$$Q \stackrel{\text{def}}{=} a.(b.c.0 + b.d.0).$$

Argue, first of all, that P and Q are not strongly bisimilar. Next show that:

1. *P and Q have the same completed traces (see Exercise 3.2);*
2. *for each process R and set of labels L, the processes*

$$(P \mid R) \setminus L \quad and \quad (Q \mid R) \setminus L$$

have the same completed traces.

So P and Q have the same deadlock behaviour in all parallel contexts, even though strong bisimilarity distinguishes them.

The lesson to be learned from these observations is that more generous notions of behavioural equivalence than bisimilarity may be necessary to validate some desirable equivalences. ◆

3.4 Weak bisimilarity

As we have seen in the previous section, strong bisimilarity affords many properties that we expect a behavioural relation to be used in implementation verification to have. (See the introduction to Chapter 3.) In particular, strong bisimilarity is an equivalence relation that is preserved by all CCS operators, it is the largest strong bisimulation, it supports a very elegant proof technique to demonstrate equivalences between process descriptions and it suffices to establish several natural equivalences. For instance, you used strong bisimilarity in

Exercise 3.12 to justify the expected equalities

$$P \mid Q \sim Q \mid P,$$
$$P \mid \mathbf{0} \sim P,$$
$$(P \mid Q) \mid R \sim P \mid (Q \mid R).$$

Moreover, a wealth of other 'structural equivalences' such as those above may be proved to hold modulo strong bisimilarity. (See Milner (1989, Propositions 7, 8).)

Should we look any further for a notion of behavioural equivalence to support implementation verification? Is there any item on our wish list that is not met by strong bisimilarity?

You might recall that we stated early on in this book that τ-actions in process behaviours are supposed to be *internal* and thus *unobservable*. This is a natural consequence of Milner's design decision to let τ indicate the result of a successful communication between two processes. Since communication is binary in CCS and since observing the behaviour of a process means communicating with it in some fashion, the unobservable nature of τ-actions is the upshot of the assumption that they cannot be used for further communication. This discussion indicates that a notion of behavioural equivalence should allow us to abstract from such steps in process behaviours.

Consider, for instance, the processes $a.\tau.0$ and $a.0$. Since τ-actions should be unobservable, we intuitively expect these to be observationally equivalent. Unfortunately, however, the processes $a.\tau.0$ and $a.0$ are *not* strongly bisimilar. In fact, the definition of strong bisimulation requires that *each* transition in the behaviour of one process should be matched by *a single* transition of the other, regardless of whether that transition is labelled by an observable action or by τ, and $a.\tau.0$ affords the trace $a\tau$ whereas $a.0$ does not.

In hindsight, this failure of strong bisimilarity to account for the unobservable nature of τ-actions should have been expected, because the definition of strong bisimulation treats internal actions as if they were ordinary observable actions. What we should like to have is a notion of bisimulation equivalence that affords all the good properties of strong bisimilarity and abstracts from τ-actions in the behaviour of processes. However, in order to fulfill this aim, first we need to understand what 'abstracting from τ-actions' actually means. Does this simply mean that we can 'erase' the τ-actions in the behaviour of a process? This would be enough to show that $a.\tau.0$ and $a.0$ are equivalent, as the former process is identical to the latter if we 'erase the τ-prefix'. But would this work in general?

To understand the issue better, let us make our old friend from the computer science department, namely the process CS defined in Table 2.1, interact with a nasty variation on the coffee machine CM from (2.1). This latest version of the

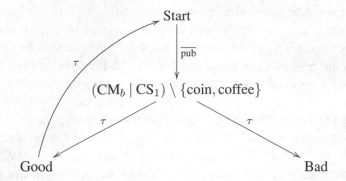

Figure 3.3 The possible behaviours of $(CM_b \mid CS) \setminus \{coin, coffee\}$:

Start $\equiv (CM_b \mid CS) \setminus \{coin, coffee\}$, $CS \stackrel{def}{=} \overline{pub}.CS_1$,
Good $\equiv (\overline{coffee}, CM_b \mid CS_2) \setminus \{coin, coffee\}$, $CS_1 \stackrel{def}{=} \overline{coin}.CS_2$,
Bad $\equiv (CM_b \mid CS_2) \setminus \{coin, coffee\}$, $CS_2 \stackrel{def}{=} coffee.CS$.

coffee machine delivered to the computer scientist's office is given by

$$CM_b \stackrel{def}{=} coin.\overline{coffee}.CM_b + coin.CM_b. \tag{3.7}$$

(The subscript b indicates that this version of the coffee machine is bad!)

Note that, upon receipt of a coin, the coffee machine CM_b can decide to go back to its initial state without delivering the coffee. You should be able to convince yourself that the sequences of transitions in Figure 3.3 describe the possible behaviours of the system $(CM_b \mid CS) \setminus \{coin, coffee\}$. In this figure, for the sake of notational convenience we use Start as a shorthand for the CCS expression

$$(CM_b \mid CS) \setminus \{coin, coffee\}.$$

The shorthands Bad and Good are also introduced in the figure, using the 'declarations'

$$Good \equiv (\overline{coffee}.CM_b \mid CS_2) \setminus \{coin, coffee\},$$
$$Bad \equiv (CM_b \mid CS_2) \setminus \{coin, coffee\}.$$

Note that there are two possible τ-transitions that stem from the process

$$(CM_b \mid CS_1) \setminus \{coin, coffee\},$$

and that one of these, namely

$$(CM_b \mid CS_1) \setminus \{coin, coffee\} \stackrel{\tau}{\rightarrow} (CM_b \mid CS_2) \setminus \{coin, coffee\},$$

leads to a deadlocked state. Albeit directly unobservable, this transition cannot be ignored in our analysis of the behaviour of this system because it pre-empts the other possible behaviour of the machine. So, unobservable actions cannot be just erased from the behaviour of processes because, in the light of their pre-emptive power in the presence of nondeterministic choices, they may affect what we may observe.

Note that the pre-emptive power of internal transitions is unimportant in the standard theory of automata, as there we are concerned only with the possibility to process our input strings correctly. Indeed, as you may recall from courses in the theory of automata, the so-called ε-transitions do *not* increase the expressive power of nondeterministic finite automata; see, for instance, the textbook (Sipser, 2005, Chapter 1). In a reactive environment, however, this power of internal transitions must be taken into account in a reasonable definition of process behaviour because it may lead to undesirable consequences, for example, the deadlock situation in Figure 3.3. We therefore expect that the behaviour of the process SmUni is *not* equivalent to that of the process $(CM_b \mid CS) \setminus \{coin, coffee\}$ since the latter may deadlock after outputting a publication whereas the former cannot.

In order to define a notion of bisimulation that allows us to abstract from internal transitions in process behaviours and to differentiate the process SmUni from $(CM_b \mid CS) \setminus \{coin, coffee\}$, we begin by introducing a new notion of transition relation between processes.

Definition 3.3 Let P and Q be CCS processes or, more generally, states in an LTS. For each action α, we shall write $P \overset{\alpha}{\Rightarrow} Q$ iff

either $\alpha \neq \tau$ and there are processes P' and Q' such that

$$P(\overset{\tau}{\rightarrow})^* P' \overset{\alpha}{\rightarrow} Q'(\overset{\tau}{\rightarrow})^* Q$$

or $\alpha = \tau$ and $P(\overset{\tau}{\rightarrow})^* Q$,

where we write $(\overset{\tau}{\rightarrow})^*$ for the reflexive and transitive closure of the relation $\overset{\tau}{\rightarrow}$. ♦

Thus $P \overset{\alpha}{\Rightarrow} Q$ holds if P can reach Q by performing an α-labelled transition, possibly preceded and followed by sequences of τ-labelled transitions. For example, $a.\tau.\mathbf{0} \overset{a}{\Rightarrow} \mathbf{0}$ and $a.\tau.\mathbf{0} \overset{a}{\Rightarrow} \tau.\mathbf{0}$ both hold, as well as $a.\tau.\mathbf{0} \overset{\tau}{\Rightarrow} a.\tau.\mathbf{0}$. In fact, we have $P \overset{\tau}{\Rightarrow} P$ for each process P.

In the LTS depicted in Figure 3.3, apart from the obvious one-step $\overline{\text{pub}}$-labelled transition, we have that

$$\text{Start} \overset{\overline{\text{pub}}}{\Rightarrow} \text{Good},$$

$$\text{Start} \overset{\overline{\text{pub}}}{\Rightarrow} \text{Bad},$$

$$\text{Start} \overset{\overline{\text{pub}}}{\Rightarrow} \text{Start}.$$

Our order of business now will be to use the new transition relations presented above to define a notion of bisimulation that can be used to equate processes that offer the same observable behaviour despite possibly having very different amounts of internal computation. The idea underlying the definition of the new notion of bisimulation is that a transition from a given process can now be matched by a sequence of transitions from another that has the same 'observational content' and leads to a state that is bisimilar to that reached by the first process.

Definition 3.4 (Weak bisimulation and observational equivalence) A binary relation $\mathcal{R}$ over the set of states of an LTS is a *weak bisimulation* iff, whenever $s_1 \mathcal{R} s_2$ and α is an action (including τ):

if $s_1 \overset{\alpha}{\to} s_1'$ then there is a transition $s_2 \overset{\alpha}{\Rightarrow} s_2'$ such that $s_1' \mathcal{R} s_2'$;
if $s_2 \overset{\alpha}{\to} s_2'$ then there is a transition $s_1 \overset{\alpha}{\Rightarrow} s_1'$ such that $s_1' \mathcal{R} s_2'$.

Two states s and s' are *observationally equivalent* (or *weakly bisimilar*), written $s \approx s'$, iff there is a weak bisimulation that relates them. Henceforth the relation $\approx$ will be referred to as *observational equivalence* or *weak bisimilarity*. ◆

Example 3.4 Let us consider the following LTS:

$$s \overset{\tau}{\longrightarrow} s_1 \overset{a}{\longrightarrow} s_2 \qquad\qquad t \overset{a}{\longrightarrow} t_1$$

Obviously $s \not\sim t$. However, $s \approx t$ because the relation

$$\mathcal{R} = \{(s, t), (s_1, t), (s_2, t_1)\}$$

is a weak bisimulation such that $(s, t) \in \mathcal{R}$. It remains to verify that $\mathcal{R}$ is indeed a weak bisimulation.

- Let us examine all possible transitions from the components of the pair (s, t). If $s \overset{\tau}{\to} s_1$ then $t \overset{\tau}{\Rightarrow} t$ and $(s_1, t) \in \mathcal{R}$. If $t \overset{a}{\to} t_1$ then $s \overset{a}{\Rightarrow} s_2$ and $(s_2, t_1) \in \mathcal{R}$.
- Let us examine all possible transitions from (s_1, t). If $s_1 \overset{a}{\to} s_2$ then $t \overset{a}{\Rightarrow} t_1$ and $(s_2, t_1) \in \mathcal{R}$. Similarly if $t \overset{a}{\to} t_1$ then $s_1 \overset{a}{\Rightarrow} s_2$ and again $(s_2, t_1) \in \mathcal{R}$.
- Consider now the pair (s_2, t_1). Since neither s_2 nor t_1 can perform any transition, it is safe to have this pair in $\mathcal{R}$.

Hence we have shown that each pair from $\mathcal{R}$ satisfies the conditions given in Definition 3.4, which means that $\mathcal{R}$ is a weak bisimulation, as claimed.   ◆

We can readily argue that $a.\mathbf{0} \approx a.\tau.\mathbf{0}$ by establishing a weak bisimulation that relates these two processes. (Do so by renaming the states in the LTS and in the bisimulation above!) However, there is no weak bisimulation that relates the process SmUni and the process Start in Figure 3.3. In fact, the process SmUni is observationally equivalent to the process

$$\text{Spec} \stackrel{\text{def}}{=} \overline{\text{pub}}.\text{Spec},$$

but the process Start is not.

Exercise 3.20 *Prove the claims that we have just made.*   ◆

Exercise 3.21 *Prove that the behavioural equivalences claimed in Exercise 2.11 hold with respect to observational equivalence (weak bisimilarity).*   ◆

The definition of weak bisimilarity is so natural, at least to our mind, that it is easy to miss some of its crucial consequences. To highlight some of these, consider the process

$$A? \stackrel{\text{def}}{=} a.\mathbf{0} + \tau.B?,$$
$$B? \stackrel{\text{def}}{=} b.\mathbf{0} + \tau.A?.$$

Intuitively, this process describes a 'polling loop' that may be seen as an implementation of a process that is willing to receive on port a or port b, and then terminate. Indeed, it is not hard to show that

$$A? \approx B? \approx a.\mathbf{0} + b.\mathbf{0}.$$

(Prove this!) This seems to be non-controversial until we note that A? and B? have a livelock (that is, a possibility of divergence), owing to the τ-loop

$$A? \stackrel{\tau}{\rightarrow} B? \stackrel{\tau}{\rightarrow} A?,$$

but $a.\mathbf{0} + b.\mathbf{0}$ does not. The above equivalences capture a main feature of observational equivalence, namely the fact that it supports what is called 'fair abstraction from divergence'. (See Baeten, Bergstra and Klop (1987), where it is shown that a proof rule embodying this idea, namely Koomen's fair-abstraction rule, is valid with respect to observational equivalence.) This means that observational equivalence assumes that if a process can escape from a loop consisting of internal transitions then it will eventually do so. This property of observational equivalence, which is by no means obvious from its definition, is crucial in using observational

$$\text{Send} \stackrel{\text{def}}{=} \text{acc.Sending} \qquad\qquad \text{Rec} \stackrel{\text{def}}{=} \text{trans.Del}$$

$$\text{Sending} \stackrel{\text{def}}{=} \overline{\text{send}}.\text{Wait} \qquad\qquad \text{Del} \stackrel{\text{def}}{=} \overline{\text{del}}.\text{Ack}$$

$$\text{Wait} \stackrel{\text{def}}{=} \text{ack.Send} + \text{error.Sending} \qquad \text{Ack} \stackrel{\text{def}}{=} \overline{\text{ack}}.\text{Rec}$$

$$\text{Med} \stackrel{\text{def}}{=} \text{send.Med}'$$

$$\text{Med}' \stackrel{\text{def}}{=} \tau.\text{Err} + \overline{\text{trans}}.\text{Med}$$

$$\text{Err} \stackrel{\text{def}}{=} \overline{\text{error}}.\text{Med}$$

Table 3.1 The sender, receiver and medium in (3.8)

equivalence as a correctness criterion in the verification of communication protocols, since the communication media may lose messages or messages may have to be retransmitted some arbitrary number of times in order to ensure their delivery.

Note moreover that $\mathbf{0}$ is observationally equivalent to the 'diverge' process,

$$\text{Div} \stackrel{\text{def}}{=} \tau.\text{Div}.$$

This means that a process that can only diverge is observationally equivalent to a deadlocked one. This may also seem odd at first sight. However, you will probably agree that, assuming that we can observe a process only by communicating with it, the systems $\mathbf{0}$ and Div are observationally equivalent since both refuse each attempt at communicating with them. (They do so for different reasons, but these reasons cannot be distinguished by an external observer.)

As an example of an application of observational equivalence to the verification of a simple protocol, consider the process Protocol defined by

$$(\text{Send} \mid \text{Med} \mid \text{Rec}) \setminus L \qquad (L = \{\text{send}, \text{error}, \text{trans}, \text{ack}\}), \qquad (3.8)$$

consisting of a sender and a receiver that communicate via a potentially faulty medium. The sender, the receiver and the medium are given in Table 3.1. (In this table, we use the port names 'acc' and 'del' as shorthand for 'accept' and 'deliver' respectively.) Note that the potentially faulty behaviour of the medium Med is described abstractly in the defining equation for the process Med' by means of an internal transition to an 'error state'. When it has entered this state, the medium informs the sender process that it has lost a message and therefore that the message must be retransmitted. The sender will receive this message when in the state Wait and will proceed to retransmit the message.

We expect the protocol to behave like a one-place buffer described thus:

$$\text{ProtocolSpec} \stackrel{\text{def}}{=} \text{acc}.\overline{\text{del}}.\text{ProtocolSpec}.$$

Note, however, that inclusion of the possibility of having to retransmit a message some arbitrary number of times before a successful delivery means that the process describing the protocol has a livelock. (Find it!) However, you should be able to prove that

$$\text{Protocol} \approx \text{ProtocolSpec},$$

by building a suitable weak bisimulation.

Exercise 3.22 *Build the aforementioned weak bisimulation.*   ◆

The following theorem is the counterpart of Theorem 3.1 for the case of weak bisimilarity. It states that $\approx$ is an equivalence relation and that it is the largest weak bisimulation.

Theorem 3.3 For all LTSs, the relation $\approx$ is

1. an equivalence relation,
2. the largest weak bisimulation, and
3. satisfies the following property:
   $s_1 \approx s_2$ iff, for each action α,

   if $s_1 \xrightarrow{\alpha} s_1'$ then there is a transition $s_2 \xRightarrow{\alpha} s_2'$ such that $s_1' \approx s_2'$;
   if $s_2 \xrightarrow{\alpha} s_2'$ then there is a transition $s_1 \xRightarrow{\alpha} s_1'$ such that $s_1' \approx s_2'$.

Proof. The proof follows the lines of that of Theorem 3.1 and is therefore omitted.   □

Exercise 3.23 *Fill in the details of the proof of the above theorem.*   ◆

Exercise 3.24 *Show that strong bisimilarity is included in observational equivalence; that is, prove that any two strongly bisimilar states are also weakly bisimilar.*   ◆

Exercise 3.25 *Consider the following LTS:*

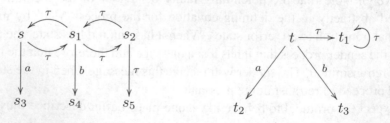

Show that $s \approx t$ by finding a weak bisimulation containing the pair (s, t).   ◆

Exercise 3.26 *Show that for all P, Q the following equivalences, which are usually referred to as Milner's τ-laws, hold:*

$$\alpha.\tau.P \approx \alpha.P, \tag{3.9}$$

$$P + \tau.P \approx \tau.P, \tag{3.10}$$

$$\alpha.(P + \tau.Q) \approx \alpha.(P + \tau.Q) + \alpha.Q. \tag{3.11}$$

Hint: Build appropriate weak bisimulations. ◆

Exercise 3.27 *Show that for all P, Q if $P \overset{\tau}{\Rightarrow} Q$ and $Q \overset{\tau}{\Rightarrow} P$ then $P \approx Q$.* ◆

Exercise 3.28 *We say that a CCS process is τ-free iff none of the states that it can reach by performing sequences of transitions affords a τ-labelled transition. For example, $a.\mathbf{0}$ is τ-free but $a.(b.\mathbf{0} \mid \bar{b}.\mathbf{0})$ is not.*

Prove that no τ-free CCS process is observationally equivalent to $a.\mathbf{0} + \tau.\mathbf{0}$. ◆

Exercise 3.29 *Prove that, for each CCS process P, the process $P \setminus (\mathsf{Act} - \{\tau\})$ is observationally equivalent to $\mathbf{0}$. Does this remain true if we consider processes modulo strong bisimilarity?* ◆

Exercise 3.30 (Mandatory) *Show that observational equivalence is the largest symmetric relation $\mathcal{R}$ satisfying that whenever $s_1 \mathcal{R} s_2$ then, for each action α (including τ), if $s_1 \overset{\alpha}{\Rightarrow} s'_1$ then there is a transition $s_2 \overset{\alpha}{\Rightarrow} s'_2$ such that $s'_1 \mathcal{R} s'_2$.*

This means that observational equivalence may be defined in the same way as strong bisimilarity but over an LTS whose transitions are $\overset{\alpha}{\Rightarrow}$, where α ranges over a set of actions including τ. ◆

Exercise 3.31 *For each sequence σ of observable actions in $\mathcal{L}$ and states s, t in an LTS, define the relation $\overset{\sigma}{\Rightarrow}$ thus:*

$s \overset{\varepsilon}{\Rightarrow} t$ iff $s \overset{\tau}{\Rightarrow} t$, and
$s \overset{a\sigma'}{\Rightarrow} t$ iff $s \overset{a}{\Rightarrow} s' \overset{\sigma'}{\Rightarrow} t$ for some s'.

A binary relation $\mathcal{R}$ over the set of states of an LTS is a weak string bisimulation iff whenever $s_1 \mathcal{R} s_2$ and σ is a (possibly empty) sequence of observable actions in $\mathcal{L}$:

if $s_1 \overset{\sigma}{\Rightarrow} s'_1$ then there is a transition $s_2 \overset{\sigma}{\Rightarrow} s'_2$ such that $s'_1 \mathcal{R} s'_2$;
if $s_2 \overset{\sigma}{\Rightarrow} s'_2$ then there is a transition $s_1 \overset{\sigma}{\Rightarrow} s'_1$ such that $s'_1 \mathcal{R} s'_2$.

Two states s and s' are weakly string bisimilar iff there is a weak string bisimulation that relates them.

Prove that weak string bisimilarity and weak bisimilarity coincide. That is, show that two states s and s' are weakly string bisimilar iff they are weakly bisimilar. ◆

The notion of observational equivalence that we have just defined seems to meet many of our desiderata. There is, however, one important property that observational equivalence does *not* enjoy: unlike strong bisimilarity, observational equivalence is *not* a congruence. This means that, in general, we cannot substitute observationally equivalent processes one for the other in a process context without affecting the overall behaviour of the system.

To see this, observe that 0 is observationally equivalent to $\tau.0$. However, it is not hard to see that

$$a.0 + 0 \not\approx a.0 + \tau.0.$$

In fact, the transition $a.0 + \tau.0 \xrightarrow{\tau} 0$ from the process $a.0 + \tau.0$ can be matched only by $a.0 + 0 \xRightarrow{\tau} a.0 + 0$, and the processes 0 and $a.0 + 0$ are not observationally equivalent. However, we still have that weak bisimilarity is a congruence with respect to the remaining CCS operators.

Theorem 3.4 Let P, Q, R be CCS processes. Assume that $P \approx Q$. Then

- $\alpha.P \approx \alpha.Q$ for each action α,
- $P \mid R \approx Q \mid R$ and $R \mid P \approx R \mid Q$ for each process R,
- $P[f] \approx Q[f]$ for each relabelling f, and
- $P \setminus L \approx Q \setminus L$ for each set of labels L.

Proof. The proof follows the lines of that of Theorem 3.2 and is left as an exercise for the reader. □

Exercise 3.32 *Prove Theorem 3.4. In the proof of the second claim in the proposition, you may find the following fact useful:*

if $Q \xRightarrow{a} Q'$ and $R \xrightarrow{\bar{a}} R'$ then $Q|R \xRightarrow{\tau} Q'|R'$.

Show this fact by induction on the number of τ-steps in the transition $Q \xRightarrow{a} Q'$. ♦

Exercise 3.33 *Give syntactic restrictions on the syntax of CCS terms such that weak bisimilarity becomes a congruence with respect to the choice operator also.* ♦

In the light of Theorem 3.4, observational equivalence is very close to being a congruence over CCS. The characterization and the study of the largest congruence relation included in observational equivalence is a very interesting chapter in process theory. It is, however, one that we hardly touch upon in this book; see, however, Exercise 3.36 below for a glimpse of this theory. The interested reader is referred to Milner (1989, Chapter 7) and Glabbeek (2005) for an in-depth treatment of this interesting topic.

Exercise 3.34 (Dijkstra's dining-philosophers problem) *In this exercise, we invite you to use the Edinburgh Concurrency Workbench – a software tool for the analysis of reactive systems specified as CCS processes – to model and analyse the dining-philosophers problem proposed by the late Edsger Dijkstra in his classic paper (Dijkstra, 1971).*

The problem is usually described as follows. Five philosophers spend their time either eating or thinking. Each philosopher usually keeps thinking, but at any point in time he might become hungry and decide that it is time to eat. The research institute where the philosophers work has a round dining table with a large bowl of spaghetti at the centre of the table. There are five plates on the table and five forks set between the plates. Each philosopher needs two forks to eat, which he picks up one at a time. The funding agency sponsoring the institute is only interested in the thinking behaviour of the philosophers and would like the institute to perform like an ideal think-factory – that is, like a system that produces thinking, rather than eating, forever.

1. *Assume, to begin with, that there are only two philosophers and two forks. Model the philosophers and the forks as CCS processes, assuming that the philosophers and the forks are numbered 1 and 2 and that the philosophers pick the forks up in increasing order (i.e. when he becomes hungry, the second philosopher begins by picking up the second fork and then picks up the first.) Argue that the system has a deadlock by finding a state in the resulting LTS that is reachable from the start state and has no outgoing transitions.*

   We encourage you to find a possible deadlock in the system by yourself, and without using the Workbench.
2. *Argue that a model of the system with five philosophers and five forks also exhibits a deadlock.*
3. *Finally, assume that there are five philosophers and five forks and that the philosophers pick the forks up in increasing order apart from the fifth, who picks up the first fork before the fifth. Use the the Edinburgh Concurrency Workbench to argue that the resulting system is observationally equivalent to the process* ThinkFactory *specified by*

$$\text{ThinkFactory} \stackrel{\text{def}}{=} \text{think.ThinkFactory}.$$

Here we are assuming that each philosopher performs the action 'think' when he is thinking and that the funding agency is not interested in knowing which specific philosopher is thinking! ◆

Exercise 3.35 (For the theoretically minded) *A binary relation $\mathcal{R}$ over the set of states of an LTS is a* branching bisimulation *(Glabbeek and Weijland, 1996) iff it is symmetric and, whenever $s \mathcal{R} t$ and α is an action (including τ):*

if $s \xrightarrow{\alpha} s'$ then
  either $\alpha = \tau$ and $s' \mathcal{R} t$
  or there is a $k \geq 0$ and a sequence of transitions

$$t = t_0 \xrightarrow{\tau} t_1 \xrightarrow{\tau} \cdots \xrightarrow{\tau} t_k \xrightarrow{\alpha} t'$$

  such that $s \mathcal{R} t_i$ for each $i \in \{0, \ldots, k\}$ and $s' \mathcal{R} t'$.

Two states s and t are branching bisimulation *equivalent (or* branching bisimilar*) iff there is a branching bisimulation that relates them. The largest branching bisimulation is called* branching bisimilarity*.*

1. *Show that branching bisimilarity is contained in weak bisimilarity.*
2. *Can you find two processes that are weakly bisimilar but not branching bisimilar?*
3. *Which of the τ-laws from Exercise 3.26 holds with respect to branching bisimilarity?*
4. *Is branching bisimilarity a congruence over the language CCS?*

In answering the last question, you may assume that branching bisimilarity is an equivalence relation. In fact, showing that branching bisimilarity is transitive is non-trivial; see, for instance, (Basten, 1996) for a proof. ◆

Exercise 3.36 *Define the binary relation $\approx^c$ over the set of states of an LTS as follows.*

$s_1 \approx^c s_2$ *iff for each action α (including τ):*
  if $s_1 \xrightarrow{\alpha} s_1'$ then there is a sequence of transitions $s_2 \xRightarrow{\tau} s_2'' \xrightarrow{\alpha} s_2''' \xRightarrow{\tau} s_2'$ such that $s_1' \approx s_2'$;
  if $s_2 \xrightarrow{\alpha} s_2'$ then there is a sequence of transitions $s_1 \xRightarrow{\tau} s_1'' \xrightarrow{\alpha} s_1''' \xRightarrow{\tau} s_1'$ such that $s_1' \approx s_2'$.

Prove the following claims.

1. *The relation $\approx^c$ is an equivalence relation.*
2. *The relation $\approx^c$ is preserved by the operators of CCS, that is, if $P \approx^c Q$ then $\alpha.P \approx^c \alpha.Q$ for each action α;*

   $P + R \approx^c Q + R$ *and* $R + P \approx^c R + Q$ *for each process R;*
   $P \mid R \approx^c Q \mid R$ *and* $R \mid P \approx^c R \mid Q$ *for each process R;*

$P[f] \approx^c Q[f]$ *for each relabelling* f; *and*
$P \setminus L \approx^c Q \setminus L$ *for each set of labels* L.

3. *Argue that* $\approx^c$ *is included in weak bisimilarity.*
4. *Find an example of two weakly bisimilar processes that are not related with respect to* $\approx^c$.

Which τ*-law from Exercise 3.26 holds with respect to* $\approx^c$? ♦

3.5 Game characterization of bisimilarity

We can naturally ask ourselves the following question:

What techniques do we have to show that two states are *not* bisimilar?

In order to prove that for two given states s and t it is the case that $s \not\sim t$, by Definition 3.2 we should enumerate all binary relations over the set of states and for each of them show that if it contains the pair (s, t) then it is not a strong bisimulation. For the transition system from Example 3.1 in Section 3.3 this translates into investigating 2^{25} different candidates and, in general, for a transition system with n states one would have to go through 2^{n^2} different binary relations. (Can you see why?) In what follows, we will introduce a game characterization of strong bisimilarity that will enable us to determine in a much more perspicuous way whether two states are strongly bisimilar.

The idea is that there are two players in the bisimulation game, called '*attacker*' and '*defender*'. The attacker is trying to show that two given states are not bisimilar while the defender aims to show the opposite. The formal definition follows.

Definition 3.5 (Strong bisimulation game) Let $(\mathsf{Proc}, \mathsf{Act}, \{\xrightarrow{\alpha} \mid \alpha \in \mathsf{Act}\})$ be an LTS. A *strong bisimulation game* starting from the pair of states $(s_1, t_1) \in \mathsf{Proc} \times \mathsf{Proc}$ is a two-player game with an '*attacker*' and a '*defender*'.

The game is played in *rounds*, and *configurations* of the game are pairs of states from $\mathsf{Proc} \times \mathsf{Proc}$. In every round exactly one configuration is called *current*; initially the configuration (s_1, t_1) is the current one.

In each round the players change the current configuration (s, t) according to the following rules.

1. The attacker chooses either the left- or the right-hand side of the current configuration (s, t) and an action α from Act.
   - If the attacker chooses left then he has to perform a transition $s \xrightarrow{\alpha} s'$ for some state $s' \in \mathsf{Proc}$.

- If the attacker chooses right then he has to perform a transition $t \xrightarrow{\alpha} t'$ for some state $t' \in \mathsf{Proc}$.
2. In this step the defender must provide an answer to the attack made in the previous step.
   - If the attacker chose left then the defender plays on the right-hand side and has to respond by making a transition $t \xrightarrow{\alpha} t'$ for some $t' \in \mathsf{Proc}$.
   - If the attacker chose right then the defender plays on the left-hand side and has to respond by making a transition $s \xrightarrow{\alpha} s'$ for some $s' \in \mathsf{Proc}$.
3. The configuration (s', t') becomes the current configuration and the game continues for another round according to the rules described above.

$\blacklozenge$

A *play* of the game is a maximal sequence of configurations formed by the players according to the rules described above and starting from the initial configuration (s_1, t_1). (A sequence of configurations is maximal if it cannot be extended while following the rules of the game.) Note that a bisimulation game can have many different plays according to the choices made by the attacker and the defender. The attacker can choose a side, an action and a transition. The defender's only choice is in selecting one of the available transitions labelled with the same action as that picked by the attacker.

We shall now define when a play is winning for the attacker and when for the defender.

A finite play is lost by the player who is stuck and cannot make a move from the current configuration (s, t) according to the rules of the game. Note that the attacker loses a finite play only if both $s \not\rightarrow$ and $t \not\rightarrow$, i.e. there is no transition from either the left- or the right-hand side of the configuration. The defender loses a finite play if he has (on his side of the configuration) no available transition under the action selected by the attacker.

It can also be the case that neither player is stuck in any configuration and the play is infinite. In this situation the defender is the winner of the play. Intuitively, this is a natural choice of outcome because if the play is infinite then the attacker has been unable to find a 'difference' in the behaviour of the two systems, which will turn out to be bisimilar.

A given play is always winning either for the attacker or the defender and it cannot be winning for both at the same time.

The following proposition relates strong bisimilarity to the corresponding game characterization (see, e.g. Stirling (1995) or Thomas (1993)).

Proposition 3.3 States s_1 and t_1 of an LTS are strongly bisimilar iff the defender has a universal winning strategy in the strong bisimulation game starting from configuration (s_1, t_1). The states s_1 and t_1 are not strongly bisimilar iff the attacker has a universal winning strategy.

By a universal winning strategy we mean that the player with that strategy can always win the game, regardless of how the other player selects his moves. If the opponent has more than one choice of how to continue from the current configuration, all these possibilities have to be considered.

The notion of a universal winning strategy is best explained by means of an example.

Example 3.5 Let us recall the transition system from Example 3.1 in Section 3.3:

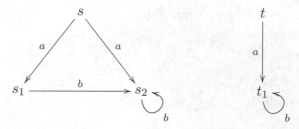

We will show that the defender has a universal winning strategy from the configuration (s, t) and hence, in the light of Proposition 3.3, that $s \sim t$. In order to do so, we have to consider all possible moves of the attacker from this configuration and define the defender's response to each of them. The attacker can make three different moves from (s, t), as follows.

1. Attacker selects right-hand side, action a and makes the move $t \xrightarrow{a} t_1$,
2. Attacker selects left-hand side, action a and makes the move $s \xrightarrow{a} s_2$.
3. Attacker selects left-hand side, action a and makes the move $s \xrightarrow{a} s_1$.

The defender's *answer to attack 1* is to play $s \xrightarrow{a} s_2$. (Even though there are more possibilities it is sufficient to provide only one suitable answer.) The current configuration becomes (s_2, t_1). The defender's *answer to attack 2* is to play $t \xrightarrow{a} t_1$. The current configuration again becomes (s_2, t_1). The defender's *answer to attack 3* is to play $t \xrightarrow{a} t_1$. The current configuration becomes (s_1, t_1).

Now it remains to show that the defender has a universal winning strategy from the configurations (s_2, t_1) and (s_1, t_1).

From (s_2, t_1) it is easy to see that any continuation of the game will always go through the same current configuration (s_2, t_1) and hence the game will be necessarily infinite. According to the definition of a winning play, the defender is the winner in this case.

From (s_1, t_1) the attacker has two possible moves. Either $s_1 \xrightarrow{b} s_2$ or $t_1 \xrightarrow{b} t_1$. In the former case the defender answers by $t_1 \xrightarrow{b} t_1$ and in the latter case by

$s_1 \xrightarrow{b} s_2$. The next configuration is in both cases (s_2, t_1), and we already know that the defender has a winning strategy from this configuration.

Hence we have shown that the defender has a universal winning strategy from the configuration (s, t) and, according to Proposition 3.3, this means that $s \sim t$. ◆

The game characterization of bisimilarity introduced above is simple yet powerful. It provides an intuitive understanding of this notion. It can be used to show that two states are strongly bisimilar and to show that they are not. The technique is particularly useful for showing the non-bisimilarity of two states. This is demonstrated by the following examples.

Example 3.6 Let us consider the following transition system (we provide only its graphical representation).

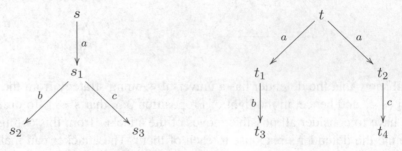

We will show that $s \not\sim t$ by describing a universal winning strategy for the attacker in the bisimulation game starting from (s, t). We will in fact show two different strategies (but of course finding one is sufficient for proving non-bisimilarity).

- In the first strategy, the attacker selects the left-hand side, action a and the transition $s \xrightarrow{a} s_1$. The defender can answer with $t \xrightarrow{a} t_1$ or $t \xrightarrow{a} t_2$. This means that we will have to consider two different configurations in the next round, namely (s_1, t_1) and (s_1, t_2). From (s_1, t_1) the attacker wins by playing the transition $s_1 \xrightarrow{c} s_3$ on the left-hand side, and the defender cannot answer as there is no c-transition from t_1. From (s_1, t_2) the attacker wins by playing $s_1 \xrightarrow{b} s_2$ and the defender has again no answer from t_2. As we have analysed all possibilities for the defender and in every one the attacker wins, we have found a universal winning strategy for the attacker. Hence s and t are not bisimilar.

- Now we provide another strategy, which is easier to describe and involves the switching of sides. Starting from (s, t) the attacker plays on the right-hand side according to the transition $t \xrightarrow{a} t_1$ and the defender can only answer by $s \xrightarrow{a} s_1$ on the left-hand side (no more configurations need to be examined as this is the only possibility for the defender). The current configuration hence becomes

(s_1, t_1). In the next round the attacker plays $s_1 \xrightarrow{c} s_3$ and wins the game as $t_1 \not\xrightarrow{c}$.

◆

Example 3.7 Let us consider a slightly more complex transition system:

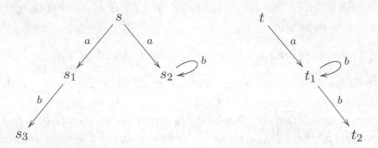

We will define the attacker's universal winning strategy from (s, t) and hence show that $s \not\sim t$.

In the first round the attacker plays on the left-hand side the move $s \xrightarrow{a} s_1$ and the defender can only answer with $t \xrightarrow{a} t_1$. The current configuration becomes (s_1, t_1). In the second round the attacker plays on the right-hand side according to the transition $t_1 \xrightarrow{b} t_1$ and the defender can only answer with $s_1 \xrightarrow{b} s_3$. The current configuration becomes (s_3, t_1). Now the attacker wins by playing again the transition $t_1 \xrightarrow{b} t_1$ (or $t_1 \xrightarrow{b} t_2$) and the defender loses because $s_3 \not\xrightarrow{}$. ◆

Exercise 3.37 *Consider the following LTS:*

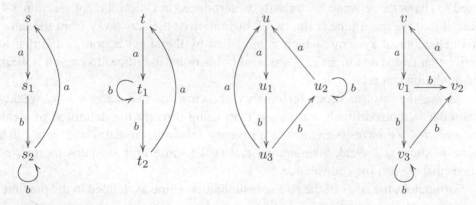

Decide whether $s \sim t$, $s \sim u$ and $s \sim v$. Support your claims by giving a universal winning strategy either for the attacker (in the negative case) or the defender (in the positive case). In the positive case you should also define a strong bisimulation relating the pair of processes in question. ◆

Exercise 3.38 (For the theoretically minded) *Prove   Proposition   3.3.   Hint:
Argue that, using the universal winning strategy for the defender you can find
a strong bisimulation and, conversely, that given a strong bisimulation you can
define a universal winning strategy for the defender.* ◆

Exercise 3.39 (For the theoretically minded) *Recall from Exercise 3.17 that a
binary relation $\mathcal{R}$ over the set of states of an LTS is a* simulation *iff, whenever
$s_1 \mathcal{R} s_2$ and a is an action,*

if $s_1 \xrightarrow{a} s_1'$ then there is a transition $s_2 \xrightarrow{a} s_2'$ such that $s_1' \mathcal{R} s_2'$.

A binary relation $\mathcal{R}$ over the set of states of an LTS is a 2-nested simulation *iff $\mathcal{R}$
is a simulation and moreover $\mathcal{R}^{-1} \subseteq \mathcal{R}$.*

Two states s and s' are in simulation preorder *(respectively in* 2-nested simulation preorder*) iff there is a simulation (respectively a 2-nested simulation) that
relates them.*

*Modify the rules of the strong bisimulation game in such a way that it charac-
terizes the simulation preorder and the 2-nested simulation preorder.* ◆

Exercise 3.40 (For the theoretically minded) *Can you change the rules of the
strong bisimulation game in such a way that it characterizes the ready-simulation
preorder introduced in Exercise 3.18?* ◆

3.5.1 Weak bisimulation games

We shall now introduce the notion of a weak bisimulation game, which can be
used to characterize weak bisimilarity as introduced in Definition 3.4, Section 3.4.
Recall that the main idea is that weak bisimilarity abstracts away from the internal behaviour of systems, which is modelled by the silent action τ, and that to
prove that two states in an LTS are weakly bisimilar it suffices to exhibit a weak
bisimulation that relates them.

As was the case for strong bisimilarity, showing that two states are *not* weakly
bisimilar is more difficult and means that, using directly the definition of weak
bisimilarity, we have to enumerate all binary relations on states and verify that
none of them is a weak bisimulation and at the same time contains the pair of
states that we test for equivalence.

Fortunately, the rules of the strong bisimulation game as defined in the previous
section need be only slightly modified in order to achieve a characterization of
weak bisimilarity in terms of weak bisimulation games.

Definition 3.6 (Weak bisimulation game) A *weak bisimulation game* is defined in
the same way as the strong bisimulation game in Definition 3.5, the only difference

being that the defender can also answer using the weak transition relation $\overset{\alpha}{\Rightarrow}$, rather that just $\overset{\alpha}{\rightarrow}$ as in the strong bisimulation game. The attacker is still only allowed to use the $\overset{\alpha}{\rightarrow}$ moves. ♦

The definitions of play and winning strategy are exactly as before and we have a similar proposition as for the strong bisimulation game.

Proposition 3.4 Two states s_1 and t_1 of an LTS are weakly bisimilar iff the defender has a universal winning strategy in the weak bisimulation game starting from the configuration (s_1, t_1). The states s_1 and t_1 are not weakly bisimilar iff the attacker has a universal winning strategy.

We remind the reader of the fact that, in the weak bisimulation game from the current configuration (s, t), if the attacker chooses a move under the silent action τ, let us say $s \overset{\tau}{\rightarrow} s'$, then the defender can (as one possibility) simply answer by doing 'nothing', i.e. by idling in the state t, since we always have $t \overset{\tau}{\Rightarrow} t$. In this case, the current configuration becomes (s', t).

Again, the notions of play and universal winning strategy in the weak bisimulation game are best explained by means of an example.

Example 3.8 Consider the following transition system:

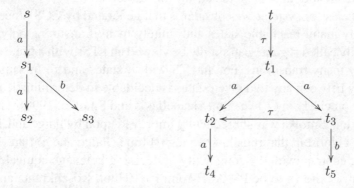

We will show that $s \not\approx t$ by defining a universal winning strategy for the attacker in the weak bisimulation game from (s, t).

In the first round, the attacker selects the left-hand side and action a and plays the move $s \overset{a}{\rightarrow} s_1$. The defender has three possible moves to answer: (i) $t \overset{a}{\Rightarrow} t_2$ via t_1, (ii) $t \overset{a}{\Rightarrow} t_2$ via t_1 and t_3 and (iii) $t \overset{a}{\Rightarrow} t_3$ via t_1. In cases (i) and (ii) the current configuration becomes (s_1, t_2) and in case (iii) it becomes (s_1, t_3).

From the configuration (s_1, t_2) the attacker wins by playing $s_1 \overset{b}{\rightarrow} s_3$, and the defender loses because $t_2 \overset{b}{\not\Rightarrow}$.

From the configuration (s_1, t_3) the attacker plays the τ-move from the right-hand side: $t_3 \xrightarrow{\tau} t_2$. The defender's only answer from s_1 is $s_1 \xRightarrow{\tau} s_1$ because no τ-actions are enabled from s_1. The current configuration becomes (s_1, t_2) and, as argued above, the attacker has a winning strategy from this pair.

This concludes the proof and shows that $s \not\approx t$ because we have found a universal winning strategy for the attacker.   ♦

Exercise 3.41 *In the weak bisimulation game the attacker is allowed to use only $\xrightarrow{a}$ moves for the attacks, but the defender can also use $\xRightarrow{a}$ moves in response. Argue that if we modify the rules of the game so that the attacker too can use moves of the form $\xRightarrow{a}$ then this does not provide any additional power for the attacker. Conclude that both versions of the game provide the same answer regarding the bisimilarity or non-bisimilarity of the two processes.*   ♦

3.6   Further results on equivalence checking

In the following few paragraphs we shall provide an overview of a number of interesting results achieved within concurrency theory in the area of equivalence checking. We shall also provide pointers to selected references in the literature that the interested reader may wish to consult for further study.

The first class of systems we consider is that generated by CCS processes which have finitely many reachable states and finitely many transitions only. Such systems, usually called *regular*, can simply be viewed an LTSs with a finite set of states and finitely many transitions. For an LTS with n states and m transitions, strong bisimilarity between any two given states is decidable in deterministic polynomial time, more precisely in $O(nm)$ time (Kanellakis and Smolka, 1990). This result of Kanellakis and Smolka was subsequently improved upon by Paige and Tarjan, who devised an algorithm that runs in $O(m \log n)$ time (Paige and Tarjan, 1987). This is in strong contrast with the complexity of deciding language equivalence, where the problem is known to be PSPACE-complete (Hunt, Rosenkrantz and Szymanski, 1976). By way of further comparison, we recall that deciding strong bisimilarity between finite LTSs is P-complete (Balcázar, Gabarró and Santha, 1992); this means that it is one of the 'hardest problems' in the class P of problems solvable in polynomial time. (P-complete problems are of interest because they appear to lack highly parallel solutions. See, for instance, the book Greenlaw, Hoover and Ruzzo (1995).)

We remind the reader that the above-mentioned complexity-results for finite LTSs are valid if the size of the input problem is measured as the number of states plus the number of transitions in the input LTS. If we assume that the size of the input is the length of the CCS equations that describe a finite transition system, then we face the so-called *state explosion problem* because relatively short CCS definitions can generate exponentially large LTSs. (For example, you should be able to convince yourself that the LTS associated with the CCS expression

$$a_1.\mathbf{0} \mid a_2.\mathbf{0} \mid \cdots \mid a_n.\mathbf{0}$$

has 2^n states.) In this case the strong-bisimilarity checking problem becomes EXPTIME-complete (Laroussinie and Schnoebelen, 2000); this means that it is one of the 'hardest problems' in the class EXPTIME of problems solvable in exponential time using deterministic algorithms.

The problem of checking observational equivalence (weak bisimilarity) over finite LTSs can be reduced to that of checking for strong bisimilarity, using a technique called *saturation*. Intuitively, saturation amounts to

1. first pre-computing the weak transition relation and then
2. constructing a new pair of finite processes whose original transitions are replaced by the weak transitions.

The question whether two states are weakly bisimilar now amounts to checking strong bisimilarity over the saturated systems. Since the computation of the weak transition relation can be carried out in polynomial time, the problem of checking for weak bisimilarity can also be decided in polynomial time.

This means that both strong and weak bisimilarity can be decided on finite-state transition systems faster than can many other equivalences. This story repeats itself also when we consider more general classes of transition systems.

Let us consider a class called BPP for *basic parallel processes*, first studied by Christensen in his Ph.D. thesis (Christensen, 1993). This is a class of infinite-state transition systems generated by a subclass of CCS expressions containing action prefixing, bounded nondeterminism and a pure-parallel composition, with neither restriction nor communication. In the case of BPP the difference between equivalence checking with respect to strong bisimilarity and other notions of equivalence is even more striking. On the one hand, it is known that language equivalence (Hirshfeld, 1994) as well as essentially any other notion of equivalence except for bisimilarity is undecidable (Hüttel, 1994). On the other hand, a surprising result by Christensen, Hirshfeld and Moller (1993) shows that strong bisimilarity is decidable in general, and Hirshfeld, Jerrum and Moller (1996b) showed that it is decidable in polynomial time for its subclass containing normed processes only. (A BPP process is *normed* iff from any of its reachable states it is possible to reach a situation where all actions are disabled.) Recently, the general bisimilarity problem for BPP has been shown to be PSPACE-complete (Jančar, 2003, Srba, 2002a).

If we want to go even further up (with respect to expressive power), we can consider the class of *Petri nets* (Petri, 1962, Reisig, 1985), a very well studied model of concurrent computation that strictly includes that of BPP processes. In fact, BPP is a subclass of Petri nets in which every transition has exactly one input place. (This is also called the communication-free subclass of Petri nets.) The problem of whether two marked Petri nets are bisimilar, as well as a number of other problems, is undecidable, as shown by Jančar (1995).

Researchers have also considered a sequential analogue to the BPP class, called BPA for *basic process algebra*, introduced by Bergstra and Klop (1982). Here, instead of the parallel operator we have a full sequential composition operator. (Action prefixing in CCS enables only a limited way of expressing sequential composition, whereas in BPA one is allowed to write down processes such as $E.F$ where both E and F can have a rather complicated behaviour.) This class also corresponds to context-free grammars in Greibach normal form, where only left-most derivations are allowed. Bar-Hillel, Perles, and Shamir (1961) showed that language equivalence for languages generated by BPA is undecidable. In fact, most studied equivalences (apart from bisimilarity, again!) are undecidable for this class of processes (Huynh and Tian, 1995, Groote and Hüttel, 1994). However, Baeten, Bergstra, and Klop showed that strong bisimilarity is decidable for normed BPA processes (Baeten, Bergstra and Klop, 1993) and there is even a polynomial-time algorithm for checking strong bisimilarity over this subclass of BPA processes, published by Hirshfeld, Jerrum and Moller (1996a).

Christensen, Hüttel, and Stirling (1995) proved that strong bisimilarity remains decidable for arbitrary (unnormed) BPA processes, but the precise complexity of the problem has not been determined yet. The problem is known to be PSPACE-hard (Srba, 2002b), yet no worse than doubly exponential (Burkart, Caucal and Steffen, 1995).

The positive-decidability trend is preserved even for a superclass of BPA called PDA, for *pushdown automata*. Even though BPA and PDA coincide with respect to language equivalence (they both generate the class of context-free languages), PDA is strictly more expressive when bisimilarity is considered as the notion of equivalence. Celebrated results of Sénizergues (1998) and Stirling (2000) both show the decidability of bisimulation equivalence over the class of pushdown automata. However, the problem of checking for weak bisimilarity over PDA is already known to be undecidable (Srba, 2002c).

There are still some open problems left in the theory, mainly concerning the decidability of weak bisimilarity. We refer the reader to an up-to-date overview in (Srba, 2004) and also to a more thorough introduction to the area available in, for instance, Burkart *et al.* (2001) or Mayr (2000).

4

Theory of fixed points and bisimulation equivalence

The aim of this chapter is to collect under one roof all the mathematical notions from the theory of partially ordered sets and lattices needed to introduce Tarski's classic fixed point theorem. You might think that this detour into some exotic looking mathematics is unwarranted in this textbook. However, we shall then put these possible doubts of yours to rest by using this fixed point theorem to give an alternative definition of strong bisimulation equivalence. This reformulation of the notion of strong bisimulation equivalence is not just mathematically pleasing but also yields an algorithm for computing the largest strong bisimulation over finite labelled transition systems (LTSs), i.e. labelled transition systems with only finitely many states, actions and transitions. This is an illustrative example of how apparently very abstract mathematical notions turn out to have algorithmic content and, possibly unexpected, applications in computer science. As you will see, we shall also put Tarski's fixed point theorem to good use in Chapter 6, where the theory developed in this chapter will allow us to understand the meaning of recursively defined properties of reactive systems.

4.1 Posets and complete lattices

We start our technical developments in this chapter by introducing the notion of a partially ordered set (also known as a poset) and some useful classes of such structures that will find application in what follows. As you will see, many examples of posets that we shall mention in this chapter are familiar.

Definition 4.1 (Partially ordered sets) A *partially ordered set* (often abbreviated to *poset*) is a pair $(D, \sqsubseteq)$, where D is a set and $\sqsubseteq$ is a binary relation over D (i.e. a subset of $D \times D$), such that:

75

$\sqsubseteq$ is *reflexive*, i.e. $d \sqsubseteq d$ for all $d \in D$;

$\sqsubseteq$ is *antisymmetric*, i.e. $d \sqsubseteq e$ and $e \sqsubseteq d$ imply $d = e$ for all $d, e \in D$;

$\sqsubseteq$ is *transitive*, i.e. $d \sqsubseteq e \sqsubseteq d'$ implies $d \sqsubseteq d'$ for all $d, d', e \in D$.

We say moreover that $(D, \sqsubseteq)$ is a *totally ordered set* if, for all $d, e \in D$, either $d \sqsubseteq e$ or $e \sqsubseteq d$ holds. ◆

Example 4.1 The following are examples of posets.

- $(\mathbb{N}, \leq)$, where $\mathbb{N}$ denotes the set of natural numbers and $\leq$ denotes the standard ordering over $\mathbb{N}$, is a poset.
- $(\mathbb{R}, \leq)$, where $\mathbb{R}$ denotes the set of real numbers and $\leq$ denotes the standard ordering over $\mathbb{R}$, is a poset.
- $(A^*, \leq)$ is a poset, where A^* is the set of strings over alphabet A and $\leq$ denotes the prefix ordering between strings, that is for all $s, t \in A^*$, we have $s \leq t$ iff there exists $w \in A^*$ such that $sw = t$. (Check that this is indeed a poset!)
- Let $(A, \leq)$ be a finite totally ordered set. Then $(A^*, \prec)$, the set of strings in A^* ordered lexicographically, is a poset. Recall that, for all $s, t \in A^*$, the relation $s \prec t$ holds with respect to the lexicographic order if one of the following conditions applies.
  1. The length of s is smaller than that of t.
  2. s and t have equal length, and either $s = \varepsilon$ or there are strings $u, v, z \in A^*$ and letters $a, b \in A$ such that $s = uav$, $t = ubz$ and $a \leq b$.
- Let $(D, \sqsubseteq)$ be a poset and S be a set. Then the collection of functions from S to D is also a poset when equipped with an ordering relation defined thus:

$$f \sqsubseteq g \quad \text{iff} \quad f(s) \sqsubseteq g(s), \text{ for each } s \in S.$$

We encourage you to think of other examples of posets with which you are familiar. ◆

Exercise 4.1 *Convince yourself that the structures mentioned in the above example are indeed posets. Which of the above posets is a totally ordered set?* ◆

As witnessed by the list of structures in Example 4.1 and by the many other examples encountered in discrete mathematics courses, posets are abundant in mathematics. Another example of a poset that will play an important role in the developments to follow is the structure $(2^S, \subseteq)$, where S is a set, 2^S stands for the set of all subsets of S and $\subseteq$ denotes set inclusion. For instance, the structure $(2^{\mathsf{Proc}}, \subseteq)$ is a poset for each set of states Proc in an LTS.

Exercise 4.2 *Is the poset $(2^S, \subseteq)$ totally ordered?* ◆

Definition 4.2 (Least upper bounds and greatest lower bounds) Let $(D, \sqsubseteq)$ be a poset, and take $X \subseteq D$.

- We say that $d \in D$ is an *upper bound* for X iff $x \sqsubseteq d$ for all $x \in X$. We say that d is the *least upper bound (lub)* of X, notation $\bigsqcup X$, iff

  d is an upper bound for X and, moreover,
  $d \sqsubseteq d'$ for every $d' \in D$ that is an upper bound for X.

- We say that $d \in D$ is a *lower bound* for X iff $d \sqsubseteq x$ for all $x \in X$. We say that d is the *greatest lower bound (glb)* of X, notation $\bigsqcap X$, iff

  d is a lower bound for X and, moreover,
  $d' \sqsubseteq d$ for every $d' \in D$ that is a lower bound for X. ◆

In the poset $(\mathbb{N}, \leq)$, all finite subsets of $\mathbb{N}$ have least upper bounds. Indeed, the least upper bound of such a set is its largest element. However, no infinite subset of $\mathbb{N}$ has an upper bound. All subsets of $\mathbb{N}$ have a least element, which is their greatest lower bound.

In $(2^S, \subseteq)$, *every* subset X of 2^S has an lub and a glb, given by $\bigcup X$ and $\bigcap X$ respectively. For example, consider the poset $(2^{\mathbb{N}}, \subseteq)$, consisting of the family of subsets of the set of natural numbers $\mathbb{N}$ ordered by inclusion. Take X to be the collection of finite sets of even numbers. Then $\bigcup X$ is the set of even numbers and $\bigcap X$ is the empty set. (Can you see why?)

Exercise 4.3 (Strongly recommended) *Let $(D, \sqsubseteq)$ be a poset, and take $X \subseteq D$. Prove that the lub and the glb of X are unique, if they exist.* ◆

Exercise 4.4
1. *Prove that the lub and the glb of a subset X of 2^S are indeed $\bigcup X$ and $\bigcap X$ respectively.*
2. *Give examples of subsets of $\{a, b\}^*$ that have upper bounds in the poset $(\{a, b\}^*, \leq)$, where $\leq$ is the prefix ordering over strings defined in the third bullet of Example 4.1. Find examples of subsets of $\{a, b\}^*$ that do not have upper bounds in that poset.* ◆

As you have seen already, a poset such as $(2^S, \subseteq)$ has the pleasing property that each of its subsets has both a least upper bound and a greatest lower bound. Posets with this property will play a crucial role in what follows, and we now introduce them formally.

Definition 4.3 (Complete lattices) A poset $(D, \sqsubseteq)$ is a *complete lattice* iff $\bigsqcup X$ and $\bigsqcap X$ exist for every subset X of D. ◆

Note that a complete lattice $(D, \sqsubseteq)$ has a least element $\bot = \bigsqcap D$, often called the *bottom element*, and a *top element* $\top = \bigsqcup D$. For example, the bottom element of the poset $(2^S, \subseteq)$ is the empty set, and the top element is S. (Why?) By Exercise 4.3 the least and top elements of a complete lattice are unique.

Exercise 4.5 *Let $(D, \sqsubseteq)$ be a complete lattice. What are $\bigsqcup \emptyset$ and $\bigsqcap \emptyset$? Hint: Each element of D is both a lower bound and an upper bound for $\emptyset$. Why?*   ♦

Example 4.2
- The poset $(\mathbb{N}, \leq)$ is *not* a complete lattice because, as remarked previously, it does not have least upper bounds for its infinite subsets.
- The poset $(\mathbb{N} \cup \{\infty\}, \sqsubseteq)$, obtained by adding a largest element ∞ to $(\mathbb{N}, \leq)$, is, however, a complete lattice and can be pictured as follows:

Here $\leq$ is the reflexive and transitive closure of the $\uparrow$ relation.
- $(2^S, \subseteq)$ is a complete lattice.

Of course, you should convince yourself of these claims!   ♦

4.2   Tarski's fixed point theorem

Now that we have some familiarity with posets and complete lattices, we are in a position to state and prove Tarski's fixed point theorem, Theorem 4.1. As you will see in due course, this apparently very abstract result plays a key role in computer science because it is a general tool that allows us to make sense of recursively defined objects. If you are interested in the uses of the theorem rather than in the reason why it holds, you can safely skip the proof of Theorem 4.1 on a first reading. None of the future applications of that result in this textbook depend on its proof, and you should feel free to use it as a 'black box'.

In the statement of Tarski's fixed point theorem, and in the applications to follow, the collection of monotonic functions will play an important role. We now proceed to define this type of function for the sake of completeness.

Definition 4.4 (Monotonic functions and fixed points) Let $(D, \sqsubseteq)$ be a poset. A function $f : D \to D$ is *monotonic* iff $d \sqsubseteq d'$ implies that $f(d) \sqsubseteq f(d')$ for all $d, d' \in D$.

An element $d \in D$ is called a *fixed point* of f iff $d = f(d)$.   ◆

For example, the function $f : 2^{\mathbb{N}} \to 2^{\mathbb{N}}$ defined, for each $X \subseteq \mathbb{N}$, by

$$f(X) = X \cup \{1, 2\}$$

is monotonic. The set $\{1, 2\}$ is a fixed point of f because

$$f(\{1, 2\}) = \{1, 2\} \cup \{1, 2\} = \{1, 2\}.$$

Exercise 4.6 *Can you give another example of a fixed point of f? Can you characterize all the fixed points of that function? Argue for your answers.*   ◆

Exercise 4.7 *Consider the function that is the same as f above except that it maps the set $\{2\}$ to $\{1, 2, 3\}$. Is such a function monotonic?*   ◆

As another example, consider the poset

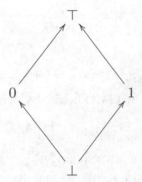

The identity function over $\{\bot, 0, 1, \top\}$ is monotonic but the function mapping $\bot$ to 0 and acting like the identity function on all other elements is not. (Why?) Note that both the posets mentioned above are in fact complete lattices.

Intuitively, if we view the partial-order relation in a poset $(D, \sqsubseteq)$ as an 'information order' – that is, if we view $d \sqsubseteq d'$ as meaning that 'd' has at least as much information as d' – then monotonic functions have the property that providing more information in the input will offer at least as much information as we had before in the output. (Our somewhat imprecise, but hopefully suggestive, slogan during lectures on this topic is that a monotonic function is one with the property that 'the more you put in, the more you get out!')

The following important theorem is due to Tarski (1955). It had been proved for the special case of lattices of sets by Knaster (1928).

Theorem 4.1 (Tarski's fixed point theorem) Let $(D, \sqsubseteq)$ be a complete lattice, and let $f : D \to D$ be monotonic. Then f has a largest fixed point z_{max} and a least fixed point z_{min} given by

$$z_{max} = \bigsqcup \{x \in D \mid x \sqsubseteq f(x)\},$$
$$z_{min} = \bigsqcap \{x \in D \mid f(x) \sqsubseteq x\}.$$

Proof. First we shall prove that z_{max} is the largest fixed point of f. This involves proving the following two statements:

1. z_{max} is a fixed point of f, i.e. $z_{max} = f(z_{max})$; and
2. for every $d \in D$ that is a fixed point of f, it holds that $d \sqsubseteq z_{max}$.

In what follows we will prove each statement separately. In the rest of the proof we let

$$A = \{x \in D \mid x \sqsubseteq f(x)\}.$$

Proof of 1. Since $\sqsubseteq$ is antisymmetric, to prove that z_{max} is a fixed point of f it is sufficient to show that

$$z_{max} \sqsubseteq f(z_{max}) \qquad (4.1)$$

and

$$f(z_{max}) \sqsubseteq z_{max}. \qquad (4.2)$$

First of all, we shall show that (4.1) holds. By definition, we have that

$$z_{max} = \bigsqcup A.$$

Thus, for every $x \in A$, it holds that $x \sqsubseteq z_{max}$. As f is monotonic, $x \sqsubseteq z_{max}$ implies that $f(x) \sqsubseteq f(z_{max})$. It follows that, for every $x \in A$,

$$x \sqsubseteq f(x) \sqsubseteq f(z_{max}).$$

Thus $f(z_{max})$ is an upper bound for the set A. By definition, z_{max} is the *least upper bound* of A. Thus $z_{max} \sqsubseteq f(z_{max})$, and we have shown (4.1).

To prove that (4.2) holds, note that, from (4.1) and the monotonicity of f, we have that $f(z_{max}) \sqsubseteq f(f(z_{max}))$. This implies that $f(z_{max}) \in A$. Therefore $f(z_{max}) \sqsubseteq z_{max}$, as z_{max} is an upper bound for A.

From (4.1) and (4.2), we have that $z_{max} \sqsubseteq f(z_{max}) \sqsubseteq z_{max}$. By antisymmetry, it follows that $z_{max} = f(z_{max})$, i.e. z_{max} is a fixed point of f.

Proof of 2. We now show that z_{max} is the largest fixed point of f. Let d be any fixed point of f. Then, in particular, we have that $d \sqsubseteq f(d)$. This implies that $d \in A$ and therefore that $d \sqsubseteq \bigsqcup A = z_{max}$.

We have thus shown that z_{max} is the largest fixed point of f. To show that z_{min} is the least fixed point of f, the second part of the theorem, we proceed in a similar fashion by proving the following two statements:

3. z_{min} is a fixed point of f, i.e. $z_{min} = f(z_{min})$; and
4. $z_{min} \sqsubseteq d$, for every $d \in D$ that is a fixed point of f.

To prove that z_{min} is a fixed point of f, it is sufficient to show that

$$f(z_{min}) \sqsubseteq z_{min} \tag{4.3}$$

and

$$z_{min} \sqsubseteq f(z_{min}). \tag{4.4}$$

Claim (4.3) can be shown by following the proof for (4.1), and claim (4.4) can be shown by following the proof for (4.2). The details are left as an exercise for the reader. Having shown that z_{min} is a fixed point of f, it is a simple matter to prove that it is indeed the least fixed point of f. (Do this as an exercise).   □

Now consider, for example, a complete lattice of the form $(2^S, \subseteq)$, where S is a set, and a monotonic function $f : S \to S$. If we instantiate the statement of the above theorem in this setting, the largest and least fixed points for f can be characterized thus:

$$z_{max} = \bigcup \{X \subseteq S \mid X \subseteq f(X)\},$$
$$z_{min} = \bigcap \{X \subseteq S \mid f(X) \subseteq X\}.$$

For instance, the largest fixed point of the function $f : 2^{\mathbb{N}} \to 2^{\mathbb{N}}$ defined by $f(X) = X \cup \{1, 2\}$ is

$$\bigcup \{X \subseteq \mathbb{N} \mid X \subseteq X \cup \{1, 2\}\} = \mathbb{N}.$$

However, the least fixed point of f is

$$\bigcap \{X \subseteq \mathbb{N} \mid X \cup \{1, 2\} \subseteq X\} = \{1, 2\}.$$

This follows because $X \cup \{1, 2\} \subseteq X$ means that X already contains 1 and 2, and the smallest set with this property is $\{1, 2\}$.

The following important theorem gives a characterization of the largest and least fixed points for monotonic functions over *finite* complete lattices. We shall see in due course how this result gives an algorithm for computing the fixed points that will find application in equivalence checking and in the developments in Chapter 6.

Definition 4.5 Let D be a set, $d \in D$, and $f : D \to D$. For each natural number n, we define $f^n(d)$ as follows:

$$f^0(d) = d$$
$$f^{n+1}(d) = f(f^n(d)).$$

$\blacklozenge$

Theorem 4.2 Let $(D, \sqsubseteq)$ be a *finite* complete lattice and let $f : D \to D$ be monotonic. Then the least fixed point for f is obtained as

$$z_{\min} = f^m(\bot),$$

for some natural number m. Furthermore the largest fixed point for f is obtained as

$$z_{\max} = f^M(\top),$$

for some natural number M.

Proof. We will prove only the first statement since the proof for the second is similar. As f is monotonic we have the following non-decreasing sequence of elements of D:

$$\bot \sqsubseteq f(\bot) \sqsubseteq f^2(\bot) \sqsubseteq \cdots \sqsubseteq f^i(\bot) \sqsubseteq f^{i+1}(\bot) \sqsubseteq \cdots$$

As D is finite, the sequence must be eventually constant, i.e. there is an m such that $f^k(\bot) = f^m(\bot)$ for all $k \geq m$. In particular,

$$f(f^m(\bot)) = f^{m+1}(\bot) = f^m(\bot),$$

which is the same as saying that $f^m(\bot)$ is a fixed point for f.

To prove that $f^m(\bot)$ is the least fixed point for f, assume that d is another fixed point for f. Then we have that $\bot \sqsubseteq d$ and therefore, as f is monotonic, that $f(\bot) \sqsubseteq f(d) = d$. By repeating this reasoning $m - 1$ more times, we get that $f^m(\bot) \sqsubseteq d$. We can therefore conclude that $f^m(\bot)$ is the least fixed point for f.

The proof of the statement that characterizes largest fixed points is similar, and is left as an exercise for the reader. $\square$

Exercise 4.8 (For the theoretically minded) *Fill in the details in the proof of the above theorem.* $\blacklozenge$

Example 4.3 Consider the function $f : 2^{\{0,1\}} \to 2^{\{0,1\}}$ defined by

$$f(X) = X \cup \{0\}.$$

This function is monotonic, and $2^{\{0,1\}}$ is a complete lattice when ordered using set inclusion with the empty set as least element and $\{0, 1\}$ as largest element. The above theorem gives an algorithm for computing the least and largest fixed points of f. To compute the least fixed point, we begin by applying f to the empty set. The result is $\{0\}$. Since we have added 0 to the input of f, we have not found our least fixed point yet. Therefore we proceed by applying f to $\{0\}$. We have that

$$f(\{0\}) = \{0\} \cup \{0\} = \{0\}.$$

It follows that, not surprisingly, $\{0\}$ is the least fixed point of the function f.

To compute the largest fixed point of f, we begin by applying f to the top element in our lattice, namely the set $\{0, 1\}$. Observe that

$$f(\{0, 1\}) = \{0, 1\} \cup \{0\} = \{0, 1\}.$$

Therefore $\{0, 1\}$ is the largest fixed point of the function f. ◆

Exercise 4.9 *Consider the function* $g : 2^{\{0,1,2\}} \to 2^{\{0,1,2\}}$ *defined by*

$$g(X) = (X \cap \{1\}) \cup \{2\}.$$

Use Theorem 4.2 to compute the least and largest fixed points of g. ◆

Exercise 4.10 (For the theoretically minded) *This exercise is for those that enjoy the mathematics of partially ordered sets. It has no direct bearing on the theory of reactive systems covered in the rest of the textbook.*

1. *Let* $(D, \sqsubseteq)$ *be a poset. An* ω-*chain in* $(D, \sqsubseteq)$ *is a sequence* d_i $(i \geq 0)$ *of elements of* D *such that* $d_i \sqsubseteq d_{i+1}$ *for each* $i \geq 0$.

   We say that $(D, \sqsubseteq)$ *is a complete partial order (cpo) if each* ω-*chain*

   $$d_0 \sqsubseteq d_1 \sqsubseteq d_2 \sqsubseteq \cdots$$

   in $(D, \sqsubseteq)$ *has a least upper bound (written* $\bigsqcup_{i \geq 0} d_i$*). A function* $f : D \to D$ *is continuous (see, for instance, Nielson and Nielson (1992), p. 103) if*

   $$f \left(\bigsqcup_{i \geq 0} d_i \right) = \bigsqcup_{i \geq 0} f(d_i),$$

   for each ω-*chain* d_i $(i \geq 0)$.

   Prove that if $(D, \sqsubseteq)$ *is a cpo and* $f : D \to D$ *is continuous then the poset*

   $$(\{x \in D \mid f(x) = x\}, \sqsubseteq),$$

   which consists of the set of fixed points of f*, is itself a cpo.*

2. *Give an example of a complete lattice* $(D, \sqsubseteq)$ *and of a monotonic function* $f : D \to D$ *such that there exist* $x, y \in D$ *that are fixed points of* f *but for which* $\bigsqcup \{x, y\}$ *is not a fixed point. Hint: Consider the complete lattice* D *pictured*

below:

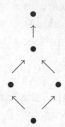

and construct such an $f : D \to D$.

3. *Let* $(D, \sqsubseteq)$ *be a complete lattice, and let* $f : D \to D$ *be monotonic. Consider a subset* X *of* $\{x \in D \mid x \sqsubseteq f(x)\}$.

   (a) *Prove that* $\bigsqcup X \in \{x \in D \mid x \sqsubseteq f(x)\}$.

   (b) *Give an example showing that, in general,*

   $$\bigsqcap X \notin \{x \in D \mid x \sqsubseteq f(x)\}.$$

   Hint: Consider the lattice pictured above turned upside down.

4. *Let* $(D, \sqsubseteq)$ *be a complete lattice, and let* $f : D \to D$ *be monotonic. Consider a subset* X *of* $\{x \in D \mid f(x) \sqsubseteq x\}$.

   (a) *Prove that* $\bigsqcap X \in \{x \in D \mid f(x) \sqsubseteq x\}$.

   (b) *Give an example showing that, in general,* $\bigsqcup X \notin \{x \in D \mid f(x) \sqsubseteq x\}$.

   Hint: Use your solution to 3(b) above.

5. *Let* $(D, \sqsubseteq)$ *be a complete lattice.*

   (a) *Let* $D \to_{\mathrm{mon}} D$ *be the set of monotonic functions from* D *to* D *and* $\preceq$ *be the relation defined on* $D \to_{\mathrm{mon}} D$ *by*

   $$f \preceq g \text{ iff } f(d) \sqsubseteq g(d) \text{ for each } d \in D.$$

   Show that $\preceq$ *is a partial order on* $D \to_{\mathrm{mon}} D$.

   (b) *Let* $\bigvee$ *and* $\bigwedge$ *be defined on* $D \to_{\mathrm{mon}} D$ *as follows.*
   If $\mathcal{F} \subseteq D \to_{\mathrm{mon}} D$ *then, for each* $d \in D$,

   $$\left(\bigvee \mathcal{F}\right)(d) = \bigsqcup \{f(d) \mid f \in \mathcal{F}\}.$$

   and

   $$\left(\bigwedge \mathcal{F}\right)(d) = \bigsqcap \{f(d) \mid f \in \mathcal{F}\}.$$

   Show that $(D \to_{\mathrm{mon}} D, \preceq)$ *is a complete lattice with* $\bigvee$ *and* $\bigwedge$ *as lub and glb.*

We invite those who would like to learn more about the mathematics of partially ordered sets and lattices to consult the book Davey and Priestley (2002) and the collection of lecture notes (Harju, 2006).

4.3 Bisimulation as a fixed point

Now that we have the theory underlying Tarski's fixed point theorem in place, it is time to put it into practice. We shall first use the theory we have just developed to provide the promised reformulation of bisimulation equivalence, and next we shall show by means of examples how this reformulation leads directly to an algorithm for computing bisimilarity over finite LTSs. The algorithm for computing bisimilarity that stems from the theory of fixed points is not the most efficient that has been devised; however, it is really pleasing to see how apparently very abstract notions from mathematics turn out to have unexpected applications in computer science.

Throughout this section, we let $(\mathsf{Proc}, \mathsf{Act}, \{\overset{\alpha}{\rightarrow} \,|\, \alpha \in \mathsf{Act}\})$ be an LTS. We recall that a relation $\mathcal{R} \subseteq \mathsf{Proc} \times \mathsf{Proc}$ is a *strong bisimulation* – see Definition 3.2 – if the following holds.

If $(p,q) \in \mathcal{R}$ then, for every $\alpha \in \mathsf{Act}$:

1. $p \overset{\alpha}{\rightarrow} p'$ implies $q \overset{\alpha}{\rightarrow} q'$ for some q' such that $(p',q') \in \mathcal{R}$;
2. $q \overset{\alpha}{\rightarrow} q'$ implies $p \overset{\alpha}{\rightarrow} p'$ for some p' such that $(p',q') \in \mathcal{R}$.

Then *strong bisimulation equivalence* (or *strong bisimilarity*) $\sim$ is defined by

$$\sim \; = \; \bigcup \left\{ \mathcal{R} \in 2^{(\mathsf{Proc} \times \mathsf{Proc})} \,\middle|\, \mathcal{R} \text{ is a strong bisimulation} \right\}.$$

In what follows we shall describe the relation $\sim$ as a fixed point to a suitable monotonic function. First we note that $(2^{(\mathsf{Proc} \times \mathsf{Proc})}, \subseteq)$ (i.e. the set of binary relations over Proc ordered by set inclusion) is a complete lattice with $\bigcup$ and $\bigcap$ as least upper bound and greatest lower bound. (Why? In fact, you should be able to realize readily that we have seen this kind of complete lattice in our previous developments!)

Consider now a binary relation $\mathcal{R}$ over Proc, that is, an element of the set $2^{(\mathsf{Proc} \times \mathsf{Proc})}$. We define the set $\mathcal{F}(\mathcal{R})$ by the following:

$(p,q) \in \mathcal{F}(\mathcal{R})$ for all $p, q \in \mathsf{Proc}$ iff

1. $p \overset{\alpha}{\rightarrow} p'$ implies $q \overset{\alpha}{\rightarrow} q'$ for some q' such that $(p',q') \in \mathcal{R}$;
2. $q \overset{\alpha}{\rightarrow} q'$ implies $p \overset{\alpha}{\rightarrow} p'$ for some p' such that $(p',q') \in \mathcal{R}$.

In other words, $\mathcal{F}(\mathcal{R})$ contains all the pairs of processes from which, in one round of the bisimulation game, the defender can make sure that the players reach a current pair of processes that is already contained in $\mathcal{R}$.

You should now convince yourself that a relation $\mathcal{R}$ is a bisimulation iff $\mathcal{R} \subseteq \mathcal{F}(\mathcal{R})$, and consequently that

$$\sim = \bigcup \left\{ \mathcal{R} \in 2^{(\mathsf{Proc} \times \mathsf{Proc})} \,\middle|\, \mathcal{R} \subseteq \mathcal{F}(\mathcal{R}) \right\}.$$

Take a minute to look at the above equality, and compare it with the characterization of the largest fixed point of a monotonic function given by Tarski's fixed point theorem (Theorem 4.1). That theorem tells us that the largest fixed point of a monotonic function f is the least upper bound of the set of elements x such that $x \sqsubseteq f(x)$; these are called the post-fixed points of the function. In our specific setting, the least upper bound of a subset of $2^{(\mathsf{Proc} \times \mathsf{Proc})}$ is given by $\bigcup$, and the post-fixed points of $\mathcal{F}$ are precisely the binary relations $\mathcal{R}$ over Proc such that $\mathcal{R} \subseteq \mathcal{F}(\mathcal{R})$. This means that the definition of $\sim$ matches that for the largest fixed point for $\mathcal{F}$ perfectly!

We note that if $\mathcal{R}, \mathcal{S} \in 2^{(\mathsf{Proc} \times \mathsf{Proc})}$ and $\mathcal{R} \subseteq \mathcal{S}$ then $\mathcal{F}(\mathcal{R}) \subseteq \mathcal{F}(\mathcal{S})$, that is, the function $\mathcal{F}$ is monotonic over $(2^{(\mathsf{Proc} \times \mathsf{Proc})}, \subseteq)$. (Check this!) Therefore, as all the conditions for Tarski's theorem are satisfied, we can conclude that $\sim$ is indeed the largest fixed point of $\mathcal{F}$. In particular, by Theorem 4.2, if Proc is finite then $\sim$ is equal to $\mathcal{F}^M(\mathsf{Proc} \times \mathsf{Proc})$ for some integer $M \geq 0$. Note how this gives us an algorithm to calculate $\sim$ for a given finite LTS, as follows.

To compute $\sim$, simply evaluate the non-increasing sequence

$$\mathcal{F}^0(\mathsf{Proc} \times \mathsf{Proc}) \supseteq \mathcal{F}^1(\mathsf{Proc} \times \mathsf{Proc}) \supseteq \mathcal{F}^2(\mathsf{Proc} \times \mathsf{Proc}) \supseteq \cdots$$

until the sequence stabilizes. (Recall that $\mathcal{F}^0(\mathsf{Proc} \times \mathsf{Proc})$ is just the top element in the complete lattice, namely $\mathsf{Proc} \times \mathsf{Proc}$.)

Example 4.4 Consider the LTS described by the following defining equations in CCS:

$$
\begin{aligned}
Q_1 &= b.Q_2 + a.Q_3, \\
Q_2 &= c.Q_4, \\
Q_3 &= c.Q_4, \\
Q_4 &= b.Q_2 + a.Q_3 + a.Q_1.
\end{aligned}
$$

In this LTS we have that

$$\mathsf{Proc} = \{Q_i \mid 1 \leq i \leq 4\}.$$

Below, we use I to denote the identity relation over Proc, that is,

$$I = \{(Q_i, Q_i) \mid 1 \leq i \leq 4\}.$$

We calculate the sequence $\mathcal{F}^i(\text{Proc} \times \text{Proc})$ for $i \geq 1$ thus:

$$\mathcal{F}^1(\text{Proc} \times \text{Proc}) = \{(Q_1, Q_4), (Q_4, Q_1), (Q_2, Q_3), (Q_3, Q_2)\} \cup I,$$
$$\mathcal{F}^2(\text{Proc} \times \text{Proc}) = \{(Q_2, Q_3), (Q_3, Q_2)\} \cup I$$

and finally

$$\mathcal{F}^3(\text{Proc} \times \text{Proc}) = \mathcal{F}^2(\text{Proc} \times \text{Proc}).$$

Therefore, the only distinct processes that are related by the largest strong bisimulation over this LTS are Q_2 and Q_3, and indeed $Q_2 \sim Q_3$. ◆

Exercise 4.11 *Using the iterative algorithm described above, compute the largest strong bisimulation over the LTS described by the following defining equations in CCS:*

$$P_1 = a.P_2,$$
$$P_2 = a.P_1,$$
$$P_3 = a.P_2 + a.P_4,$$
$$P_4 = a.P_3 + a.P_5,$$
$$P_5 = \mathbf{0}.$$

You may find it useful first to draw the LTS associated with this CCS definition. ◆

Exercise 4.12 *Use the iterative algorithm described above to compute the largest bisimulation over the LTS in Example 3.7.* ◆

Exercise 4.13 *What is the worst-case complexity of the algorithm outlined above when run on a LTS consisting of n states and m transitions? Express your answer using O-notation, and compare it with the complexity of the algorithm due to Paige and Tarjan mentioned in Section 3.6.* ◆

Exercise 4.14 *Let $(\text{Proc}, \text{Act}, \{ \xrightarrow{\alpha} \mid \alpha \in \text{Act}\})$ be a LTS. For each $i \geq 0$, define the relation $\sim_i$ over Proc as follows.*

- *$s_1 \sim_0 s_2$ holds always;*
- *$s_1 \sim_{i+1} s_2$ holds iff, for each action α,*

  if $s_1 \xrightarrow{\alpha} s_1'$ then there is a transition $s_2 \xrightarrow{\alpha} s_2'$ such that $s_1' \sim_i s_2'$;
  if $s_2 \xrightarrow{\alpha} s_2'$ then there is a transition $s_1 \xrightarrow{\alpha} s_1'$ such that $s_1' \sim_i s_2'$.

Prove that, for each $i \geq 0$,

1. *the relation $\sim_i$ is an equivalence relation,*
2. *$\sim_{i+1}$ is included in $\sim_i$, and*
3. *$\sim_i = \mathcal{F}^i(\mathsf{Proc} \times \mathsf{Proc})$.*

◆

Exercise 4.15

1. *Give a characterization of observational equivalence as a fixed point for a monotonic function similar to that presented above for strong bisimilarity.*
2. *Use your characterization to compute observational equivalence over the LTS in Example 3.8.*

What is the worst-case complexity of your algorithm?   ◆

5

Hennessy–Milner logic

5.1 Introduction to Hennessy–Milner logic

In the previous chapters we have seen that implementation verification is a natural approach to establishing the correctness of (models of) reactive systems described, for instance, in the language CCS. The reason is that CCS, like all other process algebras, can be used to describe both actual systems and their specifications. However, when establishing the correctness of our system with respect to a specification using a notion of equivalence such as observational equivalence, we are forced to specify in some way the overall behaviour of the system.

Suppose, for instance, that all we want to know about our system is whether it can perform an a-labelled transition 'now'. Phrasing this correctness requirement in terms of observational equivalence seems at best unnatural and maybe cannot be done at all! (See the paper Boudol and Larsen (1992) for an investigation of this issue.)

We can imagine a whole array of similar properties of a process that we might be interested in specifying and checking. For instance, we may wish to know whether our computer scientist of Chapter 2

- is not willing to drink tea now,
- is willing to drink both coffee and tea now,
- is willing to drink coffee, but not tea, now,
- never drinks alcoholic beverages, or
- always produces a publication after drinking coffee.

No doubt you will be able to come up with many others examples of similar properties of the computer scientist that we may wish to verify.

The verification of such properties of a process is best carried out by exploring the state space of the process in question rather than by equivalence checking.

However, before considering whether certain properties hold for a process, and checking this either manually or automatically, we need to have a language for expressing them. This language must have a formal syntax and semantics, so that it can be understood by a computer and algorithms to check whether a process affords a property may be devised. Moreover, the use of a language with a well-defined and intuitively understandable semantics will also allow us to overcome the imprecision that often accompanies natural-language descriptions. For instance, what do we really mean when we say that

> our computer scientist is willing to drink both coffee and tea now?

Do we mean that, in his or her current state, the computer scientist can perform both a coffee-labelled transition and a tea-labelled one? Do we mean that these transitions should be possible one after the other? And could these transitions be preceded and/or followed by sequences of internal steps? Whether our computer scientist affords the specified property clearly depends on the answer to the questions above, and the use of a language with a formal semantics will help us to understand precisely what is meant. Moreover, giving a formal syntax to our specification language will tell us the properties we can hope to express using it.

The approach to the specification and verification of reactive systems that we shall begin exploring in this chapter is often referred to as 'model checking'. In this approach we normally use different languages for describing actual systems and their specifications. For instance, we may use CCS expressions or the LTSs that they denote to describe actual systems, and some kind of logic to describe specifications. In what follows, we shall present a property language that was introduced in process theory by Hennessy and Milner (1985). This logic is often referred to as *Hennessy–Milner logic* (HML) and, as we shall see in due course, has a very pleasing connection with the notion of bisimilarity.

Definition 5.1 The set $\mathcal{M}$ of *Hennessy-Milner formulae* over a set of actions Act is given by the following abstract syntax:

$$F, G ::= tt \mid ff \mid F \wedge G \mid F \vee G \mid \langle a \rangle F \mid [a]F,$$

where $a \in$ Act and we use tt and ff to denote 'true' and 'false', respectively. If $A = \{a_1, \ldots, a_n\} \subseteq$ Act $(n \geq 0)$, we use the abbreviation $\langle A \rangle F$ for the formula $\langle a_1 \rangle F \vee \cdots \vee \langle a_n \rangle F$ and $[A]F$ for the formula $[a_1]F \wedge \cdots \wedge [a_n]F$. (If $A = \emptyset$ then $\langle A \rangle F = ff$ and $[A]F = tt$.)   ♦

We are interested in using the above logic to describe properties of CCS processes or, more generally, of states in an LTS over the set of actions Act. The meaning of a formula in the language $\mathcal{M}$ is given by characterizing the collection of processes that satisfy it. Intuitively this can be described as follows.

- All processes satisfy *tt*.
- No process satisfies *ff*.
- A process satisfies $F \wedge G$ (respectively $F \vee G$) iff it satisfies both F and G (respectively either F or G).
- A process satisfies $\langle a \rangle F$ for some $a \in \mathsf{Act}$ iff it affords an a-labelled transition leading to a state satisfying F.
- A process satisfies $[a]F$ for some $a \in \mathsf{Act}$ iff all its a-labelled transitions lead to a state satisfying F.

So, intuitively, a formula of the form $\langle a \rangle F$ states that it is *possible* to perform action a and thereby satisfy property F, whereas a formula of the form $[a]F$ states that, no matter how a process performs action a, the state it reaches in doing so will *necessarily* satisfy the property F.

Logics that involve the use of expressions such as *possibly* and *necessarily* are usually called *modal logics* and, in some form or another, have been studied by philosophers throughout history, notably by Aristotle and by philosophers in the middle ages. So Hennessy–Milner logic is a modal logic, in fact, a so-called multi-modal logic since it involves modal operators that are parameterized by actions. The semantics of formulae is defined with respect to a given LTS

$$(\mathsf{Proc}, \mathsf{Act}, \{\xrightarrow{a} \mid a \in \mathsf{Act}\}).$$

We shall use $\llbracket F \rrbracket$ to denote the set of processes in Proc that satisfy F. We now proceed to define this notation formally.

Definition 5.2 (Denotational semantics) We define $\llbracket F \rrbracket \subseteq \mathsf{Proc}$ for $F \in \mathcal{M}$ by

1. $\llbracket tt \rrbracket = \mathsf{Proc}$,
2. $\llbracket ff \rrbracket = \emptyset$,
3. $\llbracket F \wedge G \rrbracket = \llbracket F \rrbracket \cap \llbracket G \rrbracket$,
4. $\llbracket F \vee G \rrbracket = \llbracket F \rrbracket \cup \llbracket G \rrbracket$,
5. $\llbracket \langle a \rangle F \rrbracket = \langle \cdot a \cdot \rangle \llbracket F \rrbracket$,
6. $\llbracket [a]F \rrbracket = [\cdot a \cdot] \llbracket F \rrbracket$,

where we have used the set operators $\langle \cdot a \cdot \rangle, [\cdot a \cdot] : 2^{\mathsf{Proc}} \to 2^{\mathsf{Proc}}$ defined by

$$\langle \cdot a \cdot \rangle S = \{p \in \mathsf{Proc} \mid p \xrightarrow{a} p' \text{ and } p' \in S \text{ for some } p'\},$$
$$[\cdot a \cdot] S = \{p \in \mathsf{Proc} \mid p \xrightarrow{a} p' \text{ implies } p' \in S \text{ for each } p'\}.$$

We write $p \models F$, read as 'p satisfies F', iff $p \in \llbracket F \rrbracket$.

Two formulae are *equivalent* iff they are satisfied by the same processes in every transition system. $\blacklozenge$

Example 5.1 In order to understand the definition of the set operators $\langle \cdot a \cdot \rangle$ and $[\cdot a \cdot]$ introduced above, it is instructive to look at an example. Consider the following LTS:

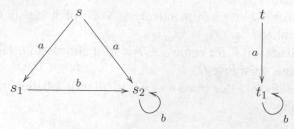

Then on the one hand

$$\langle \cdot a \cdot \rangle \{s_1, t_1\} = \{s, t\}.$$

This means that $\langle \cdot a \cdot \rangle \{s_1, t_1\}$ is the collection of states from which it is possible to perform an a-labelled transition ending up in either s_1 or t_1. On the other hand,

$$[\cdot a \cdot]\{s_1, t_1\} = \{s_1, s_2, t, t_1\}.$$

The idea here is that $[\cdot a \cdot]\{s_1, t_1\}$ consists of the set of all processes that become either s_1 or t_1 no matter how they perform an a-labelled transition. Clearly, s does not have this property because it can perform the transition $s \xrightarrow{a} s_2$, whereas t does have the property because its only a-labelled transition ends up in t_1. But why are s_1, s_2 and t_1 in $[\cdot a \cdot]\{s_1, t_1\}$? To see this, look at the formal definition of the set:

$$[\cdot a \cdot]\{s_1, t_1\} = \{p \in \mathsf{Proc} \mid p \xrightarrow{a} p' \text{ implies } p' \in \{s_1, t_1\} \text{ for each } p'\}.$$

Since s_1, s_2 and t_1 do *not* afford a-labelled transitions, it is vacuously true that all of their a-labelled transitions end up in either s_1 or t_1! This is the reason why those states are in the set $[\cdot a \cdot]\{s_1, t_1\}$.

We shall come back to this important point repeatedly in what follows.   ◆

Exercise 5.1 *Consider the LTS in the example above. What are* $\langle \cdot b \cdot \rangle \{s_1, t_1\}$ *and* $[\cdot b \cdot]\{s_1, t_1\}$?   ◆

Let us now re-examine the properties of our computer scientist that we mentioned earlier, and let us see whether we can express them using HML. First of all, note that, for the time being, we have defined the semantics of formulae in $\mathcal{M}$ in terms of the one-step transitions $\xrightarrow{a}$. This means, in particular, that we are not considering τ-actions as unobservable. So, if we say that 'a process P can do action a now' then we really mean that the process can perform a transition of the form $P \xrightarrow{a} Q$ for some Q.

How can we express, for instance, that our computer scientist is willing to drink coffee now? Well, one way to say so using our logic is to say that the computer scientist has the possibility of making a coffee-labelled transition. This suggests that we use a formula of the form $\langle\text{coffee}\rangle F$ for some property F that will be satisfied by the state reached by the computer scientist after having drunk her coffee. What should this F be? Since we do not need to know anything about the subsequent behaviour of the computer scientist, it makes sense to set $F = tt$. So, it looks as if we can express our natural-language requirement in terms of the formula $\langle\text{coffee}\rangle tt$. In fact, since our property language has a formal semantics, we can actually prove that our proposed formula is satisfied exactly by all the processes that have an outgoing coffee-labelled transition. This can be done as follows:

$$
\begin{aligned}
[\![\langle\text{coffee}\rangle tt]\!] &= \langle\cdot\text{coffee}\cdot\rangle\,[\![tt]\!]\\
&= \langle\cdot\text{coffee}\cdot\rangle\,\textsf{Proc}\\
&= \{P \mid P \stackrel{\text{coffee}}{\rightarrow} P' \text{ for some } P' \in \textsf{Proc}\}\\
&= \{P \mid P \stackrel{\text{coffee}}{\rightarrow}\}.
\end{aligned}
$$

So the formula we have come up with does in fact say what we wanted.

Can we express that the computer scientist cannot drink tea now using HML? Consider the formula $[\text{tea}]\,ff$. Intuitively this formula says that all the states that a process can reach by doing a tea-labelled transition must satisfy the formula ff, i.e. false. Since no state has the property 'false', the only way that a process can satisfy the property $[\text{tea}]\,ff$ is that it has no tea-labelled transition. To prove formally that our proposed formula is satisfied exactly by all the processes that have no outgoing tea-labelled transition, we proceed as follows:

$$
\begin{aligned}
[\![[\text{tea}]\,ff]\!] &= [\cdot\text{tea}\cdot]\,[\![ff]\!]\\
&= [\cdot\text{tea}\cdot]\,\emptyset\\
&= \{P \mid P \stackrel{\text{tea}}{\rightarrow} P' \text{ implies } P' \in \emptyset \text{ for each } P'\}\\
&= \{P \mid P \stackrel{\text{tea}}{\nrightarrow}\}.
\end{aligned}
$$

The last equality above follows from the fact that, for each process P,

$$
P \stackrel{\text{tea}}{\nrightarrow} \text{ iff } (P \stackrel{\text{tea}}{\rightarrow} P' \text{ implies } P' \in \emptyset \text{ for each } P').
$$

To see that this holds, observe first of all that if $P \stackrel{\text{tea}}{\rightarrow} Q$ for some Q then it is not true that $P' \in \emptyset$ for all P' such that $P \stackrel{\text{tea}}{\rightarrow} P'$. In fact, Q is a counter-example to the latter statement. So the implication from right to left is true. To establish the implication from left to right, assume that $P \stackrel{\text{tea}}{\nrightarrow}$. Then it is vacuously true that

$P' \in \emptyset$ for all P' such that $P \stackrel{\text{tea}}{\rightarrow} P'$; indeed, since there is no such P', there is no counter-example to that statement!

To sum up, we can express that a process *cannot* perform action $a \in$ Act with the formula $[a]\mathit{ff}$.

Suppose now that we want to say that the computer scientist must have a biscuit after drinking coffee. This means that it must be possible for the computer scientist to have a biscuit in all the states that she can reach by drinking coffee. This can be expressed by means of the formula

$$[\text{coffee}]\langle\text{biscuit}\rangle t\!t.$$

Exercise 5.2 (Recommended)

1. *Use the semantics of the logic to check that the above formula expresses the desired property of the computer scientist.*
2. *Give formulae that express the following natural language requirements:*
   * *the process is willing to drink either coffee or tea now;*
   * *the process is willing to drink coffee but not tea now;*
   * *the process can always drink tea immediately after having drunk two coffees in a row.*
3. *What do the formulae $\langle a\rangle\mathit{ff}$ and $[a]t\!t$ express?*

♦

Exercise 5.3 *Consider the following LTS:*

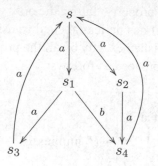

1. *Decide whether the following statements hold:*

$$s \overset{?}{\models} \langle a\rangle t\!t,$$

$$s \overset{?}{\models} \langle b\rangle t\!t,$$

$$s \overset{?}{\models} [a]\mathit{ff},$$

$$s \overset{?}{\models} [b]\mathit{ff},$$

$$s \overset{?}{\models} [a]\langle b\rangle t\!t,$$

$$s \overset{?}{\models} \langle a\rangle\langle b\rangle t\!t,$$

$$s \overset{?}{\models} [a]\langle a\rangle[a][b] f\!f,$$

$$s \overset{?}{\models} \langle a\rangle(\langle a\rangle t\!t \wedge \langle b\rangle t\!t),$$

$$s \overset{?}{\models} [a](\langle a\rangle t\!t \vee \langle b\rangle t\!t),$$

$$s \overset{?}{\models} \langle a\rangle([b][a] f\!f \wedge \langle b\rangle t\!t),$$

$$s \overset{?}{\models} \langle a\rangle([a](\langle a\rangle t\!t \wedge [b] f\!f) \wedge \langle b\rangle f\!f).$$

2. *Compute the following sets using the denotational semantics for Hennessy–Milner logic.*

$$[\![[a][b] f\!f]\!] = ?,$$
$$[\![\langle a\rangle(\langle a\rangle t\!t \wedge \langle b\rangle t\!t)]\!] = ?,$$
$$[\![[a][a][b] f\!f]\!] = ?,$$
$$[\![[a](\langle a\rangle t\!t \vee \langle b\rangle t\!t)]\!] = ?.$$

◆

Exercise 5.4 *Consider an everlasting clock whose behaviour is defined thus:*

$$\text{Clock} \overset{\text{def}}{=} \text{tick.Clock}.$$

Prove that the process Clock *satisfies the formula*

$$[\text{tick}](\langle\text{tick}\rangle t\!t \wedge [\text{tock}] f\!f).$$

Show also that, for each $n \geq 0$, the process Clock *satisfies the formula*

$$\underbrace{\langle\text{tick}\rangle \cdots \langle\text{tick}\rangle}_{n \text{ times}} t\!t.$$

◆

Exercise 5.5 (Mandatory) *Find a formula in $\mathcal{M}$ that is satisfied by $a.b.\mathbf{0} + a.c.\mathbf{0}$ but not by $a.(b.\mathbf{0} + c.\mathbf{0})$.*

Now find a formula in $\mathcal{M}$ that is satisfied by $a.(b.c.\mathbf{0} + b.d.\mathbf{0})$ but not by $a.b.c.\mathbf{0} + a.b.d.\mathbf{0}$. ◆

It is sometimes useful to have an alternative characterization of the satisfaction relation $\models$ presented in Definition 5.2. This can be obtained by defining the binary relation $\models$ relating processes to formulae by structural induction on formulae thus:

$$P \models tt \text{ for each } P,$$
$$P \models ff \text{ for no } P,$$
$$P \models F \wedge G \text{ iff } P \models F \text{ and } P \models G,$$
$$P \models F \vee G \text{ iff } P \models F \text{ or } P \models G,$$
$$P \models \langle a \rangle F \text{ iff } P \xrightarrow{a} P' \text{ for some } P' \text{ such that } P' \models F,$$
$$P \models [a]F \text{ iff } P' \models F \text{ for each } P' \text{ such that } P \xrightarrow{a} P'.$$

Exercise 5.6 *Show that the above definition of the satisfaction relation is equivalent to that given in Definition 5.2. Hint: Use induction on the structure of formulae.*   ◆

Exercise 5.7 *Find an LTS with initial state s that satisfies all the following properties:*

$$\langle a \rangle (\langle b \rangle \langle c \rangle tt \wedge \langle c \rangle tt),$$
$$\langle a \rangle \langle b \rangle ([a]ff \wedge [b]ff \wedge [c]ff),$$
$$[a]\langle b \rangle ([c]ff \wedge \langle a \rangle tt).$$

◆

Note that logical negation is *not* one of the constructs in the abstract syntax for $\mathcal{M}$. However, the language $\mathcal{M}$ *is* closed under negation in the sense that, for each formula $F \in \mathcal{M}$, there is a formula $F^c \in \mathcal{M}$ that is equivalent to the negation of F. This formula F^c is defined inductively on the structure of F as follows.

1. $tt^c = ff$,
2. $ff^c = tt$,
3. $(F \wedge G)^c = F^c \vee G^c$,
4. $(F \vee G)^c = F^c \wedge G^c$,
5. $(\langle a \rangle F)^c = [a]F^c$,
6. $([a]F)^c = \langle a \rangle F^c$.

Note, for instance, that

$$(\langle a \rangle tt)^c = [a]ff,$$
$$([a]ff)^c = \langle a \rangle tt.$$

Proposition 5.1 Let $(\mathsf{Proc}, \mathsf{Act}, \{\xrightarrow{a} \mid a \in \mathsf{Act}\})$ be an LTS. Then, for every formula $F \in \mathcal{M}$, it holds that $[\![F^c]\!] = \mathsf{Proc} \setminus [\![F]\!]$.

Proof. The proposition can be proved by structural induction on F. The details are left as an exercise to the reader.   □

Exercise 5.8

1. Prove Proposition 5.1.

2. Prove, furthermore, that $(F^c)^c = F$ for every formula $F \in \mathcal{M}$. Hint: Use structural induction on F.

◆

As a consequence of Proposition 5.1 we have that, for each process P and formula F, exactly one of $P \models F$ and $P \models F^c$ holds. In fact, each process is either contained in $[\![F]\!]$ or in $[\![F^c]\!]$.

In Exercise 5.5 you were asked to come up with formulae that distinguished between processes that we know are not strongly bisimilar. As a further example, consider the processes

$$A \overset{\mathrm{def}}{=} a.A + a.0,$$
$$B \overset{\mathrm{def}}{=} a.a.B + a.0.$$

These two processes are *not* strongly bisimilar. In fact, A affords the transition

$$A \overset{a}{\to} A.$$

This transition can be matched only by either

$$B \overset{a}{\to} 0$$

or

$$B \overset{a}{\to} a.B.$$

On the one hand, neither 0 nor $a.B$ is strongly bisimilar to A because this process can perform an a-labelled transition and become 0 in doing so. On the other hand,

$$a.B \overset{a}{\to} B$$

is the only transition that is possible from $a.B$, and B is not strongly bisimilar to 0.

On the basis of this analysis, it seems that a property distinguishing the processes A and B is $\langle a \rangle \langle a \rangle [a] \mathit{ff}$, that is, the property that a process can perform a sequence of two a-labelled transitions and in so doing reach a state from which no a-labelled transition is possible. In fact, you should be able to establish that A satisfies this property but B does not. (Do so!)

Again, faced with two non-bisimilar processes, we have been able to find a formula, in the logic $\mathcal{M}$, that distinguishes them in the sense that one process satisfies it but the other does not. Is this true in general? And what can we say about two processes that satisfy precisely the same formulae in $\mathcal{M}$? Are they guaranteed to be strongly bisimilar?

5.2   Hennessy–Milner theorem

We shall now present a seminal theorem, due to Hennessy and Milner, that answers both of these questions at once by establishing a satisfying, and very fruitful, connection between the apparently unrelated notions of strong bisimilarity and the logic $\mathcal{M}$. The theorem applies to a class of processes that we now proceed to define.

Definition 5.3 (Image-finite process) A process P is *image finite* iff the collection $\{P' \mid P \xrightarrow{a} P'\}$ is finite for each action a. An LTS is image finite if so is each of its states.   ♦

For example, the process A_{rep} (for 'A replicated') defined by

$$A_{rep} \stackrel{\text{def}}{=} a.\mathbf{0} \mid A_{rep}$$

is *not* image finite. In fact, you should be able to prove by induction on n that, for each $n \geq 1$,

$$A_{rep} \xrightarrow{a} \underbrace{a.\mathbf{0} \mid \cdots \mid a.\mathbf{0}}_{n \text{ times}} \mid \mathbf{0} \mid A_{rep}.$$

Another example of a process that is not image finite is

$$A^{<\omega} \stackrel{\text{def}}{=} \sum_{i \geq 0} a^i, \tag{5.1}$$

where $a^0 = \mathbf{0}$ and $a^{i+1} = a.a^i$. However, all the other processes that we have met so far in this text are image finite.

Theorem 5.1 (Hennessy and Milner, 1985) Let

$$(\mathsf{Proc}, \mathsf{Act}, \{\xrightarrow{a} \mid a \in \mathsf{Act}\})$$

be an image-finite LTS. Assume that P, Q are states in Proc. Then $P \sim Q$ iff P and Q satisfy exactly the same formulae in Hennessy–Milner logic.

Proof. We prove the two implications separately.

- Assume that $P \sim Q$ and $P \models F$ for some formula $F \in \mathcal{M}$. Using structural induction on F, we can prove that $Q \models F$. By symmetry, this is enough to establish that P and Q satisfy the same formulae in $\mathcal{M}$.

  The proof proceeds by a case analysis on the form of F. We present the details only for the case $F = [a]G$ for some action a and formula G. Our inductive hypothesis is that, for all processes R and S, if $R \sim S$ and $R \models G$ then $S \models G$. Using this hypothesis, we shall prove that $Q \models [a]G$. To this end, assume that

$Q \xrightarrow{a} Q'$ for some Q'. We wish to show that $Q' \models G$. Now, since $P \sim Q$ and $Q \xrightarrow{a} Q'$, there is a process P' such that $P \xrightarrow{a} P'$ and $P' \sim Q'$. (Why?) By our assumption that $P \models [a]G$, we have that $P' \models G$. The inductive hypothesis yields that $Q' \models G$. Therefore, each Q' such that $Q \xrightarrow{a} Q'$ satisfies G and we may conclude that $Q \models [a]G$, which was to be shown.

- Assume that P and Q satisfy the same formulae in $\mathcal{M}$. We shall prove that P and Q are strongly bisimilar. To this end, note that it is sufficient to show that the relation

$$\mathcal{R} = \{(R, S) \mid R, S \in \mathsf{Proc} \text{ satisfy the same formulae in } \mathcal{M}\}$$

is a strong bisimulation.

Assume that $R \mathcal{R} S$ and $R \xrightarrow{a} R'$. We shall now argue that there is a process S' such that $S \xrightarrow{a} S'$ and $R' \mathcal{R} S'$. Since $\mathcal{R}$ is symmetric, this suffices to establish that $\mathcal{R}$ is a strong bisimulation.

Now assume, towards a contradiction, that there is no S' such that $S \xrightarrow{a} S'$ and S' satisfies the same properties as R'. Since S is image finite, the set of processes that S can reach by performing an a-labelled transition is finite, say $\{S_1, \ldots, S_n\}$ with $n \geq 0$. By our assumption, none of the processes in the above set satisfies the same formulae as R'. So, for each $i \in \{1, \ldots, n\}$, there is a formula F_i such that

$$R' \models F_i \text{ and } S_i \not\models F_i.$$

(Why? Could it not be that $R' \not\models F_i$ and $S_i \models F_i$ for some $i \in \{1, \ldots, n\}$?) We are finally in a position to construct a formula that is satisfied by R but not by S, contradicting our assumption that R and S satisfy the same formulae. In fact, the formula

$$\langle a \rangle (F_1 \wedge F_2 \wedge \cdots \wedge F_n)$$

is satisfied by R but not by S. The easy verification of this is left to the reader.

The proof of the theorem is now complete. □

Exercise 5.9 (Mandatory) *Fill in the details that we have omitted in the above proof. What is the formula that we have constructed to distinguish R and S in the proof of the implication from right to left, if $n = 0$?* ♦

Remark 5.1 In fact, the implication from left to right in the above theorem holds for arbitrary processes, not just image-finite ones. ♦

The above theorem has many applications in the theory of processes and in verification technology. For example, a consequence of its statement is that if two image-finite processes are not strongly bisimilar then there is a formula in $\mathcal{M}$ that tells us one reason why they are not. Moreover, as the proof of the theorem suggests, we can always construct this distinguishing formula.

Note, moreover, that this characterization theorem for strong bisimilarity is very general. For instance, in the light of the answer to Exercise 3.30, it also applies to observational equivalence provided that we interpret HML over the LTS whose set of actions consists of all the observable actions and of the label τ and whose transitions are precisely the 'weak transitions' whose labels are either observable actions or τ.

Exercise 5.10 *Consider the following LTS:*

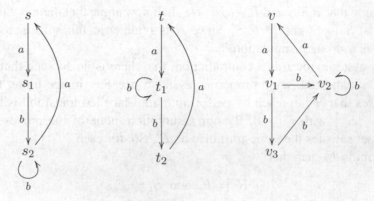

Argue that $s \not\sim t$, $s \not\sim v$ and $t \not\sim v$. Next, find a distinguishing formula of Hennessy–Milner logic for each of the pairs

$$s \text{ and } t, \quad s \text{ and } v, \quad t \text{ and } v.$$

Verify your claims in the Edinburgh Concurrency Workbench (use the `strongeq` *and* `checkprop` *commands) and check whether you have found the shortest distinguishing formula (use the* `dfstrong` *command).* ◆

Exercise 5.11 *For each of the following pairs of CCS expressions, decide whether they are strongly bisimilar and, if they are not, find a distinguishing formula in Hennessy–Milner logic:*

$$b.a.\mathbf{0} + b.\mathbf{0} \quad and \quad b.(a.\mathbf{0} + b.\mathbf{0});$$
$$a.(b.c.\mathbf{0} + b.d.\mathbf{0}) \quad and \quad a.b.c.\mathbf{0} + a.b.d.\mathbf{0};$$
$$a.\mathbf{0} \mid b.\mathbf{0} \quad and \quad a.b.\mathbf{0} + b.a.\mathbf{0}; \quad and$$
$$(a.\mathbf{0} \mid b.\mathbf{0}) + c.a.\mathbf{0} \quad and \quad a.\mathbf{0} \mid (b.\mathbf{0} + c.\mathbf{0}).$$

Verify your claims in the Edinburgh Concurrency Workbench (use the `strongeq` *and* `checkprop` *commands) and check whether you have found the shortest distinguishing formula (use the* `dfstrong` *command).*   ◆

Exercise 5.12 (For the theoretically minded) *Let* $(\mathsf{Proc}, \mathsf{Act}, \{\xrightarrow{a} \mid a \in \mathsf{Act}\})$ *be image finite. Show that*

$$\sim \; = \bigcap_{i \geq 0} \sim_i,$$

where $\sim_i$, $i \geq 0$, *is the sequence of equivalence relations defined in Exercise 4.14.*   ◆

Exercise 5.13 (For the theoretically minded) *Consider the process* A^ω *given by*

$$\mathrm{A}^\omega \stackrel{\text{def}}{=} a.\mathrm{A}^\omega.$$

Show that the processes $\mathrm{A}^{<\omega}$ *and* $\mathrm{A}^\omega + \mathrm{A}^{<\omega}$, *where* $\mathrm{A}^{<\omega}$ *is defined in (5.1),*

1. *are not strongly bisimilar, but*
2. *satisfy the same properties in* $\mathcal{M}$.

Conclude that Theorem 5.1 does not hold for processes that are not image finite. Hint: To prove that the two processes satisfy the same formulae in $\mathcal{M}$, *use structural induction on formulae. You will find it useful first to establish the following statement:*

A^ω satisfies a formula $F \in \mathcal{M}$ iff a^i, where i is the modal depth of F, also satisfies the formula.

The modal depth of a formula is the maximum nesting of the modal operators in it.   ◆

6

Hennessy–Milner logic with recursive definitions

Introduction

An HML formula can only describe a *finite* part of the overall behaviour of a process. In fact, as each modal operator allows us to explore the effect of taking one step in the behaviour of a process, using a single HML formula we can only describe properties of a fixed small part of the computations of a process. As those who solved Exercise 5.13 have already discovered, how much of the behaviour of a process we can explore using a single formula is entirely determined by its so-called *modal depth*, i.e. by the maximum nesting of modal operators in it. For example, the formula $([a]\langle a\rangle f\!f) \vee \langle b\rangle t\!t$ has modal depth 2, and checking whether a process satisfies it involves only an analysis of its sequences of transitions whose length is at most 2. (We will return to this issue in Section 6.6, where a formal definition of the modal depth of a formula will be given.)

However, we often wish to describe properties that describe a state of affairs that may or must occur in arbitrarily long computations of a process. If we want to express properties such as, for example, that a process is *always* able to perform a given action, we have to extend the logic. As the following example indicates, one way of doing so is to allow for infinite conjunctions and disjunctions in our property language.

Example 6.1 Consider the processes p and q in Figure 6.1. It is not hard to come up with an HML formula that p satisfies and q does not. In fact, after performing one a-action, p will always be able to perform another whereas q may fail to do so. This can be captured formally in HML as follows:

$$p \models [a]\langle a\rangle t\!t$$

102

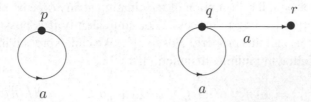

Figure 6.1 Two processes, p and q.

but

$$q \not\models [a]\langle a \rangle tt.$$

Since a difference in the behaviour of the two processes can already be found by examining their behaviour after two transitions, a formula that distinguishes them is 'small'.

Assume, however, that we modify the LTS for q by adding a sequence of transitions to r thus:

$$r = r_0 \xrightarrow{a} r_1 \xrightarrow{a} r_2 \xrightarrow{a} \cdots \xrightarrow{a} r_{n-1} \xrightarrow{a} r_n \quad (n \geq 0).$$

No matter how we choose the non-negative integer n, there is an HML formula that distinguishes the processes p and q. In fact, we have that

$$p \models [a]^{n+1}\langle a \rangle tt$$

but

$$q \not\models [a]^{n+1}\langle a \rangle tt,$$

where $[a]^{n+1}$ stands for a sequence of modal operators $[a]$ of length $n+1$. However, no formula in HML would work for all values of n. (Prove this claim!) This is unsatisfactory, as there appears to be a general reason why the behaviours of p and q are different. Indeed, the process p in Figure 6.1 can always (i.e. at any point in each of its computations) perform an a-action, that is, $\langle a \rangle tt$ is always true. Let us call this *invariance* property $Inv(\langle a \rangle tt)$. We could describe it in an extension of HML as an infinite conjunction thus:

$$Inv(\langle a \rangle tt) = \langle a \rangle tt \wedge [a]\langle a \rangle tt \wedge [a][a]\langle a \rangle tt \wedge \cdots = \bigwedge_{i \geq 0} [a]^i \langle a \rangle tt.$$

This formula can be read as follows:

> In order for a process always to be able to perform an a-action, this action should be possible now (as expressed by the conjunct $\langle a \rangle tt$) and, for each positive integer i, it should be possible in each state that the process can reach by performing a sequence of i actions (as expressed by the conjunct $[a]^i \langle a \rangle tt$, because a is the only action in our example LTS).

However, the process q has the option of terminating at any time by performing the a-labelled transition leading to process r, or equivalently it is possible from q to satisfy $[a]ff$. Let us call this property $Pos([a]ff)$. We can express it in an extension of HML as the following infinite disjunction:

$$Pos([a]ff) = [a]ff \vee \langle a \rangle [a]ff \vee \langle a \rangle \langle a \rangle [a]ff \vee \cdots = \bigvee_{i \geq 0} \langle a \rangle^i [a]ff,$$

where $\langle a \rangle^i$ stands for a sequence of modal operators $\langle a \rangle$ of length i. This formula can be read as follows:

> In order for a process to have the possibility of refusing an a-action at some point, this action should either be refused now (as expressed by the disjunct $[a]ff$) or, for some positive integer i, it should be possible to reach a state in which an a-action can be refused by the performing of a sequence of i actions (as expressed by the disjunct $\langle a \rangle^i [a]ff$, because a is the only action in our example LTS).

$\blacklozenge$

Even if it is theoretically possible to extend HML with infinite conjunctions and disjunctions, infinite formulae are not particularly easy to handle (for instance they are infinitely long, and we would have a hard time using them as inputs for an algorithm). What do we do instead? The answer is in fact both simple and natural for a computer scientist; let us introduce *recursion* into our logic. Assuming for the moment that a is the only action, we can then express $Inv(\langle a \rangle tt)$ by means of the following recursive equation:

$$X \equiv \langle a \rangle tt \wedge [a]X, \tag{6.1}$$

where we write $F \equiv G$ iff formulae F and G are satisfied by exactly the same processes, i.e. if $[\![F]\!] = [\![G]\!]$. The above recursive equation captures the intuition that a process that can invariantly perform an a-labelled transition, i.e. one that can perform an a-labelled transition in all its reachable states, can certainly perform one now and, moreover, that each state reached by the process via one such transition can invariantly perform an a-labelled transition. This looks deceptively easy and natural. However, the mere fact of writing down an equation like (6.1) does not mean that this equation makes sense! Indeed, equations may be seen as implicitly defining the set of their solutions, and we are all familiar with equations that have no solutions at all. For instance, the equation

$$x = x + 1 \tag{6.2}$$

has no solution over the set of natural numbers, and there is no $X \subseteq \mathbb{N}$ such that

$$X = \mathbb{N} \setminus X. \tag{6.3}$$

However, there are uncountably many $X \subseteq \mathbb{N}$ such that

$$X = \{2\} \cup X, \tag{6.4}$$

namely all the sets of natural numbers that contain the number 2. There are also equations that have a finite number of solutions rather than a unique solution. As an example, consider the equation

$$X = \{10\} \cup \{n - 1 \mid n \in X, \, n \neq 0\}. \tag{6.5}$$

The finite set that is the solution for this equation is the set $\{0, 1, \ldots, 10\}$ and the infinite solution is $\mathbb{N}$ itself; thus the equation has two solutions.

Exercise 6.1 *Check the claims that we have just made.* ♦

Exercise 6.2 *Reconsider (6.2)–(6.5).*

1. *Why cannot Tarski's fixed point theorem be used to yield a solution to the first two of these equations?*
2. *Consider the structure introduced in the second bullet point of Example 4.2. For each $d \in \mathbb{N} \cup \{\infty\}$, define*

$$\infty + d = d + \infty = \infty.$$

   Does (6.2) have a solution in the resulting structure? How many solutions does it have?
3. *Use Tarski's fixed point theorem to find the largest and least solutions of (6.5).*

♦

Since an equation like (6.1) is meant to describe a formula, it is therefore natural to ask ourselves the following questions.

- Does (6.1) have a solution? And what precisely do we mean by that?
- If (6.1) has more than one solution, which do we choose?
- How can we compute whether a process satisfies the formula described by (6.1)?

Precise answers to these questions will be given in the remainder of this chapter. However, to motivate our subsequent technical developments, it is appropriate here to discuss briefly the first two questions above.

Recall that the meaning of a formula (with respect to a labelled transition system) is the set of processes that satisfy it. Therefore, it is natural to expect that a set S of processes that satisfy the formula described by (6.1) should be such that

$$S = \langle \cdot a \cdot \rangle \mathsf{Proc} \cap [\cdot a \cdot] S.$$

It is clear that $S = \emptyset$ is a solution to the equation (as no process can satisfy both $\langle a \rangle tt$ and $[a] ff$). However, the process p in Figure 6.1 can perform an a-transition invariantly and $p \notin \emptyset$, so this cannot be the solution for which we are looking. Actually it turns out that it is the *largest* solution we need here, namely $S = \{p\}$. The set $S = \emptyset$ is the *least solution*.

In other cases it is the least solution in which we are interested. For instance, we can express $Pos([a] ff)$ by the following equation:

$$Y \equiv [a] ff \vee \langle a \rangle Y.$$

Here the largest solution is $Y = \{p, q, r\}$ but, as the process p in Figure 6.1 cannot terminate at all, this is clearly not the solution in which we are interested. The least solution of the above equation over the LTS in Figure 6.1 is $Y = \{q, r\}$ and is exactly the set of processes in that labelled transition system that intuitively satisfy $Pos([a] ff)$.

When we write down a recursively defined property, we can indicate whether we desire the least or the largest solution by adding this information above the equality sign. For $Inv(\langle a \rangle tt)$ we want the largest solution, and so in this case we write

$$X \stackrel{\max}{=} \langle a \rangle tt \wedge [a] X.$$

For $Pos([a] ff)$ we write

$$Y \stackrel{\min}{=} [a] ff \vee \langle a \rangle Y.$$

More generally we can express that the formula F holds for each reachable state in an LTS having a set of actions Act (this property is written as $Inv(F)$ and read as 'invariantly F') by means of the equation

$$X \stackrel{\max}{=} F \wedge [\mathsf{Act}] X$$

and that F possibly holds at some point (written as $Pos(F)$) by

$$Y \stackrel{\min}{=} F \vee \langle \mathsf{Act} \rangle Y.$$

Intuitively, we use largest solutions for those properties of a process that hold unless it has a finite computation that disproves the property. For instance, process q does *not* have property $Inv(\langle a \rangle tt)$ because it can reach a state in which no a-labelled transition is possible. Conversely, we use least solutions for those properties of a process that hold if it has a finite computation sequence which 'witnesses' the property. For instance, a process has the property $Pos(\langle a \rangle tt)$ if it has a computation leading to a state that can perform an a-labelled transition. This computation witnesses to the fact that the process can perform an a-labelled transition at some point in its behaviour.

We shall appeal to the intuition given above in the following section, where we present examples of recursively defined properties.

Exercise 6.3 *Give a formula, built using HML and the temporal operators Pos and/or Inv, that expresses a property satisfied by exactly one of the processes in Exercise 5.13.* ◆

6.1 Examples of recursive properties

Adding recursive definitions to Hennessy–Milner logic gives us a very powerful language for specifying properties of processes. In particular this extension allows us to express different kinds of safety and liveness properties. Before developing the theory of HML with recursion, we give some more examples of its uses.

Consider the formula $Safe(F)$, which is satisfied by a process p whenever it has a complete transition sequence

$$p = p_0 \xrightarrow{a_1} p_1 \xrightarrow{a_2} p_2 \cdots,$$

where each process p_i satisfies F. (A transition sequence is *complete* if it is infinite or its last state affords no transition.) This *invariance of F under some computation* can be expressed in the following way:

$$X \stackrel{\max}{=} F \wedge ([\mathsf{Act}] \mathit{ff} \vee \langle \mathsf{Act} \rangle X).$$

It turns out to be the largest solution that is of interest here; we will argue this formally later.

Intuitively, the recursively defined formula above states that a process p has a complete transition sequence all of whose states satisfy the formula F iff

- p itself satisfies F, and
- either p has no outgoing transition (in which case p will satisfy the formula $[\mathsf{Act}] \mathit{ff}$) or p has a transition leading to a state that has a complete transition sequence all of whose states satisfy the formula F.

A process p satisfies the property $Even(F)$, read as 'eventually F', if each of its complete transition sequences will contain at least one state that has the property F. This means that either p satisfies F or p can perform some transition and every state that it can reach by performing a transition can itself eventually reach a state that has property F. This can be expressed by means of the following equation:

$$Y \overset{\min}{=} F \vee (\langle \text{Act} \rangle tt \wedge [\text{Act}]Y).$$

In this case we are interested in the least solution because $Even(F)$ should be satisfied only by those processes that are guaranteed to reach a state satisfying F in all their computation paths.

Note that the definitions of $Safe(F)$ and $Even(F)$, and respectively $Inv(F)$ and $Pos(F)$, are mutually *dual*, i.e. they can be obtained from one another by replacing $\vee$ by $\wedge$, $[\text{Act}]$ by $\langle \text{Act} \rangle$ and $\overset{\min}{=}$ by $\overset{\max}{=}$. One can show that $\neg Safe(F) \equiv Even(\neg F)$ and $\neg Inv(F) \equiv Pos(\neg F)$, where we write $\neg$ for logical negation.

It is also possible to express that F should be satisfied in each transition sequence until G becomes true. There are two well-known variants of this construction:

- $F \mathcal{U}^s G$, the so-called *strong until*, which says that sooner or later p reaches a state where G is true and in all the states it traverses before this happens F must hold;
- $F \mathcal{U}^w G$, the so-called *weak until*, which says that F must hold in all the states p traverses until it reaches a state where G holds (but maybe this will never happen!).

We express these operators as follows:

$$F \mathcal{U}^s G \overset{\min}{=} G \vee (F \wedge \langle \text{Act} \rangle tt \wedge [\text{Act}](F \mathcal{U}^s G)),$$
$$F \mathcal{U}^w G \overset{\max}{=} G \vee (F \wedge [\text{Act}](F \mathcal{U}^w G)).$$

It should be clear that, as the names indicate, *strong until* is a stronger condition than *weak until*. We can use the 'until' operators to express $Even(F)$ and $Inv(F)$. In fact, $Even(G) \equiv tt \, \mathcal{U}^s G$ and $Inv(F) \equiv F \mathcal{U}^w \, ff$.

Properties such as 'at some time in the future' and 'until' are examples of what we call *temporal properties*. *Tempora* is Latin – it is plural for *tempus*, which means 'time' – and a logic that expresses properties that depend on time is called a *temporal logic*. The study of temporal logics is very old and can be traced back to Aristotle. Within the last 30 years, researchers in computer science have started to show interest in temporal logics as, within this framework, it is possible to express properties of the behaviour of programs that change over time (Clarke, Emerson and Sistla, 1986, Manna and Pnueli, 1992, Pnueli, 1977).

The modal μ-calculus (Kozen, 1983) is a generalization of Hennessy–Milner logic with recursion that allows for largest- and least-fixed-point definitions to be mixed freely. It has been shown that the modal μ-calculus is expressive enough to describe any standard operator that occurs in the framework of temporal logic.

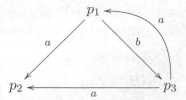

Figure 6.2 A process.

In this sense, by extending Hennessy–Milner logic with recursion we obtain a temporal logic.

From the examples in this section we can see that least fixed points are used to express that something will happen sooner or later, whereas largest fixed points are used to express the invariance of some state of affairs during computations or that something does *not* happen as a system evolves.

6.2 Syntax and semantics of HML with recursion

The first step towards introducing recursion in HML is to add variables to the syntax. To start with, we consider only *one* recursively defined property. We will study the more general case of properties defined by *mutual recursion* later.

The syntax for Hennessy–Milner logic with one variable X, denoted by $\mathcal{M}_{\{X\}}$, is given by the following grammar:

$$F ::= X \mid t\!t \mid f\!f \mid F_1 \wedge F_2 \mid F_1 \vee F_2 \mid \langle a \rangle F \mid [a] F.$$

Semantically a formula F (which may contain a variable X) is interpreted as a function $\mathcal{O}_F : 2^{\mathsf{Proc}} \to 2^{\mathsf{Proc}}$ that, given a set of processes that are assumed to satisfy X, gives us the set of processes that satisfy F.

Example 6.2 Consider the formula $F = \langle a \rangle X$ and let Proc be the set of states in the transition graph in Figure 6.2. If X is satisfied by p_1 then $\langle a \rangle X$ will be satisfied by p_3, i.e. we expect that

$$\mathcal{O}_{\langle a \rangle X}(\{p_1\}) = \{p_3\}.$$

If the set of states satisfying X is $\{p_1, p_2\}$ then $\langle a \rangle X$ will be satisfied by $\{p_1, p_3\}$. Therefore we expect that

$$\mathcal{O}_{\langle a \rangle X}(\{p_1, p_2\}) = \{p_1, p_3\}.$$

What is the set $\mathcal{O}_{[b]X}(\{p_2\})$? ♦

The above intuition is captured formally in the following definition.

Definition 6.1 Let $(\mathsf{Proc}, \mathsf{Act}, \{ \xrightarrow{a} \mid a \in \mathsf{Act}\})$ be a labelled transition system. For each $S \subseteq \mathsf{Proc}$ and formula F, we define $\mathcal{O}_F(S)$ inductively as follows:

$$\mathcal{O}_X(S) = S,$$
$$\mathcal{O}_{t\!t}(S) = \mathsf{Proc},$$
$$\mathcal{O}_{f\!f}(S) = \emptyset,$$
$$\mathcal{O}_{F_1 \wedge F_2}(S) = \mathcal{O}_{F_1}(S) \cap \mathcal{O}_{F_2}(S),$$
$$\mathcal{O}_{F_1 \vee F_2}(S) = \mathcal{O}_{F_1}(S) \cup \mathcal{O}_{F_2}(S),$$
$$\mathcal{O}_{\langle a \rangle F}(S) = \langle \cdot a \cdot \rangle \mathcal{O}_F(S),$$
$$\mathcal{O}_{[a]F}(S) = [\cdot a \cdot] \mathcal{O}_F(S).$$

◆

A few words of explanation for the above definition are in order here. Intuitively, the first equality in Definition 6.1 expresses the trivial observation that if we assume that S is the set of states that satisfy X then the set of states satisfying X is S. The second equation states the fact, equally obvious, that every state satisfies $t\!t$ irrespective of the set of states that are assumed to satisfy X. The last equation, however, says that to calculate the set of states satisfying the formula $[a]F$ under the assumption that the states in S satisfy X, it is sufficient to

1. compute the set of states satisfying the formula F under the assumption that the states in S satisfy X, and then
2. find the collection of states that will end up in that set no matter how they perform an a-labelled transition.

Exercise 6.4 *Given the transition graph from Example 6.2, use the above definition to calculate* $\mathcal{O}_{[b]f\!f \wedge [a]X}(\{p_2\})$. ◆

One can show that, for every formula F, the function $\mathcal{O}_F$ is *monotonic* (see Definition 4.4) over the complete lattice $(2^{\mathsf{Proc}}, \subseteq)$. In other words, for all subsets S_1, S_2 of Proc, if $S_1 \subseteq S_2$ then $\mathcal{O}_F(S_1) \subseteq \mathcal{O}_F(S_2)$.

Exercise 6.5 *Show that $\mathcal{O}_F$ is monotonic for all F. Consider what will happen if we introduce negation into our logic. Hint: Use structural induction on F.* ◆

As mentioned before, the idea underlying the definition of the function $\mathcal{O}_F$ is that if $[\![X]\!] \subseteq \mathsf{Proc}$ gives the set of processes that satisfy X then $\mathcal{O}_F([\![X]\!])$ will be the set of processes that satisfy F. What then is this set $[\![X]\!]$? Syntactically we shall assume that $[\![X]\!]$ is implicitly given by a recursive equation for X of the form

$$X \stackrel{\mathrm{min}}{=} F_X \ \text{ or } \ X \stackrel{\mathrm{max}}{=} F_X.$$

As shown in the previous section, such an equation can be interpreted as the set equation

$$[\![X]\!] = \mathcal{O}_{F_X}([\![X]\!]).\tag{6.6}$$

As $\mathcal{O}_{F_X}$ is a monotonic function over a complete lattice we know that (6.6) has solutions, i.e. that $\mathcal{O}_{F_X}$ has fixed points. In particular Tarski's fixed point theorem (Theorem 4.1) gives us that there is a unique *largest* fixed point, which we now denote FIX $\mathcal{O}_{F_X}$, and also a unique *least* one, which we denote fix $\mathcal{O}_{F_X}$. These are given respectively by

$$\text{FIX } \mathcal{O}_{F_X} = \bigcup \{S \subseteq \mathsf{Proc} \mid S \subseteq \mathcal{O}_{F_X}(S)\},$$
$$\text{fix } \mathcal{O}_{F_X} = \bigcap \{S \subseteq \mathsf{Proc} \mid \mathcal{O}_{F_X}(S) \subseteq S\}.$$

A set S with the property that $S \subseteq \mathcal{O}_{F_X}(S)$ is called a *post-fixed point* for $\mathcal{O}_{F_X}$. Correspondingly S is a *pre-fixed point* for $\mathcal{O}_{F_X}$ if $\mathcal{O}_{F_X}(S) \subseteq S$.

In what follows, for a function $f : 2^{\mathsf{Proc}} \longrightarrow 2^{\mathsf{Proc}}$ we define

$$f^0 = \text{id} \quad \text{(the identity function on } 2^{\mathsf{Proc}}),$$
$$f^{m+1} = f \circ f^m.$$

When Proc is finite we have the following characterization of the largest and least fixed points.

Theorem 6.1 If Proc is finite then FIX $\mathcal{O}_{F_X} = (\mathcal{O}_{F_X})^M(\mathsf{Proc})$ for some M and fix $\mathcal{O}_{F_X} = (\mathcal{O}_{F_X})^m(\emptyset)$ for some m.

Proof. This follows directly from the fixed point theorem for finite complete lattices. See Theorem 4.2 for the details. $\qquad\square$

The above theorem gives us an algorithm for computing the least and largest set of processes solving an equation of the form (6.6). Consider, by way of example, the formula

$$X \overset{\text{max}}{=} F_X,$$

where $F_X = \langle b \rangle t\!t \wedge [b]X$. The set of processes in the LTS, shown below,

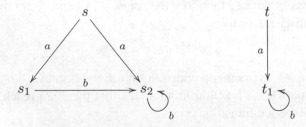

that satisfy this property is the largest solution to the equation

$$[\![X]\!] = (\langle \cdot b \cdot \rangle \{s, s_1, s_2, t, t_1\}) \cap [\cdot b \cdot][\![X]\!].$$

This solution is simply the largest fixed point of the set function defined by the right-hand side of the above equation – that is, the function mapping each set of states S to the set

$$\mathcal{O}_{F_X}(S) = (\langle \cdot b \cdot \rangle \{s, s_1, s_2, t, t_1\}) \cap [\cdot b \cdot] S.$$

Since we are looking for the largest fixed point of this function, we begin the iterative algorithm by taking $S = \{s, s_1, s_2, t, t_1\}$, the set of all states in our LTS. We therefore have that our first approximation to the largest fixed point is the set

$$\begin{aligned}
\mathcal{O}_{F_X}(\{s, s_1, s_2, t, t_1\}) &= (\langle \cdot b \cdot \rangle \{s, s_1, s_2, t, t_1\}) \cap [\cdot b \cdot]\{s, s_1, s_2, t, t_1\} \\
&= \{s_1, s_2, t_1\} \cap \{s, s_1, s_2, t, t_1\} \\
&= \{s_1, s_2, t_1\}.
\end{aligned}$$

Note that our candidate solution to the equation has shrunk in size, since an application of $\mathcal{O}_{F_X}$ to the set of all processes has removed the states s and t from this solution. Intuitively, this follows because, by applying $\mathcal{O}_{F_X}$ to the set of all states, we have found a reason why s and t do *not* afford the property specified by

$$X \stackrel{\mathrm{max}}{=} \langle b \rangle t\!t \wedge [b]X,$$

namely that s and t do not have a b-labelled outgoing transition and therefore that neither is in the set $\langle \cdot b \cdot \rangle \{s, s_1, s_2, t, t_1\}$.

Following our iterative algorithm for the computation of the largest fixed point, we now apply the function $\mathcal{O}_{F_X}$ to the new candidate largest solution, namely $\{s_1, s_2, t_1\}$. We now have that

$$\begin{aligned}
\mathcal{O}_{F_X}(\{s_1, s_2, t_1\}) &= (\langle \cdot b \cdot \rangle \{s, s_1, s_2, t, t_1\}) \cap [\cdot b \cdot]\{s_1, s_2, t_1\} \\
&= \{s_1, s_2, t_1\} \cap \{s, s_1, s_2, t, t_1\} \\
&= \{s_1, s_2, t_1\}.
\end{aligned}$$

(You should convince yourself that the above calculations are correct!) We have found that $\{s_1, s_2, t_1\}$ is a fixed point of the function $\mathcal{O}_{F_X}$. By Theorem 6.1, this is the largest fixed point and therefore the states s_1, s_2 and t_1 are the only states in our LTS that satisfy the property

$$X \stackrel{\mathrm{max}}{=} \langle b \rangle t\!t \wedge [b]X.$$

This is in complete agreement with our intuition, because those are the only states that can perform a b-action in all states that they can reach by performing sequences of b-labelled transitions.

Exercise 6.6 *Consider the property*

$$Y \stackrel{\min}{=} \langle b \rangle tt \vee \langle \{a, b\} \rangle Y.$$

Use Theorem 6.1 to compute the set of processes in the LTS above that satisfy this property. ♦

6.3 Largest fixed points and invariant properties

In this section we shall have a closer look at the meaning of formulae defined by means of largest fixed points. More precisely we consider an equation of the form

$$X \stackrel{\max}{=} F_X,$$

and define $[\![X]\!] \subseteq \text{Proc}$ by

$$[\![X]\!] = \text{FIX } \mathcal{O}_{F_X}.$$

We have previously given an informal argument for why *invariant* properties are obtained as largest fixed points. In what follows we will formalize this argument and prove its correctness.

As we saw in the previous section, the property $Inv(F)$ is obtained as the largest fixed point to the recursive equation

$$X = F \wedge [\text{Act}]X.$$

We will now show that $Inv(F)$ defined in this way indeed expresses that F *holds at all states in all transition sequences*.

For this purpose we let $\mathcal{I} : 2^{\text{Proc}} \longrightarrow 2^{\text{Proc}}$ be the corresponding semantic function, i.e.

$$\mathcal{I}(S) = [\![F]\!] \cap [\cdot\text{Act}\cdot]S.$$

By Tarski's fixed point theorem this equation has exactly one largest solution, given by

$$\text{FIX } \mathcal{I} = \bigcup \{S \mid S \subseteq \mathcal{I}(S)\}.$$

To show that FIX $\mathcal{I}$ indeed characterizes precisely the set of processes for which all states in all computations satisfy the property F, we need a direct (and obviously correct) formulation of this set. This is given by the set Inv, defined as follows:

$$Inv = \{p \mid p \stackrel{\sigma}{\to} p' \text{ implies } p' \in [\![F]\!] \text{ for each } \sigma \in \text{Act}^* \text{ and } p' \in \text{Proc}\}.$$

The correctness of $Inv(F)$ with respect to this description can now be formulated as follows.

Theorem 6.2 For every LTS (Proc, Act, $\{ \xrightarrow{a} \mid a \in \text{Act}\}$), $Inv = \text{FIX } \mathcal{I}$ holds.

Proof. We show the validity of the statement by proving each of the inclusions $Inv \subseteq \text{FIX } \mathcal{I}$ and $\text{FIX } \mathcal{I} \subseteq Inv$ separately.

$Inv \subseteq \text{FIX } \mathcal{I}$. To prove this inclusion it is sufficient to show that $Inv \subseteq \mathcal{I}(Inv)$. (Why?) To this end, let $p \in Inv$. Then, for all $\sigma \in \text{Act}^*$ and $p' \in \text{Proc}$,

$$p \xrightarrow{\sigma} p' \text{ implies } p' \in [\![F]\!]. \tag{6.7}$$

We must establish that $p \in \mathcal{I}(Inv)$ or, equivalently, that $p \in [\![F]\!]$ and $p \in [\cdot \text{Act} \cdot] Inv$. We obtain the first of these two statements by taking $\sigma = \varepsilon$ in (6.7), because $p \xrightarrow{\varepsilon} p$ always holds.

To prove that $p \in [\cdot \text{Act} \cdot] Inv$, we have to show that, for each process p' and action a,

$$p \xrightarrow{a} p' \text{ implies } p' \in Inv.$$

This is equivalent to proving that, for each sequence of actions σ' and process p'',

$$p \xrightarrow{a} p' \text{ and } p' \xrightarrow{\sigma'} p'' \text{ imply } p'' \in [\![F]\!].$$

However, this follows immediately by letting $\sigma = a\sigma'$ in (6.7).

$\text{FIX } \mathcal{I} \subseteq Inv$. First we note that, since $\text{FIX } \mathcal{I}$ is a fixed point of $\mathcal{I}$, it holds that

$$\text{FIX } \mathcal{I} = [\![F]\!] \cap [\cdot \text{Act} \cdot] \text{FIX } \mathcal{I}. \tag{6.8}$$

To prove that $\text{FIX } \mathcal{I} \subseteq Inv$, assume that $p \in \text{FIX } \mathcal{I}$ and that $p \xrightarrow{\sigma} p'$. We shall show that $p' \in [\![F]\!]$ by induction on $|\sigma|$, the length of σ.

Base case $\sigma = \varepsilon$. For this case $p = p'$ and therefore, by (6.8) and our assumption that $p \in \text{FIX } \mathcal{I}$, it holds that $p' \in [\![F]\!]$, which was to be shown.

Inductive step $\sigma = a\sigma'$. Now $p \xrightarrow{a} p'' \xrightarrow{\sigma'} p'$ for some p''. By (6.8) and our assumption that $p \in \text{FIX } \mathcal{I}$, it follows that $p'' \in \text{FIX } \mathcal{I}$. As $|\sigma'| < |\sigma|$ and $p'' \in \text{FIX } \mathcal{I}$, by the induction hypothesis we may conclude that $p' \in [\![F]\!]$, as required.

This completes the proof of the second inclusion.

The proof of the theorem is now complete. $\qquad\qquad\qquad\qquad\qquad\qquad\quad\Box$

6.4 A game characterization for HML with recursion

Let us recall the definition of Hennessy–Milner logic with one recursively defined variable X. The formulae are defined using the following abstract syntax:

$$F ::= X \mid t t \mid f f \mid F_1 \wedge F_2 \mid F_1 \vee F_2 \mid \langle a \rangle F \mid [a]F,$$

where $a \in \mathsf{Act}$ and there is exactly one defining equation for the variable X, which is either of the form

$$X \stackrel{\min}{=} F_X$$

or of the form

$$X \stackrel{\max}{=} F_X.$$

Here F_X is a formula of the logic that may contain occurrences of the variable X.

Let $(\mathsf{Proc}, \mathsf{Act}, \{\stackrel{a}{\rightarrow} \mid a \in \mathsf{Act}\})$ be an LTS and F a formula of Hennessy–Milner logic with one (recursively defined) variable X. Let $s \in \mathsf{Proc}$. We shall describe a game between an 'attacker' and a 'defender' that has the following goal.

The attacker is aiming to prove that $s \not\models F$ while
The defender is aiming to prove that $s \models F$.

The *configurations* of the game are pairs of the form (s, F), where $s \in \mathsf{Proc}$ and F is a formula of Hennessy–Milner logic with one variable X. For every configuration we define the following successor configurations according to the structure of the formula F (here s ranges over Proc):

- $(s, t t)$ and $(s, f f)$ have no successor configurations;
- $(s, F_1 \wedge F_2)$ and $(s, F_1 \vee F_2)$ both have two successor configurations, namely (s, F_1) and (s, F_2);
- $(s, \langle a \rangle F)$ and $(s, [a]F)$ both have the successor configurations (s', F) for every s' such that $s \stackrel{a}{\rightarrow} s'$; and
- (s, X) has only one successor configuration (s, F_X), where X is defined via either $X \stackrel{\max}{=} F_X$ or $X \stackrel{\min}{=} F_X$.

A *play* of the game starting from (s, F) is a maximal sequence of configurations formed by the players according to the following rules.

The attacker picks a successor configuration for every current configuration of the form $(s, F_1 \wedge F_2)$ and $(s, [a]F)$.
The defender picks a successor configuration for every current configuration of the form $(s, F_1 \vee F_2)$ and $(s, \langle a \rangle F)$.

Note that the successor configuration of (s, X) is always uniquely determined; we will denote this move by $(s, X) \rightarrow (s, F_X)$. (It is suggestive to think of these moves that unwind fixed points as moves made by a referee of the game.) Furthermore, successor configurations selected by the attacker will be denoted by $\xrightarrow{A}$ moves and those chosen by the defender by $\xrightarrow{D}$ moves.

We also notice that

- every play terminates in (s, tt) or (s, ff), or
- the attacker (or the defender) gets stuck in the current configuration $(s, [a]F)$ (or $(s, \langle a \rangle F)$) whenever $s \xrightarrow{a}\!\!\!\!\!/\,$, or
- the play is infinite.

The following rules decide who is the winner of a play.

The attacker is the winner in every play ending in a configuration of the form (s, ff) or in a play in which the defender gets stuck and cannot make any further moves.

The defender is the winner in every play ending in a configuration of the form (s, tt) or in a play in which the attacker gets stuck and cannot make any further moves.

The attacker is the winner in every infinite play provided that X is defined via $X \stackrel{\min}{=} F_X$; the defender is a winner in every infinite play provided that X is defined via $X \stackrel{\max}{=} F_X$.

Remark 6.1 The intuition for the least and largest fixed point is as follows. If X is defined as a least fixed point then the defender has to prove in finitely many rounds that this property is satisfied. If a play of the game is infinite then the defender has failed to do so, and the attacker wins. If instead X is defined as a largest fixed point then it is the attacker who has to disprove in finitely many rounds that the formula is satisfied. If a play of the game is infinite then the attacker has failed to do so, and the defender wins.   ◆

Theorem 6.3 (Game characterization) Let $(\mathsf{Proc}, \mathsf{Act}, \{\xrightarrow{a} \mid a \in \mathsf{Act}\})$ be an LTS and F a formula of Hennessy–Milner logic with one (recursively defined) variable X. Let $s \in \mathsf{Proc}$. Then the following statements hold.

- State s satisfies F iff the defender has a universal winning strategy starting from (s, F).
- State s does not satisfy F iff the attacker has a universal winning strategy starting from (s, F).

The proof of this result is beyond the scope of this introductory textbook. We refer the reader to Stirling (2001) for a proof of the above result and more information on model checking games.

6.4.1 Examples of use

In this section let us consider the following LTS:

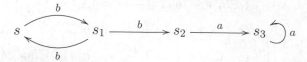

Example 6.3 We start with an example which does not use any recursively defined variable. We shall demonstrate that $s \models [b](\langle b \rangle [b] \mathit{ff} \wedge \langle b \rangle [a] \mathit{ff})$ by defining a universal winning strategy for the defender. As remarked before, we will use $\xrightarrow{A}$ to denote that the successor configuration was selected by the attacker and $\xrightarrow{D}$ to denote that it was selected by the defender. The game starts from

$$(s, [b](\langle b \rangle [b] \mathit{ff} \wedge \langle b \rangle [a] \mathit{ff})).$$

Because $[b]$ is the outermost operation the attacker selects the successor configuration, and he has only one possibility, namely

$$(s, [b](\langle b \rangle [b] \mathit{ff} \wedge \langle b \rangle [a] \mathit{ff})) \xrightarrow{A} (s_1, \langle b \rangle [b] \mathit{ff} \wedge \langle b \rangle [a] \mathit{ff}).$$

Now the topmost operation is $\wedge$ so the attacker has two possibilities:

$$(s_1, \langle b \rangle [b] \mathit{ff} \wedge \langle b \rangle [a] \mathit{ff}) \xrightarrow{A} (s_1, \langle b \rangle [b] \mathit{ff})$$

or

$$(s_1, \langle b \rangle [b] \mathit{ff} \wedge \langle b \rangle [a] \mathit{ff}) \xrightarrow{A} (s_1, \langle b \rangle [a] \mathit{ff}).$$

We have to show that the defender wins from either of these configurations (we have to find a universal winning strategy).

- From $(s_1, \langle b \rangle [b] \mathit{ff})$ it is the defender who makes the next move; suppose that he plays $(s_1, \langle b \rangle [b] \mathit{ff}) \xrightarrow{D} (s_2, [b] \mathit{ff})$. Now the attacker should continue, but $s_2 \xrightarrow{b}\!\!\!\!/\,$ so he is stuck and the defender wins this play.
- From $(s_1, \langle b \rangle [a] \mathit{ff})$ it is also the defender who makes the next move; suppose that he plays $(s_1, \langle b \rangle [a] \mathit{ff}) \xrightarrow{D} (s, [a] \mathit{ff})$. Now the attacker should continue, but $s \xrightarrow{a}\!\!\!\!/\,$ so he is stuck again and the defender wins this play too.

Hence the defender has a universal winning strategy. ◆

Example 6.4 Let $X \stackrel{\min}{=} \langle a \rangle t\!t \vee \langle b \rangle X$. This property informally says that it is possible to perform a sequence of b-actions leading to a state where action a is enabled. We will show that $s \models X$ by defining a universal winning strategy for a defender starting from (s, X). The strategy looks as follows (note that it consists solely of the defender's moves $\stackrel{D}{\rightarrow}$ or the referee's moves $\rightarrow$ for expanding the variable X, so it is truly a universal winning strategy):

$$(s, X) \rightarrow (s, \langle a \rangle t\!t \vee \langle b \rangle X) \stackrel{D}{\rightarrow} (s, \langle b \rangle X) \stackrel{D}{\rightarrow} (s_1, X)$$
$$\rightarrow (s_1, \langle a \rangle t\!t \vee \langle b \rangle X) \stackrel{D}{\rightarrow} (s_1, \langle b \rangle X) \stackrel{D}{\rightarrow} (s_2, X)$$
$$\rightarrow (s_2, \langle a \rangle t\!t \vee \langle b \rangle X) \stackrel{D}{\rightarrow} (s_2, \langle a \rangle t\!t) \stackrel{D}{\rightarrow} (s_3, t\!t).$$

According to the definition of the winner of a play (given before Remark 6.1), $(s_3, t\!t)$ is a winning configuration for the defender.   ♦

Example 6.5 Let $X \stackrel{\max}{=} \langle b \rangle t\!t \wedge [b] X$. This property informally says that along every path where the edges are labelled by the action b, this action never becomes disabled. It is easy to see that $s \not\models X$ and we will prove this by finding a universal winning strategy for an attacker starting from (s, X). As before, the attacker's strategy will not give any selection possibility to the defender and hence it is a universal one:

$$(s, X) \rightarrow (s, \langle b \rangle t\!t \wedge [b] X) \stackrel{A}{\rightarrow} (s, [b] X) \stackrel{A}{\rightarrow} (s_1, X)$$
$$\rightarrow (s_1, \langle b \rangle t\!t \wedge [b] X) \stackrel{A}{\rightarrow} (s_1, [b] X) \stackrel{A}{\rightarrow} (s_2, X)$$
$$\rightarrow (s_2, \langle b \rangle t\!t \wedge [b] X) \stackrel{A}{\rightarrow} (s_2, \langle b \rangle t\!t).$$

From the last configuration $(s_2, \langle b \rangle t\!t)$ the defender is supposed to continue, but he is stuck since $s_2 \stackrel{b}{\not\rightarrow}$ and hence the attacker wins.   ♦

Example 6.6 Let $X \stackrel{\max}{=} \langle a \rangle t\!t \wedge [a] X$. This is the same property as in the previous example (with a exchanged for b). We will show that $s_2 \models X$ by finding a universal winning strategy for the defender from (s_2, X). In the first round we expand the variable X by the move $(s_2, X) \rightarrow (s_2, \langle a \rangle t\!t \wedge [a] X)$ and in the second round the attacker can play either

$$(s_2, \langle a \rangle t\!t \wedge [a] X) \stackrel{A}{\rightarrow} (s_2, \langle a \rangle t\!t)$$

or

$$(s_2, \langle a \rangle t\!t \wedge [a] X) \stackrel{A}{\rightarrow} (s_2, [a] X).$$

It is easy to see that the defender wins from the configuration $(s_2, \langle a \rangle t\!t)$ by the move $(s_2, \langle a \rangle t\!t) \stackrel{D}{\rightarrow} (s_3, t\!t)$, so we shall investigate only the continuation of the game from $(s_2, [a]X)$. The attacker has only the move $(s_2, [a]X) \xrightarrow{A} (s_3, X)$. After expanding the variable X the game continues from $(s_3, \langle a \rangle tt \wedge [a]X)$. Again the attacker can play either

$$(s_3, \langle a \rangle tt \wedge [a]X) \xrightarrow{A} (s_3, \langle a \rangle tt)$$

or

$$(s_3, \langle a \rangle tt \wedge [a]X) \xrightarrow{A} (s_3, [a]X).$$

In the first case the attacker loses as before. In the second case, the only contin-uation of the game is $(s_3, [a]X) \xrightarrow{A} (s_3, X)$. However, we have already seen this configuration, earlier in the game. To sum up, either the attacker loses in finitely many steps or the game is infinite. As we are considering the largest fixed point, in both cases the defender is the winner of the game. $\blacklozenge$

Example 6.7 Let $X \stackrel{\min}{=} \langle a \rangle tt \vee ([b]X \wedge \langle b \rangle tt)$. This property informally says that along each b-labelled sequence there is eventually a state where the action a is enabled. We shall argue that $s_1 \not\models X$ by finding a winning strategy for the attacker starting from (s_1, X). The first move of the game is

$$(s_1, X) \rightarrow (s_1, \langle a \rangle tt \vee ([b]X \wedge \langle b \rangle tt)),$$

and then the defender has two options, namely

$$(s_1, \langle a \rangle tt \vee ([b]X \wedge \langle b \rangle tt)) \xrightarrow{D} (s_1, \langle a \rangle tt)$$

or

$$(s_1, \langle a \rangle tt \vee ([b]X \wedge \langle b \rangle tt)) \xrightarrow{D} (s_1, [b]X \wedge \langle b \rangle tt).$$

In the first case the defender loses, as he needs to pick an a-successor of the state s_1 but $s_1 \xrightarrow{a} \!\!\!\!\!/\,$. In the second case the attacker proceeds as follows:

$$(s_1, [b]X \wedge \langle b \rangle tt) \xrightarrow{A} (s_1, [b]X) \xrightarrow{A} (s, X).$$

The game now continues from (s, X) by the move

$$(s, X) \rightarrow (s, \langle a \rangle tt \vee ([b]X \wedge \langle b \rangle tt)).$$

Again, if the defender were to play $(s, \langle a \rangle tt \vee ([b]X \wedge \langle b \rangle tt)) \xrightarrow{D} (s, \langle a \rangle tt)$ then he would lose in the next round, so he has to play

$$(s, \langle a \rangle tt \vee ([b]X \wedge \langle b \rangle tt)) \xrightarrow{D} (s, [b]X \wedge \langle b \rangle tt).$$

The attacker continues with $(s, [b]X \wedge \langle b \rangle tt) \xrightarrow{A} (s, [b]X) \xrightarrow{A} (s_1, X)$, and the situation (s_1, X) has been seen before. This means that the game is infinite (unless the defender loses in finitely many rounds) and hence the attacker is the winner of the game (since we are considering a least fixed point).   ♦

Exercise 6.7 *Consider the LTS*

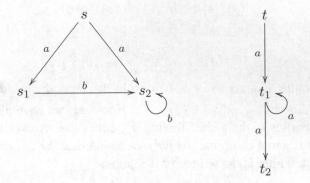

Use the game characterization for HML with recursion to show that:

1. s_1 satisfies the formula

$$X \overset{\max}{=} \langle b \rangle tt \wedge [b]X;$$

2. s satisfies the formula

$$Y \overset{\min}{=} \langle b \rangle tt \vee \langle \{a, b\} \rangle Y$$

but t does not.

Find a recursively defined property that t satisfies and argue that it does so using the game characterization of satisfaction presented in this section.   ♦

6.5   Mutually recursive equational systems

As you may have noticed, so far we have only allowed one equation with one variable in our recursive definitions of formulae. However, as is the case in the specification of process behaviours in CCS, it is sometimes useful, even when not altogether necessary, to define formulae recursively using two or more variables.

By way of example, consider the following property.

>   It is always the case that a process can perform an a-labelled transition lead-ing to a state where b-transitions can be executed forever.

Using the template for the specification of invariance properties we presented at the start of Section 6.1, we can specify the above requirement in terms of the following recursive equation:

$$Inv(\langle a\rangle\text{Forever}(b)) \stackrel{\text{max}}{=} \langle a\rangle\text{Forever}(b) \wedge [\text{Act}]Inv(\langle a\rangle\text{Forever}(b)),$$

where the formula $\text{Forever}(b)$ is one that expresses that b-transitions can be executed forever. The formula $\text{Forever}(b)$ is itself specified recursively, thus:

$$\text{Forever}(b) \stackrel{\text{max}}{=} \langle b\rangle\text{Forever}(b).$$

Our informally specified requirement is therefore formally expressed by means of two recursive equations.

In general, a *mutually recursive equational system* has the form

$$X_1 = F_{X_1},$$

$$\vdots$$

$$X_n = F_{X_n},$$

where $\mathcal{X} = \{X_1, \ldots, X_n\}$ is a set of variables and, for $1 \leq i \leq n$, the formula F_{X_i} is in $\mathcal{M}_{\mathcal{X}}$ and can therefore contain any variable from $\mathcal{X}$. An example of such an equational system is

$$X = [a]Y,$$

$$Y = \langle a\rangle X.$$

An equational system is sometimes given by specifying a (finite) set of variables $\mathcal{X}$ together with a declaration. A *declaration* is a function $D : \mathcal{X} \to \mathcal{M}_{\mathcal{X}}$ that associates a formula with each variabls; $D(X) = F_X$ in the notation used above. As in the example presented above, in what follows we shall assume that either the largest solution is sought for all the equations in an equational system (or the declaration that represents it) or the least solution is sought for all of them. This requirement will be lifted in Section 6.7, where we shall discuss briefly formulae specified by equational systems for which the largest and least fixed points can be mixed.

An equational system generalizes the recursive definition of a single formula in much the same way as, in standard algebra, a system of equations is a generalization of a single equation. The intended meaning of an equational system, which we now proceed to present formally, is therefore, naturally enough, a generalization of the semantics of a single recursively defined formula.

Recall that an equation of the form

$$X = F,$$

where F is a formula in Hennessy–Milner logic that may contain occurrences of the variable X, is intended to describe a set of processes S such that

$$S = \mathcal{O}_F(S).$$

As a natural generalization of this idea, an equational system like

$$X_1 = F_{X_1},$$
$$\vdots$$
$$X_n = F_{X_n},$$

where each formula F_{X_i} may contain any of the variables $X_1, \ldots, X_n$, is meant to describe a vector $(S_1, \ldots, S_n)$ of sets of processes such that

$$S_1 = \mathcal{O}_{F_{X_1}}(S_1, \ldots, S_n),$$
$$\vdots$$
$$S_n = \mathcal{O}_{F_{X_n}}(S_1, \ldots, S_n).$$

To define the semantics of an equational system over a set of variables $\mathcal{X}$, it is therefore not enough to consider simply the complete lattice consisting of subsets of processes. Instead such a system is interpreted over *n-dimensional vectors* of sets of processes, where n is the number of variables in $\mathcal{X}$. Thus the new domain is $\mathcal{D} = (2^{\mathsf{Proc}})^n$ (n times the cross product of 2^{Proc} with itself), with a partial order defined component-wise:

$$(S_1, \ldots, S_n) \sqsubseteq (S'_1, \ldots, S'_n) \text{ if } S_1 \subseteq S'_1 \text{ and } S_2 \subseteq S'_2 \text{ and } \cdots \text{ and } S_n \subseteq S'_n.$$

$(\mathcal{D}, \sqsubseteq)$ defined in this way yields a complete lattice with the least upper bound and the greatest lower bound also defined component-wise:

$$\bigsqcup\{(A_1^i, \ldots, A_n^i) \mid i \in I\} = (\bigcup\{A_1^i \mid i \in I\}, \ldots, \bigcup\{A_n^i \mid i \in I\}),$$
$$\bigsqcap\{(A_1^i, \ldots, A_n^i) \mid i \in I\} = (\bigcap\{A_1^i \mid i \in I\}, \ldots, \bigcap\{A_n^i \mid i \in I\}),$$

where I is an index set.

Let D be a declaration over the set of variables $\mathcal{X} = \{X_1, \ldots, X_n\}$ that associates a formula F_{X_i} with each variable X_i, $1 \leq i \leq n$. The semantic function $[\![D]\!] : \mathcal{D} \to \mathcal{D}$ that is used to obtain the largest and least solutions of the system of recursive equations described by the declaration D is obtained from the syntax in the following way:

$$[\![D]\!](S_1, \ldots, S_n) = (\mathcal{O}_{F_{X_1}}(S_1, \ldots, S_n), \ldots, \mathcal{O}_{F_{X_n}}(S_1, \ldots, S_n)), \quad (6.9)$$

where each argument S_i, $1 \leq i \leq n$, is an arbitrary subset of the set of processes Proc. By analogy with our previous developments, for each formula F in $\mathcal{M}_{\mathcal{X}}$,

$$\mathcal{O}_F(S_1, \ldots, S_n)$$

stands for the set of processes that satisfy F under the assumption that S_i is the collection of processes satisfying X_i, for each $1 \leq i \leq n$.

For each formula F that may contain occurrences of the variables $X_1, \ldots, X_n$, the set $\mathcal{O}_F(S_1, \ldots, S_n)$ is defined exactly as in Definition 6.1 but with

$$\mathcal{O}_{X_i}(S_1, \ldots, S_n) = S_i \quad (1 \leq i \leq n).$$

The function $\llbracket D \rrbracket$ turns out to be monotonic over the complete lattice $(\mathcal{D}, \sqsubseteq)$, and we can obtain both the largest and least fixed points for the equational system in the same way as for the case of one variable.

Consider, for example, the mutually recursive formulae described by the system of equations below:

$$X \stackrel{\text{max}}{=} \langle a \rangle Y \wedge [a]Y \wedge [b]\mathit{ff},$$
$$Y \stackrel{\text{max}}{=} \langle b \rangle X \wedge [b]X \wedge [a]\mathit{ff}.$$

We wish to find out the set of states, in the following LTS, that satisfies the formula X:

To this end, we can again apply the iterative algorithm for computing the largest fixed point of the function determined by the above system of equations. Note that, as formally explained before, such a function maps a pair of sets of states (S_1, S_2) to the pair of sets of states

$$(\langle \cdot a \cdot \rangle S_2 \cap [\cdot a \cdot]S_2 \cap \{s, s_2\}, \ \langle \cdot b \cdot \rangle S_1 \cap [\cdot b \cdot]S_1 \cap \{s_1, s_3\}). \tag{6.10}$$

Here

- S_1 stands for the set of states that are assumed to satisfy X,
- S_2 stands for the set of states that are assumed to satisfy Y,
- $\langle \cdot a \cdot \rangle S_2 \cap [\cdot a \cdot]S_2 \cap \{s, s_2\}$ is the set of states that satisfy the right-hand side of the defining equation for X under these assumptions, and
- $\langle \cdot b \cdot \rangle S_1 \cap [\cdot b \cdot]S_1 \cap \{s_1, s_3\}$ is the set of states that satisfy the right-hand side of the defining equation for Y under these assumptions.

To compute the largest solution of the system of equations above, we use the iterative algorithm provided by Theorem 6.1, starting from the top element in our complete lattice, namely the pair

$$(\{s, s_1, s_2, s_3\}, \{s, s_1, s_2, s_3\}).$$

This corresponds to assuming that all states satisfy both X and Y. To obtain the next approximation to the largest solution of our system of equations, we compute the pair (6.10) taking $S_1 = S_2 = \{s, s_1, s_2, s_3\}$. The result is the pair

$$(\{s, s_2\}, \{s_1, s_3\}).$$

Note that we have shrunk both the components in our original estimate to the largest solution. This means that we have not yet found the largest solution, which is the solution for which we are looking. We therefore compute the pair (6.10) again, taking the above pair as our new input (S_1, S_2). You should convince yourself that the result of this computation is the pair

$$(\{s, s_2\}, \{s_1\}).$$

Note that the first component in the pair has not changed since our previous approximation but that s_3 has been removed from the second component. The reason is that at this point we have discovered that, for instance, s_3 does not afford a b-labelled transition ending up in either s or s_2.

Since we have not yet found a fixed point, we compute the pair (6.10) again, taking $(\{s, s_2\}, \{s_1\})$ as our new input (S_1, S_2). The result of this computation is the pair

$$(\{s\}, \{s_1\}).$$

Intuitively, at this iteration we have discovered a reason why s_2 does not afford property X – namely, that s_2 has an a-labelled transition leading to state s_3, which, as we saw before, does not have property Y.

If we now compute the pair (6.10) again, taking $(\{s\}, \{s_1\})$ as our new input (S_1, S_2), we obtain $(\{s\}, \{s_1\})$. We have therefore found the largest solution to our system of equations. It follows that process s satisfies X and process s_1 satisfies Y.

Exercise 6.8

1. Show that $((2^{\mathsf{Proc}})^n, \sqsubseteq)$, with $\sqsubseteq$, $\bigsqcup$ and $\bigsqcap$ defined as described in the text above, is a complete lattice.

2. Show that (6.9) defines a monotonic function

$$[\![D]\!] : (2^{\mathsf{Proc}})^n \longrightarrow (2^{\mathsf{Proc}})^n.$$

3. Compute the least and largest solutions of the system of equations

$$X = [a]Y,$$
$$Y = \langle a \rangle X,$$

over the transition system associated with the CCS term

$$A_0 = a.A_1 + a.a.0,$$

where

$$A_1 = a.A_2 + a.0,$$
$$A_2 = a.A_1.$$

◆

Exercise 6.9 *Compute the largest solution of the equational system*

$$X = [a]Y,$$
$$Y = \langle a \rangle X$$

over the following LTS:

◆

6.6 Characteristic properties

The characterization theorem for bisimulation equivalence in terms of Hennessy–Milner logic (Theorem 5.1) tells us that if our transition system is image finite then the equivalence classes of bisimulation equivalence are completely characterized by the logic; see Hennessy and Milner (1985) for the original reference. More precisely, for image-finite processes, the equivalence class that contains p consists exactly of the set of processes that satisfy the same formulae in HML as p – that is, letting $[p]_\sim = \{q \mid q \sim p\}$ we have that

$$[p]_\sim = \{q \mid p \models F \text{ implies } q \models F, \text{ for each } F \in \mathcal{M}\}.$$

Exercise 6.10 *Note that in the above rephrasing of the characterization theorem for HML, we require only that each formula satisfied by p is also satisfied by q, not the converse. Show, however, that if q satisfies all the formulae in HML satisfied by p then p and q satisfy the same formulae in HML.* ◆

In this section, following Ingolfsdottir, Godskesen and Zeeberg (1987) and Steffen and Ingolfsdottir (1994) we will show that if our transition system is finite then, by extending the logic with recursion, we can characterize the equivalence classes for strong bisimulation with a *single* formula. (See also Graf and Sifakis (1986) for a translation from CCS expressions describing terminating behaviours into modal formulae.) The formula that characterizes the bisimulation equivalence class for p is called the *characteristic formula* for p and will use the facility for mutually recursive definitions that we introduced in Section 6.5. (Since the material in this section depends on that in Section 6.5, you might wish to review your knowledge of the syntax and semantics for mutually recursive formulae while reading the technical material to follow.) That such a characteristic formula is unique from a semantic point of view is obvious, as the semantics for such a formula is exactly the equivalence class $[p]_\sim$.

Our aim in this section is, therefore, given a process p in a finite transition system, to find a formula $F_p \in \mathcal{M}_\mathcal{X}$ for a suitable set of variables $\mathcal{X}$ such that, for all processes q,

$$q \models F_p \quad \text{iff} \quad q \sim p.$$

Let us start by giving an example which shows that, in general, bisimulation equivalence cannot be characterized by a recursion-free formula.

Example 6.8 Assume that $\mathsf{Act} = \{a\}$ and that the process p is given by the equation

$$X \stackrel{\text{def}}{=} a.X.$$

We will show that p cannot be characterized up to bisimulation equivalence by a single recursion-free formula. To see this we will assume that such a formula exists and show that this leads to a contradiction. Towards a contradiction, we assume that, for some $F_p \in \mathcal{M}$,

$$\llbracket F_p \rrbracket = [p]_\sim. \tag{6.11}$$

In particular we have that

$$p \models F_p \text{ and } (q \models F_p \text{ implies } q \sim p \text{ for each } q). \tag{6.12}$$

We will obtain a contradiction by proving that (6.12) cannot hold for any formula F_p. Before we prove our statement we have to introduce some notation.

Recall that, by the *modal depth* of a formula F, notation $md(F)$, we mean the maximum number of nested occurrences of the modal operators in F. Formally, this is defined by the following recursive definition:

$$md(t\!t) = md(f\!f) = 0,$$
$$md([a]F) = md(\langle a \rangle F) = 1 + md(F),$$
$$md(F_1 \vee F_2) = md(F_1 \wedge F_2) = \max\{md(F_1), md(F_2)\}.$$

Next we define a sequence $p_0, p_1, p_2, \ldots$ of processes inductively as follows:

$$p_0 = \mathbf{0},$$
$$p_{i+1} = a.p_i.$$

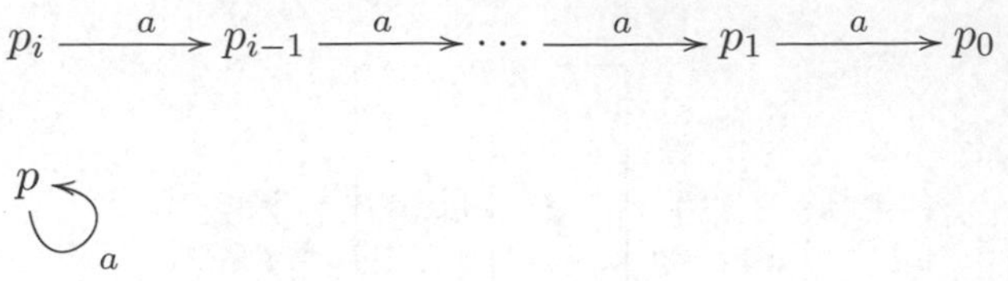

$$p_i \xrightarrow{\quad a \quad} p_{i-1} \xrightarrow{\quad a \quad} \cdots \xrightarrow{\quad a \quad} p_1 \xrightarrow{\quad a \quad} p_0$$

Figure 6.3 The processes p and p_i.

The processes p and p_i, for $i \geq 1$, are depicted in Figure 6.3. Observe that each process p_i can perform a sequence of i a-labelled transitions in a row and terminate in doing so. Moreover, this is the only behaviour that p_i affords.

Now we can prove the following:

$$p \models F \text{ implies } p_{md(F)} \models F \text{ for each } F. \tag{6.13}$$

The statement in (6.13) can be proved by structural induction on F and is left as an exercise for the reader. As obviously p and p_i are not bisimulation equivalent for any i (why?), the statement in (6.13) contradicts (6.12). Indeed, (6.12) and (6.13) imply that p is bisimilar to p_k, where k is the modal depth of the formula F_p.

As (6.12) is a consequence of (6.11), we can therefore conclude that no recursion-free formula F_p can characterize the process p up to bisimulation equivalence. ◆

Exercise 6.11 *Prove statement (6.13).* ◆

Exercise 6.12 (Recommended) *Before reading on, you might want to try to define a characteristic formula for some processes for which HML suffices. If you fancy this challenge, we encourage you to read Example 6.9 below for inspiration.*

Assume that a is the only action. For each $i \geq 0$, construct an HML formula that is a characteristic formula for process p_i in Figure 6.3. Hint: First give a characteristic formula for p_0. Next show how to construct a characteristic formula for p_{i+1} from that for p_i. ◆

Example 6.8 showed us that in order to obtain a characteristic formula even for finite LTSs we need to make use of the recursive extension of Hennessy–Milner logic.

The construction of a characteristic formula involves two steps. First of all, we need to construct an equational system that describes the formula; next we must decide whether to adopt the least or the largest solution to this system. We start our search for the characteristic formula by giving the equational system and afterwards choose a suitable interpretation for the fixed points.

We start by assuming that we have a finite transition system

$$(\{p_1, \ldots, p_n\}, \mathsf{Act}, \{\xrightarrow{a} \mid a \in \mathsf{Act}\})$$

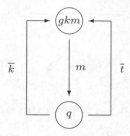

Figure 6.4 The coffee machine gkm.

and a set of variables $\mathcal{X} = \{X_{p_1}, \ldots, X_{p_n}, \ldots\}$ that contains (at least) as many variables as there are states in the transition system. Intuitively X_p is the syntactic symbol for the characteristic formula for p and its meaning will be given in terms of an equational system.

A characteristic formula for a process has to describe which actions the process *can perform*, which actions it *cannot perform* and what happens to it *after it has performed* each action. The following example illustrates these issues.

Example 6.9 A coffee machine is shown schematically in Figure 6.4. We can construct a characteristic formula for it as follows.

Let gkm be the initial state of the coffee machine. Then we see that gkm can perform an m-action and that this is the only action it can perform in this state. The diagram also shows us that by performing the m-action gkm will necessarily end up in state q. These properties can be expressed as follows.

1. The state gkm can perform m and become q.
2. No matter how gkm performs m it becomes q.
3. The state gkm cannot perform any action other than m.

If we let X_{gkm} and X_q denote the characteristic formula for gkm and q respectively, X_{gkm} can be expressed as

$$X_{gkm} \equiv \langle m \rangle X_q \wedge [m] X_q \wedge [\{\bar{t}, \bar{k}\}] \mathit{ff},$$

where $\langle m \rangle X_q$ expresses property 1 above, $[m] X_q$ expresses property 2 and the last conjunct $[\{\bar{t}, \bar{k}\}] \mathit{ff}$ expresses property 3. To obtain the characteristic formula for gkm we have to define a recursive formula for X_q following the same strategy. We observe that q can perform two actions, namely $\bar{t}$ and $\bar{k}$, and that in both cases it becomes gkm. X_q can therefore be expressed as

$$X_q \equiv \langle \bar{t} \rangle X_{gkm} \wedge \langle \bar{k} \rangle X_{gkm} \wedge [\{\bar{t}, \bar{k}\}] X_{gkm} \wedge [m] \mathit{ff}.$$

In the recursive formula above, the first conjunct $\langle \bar{t} \rangle X_{gkm}$ states that a process that is bisimilar to q should be able to perform a $\bar{t}$-labelled transition and thereby end up in a state that is bisimilar to gkm, i.e. a state that satisfies the characteristic property X_{gkm} for state gkm. The interpretation of the second conjunct is similar. The third conjunct states that all the outgoing transitions from a state which is bisimilar to q that are labelled with $\bar{t}$ or $\bar{k}$ will end up in a state which is bisimilar to gkm. Finally, the fourth and last conjunct says that a process that is bisimilar to q cannot perform action m. ◆

Now we can generalize the strategy employed in the above example, as follows. Let

$$Der(a, p) = \{p' \mid p \xrightarrow{a} p'\}$$

be the set of states that can be reached from p by the performing of action a. If $p' \in Der(a, p)$ and p' has a characteristic property $X_{p'}$ then p has the property $\langle a \rangle X_{p'}$. We therefore have that

$$p \models \bigwedge_{a, p' . p \xrightarrow{a} p'} \langle a \rangle X_{p'}.$$

Furthermore, if $p \xrightarrow{a} p'$ then $p' \in Der(a, p)$. Therefore p has the property

$$[a] \left(\bigvee_{p' . p \xrightarrow{a} p'} X_{p'} \right),$$

for each action a. The above property states that, by performing action a, process p (and any other process that is bisimilar to it) must become a process satisfying the characteristic property of a state in $Der(a, p)$. (Note that if $p \not\xrightarrow{a}$ then $Der(a, p)$ is empty. In that case, since an empty disjunction is just the formula ff, the above formula becomes simply $[a] ff$, which is what we would expect.)

Since action a is arbitrary, we have that

$$p \models \bigwedge_{a} [a] \left(\bigvee_{p' . p \xrightarrow{a} p'} X_{p'} \right).$$

If we summarize the above requirements, we have that

$$p \models \bigwedge_{a, p' . p \xrightarrow{a} p'} \langle a \rangle X_{p'} \wedge \bigwedge_{a} [a] \left(\bigvee_{p' . p \xrightarrow{a} p'} X_{p'} \right).$$

As this property is clearly a complete description of the behaviour of process p, this is our candidate for its characteristic property. X_p is therefore defined as a

Figure 6.5 Simple infinite process p.

solution to the equational system obtained by giving the following equation for each $q \in \mathsf{Proc}$:

$$X_q = \bigwedge_{a,q'.q \xrightarrow{a} q'} \langle a \rangle X_{q'} \wedge \bigwedge_a [a] \left(\bigvee_{q'.q \xrightarrow{a} q'} X_{q'} \right). \tag{6.14}$$

This solution could either be the least or the largest one (or, in fact, any other fixed point, by what we know at this stage).

The following example shows that the least solution to (6.14) in general does not yield the characteristic property for a process.

Example 6.10 Let p be the process given in Figure 6.5. In this case, assuming for the sake of simplicity that a is the only action, the equational system obtained by using (6.14) will have the form

$$X_p = \langle a \rangle X_p \wedge [a] X_p.$$

Since $\langle \cdot a \cdot \rangle \emptyset = \emptyset$, you should be able to convince yourself that $\llbracket X_p \rrbracket = \emptyset$ is the least solution to this equation. This corresponds to taking $X_p = \mathit{ff}$ as the characteristic formula for p. However, p does not have the property ff, which therefore cannot be the characteristic property for p. ♦

In what follows we will show that the largest solution to (6.14) yields the characteristic property for all $p \in \mathsf{Proc}$. (Readers of Section 4.3 will have noticed that this is in line with our characterization of bisimulation equivalence as the largest fixed point of a suitable monotonic function.) This is the content of the following theorem, whose proof you can skip unless you are especially interested in the mathematical developments.

Theorem 6.4 Let $(\mathsf{Proc}, \mathsf{Act}, \{\xrightarrow{a} \mid a \in \mathsf{Act}\})$ be a finite transition system and, for each $p \in \mathsf{Proc}$, let X_p be defined by

$$X_p \stackrel{\mathrm{max}}{=} \bigwedge_{a,p'.p \xrightarrow{a} p'} \langle a \rangle X_{p'} \wedge \bigwedge_a [a] \left(\bigvee_{p'.p \xrightarrow{a} p'} X_{p'} \right). \tag{6.15}$$

Then X_p is the characteristic property for p, i.e. $q \models X_p$ iff $p \sim q$ for each $q \in$ Proc.

The assumption that Proc and Act are finite ensures that there is only a finite number of variables involved in the definition of the characteristic formula and that we obtain a formula with only finite conjunctions and disjunctions on the right-hand side of each equation.

In the proof of the theorem we will let D_K be the declaration defined by

$$D_K(X_p) = \bigwedge_{a,p.p \xrightarrow{a} p'} \langle a \rangle X_{p'} \wedge \bigwedge_a [a] \left(\bigvee_{p'.p \xrightarrow{a} p'} X_{p'} \right).$$

From our previous discussion, we have that X_p is the characteristic property for p iff for the largest solution $[\![X_p]\!]$, where $p \in$ Proc, we have that $[\![X_p]\!] = [p]_\sim$. In what follows, we write $q \models_{\max} X_p$ if q belongs to $[\![X_p]\!]$ in the largest solution for D_K.

In order to prove Theorem 6.4, we shall establish the following two statements separately, for each process $q \in$ Proc:

1. if $q \models_{\max} X_p$ then $p \sim q$, and
2. if $p \sim q$ then $q \models_{\max} X_p$.

As the first step in the proof of Theorem 6.4, we prove the following lemma, to the effect that the former statement holds.

Lemma 6.1 Let X_p be defined as in (6.15). Then, for each $q \in$ Proc, we have that

$$q \models_{\max} X_p \Rightarrow p \sim q.$$

Proof. Let $R = \{(p, q) \mid q \models_{\max} X_p\}$. We will prove that R is a bisimulation and thus that $p \sim q$ whenever $q \models_{\max} X_p$. To this end, we have to prove the following two claims, where b is an arbitrary action in Act and p_1, q_1 are processes in Proc:

1. $(p, q) \in R$ and $p \xrightarrow{b} p_1 \Rightarrow \exists q_1. q \xrightarrow{b} q_1$ and $(p_1, q_1) \in R$;
2. $(p, q) \in R$ and $q \xrightarrow{b} q_1 \Rightarrow \exists p_1. p \xrightarrow{b} p_1$ and $(p_1, q_1) \in R$.

We shall prove these two claims separately.

Proof of 1. Assume that $(p, q) \in R$ and $p \xrightarrow{b} p_1$. This means that

$$q \models_{\max} X_p \quad \text{and} \quad p \xrightarrow{b} p_1.$$

From (6.15) it follows that

$$q \models_{\max} \left(\bigwedge_{a,p'.p \xrightarrow{a} p'} \langle a \rangle X_{p'} \right) \wedge \left(\bigwedge_a [a] \left(\bigvee_{p'.p \xrightarrow{a} p'} X_{p'} \right) \right).$$

As $p \xrightarrow{b} p_1$, we obtain, in particular, that $q \models_{\max} \langle b \rangle X_{p_1}$, which means that, for some $q_1 \in \text{Proc}$,

$$q \xrightarrow{b} q_1 \quad \text{and} \quad q_1 \models_{\max} X_{p_1}.$$

Using the definition of R, we have that

$$q \xrightarrow{b} q_1 \quad \text{and} \quad (p_1, q_1) \in R,$$

as required.

Proof of 2. Assume that $(p, q) \in R$ and $q \xrightarrow{b} q_1$. This means that

$$q \models_{\max} X_p \quad \text{and} \quad q \xrightarrow{b} q_1.$$

As before, since $q \models_{\max} X_p$ we have that

$$q \models_{\max} \left(\bigwedge_{a,p'.p \xrightarrow{a} p'} \langle a \rangle X_{p'} \right) \wedge \left(\bigwedge_a [a] \left(\bigvee_{p'.p \xrightarrow{a} p'} X_{p'} \right) \right).$$

In particular, it follows that

$$q \models_{\max} [b] \bigvee_{p'.p \xrightarrow{b} p'} X_{p'}.$$

As we know that $q \xrightarrow{b} q_1$, we obtain that

$$q_1 \models_{\max} \bigvee_{p'.p \xrightarrow{b} p'} X_{p'}.$$

Therefore there must exist a p_1 such that $q_1 \models_{\max} X_{p_1}$ and $p \xrightarrow{b} p_1$.
We have therefore proved that

$$\exists p_1. p \xrightarrow{b} p_1 \quad \text{and} \quad (p_1, q_1) \in R,$$

as required.

We have now shown that R is a bisimulation, and therefore that

$$q \models_{\max} X_p \quad \text{implies} \quad p \sim q.$$

This proves the lemma.   □

The next lemma completes the proof of Theorem 6.4, our main theorem of this section. In the statement of this lemma and in its proof we will assume for notational convenience that $\mathsf{Proc} = \{p_1, \ldots, p_n\}$.

Lemma 6.2 $([p_1]_\sim, \ldots, [p_n]_\sim) \sqsubseteq [\![D_K]\!]([p_1]_\sim, \ldots, [p_n]_\sim)$, where D_K is the declaration defined after the statement of Theorem 6.4.

Proof. Assume that $q \in [p]_\sim$, where p is one of $p_1, \ldots, p_n$. To prove our claim, it is sufficient to show that

$$q \in \left(\bigcap_{a, p'. p \xrightarrow{a} p'} \langle \cdot a \cdot \rangle [p']_\sim \right) \cap \left(\bigcap_a [\cdot a \cdot] \left(\bigcup_{p'. p \xrightarrow{a} p'} [p']_\sim \right) \right).$$

(Can you see why?) As before, the proof can be divided into two parts, namely:

1. $q \in \bigcap_{a, p'. p \xrightarrow{a} p'} \langle \cdot a \cdot \rangle [p']_\sim$; and

2. $q \in \bigcap_a [\cdot a \cdot] \left(\bigcup_{p'. p \xrightarrow{a} p'} [p']_\sim \right).$

We proceed by proving these claims in turn.

Proof of 1. We recall that $q \sim p$. Assume that $p \xrightarrow{a} p'$ for some action a and process p'. Then there is a q', where $q \xrightarrow{a} q'$ and $q' \sim p'$. We have therefore shown that, for all a and p', there is a q' such that

$$q \xrightarrow{a} q' \quad \text{and} \quad q' \in [p']_\sim.$$

This means that, for each a and p' such that $p \xrightarrow{a} p'$, we have that

$$q \in \langle \cdot a \cdot \rangle [p']_\sim.$$

We may therefore conclude that

$$q \in \bigcap_{a, p'. p \xrightarrow{a} p'} \langle \cdot a \cdot \rangle [p']_\sim,$$

as required.

Proof of 2. Let $a \in \mathsf{Act}$ and $q \xrightarrow{a} q'$. We have to show that $q' \in \bigcup_{p'. p \xrightarrow{a} p'} [p']_\sim$. To this end, observe that, as $q \xrightarrow{a} q'$ and $p \sim q$, there exists a p' such that $p \xrightarrow{a} p'$ and $p' \sim q'$. For this q' we have that $q' \in [p']_\sim$. We have therefore proved that, for all a and q',

$$q \xrightarrow{a} q' \Rightarrow \exists p'. p \xrightarrow{a} p' \quad \text{and} \quad q \in [p']_\sim,$$

which is equivalent to

$$q \in \bigcap_a [\cdot a \cdot] \left(\bigcup_{p' . p \xrightarrow{a} p'} [p']_\sim \right).$$

Statements 1 and 2 above yield

$$([p_1]_\sim, \dots, [p_n]_\sim) \sqsubseteq [\![D_K]\!]([p_1]_\sim, \dots, [p_n]_\sim),$$

as required.   □

Theorem 6.4 can now be expressed as the following lemma, whose proof completes the argument for that result.

Lemma 6.3 For each $p \in$ Proc, we have that $[\![X_p]\!] = [p]_\sim$.

Proof. Lemma 6.2 yields that

$$([p_1]_\sim, \dots, [p_n]_\sim) \sqsubseteq ([\![X_{p_1}]\!], \dots, [\![X_{p_n}]\!]),$$

which means that

$$[p]_\sim \subseteq [\![X_p]\!]$$

for each $p \in$ Proc. (Why?) Furthermore Lemma 6.1 gives that $[\![X_p]\!] \subseteq [p]_\sim$ for every $p \in$ Proc, which proves the statement of the lemma.   □

Exercise 6.13 *What are the characteristic formulae for the processes p and q in Figure 6.1?*   ♦

Exercise 6.14 *Define characteristic formulae for the simulation and ready simulation preorders as defined in Exercises 3.17 and 3.18, respectively.*   ♦

6.7   Mixing largest and least fixed points

Assume that we are interested in using HML with recursive definitions to specify the following property of systems.

It is possible for the system to reach a state which has a livelock.

We saw just before the start of Section 6.1 how to describe a property of the form 'it is possible for the system to reach a state satisfying F' using the template formula $Pos(F)$, namely

$$Pos(F) \stackrel{\mathrm{min}}{=} F \vee \langle \mathsf{Act} \rangle Pos(F).$$

Therefore, all that we need to do to specify the above property using HML with recursion is to 'plug in' a specification of the property 'the state has a livelock' in lieu of F. How can we describe a property of the form 'the state has a livelock' using HML with recursion? A livelock is an infinite sequence of internal steps of the system. So a state p in an LTS has a livelock if it affords a computation of the form

$$p = p_0 \xrightarrow{\tau} p_1 \xrightarrow{\tau} p_2 \xrightarrow{\tau} p_3 \xrightarrow{\tau} \cdots$$

for some sequence of states $p_1, p_2, p_3 \ldots$. In other words, a state p has a livelock now if it affords a τ-labelled transition leading to a state p_1 that has a livelock now. This immediately suggests the following recursive specification of a property LivelockNow:

$$\text{LivelockNow} = \langle \tau \rangle \text{LivelockNow}.$$

As usual, we are faced with a choice in selecting a suitable solution for the above equation. Since we are specifying a state of affairs that should hold forever, in this case we should select the largest solution to the equation above. It follows that our HML specification of the property 'the state has a livelock' is

$$\text{LivelockNow} \stackrel{\max}{=} \langle \tau \rangle \text{LivelockNow}.$$

Exercise 6.15 *What would be the least solution of the above equation?* ♦

Exercise 6.16 (Mandatory) *Consider the LTS below.*

$$s \xrightarrow{\ \ a\ \ } p \xrightarrow{\ \ \tau\ \ } q \xrightarrow{\ \ \tau\ \ } r$$
$$p \circlearrowleft \tau$$

Use the iterative algorithm for computing the set of states in this LTS that satisfies the formula LivelockNow *defined above.* ♦

Exercise 6.17 *This exercise is for those who feel they need more practice in computing fixed points using the iterative algorithm.*
 Consider the LTS below.

$$s \underset{\tau}{\overset{\tau}{\rightleftarrows}} s_1 \xleftarrow{\ \ a\ \ } s_2 \xrightarrow{\ \ \tau\ \ } s_3 \circlearrowright \tau$$

Use the iterative algorithm for computing the set of states in this LTS that satisfies the formula LivelockNow *defined above.* ♦

In the light of the above discussion, a specification of the property mentioned at the beginning of this section using HML with recursive definitions can be given using the following system of equations:

$$Pos(\text{LivelockNow}) \stackrel{\text{min}}{=} \text{LivelockNow} \vee \langle \text{Act} \rangle Pos(\text{LivelockNow}),$$
$$\text{LivelockNow} \stackrel{\text{max}}{=} \langle \tau \rangle \text{LivelockNow}.$$

This looks natural and innocuous. However, first appearances can be deceptive! Indeed, the equational systems we have considered so far have only allowed us to express formulae purely in terms of the largest or least solutions to systems of recursion equations. (See Section 6.5.) For instance, in defining the characteristic formulae for bisimulation equivalence, we used only systems of equations in which the largest solution was sought for *all* the equations in the system.

Our next question is whether we can extend our framework in such a way that it can treat *systems of equations with mixed solutions* like the one describing the formula $Pos(\text{LivelockNow})$ above. How can we, for instance, compute the set of processes in the LTS

$$s \xrightarrow{\ a\ } p \xrightarrow{\ \tau\ } q \xrightarrow{\ \tau\ } r$$
$$\underset{\tau}{\circlearrowright}$$

that satisfy the formula Pos (LivelockNow)? In this case, the answer is not overly difficult. In fact, you might have already noted that we can compute the set of processes satisfying the formula $Pos(\text{LivelockNow})$ once we have in our hands the collection of processes satisfying the formula LivelockNow. As in Exercise 6.16, the only state in the above LTS satisfying the formula LivelockNow is p. Therefore, we may obtain the collection of states satisfying the formula $Pos(\text{LivelockNow})$ as the *least* solution of the set equation

$$S = \{p\} \cup \langle \cdot \text{Act} \cdot \rangle S, \tag{6.16}$$

where S ranges over subsets of $\{s, p, q, r\}$. We can calculate the least solution of this equation using the iterative methods introduced in Section 6.2.

Since we are looking for the least solution of the above equation, we begin by obtaining our first approximation $S^{(1)}$ to the solution by computing the value of the expression on the right-hand side of the equation when $S = \emptyset$, which is the least element in the complete lattice consisting of the subsets of $\{s, p, q, r\}$ ordered by inclusion. We have that

$$S^{(1)} = \{p\} \cup \langle \cdot \text{Act} \cdot \rangle \emptyset = \{p\}.$$

Intuitively, we have so far discovered the (obvious!) fact that p has the possibility of reaching a state where a livelock may arise because p has a livelock now.

Our second approximation $S^{(2)}$ is found by computing the set obtained by evaluating the expression on the right-hand side of (6.16) when $S = S^{(1)} = \{p\}$. The result is

$$S^{(2)} = \{p\} \cup \langle \cdot \text{Act} \cdot \rangle \{p\} = \{s, p\}.$$

Intuitively, we have now discovered the new fact that s has the possibility of reaching a state where a livelock may arise because s has a transition leading to p, which, as we found out in the previous approximation, has itself the possibility of reaching a livelock.

You should now be able to convince yourself that the set $\{s, p\}$ is indeed a fixed point of equation (6.16), i.e. that

$$\{s, p\} = \{p\} \cup \langle \cdot \text{Act} \cdot \rangle \{s, p\}.$$

It follows that $\{s, p\}$ is the least solution of (6.16) and that the states s and p are the only ones in our example LTS that satisfy the formula $Pos(\text{LivelockNow})$. This makes perfect sense intuitively, because s and p are the only states in that LTS that afford a sequence of transitions leading to a state from which an infinite computation consisting of τ-labelled transitions is possible. (In the case of p, this sequence is empty since p can embark on a τ-loop immediately.)

Note that we could find the set of states satisfying $Pos(\text{LivelockNow})$ by first computing $[\![\text{LivelockNow}]\!]$ and then using this set to compute

$$[\![Pos(\text{LivelockNow})]\!],$$

because the specification of the formula LivelockNow is independent of that for $Pos(\text{LivelockNow})$. In general, we can apply this strategy if the collection of equations can be partitioned into a sequence of 'blocks' such that

- the equations in the same block are all either largest-fixed-point equations or least-fixed-point equations, and
- equations in each block use only variables defined in that block or in preceding ones.

The following definition formalizes this class of systems of equations.

Definition 6.2 A n-nested mutually recursive equational system E is an n-tuple

$$\langle (D_1, \mathcal{X}_1, m_1), (D_2, \mathcal{X}_2, m_2), \dots, (D_n, \mathcal{X}_n, m_n) \rangle,$$

where the $\mathcal{X}_i$ are pairwise-disjoint finite sets of variables and, for each $1 \leq i \leq n$,

- D_i is a declaration mapping the variables in the set $\mathcal{X}_i$ to formulae in HML with recursion that may use variables in the set $\bigcup_{1 \leq j \leq i} \mathcal{X}_j$,
- $m_i = \max$ or $m_i = \min$, and
- $m_i \neq m_{i+1}$.

We refer to $(D_i, \mathcal{X}_i, m_i)$ as the ith block of E and say that it is a maximal block if $m_i = \max$ and a minimal block otherwise.   ♦

Observe that our earlier specification of the formula Pos(LivelockNow) was given in terms of a 2-nested mutually recursive equational system. In fact, take $\mathcal{X}_1 = \{$LivelockNow$\}$ and $\mathcal{X}_2 = \{Pos($LivelockNow$)\}$. You can easily check that the constraints in the above definition are met. However, the mixed equational system

$$X \stackrel{\max}{=} \langle a \rangle Y,$$
$$Y \stackrel{\min}{=} \langle b \rangle X$$

does not meet these requirements because the variables X and Y are both defined in mutually recursive fashion and their definitions refer to different types of fixed point. If we allow fixed points to be mixed completely freely we obtain the *modal μ-calculus* (Kozen, 1983), which was mentioned in Section 6.1. In this book we shall not allow a full freedom in mixing fixed points in declarations, however, but will restrict ourselves to systems of equations satisfying the constraints in Definition 6.2. Note that employing the approach described above, using our running example in this section, such systems of equations have a unique solution, obtained by solving the first block and then proceeding with the others using the solutions already obtained for the preceding blocks.

Finally if F is a Hennessy–Milner formula defined over a set of variables $\mathcal{Y} = \{Y_1, \ldots, Y_k\}$ that are declared by an n-nested mutually recursive equational system E then $[\![F]\!]$ is well defined and can be expressed by

$$[\![F]\!] = \mathcal{O}_F([\![Y_1]\!], \ldots, [\![Y_k]\!]), \tag{6.17}$$

where $[\![Y_1]\!], \ldots, [\![Y_k]\!]$ are the sets of states satisfying the recursively defined formulae associated with the variables $Y_1, \ldots, Y_k$.

Exercise 6.18 *Consider the LTS in Exercise 6.17. Use (6.17) to compute the set of states satisfying the formula*

$$F = \langle \mathsf{Act} \rangle Pos(\text{LivelockNow}).$$

♦

Exercise 6.19 *Consider the following property expressed in natural language.*

It is always the case that each request is eventually followed by a grant.

Express this property using HML with recursion. Next, construct a rooted LTS that satisfies the property and one that does not. Check your constructions by computing the set of states in the LTSs you have built that satisfy the formula.   ♦

6.8 Further results on model checking

We shall now present an overview of results in connection with model checking for various modal and temporal logics over several classes of processes, as we did for equivalence-checking problems in Section 3.6.

We consider only the logics mentioned in the above text. They form the following natural expressiveness hierarchy:

- Hennessy–Milner logic (HML),
- Hennessy–Milner logic with one recursively defined variable (1HML), and
- the modal μ-calculus (Kozen, 1983), i.e. Hennessy–Milner logic with arbitrarily many nested and recursively defined variables.

These logics are typical representatives of the so-called *branching-time* logics. The view of time taken by these logics is that each moment in time may branch into several distinct possible futures. Therefore, the structures used for interpreting branching-time logics can be viewed as computation trees. This means that in order to check for the validity of a formula, one has to consider a whole tree of states reachable from the root. Another typical and well-known branching-time logic is *computation-tree logic* or CTL (Clarke and Emerson, 1981), which uses *until* (in nested form) as the only temporal operator, the next-time modality X and existential and universal path quantifiers.

Another collection of temporal logics is the so-called *linear-time* logics. The view of time taken by these logics is that each moment in time has a unique successor. Suitable models for formulae in such logics are therefore computation sequences. Here the validity of a formula is determined for a particular (fixed) trace of the system and possible branching is not taken into account. A process satisfies a linear-time formula if all its computation sequences satisfy it. *Linear temporal logic* or LTL (Pnueli, 1977) is probably the most studied logic of this type, in particular with its connection to the automata-theoretic approach to model checking (Vardi, 1995) and its implementation in tools such as SPIN (Holzmann, 2003) and COSPAN (Har'El and Kurshan, 1987)

We shall first have a look at the decidability of model checking for the logics HML, 1HML and the modal μ-calculus over finite LTSs. The model-checking problem for the μ-calculus, which is the most expressive of those three logics, is decidable and belongs to both the classes NP and co-NP. In fact it was proved by Jurdziński (1998) that the problem is even in UP $\cap$ co-UP, which is the class of problems that can be decided by polynomial-time nondeterministic Turing machines with the extra restriction that, for each input, there is at most *one* accepting computation of the Turing machine. It has been widely conjectured that the problem is indeed decidable in deterministic polynomial time. However, this is still one of the major open questions in this theory. The logics HML and 1HML are fragments of the μ-calculus. Their model-checking problems are both decidable in polynomial (more precisely in linear) time on finite LTSs (Cleaveland and Steffen, 1992). It is worth remarking here that the model checking problem for LTL over finite LTSs is instead PSPACE-complete (Sistla and Clarke, 1985).

The aforementioned results on the complexity of model checking are based on the use of LTSs as our model for reactive systems. However, in practice, most reactive systems contain several communicating components and may be modelled as parallel compositions of (restricted classes of) LTSs. As with equivalence checking, model checking suffers from the so-called state-explosion problem in the presence of concurrency. Hence a characterization of the complexity of the model-checking problem in the presence of concurrency yields a more realistic assessment of the hardness of the task of model checking for reactive systems. The picture that emerges from the results presented in the literature on the complexity of model checking, when the size of a concurrent process is measured in terms of the 'length of its description' rather than by the size of the LTS that describes all its possible computations, is somewhat bleak. The complexity of CTL model checking and of reachability for concurrent programs is PSPACE-complete (Kupferman, Vardi and Wolper, 2000, Kozen, 1977) and that for the (alternation-free) μ-calculus is EXPTIME-complete (Kupferman *et al.*, 2000).

If we consider classes of sequential systems with infinitely many reachable states, such as for example pushdown automata, the model-checking problem for the μ-calculus remains decidable. More precisely, it is EXPTIME-complete, as shown in Walukiewicz (2001).

In fact even more powerful logics, such as monadic second-order logic – see, for instance, Libkin (2004, Chapter 7) for a textbook introduction – are still decidable over sequential infinite-state systems (Caucal, 1996, Muller and Schupp, 1985). The EXPTIME-hardness of model-checking μ-calculus formulae over pushdown automata is valid even in the case where the size of the formula is assumed to be constant (fixed). However, for fixed formulae and processes in the BPA class (pushdown automata with a single control state), the problem is decidable in polynomial time (Burkart and Steffen, 1997, Walukiewicz, 2001). The model checking of HML is PSPACE-complete for BPA but, for a fixed formula, this problem is again in P (Mayr, 1998).

The situation is, however, not so promising once we move from sequential infinite-state systems to parallel infinite-state systems. Both for the class of Petri nets (PN) and for its communication-free fragment BPP (CCS with parallel composition, recursion and action prefixing only), essentially all branching-time logics with at least one recursively defined variable are undecidable. More precisely, the EG logic which can express the property that there exists a computation during which some HML formula is invariantly true is undecidable for BPP (Esparza and Kiehn, 1995) (and hence also for PN). The EF logic, which essentially can express reachability properties, is decidable for BPP (Esparza, 1997) but undecidable for PN (Esparza, 1994). However, the linear-time logic LTL (with a certain restriction) is decidable for Petri nets and BPP (Esparza, 1994). This is an example for which LTL turns out to be more tractable than branching-time logics. A thorough discussion of the relative merits of linear- and branching-time logics from a complexity-theoretic perspective may be found in, for example, the paper Vardi (2001).

For further references and more detailed overviews we refer the reader to, for example, the references Burkart *et al.* (2001) and Burkart and Esparza (1997).

7

Modelling and analysis of mutual exclusion algorithms

Introduction

In the previous chapters of this book, we have illustrated the use of the ingredients in our methodology for the description and analysis of reactive systems by means of simple but, it is hoped, illustrative examples. As we have mentioned repeatedly, the difficulty in understanding and reasoning reliably about even the simplest reactive systems has long been recognized. Apart from the intrinsic scientific and intellectual interest of a theory of reactive computation, this realization has served as a powerful motivation for the development of the theory we have presented so far and its associated verification techniques.

In order to offer you further evidence for the usefulness of the theory you have learned so far in the modelling and analysis of reactive systems, we shall now use it to model and analyse some well-known mutual exclusion algorithms. These algorithms are amongst the most classic ones in the theory of concurrent algorithms and have been investigated by many authors using a variety of techniques; see, for instance, the classic papers Dijkstra (1965), Knuth (1966) and Lamport (1986). Here, they will give us the opportunity to introduce some modelling and verification techniques that have proved their worth in the analysis of many different kinds of reactive system.

In order to illustrate concretely the steps that have to be taken in modelling and verification problems, we shall consider a very elegant solution to the mutual exclusion problem proposed by Peterson and discussed in Peterson and Silberschatz (1985).

In Peterson's algorithm for mutual exclusion, there are two processes P_1 and P_2, two boolean variables b_1 and b_2 and an integer variable k that may take the values 1 and 2. The boolean variables b_1 and b_2 have initial value 'false', whereas the initial value of the variable k is arbitrary. In order to ensure mutual exclusion, each process P_i, $i \in \{1, 2\}$, executes the following algorithm, where we use j to denote the index of the other process.

> **while true do**
> **begin**
> > 'noncritical section';
> > $b_i := $ **true**;
> > $k := j$;
> > **while** (b_j **and** $k = j$) **do skip**;
> > 'critical section';
> > $b_i := $ **false**;
> **end**

As for many concurrent algorithms in the literature, Peterson's mutual exclusion algorithm is presented in pseudocode. Therefore one of our tasks, when modelling the above algorithm, is to translate the pseudocode description of the behaviour of the processes P_1 and P_2 into the model of LTSs or into Milner's CCS. Moreover, the algorithm uses variables that are manipulated by the processes P_1 and P_2. Variables are not part of CCS because, as discussed in Section 1.2, process calculi like CCS are based on the message-passing paradigm and not on shared variables. However, this is not a major problem. In fact, following the message-passing paradigm, we can view variables as processes which are willing to communicate with other computing agents in their environment that need to read and/or write them.

By way of example, let us consider how to represent the boolean variable b_1 as a process. This variable will be encoded as a process with two states, namely B_{1t} and B_{1f}. The former state will describe the behaviour whereby the variable b_1 holds the value 'true', and the latter the behaviour whereby the variable b_1 holds the value 'false'. No matter what its value is, the variable b_1 can be read (yielding information on its value to the reading process) or written (possibly changing its value). We need to describe these possibilities in CCS. To this end, we shall assume that processes read and write variables by communicating with them using suitable communication ports. For instance, a process wishing to read the value 'true' from variable b_1 will try to synchronize with the process representing that variable on a specific communication channel, say b1rt; this acronym means, read the value 'true' from b_1. Similarly, a process wishing to write the value 'false' into variable b_1 will try to synchronize with the process representing that variable on the communication channel b1wf; here the acronym means, write 'false' into b_1.

Using these ideas, the behaviour of the process describing the variable b_1 can be represented by the following CCS expressions:

$$B_{1f} \stackrel{def}{=} \overline{b1rf}.B_{1f} + b1wf.B_{1f} + b1wt.B_{1t},$$

$$B_{1t} \stackrel{def}{=} \overline{b1rt}.B_{1t} + b1wf.B_{1f} + b1wt.B_{1t}.$$

Intuitively, when in state B_{1t} the above process is willing to tell its environment that its value is 'true' and to receive writing requests from other processes. The communication of the value of the variable to its environment does not change the state of the variable, whereas a writing request from a process in the environment may do so.

The behaviour of the process describing the variable b_2 can be represented in similar fashion:

$$B_{2f} \stackrel{def}{=} \overline{b2rf}.B_{2f} + b2wf.B_{2f} + b2wt.B_{2t},$$

$$B_{2t} \stackrel{def}{=} \overline{b2rt}.B_{2t} + b2wf.B_{2f} + b2wt.B_{2t}.$$

The CCS representation of the behaviour of the variable k in the algorithm is as follows:

$$K_1 \stackrel{def}{=} \overline{kr1}.K_1 + kw1.K_1 + kw2.K_2,$$

$$K_2 \stackrel{def}{=} \overline{kr2}.K_2 + kw1.K_1 + kw2.K_2.$$

Again, the process representing the variable k has two states, denoted by the constants K_1 and K_2 above, because the variable k can only take the two values 1 and 2.

Exercise 7.1 *You should now be in a position to generalize the above examples. Assume that we have a variable v taking values over a data domain D. Can you represent this variable using a CCS process?* ♦

Having described the variables used in Peterson's algorithm as processes, we are now left to represent the pseudocode algorithms for the processes P_1 and P_2 as CCS expressions. Note that, in doing so, we are making a step of formalization, because pseudocode is a semi-formal notation without a precise syntax and semantics whereas both the syntax and the semantics of CCS are unambiguously specified.

In our CCS formalization of the behaviour of processes P_1 and P_2, we shall ignore what the processes do outside and within their critical sections and focus on their entering and exiting the critical section. After all, this is the interesting part of their behaviour as far as ensuring mutual exclusion is concerned! Moreover, we shall assume, for the sake of simplicity, that processes cannot fail or terminate within the critical section. Under these assumptions, the initial behaviour of process P_1 can be described by the following CCS expression:

$$P_1 \stackrel{\text{def}}{=} \overline{b1wt}.\overline{kw2}.P_{11}.$$

The above expression says that process P_1 begins by writing 'true' in variable b_1 and 2 in variable k. Having done so, it will enter a new state that will be represented by the constant P_{11}. This new constant will intuitively describe the behaviour of process P_1 while it is executing the following line of pseudocode:

while (b_j **and** $k = j$) **do skip**.

To simulate this 'busy waiting' behaviour, we expect that process P_{11} will

- read the value of the variables b_j and k,
- loop back to P_{11} if b_j is true and k is equal to 2, and
- move to a new state, say P_{12}, otherwise. In state P_{12}, we expect that process P_1 will enter and then exit the critical section.

The first thing to note here is that we need to make a decision about the precise semantics of the informal pseudocode expression

$$b_j \text{ and } k = j.$$

How is this boolean conjunction evaluated? Is it evaluated from left to right or from right to left? Assuming that it is evaluated from left to right, is the second conjunct evaluated if the first turns out to yield 'false'? Different answers to these questions will produce different CCS processes. In what follows, we shall present a CCS description for process P_{11} under the assumption that conjunctions are evaluated from left to right and that the second conjunct is *not* evaluated if the value of the first is equal to 'false'. Under these assumptions, we can write

$$P_{11} \stackrel{\text{def}}{=} b2rf.P_{12} + b2rt.(kr2.P_{11} + kr1.P_{12}).$$

Exercise 7.2 *Would it have been a good idea to define* P_{11} *thus:*

$$P_{11} \stackrel{\text{def}}{=} b2rf.P_{12} + b2rt.kr2.P_{11} + b2rt.kr1.P_{12}?$$

Argue for your answer. ◆

To complete the description of the behaviour of the process P_1 we are left to present the defining equation for the constant P_{12}, describing the access to, and exit from, the critical section and the setting of the variable b_1 to 'false':

$$P_{12} \stackrel{\text{def}}{=} enter1.exit1.\overline{b1wf}.P_1.$$

In the above CCS expression, we have labelled the enter and exit actions in a way that makes it clear that it is process P_1 that is entering and exiting the critical section.

The CCS process describing the behaviour of process P_2 in Peterson's algorithm is entirely symmetric to the one we have just provided and is defined thus:

$$P_2 \stackrel{\text{def}}{=} \overline{\text{b2wt}}.\overline{\text{kw1}}.P_{21},$$

$$P_{21} \stackrel{\text{def}}{=} \text{b1rf}.P_{22} + \text{b1rt}.(\text{kr1}.P_{21} + \text{kr2}.P_{22}),$$

$$P_{22} \stackrel{\text{def}}{=} \text{enter2}.\text{exit2}.\overline{\text{b2wf}}.P_2.$$

The CCS process term representing the whole of Peterson's algorithm consists of the parallel composition of the terms describing the two processes running the algorithm and of those describing the variables. Since we are only interested in the behaviour of the algorithm pertaining to the access to, and exit from, their critical sections, we shall restrict all the communication channels that are used to read from, and write to, the variables. We shall use L to stand for that set of channel names. Assuming that the initial value of the variable k is 1, our CCS description of Peterson's algorithm is therefore given by the term

$$\text{Peterson} \stackrel{\text{def}}{=} (P_1 \mid P_2 \mid B_{1f} \mid B_{2f} \mid K_1) \setminus L.$$

Exercise 7.3 (Mandatory!) *Give a CCS process that describes the behaviour of Hyman's 'mutual exclusion' algorithm. Hyman's algorithm was proposed in (Hyman, 1966). It uses the same variables as Peterson's.*

In Hyman's algorithm, each process P_i, $i \in \{1, 2\}$, executes the algorithm given below, where again we use j to denote the index of the other process.   ♦

```
while true do
begin
      'noncritical section';
      b_i := true;
      while k ≠ j do begin
                        while b_j do skip;
                        k := i
                  end;
      'critical section';
      b_i := false;
end
```

Now that we have a formal description of Peterson's algorithm, we can set ourselves the goal of analysing its behaviour, either manually or with the assistance of a software tool that can handle specifications of reactive systems given in the language CCS. In order to do so, however, we first need to specify precisely what it means for an algorithm to 'ensure mutual exclusion'. In our formalization, it seems natural to identify 'ensuring mutual exclusion' with the following requirement.

At no point in the execution of the algorithm will processes P_1 and P_2 both be in their critical sections at the same time.

How can we formalize this requirement? There are at least two options for doing so, depending on whether we wish to use HML with recursion or CCS processes, i.e. LTSs, as our specification formalism. In order to gain experience in the use of both these approaches to specification and verification, in what follows we shall present specifications for mutual exclusion using HML with recursion and CCS.

7.1 Specifying mutual exclusion in HML

Hennessy–Milner logic with recursion is an excellent formalism for specifying our informal correctness condition for Peterson's algorithm. To see this, observe first of all that the aforementioned desideratum is really a safety property, in that it intuitively states that a desirable state of affairs – namely that 'it is not possible for both processes to be in their critical sections at the same time' – is maintained throughout the execution of the process Peterson. We have seen already, in Chapter 6, that safety properties can be specified in HML with recursion using formulae of the form $Inv(F)$, where F is the 'desirable property' that we wish to hold at all points in the execution of the process. Recall that $Inv(F)$ is nothing but a short-hand for the recursively defined formula

$$Inv(F) \overset{\max}{=} F \wedge [\mathsf{Act}]Inv(F).$$

So, all that we are left to do in order to specify mutual exclusion is to give a formula F in HML describing the following requirement.

It is not possible for both processes to be in their critical sections at the same time.

In the light of our CCS formalization of the processes P_1 and P_2, we know that process P_i, $i \in \{1, 2\}$, is in its critical section precisely when it can perform the action exit_i. So our formula F can be taken to be

$$F \overset{\mathrm{def}}{=} [\mathrm{exit}_1]\mathit{ff} \vee [\mathrm{exit}_2]\mathit{ff}.$$

The formula $Inv(F)$ now states that it is invariably the case that either P_1 is not in the critical section or P_2 is not in the critical section, which is an equivalent formulation of our correctness criterion.

Throughout this chapter, we are interpreting the modalities in HML over the transition system whose states are CCS processes and whose transitions are weak transitions of the form $\overset{\alpha}{\Rightarrow}$ for any action α including τ. So a formula like $[\text{exit}_1]\mathit{ff}$ is satisfied by all processes that do not afford an $\overset{\text{exit}_1}{\Rightarrow}$-labelled transition, i.e. by those processes that cannot perform action exit_1 no matter how many internal steps they do beforehand.

Exercise 7.4 *Consider the formula* $Inv(G)$*, where* G *is*

$$([\text{enter}_1][\text{enter}_2]\mathit{ff}) \wedge ([\text{enter}_2][\text{enter}_1]\mathit{ff}).$$

Would such a formula be a good specification for our correctness criterion? What if we took G *to be the formula*

$$(\langle\text{enter}_1\rangle[\text{enter}_2]\mathit{ff}) \wedge (\langle\text{enter}_2\rangle[\text{enter}_1]\mathit{ff})?$$

Argue for your answers!   ◆

Now that we have a formal description of Peterson's algorithm, and a specification of a correctness criterion for it, we could try to establish whether process Peterson satisfies the formula $Inv(F)$.

With some painstaking effort, this could be done manually either by showing that the set of states of the process Peterson is a post-fixed point of the set function associated with the mapping

$$S \mapsto [\![F]\!] \cap [\cdot\text{Act}\cdot]S$$

or by iteratively computing the largest fixed point of the above mapping. The good news, however, is that we do *not* need to do either of these! One benefit of having formal specifications of systems and of their correctness criteria is that, at least in principle, they can be used as inputs for algorithms and tools that do the analysis for us.

One such verification tool for reactive systems that is often used for educational purposes is the so-called Edinburgh Concurrency Workbench (henceforth abbreviated to CWB), which is freely available at

http://homepages.inf.ed.ac.uk/perdita/cwb/.

The CWB accepts inputs specified in CCS and HML with recursive definitions and implements, amongst others, algorithms that check whether a CCS process satisfies a formula in HML with recursion. One of its commands (namely, `checkprop`) allows us to check, at the press of a button, that Peterson does indeed satisfy property $Inv(F)$ above and therefore that it preserves mutual exclusion, as its proposer intended.

Exercise 7.5 *Use the CWB to check whether* Peterson *satisfies the two candidate formulae* $Inv(G)$ *in Exercise 7.4.* ♦

Exercise 7.6 (Mandatory) *Use the CWB to check whether the CCS process for Hyman's algorithm that you gave in your answer to Exercise 7.3 satisfies the formula* $Inv(F)$ *specifying mutual exclusion.* ♦

7.2 Specifying mutual exclusion using CCS itself

In the previous section, we saw how to specify and verify the correctness of Peterson's mutual exclusion algorithm, using HML with recursion and the model-checking approach to the correctness problem. We also hinted at the usefulness of an automatic verification tool like the CWB in the verification of even rather simple concurrent algorithms such as Peterson's algorithm. (Process Peterson has 69 states and cannot be considered a 'large reactive system'. Even so, its manual analysis requires a fair amount of work and care.)

As mentioned previously in this book (see Chapter 3), implementation verification (or equivalence checking) is another natural approach to the specification and verification of reactive systems. Recall that, in implementation verification, both actual systems and their specifications are represented as terms in the same model of concurrent computation, for instance as CCS terms or LTSs. The correctness criterion in this setting is that in some suitable formal sense the term describing the implementation is equivalent to, or a suitable approximation of, that standing for the specification of the desired behaviour. As we saw in Chapter 3, in this approach an important ingredient in the theory of reactive systems is therefore a notion of behavioural equivalence or approximation between process descriptions. Such a notion of equivalence can be used as our yardstick for correctness.

Unfortunately, there is no single notion of behavioural equivalence that fits all purposes. We have already met notions of equivalence such as trace equivalence (Section 3.2), strong bisimilarity (Section 3.3) and weak bisimilarity (Section 3.4). Moreover, this is just the tip of the iceberg of 'reasonable' notions of equivalence or approximation between reactive systems. (The interested, and very keen, reader may wish to consult van Glabbeek's encyclopaedic studies (Glabbeek, 1990, 1993, 2001) for an in-depth investigation of the notions of behavioural equivalence that have been proposed in the literature on concurrency theory.) So, when using implementation verification to establish the correctness of an implementation such as our description of Peterson's mutual exclusion algorithm, we need to

1. express our specification of the desired behaviour of the implementation using our model for reactive systems – in our setting as a CCS term – and

2. choose a suitable notion of behavioural equivalence to be used in checking
   that the model of the implementation is correct with respect to the chosen
   specification.

As you can see, in both these steps we need to make creative choices – putting to
rest the usual perception that verifying the correctness of computing systems is a
purely mechanical endeavour.

So let us try to verify the correctness of Peterson's algorithm for mutual exclusion using implementation verification. According to the above checklist, the first
thing that we need to do is to express the desired behaviour of a mutual exclusion
algorithm using a CCS process term.

Intuitively, we expect that a mutual exclusion algorithm like Peterson's initially
allows both processes P_1 and P_2 to enter their critical sections. However, once one
of the two processes, say P_1, has entered its critical section, the other process cannot enter its own critical section until P_1 has exited its critical section. A suitable
specification of the behaviour of a mutual exclusion algorithm seems therefore to
be given by the CCS term

$$\text{MutexSpec} \stackrel{\text{def}}{=} \text{enter}_1.\text{exit}_1.\text{MutexSpec} + \text{enter}_2.\text{exit}_2.\text{MutexSpec}. \qquad (7.1)$$

Assuming that this is our specification of the expected behaviour of a mutual exclusion algorithm, our next task is to prove that the process Peterson is equivalent to,
or a suitable approximation of, MutexSpec. What notion of equivalence or approximation should we use for this purpose?

You should be able to convince yourself readily that trace equivalence or strong
bisimilarity, as presented in Sections 3.2 and 3.3, will not do. (Why?) One possible
approach would be to use observational equivalence (Definition 3.4) as our formal
embodiment of the notion of correctness. Unfortunately, however, this would *not*
work either! Indeed, you should be able to check easily that on the one hand the
process Peterson affords the weak transition

$$\text{Peterson} \stackrel{\tau}{\Rightarrow} (P_{12} \mid P_{21} \mid B_{1t} \mid B_{2t} \mid K_1) \setminus L$$

and that the state that is the target of that transition affords an enter_1-labelled transition but cannot perform any weak enter_2-labelled transition. On the other hand,
the only state that process MutexSpec can reach by performing internal transitions
is itself, and in that state both enter transitions are always enabled. It follows that
Peterson and MutexSpec are *not* observationally equivalent.

Exercise 7.7 *What sequence of τ-transitions will bring process* Peterson *into state*
$(P_{12} \mid P_{21} \mid B_{1t} \mid B_{2t} \mid K_1) \setminus L$? *(You will need five τ-steps.)*

Argue that, as we claimed above, this state affords an enter$_1$*-labelled transition but cannot perform a weak* enter$_2$*-labelled transition.* ◆

This sounds like very bad news indeed. Observational equivalence allows us to ignore some internal steps, in the evolution of process Peterson, but obviously not enough in this specific setting. We seem to need a more abstract notion of equivalence to establish the, seemingly obvious, correctness of Peterson's algorithm with respect to our specification.

Observe that if we could show that the 'observable content' of each sequence of actions performed by process Peterson is a trace of the process MutexSpec then we could certainly conclude that Peterson does ensure mutual exclusion. In fact, this would mean that at no point in its behaviour can process Peterson perform two exit actions in a row – possibly with some internal steps in between them. But what do we mean precisely by the 'observable content' of a sequence of actions? The following definition formalizes this notion in a very natural way.

Definition 7.1 (Weak traces and weak trace equivalence) A *weak trace* of a process P is a sequence $a_1 \cdots a_k$, $k \geq 1$, of observable actions such that there exists a sequence of transitions

$$P = P_0 \overset{a_1}{\Rightarrow} P_1 \overset{a_2}{\Rightarrow} \cdots \overset{a_k}{\Rightarrow} P_k,$$

for some $P_1, \ldots, P_k$. Moreover, each process affords the weak trace ε.

We say that a process P is a *weak trace approximation* of process Q if the set of weak traces of P is included in that of Q. Two processes are *weak trace equivalent* if they afford the same weak traces. ◆

Note that the collection of weak traces coincides with that of traces for processes that, like MutexSpec, do not afford internal transitions. (Why?)

We claim that the processes Peterson and MutexSpec are weak trace equivalent, and therefore that Peterson does meet our specification of mutual exclusion *modulo weak trace equivalence*. This can be checked automatically using the command `mayeq` provided by the CWB. (Do so!) This equivalence tells us not only that each weak trace of process Peterson is allowed by the specification MutexSpec but also that process Peterson can exhibit as a weak trace each trace permitted by the specification.

If we are just satisfied with checking the pure safety condition that no trace of process Peterson violates the mutual exclusion property, then it suffices to show that Peterson is a weak trace approximation of MutexSpec. A useful proof technique that can be used to establish this result is given by the notion of *weak simulation*. (Compare with the notion of simulation defined in Exercise 3.17.)

Definition 7.2 (Weak simulation) Let us say that a binary relation $\mathcal{R}$ over the set of states of an LTS is a *weak simulation* iff, whenever $s_1 \, \mathcal{R} \, s_2$ and α is an action (including τ),

if $s_1 \xrightarrow{\alpha} s_1'$ then there is a transition $s_2 \xRightarrow{\alpha} s_2'$ such that $s_1' \, \mathcal{R} \, s_2'$.

We say that s' *weakly simulates* s iff there is a weak simulation $\mathcal{R}$ with $s \, \mathcal{R} \, s'$. ◆

Proposition 7.1 For all states s, s', s'' in an LTS, the following statements hold.

1. State s weakly simulates itself.
2. If s' weakly simulates s and s'' weakly simulates s' then s'' weakly simulates s.
3. If s' weakly simulates s then each weak trace of s is also a weak trace of s'.

In the light of the above proposition, to show that Peterson is a weak trace approximation of MutexSpec it suffices to build a weak simulation that relates Peterson to MutexSpec. The existence of such a weak simulation can be checked using the command `pre` offered by the CWB. (Do so!)

Exercise 7.8 *Prove Proposition 7.1.*   ◆

Exercise 7.9 *Assume that s' weakly simulates s and that s weakly simulates s'. Is it true that s and s' are observationally equivalent? Argue for your answer.*   ◆

Exercise 7.10 *Assume that the CCS process Q weakly simulates P. Show that $Q + R$ weakly simulates P and $P + R$, for each CCS process R.*   ◆

Exercise 7.11
1. *Show that the processes $\alpha.P + \alpha.Q$ and $\alpha.(P + Q)$ are weak trace equivalent for each action α and terms P, Q.*
2. *Show that weak trace equivalence is preserved by all the operators of CCS.*
                                                                                                ◆

7.3 Testing mutual exclusion

Another approach to establishing the correctness of Peterson's algorithm is to use a notion of 'testing'. Recall that what we mean by ensuring mutual exclusion is that at no point in the execution of process Peterson will both processes be in their critical sections at the same time. Such a situation would arise if there is some execution of process Peterson in which two enter actions occur one after the other without any exit action in between them. For instance, process P_1 might perform action $enter_1$ and the next observable action might be $enter_2$ – causing both processes to be in their critical sections at the same time. A way to check whether this undesirable situation can ever occur in the behaviour of process Peterson is to make it interact with a 'monitor process' that observes its behaviour and reports an error if and when the undesirable situation arises. This is a conceptually simple, but very useful, technique that has arisen in various forms over and over again in the study of verification techniques for reactive systems and probably finds its most theoretically satisfying embodiment in the classic automata-theoretic approach to verification; see, for instance, the references Vardi (1991) and Vardi and Wolper (1994).

So, how can we construct a monitor process that reports a failure in ensuring mutual exclusion if any arises? Intuitively, such a process would observe the enter and exit actions performed by process Peterson. Whenever an enter action is observed, the monitor process reaches a state in which it is ready to report that something bad has happened if it observes that the other process can now enter its critical section as well. If our monitor process observes the relevant exit action as expected, it gladly returns to its initial state, ready to observe the next round of the execution of the algorithm. A CCS process term describing the above behaviour is, for instance,

$$\text{MutexTest} \stackrel{\text{def}}{=} \overline{\text{enter}_1}.\text{MutexTest}_1 + \overline{\text{enter}_2}.\text{MutexTest}_2,$$

$$\text{MutexTest}_1 \stackrel{\text{def}}{=} \overline{\text{exit}_1}.\text{MutexTest} + \overline{\text{enter}_2}.\overline{\text{bad}}.\mathbf{0},$$

$$\text{MutexTest}_2 \stackrel{\text{def}}{=} \overline{\text{exit}_2}.\text{MutexTest} + \overline{\text{enter}_1}.\overline{\text{bad}}.\mathbf{0},$$

where we have assumed that our monitor process outputs on channel name 'bad' when it discovers that two enter actions have occurred without an intervening exit.

In order to check whether process Peterson ensures mutual exclusion, it is now sufficient to let it interact with MutexTest and ask whether the resulting system

$$(\text{Peterson} \mid \text{MutexTest}) \setminus \{\text{enter}_1, \text{enter}_2, \text{exit}_1, \text{exit}_2\}$$

can initially perform the action $\overline{\text{bad}}$. Indeed, we have the following result.

Proposition 7.2 Let P be a CCS process whose only visible actions are contained in the set $L' = \{\text{enter}_1, \text{enter}_2, \text{exit}_1, \text{exit}_2\}$. Then $(P \mid \text{MutexTest}) \setminus L' \stackrel{\overline{\text{bad}}}{\Rightarrow}$ iff either $P \stackrel{\sigma}{\Rightarrow} P' \stackrel{\text{enter}_1}{\Rightarrow} P'' \stackrel{\text{enter}_2}{\Rightarrow} P'''$ or $P \stackrel{\sigma}{\Rightarrow} P' \stackrel{\text{enter}_2}{\Rightarrow} P'' \stackrel{\text{enter}_1}{\Rightarrow} P'''$, for some P', P'', P''' and some sequence of actions σ in the regular language $(\text{enter}_1\text{exit}_1 + \text{enter}_2\text{exit}_2)^*$.

Proof. For the 'if' implication, assume, without loss of generality, that

$$P \stackrel{\sigma}{\Rightarrow} P' \stackrel{\text{enter}_1}{\Rightarrow} P'' \stackrel{\text{enter}_2}{\Rightarrow} P''',$$

for some P', P'', P''' and sequence of actions $\sigma \in (\text{enter}_1\text{exit}_1 + \text{enter}_2\text{exit}_2)^*$. We shall argue that $(P \mid \text{MutexTest}) \setminus L' \stackrel{\overline{\text{bad}}}{\Rightarrow}$. To see this note that, using induction on the length of the sequence σ, it is not hard to prove that

$$(P \mid \text{MutexTest}) \setminus L' \stackrel{\tau}{\Rightarrow} (P' \mid \text{MutexTest}) \setminus L'.$$

Since $P' \stackrel{\text{enter}_1}{\Rightarrow} P'' \stackrel{\text{enter}_2}{\Rightarrow} P'''$, we have that

$$(P' \mid \text{MutexTest}) \setminus L' \stackrel{\tau}{\Rightarrow} (P'' \mid \text{MutexTest}_1) \setminus L' \stackrel{\tau}{\Rightarrow} (P''' \mid \overline{\text{bad}}.0) \setminus L' \stackrel{\overline{\text{bad}}}{\rightarrow}.$$

Combining the above sequences of transitions, we may conclude that

$$(P \mid \text{MutexTest}) \setminus L' \stackrel{\overline{\text{bad}}}{\Rightarrow},$$

as required.

Conversely, assume that $(P \mid \text{MutexTest}) \setminus L' \stackrel{\overline{\text{bad}}}{\Rightarrow}$. Since $\overline{\text{bad}}.0$ is the only state of process MutexTest that can perform a $\overline{\text{bad}}$-action, this means that, for some P''',

$$(P \mid \text{MutexTest}) \setminus L' \stackrel{\tau}{\Rightarrow} (P''' \mid \overline{\text{bad}}.0) \setminus L' \stackrel{\overline{\text{bad}}}{\rightarrow}.$$

Because of the way MutexTest is constructed, the above trasition holds because, for some P' and P'' such that either $P' \stackrel{\text{enter}_1}{\Rightarrow} P'' \stackrel{\text{enter}_2}{\Rightarrow} P'''$ or $P' \stackrel{\text{enter}_2}{\Rightarrow} P'' \stackrel{\text{enter}_1}{\Rightarrow} P'''$,

$$(P \mid \text{MutexTest}) \setminus L' \stackrel{\tau}{\Rightarrow} (P' \mid \text{MutexTest}) \setminus L'$$
$$\stackrel{\tau}{\Rightarrow} (P'' \mid \text{MutexTest}_i) \setminus L' \quad (i \in \{1,2\})$$
$$\stackrel{\tau}{\Rightarrow} (P''' \mid \overline{\text{bad}}.0) \setminus L'.$$

Using induction on the number of $\stackrel{\tau}{\rightarrow}$-steps in the weak transition

$$(P \mid \text{MutexTest}) \setminus L' \stackrel{\tau}{\Rightarrow} (P' \mid \text{MutexTest}) \setminus L',$$

we can now argue that $P \stackrel{\sigma}{\Rightarrow} P'$ for some sequence of actions σ in the regular language $(\text{enter}_1\text{exit}_1 + \text{enter}_2\text{exit}_2)^*$. This completes the proof.   □

Exercise 7.12 *Fill in the details in the above proof.*   ♦

Aside: Testable formulae in Hennessy–Milner logic   *This section is for theoretically minded readers who would like a glimpse of some technical results related to testing formulae in HML with recursion; it is meant as a pointer for further self-study.*

Those who solved Exercise 7.4 might have realized already that, intuitively, the monitor process MutexTest is 'testing' whether the process it observes satisfies the formula $Inv(G)$, where G is

$$([\text{enter}_1][\text{enter}_2]\mathit{ff}) \wedge ([\text{enter}_2][\text{enter}_1]\mathit{ff}).$$

A natural question to ask is whether each formula in the language HML with recursion can be tested as we have just done for the above formula $Inv(G)$. In order to make this question precise, we need to define the collection of allowed *tests* and the notion of *property testing*. Informally, testing involves the parallel composition of the tested process (described by a state in an LTS or by a CCS process) with a test. Following the spirit of the classic approach of De Nicola and Hennessy (De Nicola and Hennessy, 1984, Hennessy, 1988) and our developments above, we say that the tested state fails a test if the distinguished reject action $\overline{\mathsf{bad}}$ can be performed by the test while it interacts with it, and passes otherwise. The formal definition of testing then involves the definition of what a test is, how interaction takes place and when the test has failed or succeeded. We now proceed to make these notions precise.

Definition 7.3 (Tests) A *test* is a finite rooted LTS T over the set of actions $\mathsf{Act} \cup \{\overline{\mathsf{bad}}\}$, where bad is a distinguished channel name not occurring in Act. We use $\mathsf{root}(T)$ to denote the start state of the LTS T. ♦

As above, the idea is that a test acts as a monitor that 'observes' the behaviour of a process and reports any occurrence of an undesirable situation by performing a $\overline{\mathsf{bad}}$-labelled transition.

In the remainder of this section, tests will often be described concisely using the regular fragment of Milner's CCS, i.e. the fragment of CCS given by the following grammar:

$$T ::= \mathbf{0} \mid \alpha.T \mid T + T \mid X,$$

where α can be any action in Act as well as the distinguished action $\overline{\mathsf{bad}}$, and X is a constant drawn from a given finite set of process names. The right-hand side of the defining equations for a constant can only be a term generated by the above grammar. For example, the process MutexTest that we specified above is a regular CCS process, but the term

$$X \stackrel{\mathrm{def}}{=} a.(b.\mathbf{0} \mid X)$$

is not.

We now proceed to describe formally how tests can be used to check whether a process satisfies a formula expressed in HML with recursion.

Definition 7.4 (Testing properties) Let F be a formula in HML with recursion, and let T be a test.

- For every state s of an LTS, we say that s passes the test T iff

$$(s \mid \mathsf{root}(T)) \setminus \mathcal{L} \stackrel{\overline{\mathsf{bad}}}{\nRightarrow} .$$

(Recall that $\mathcal{L}$ stands for the collection of observable actions in CCS except for the action bad.) Otherwise we say that s fails the test T.

- We say that the test T *tests* for the formula F (and that F is *testable*) iff for every LTS $\mathcal{T}$ and every state s of $\mathcal{T}$,

$$s \models F \text{ iff } s \text{ passes the test } T.$$

- A collection of formulae in HML with recursion is testable iff each formula in it is testable.

◆

Example 7.1 The formula $[a]\mathit{ff}$ is satisfied by those processes that do not afford an $\overset{a}{\Rightarrow}$-transition. We therefore expect that a suitable test for such a property is $T \equiv \bar{a}.\overline{\text{bad}}.\mathbf{0}$. Indeed, the reader will easily realize that $(s \mid T) \setminus \mathcal{L} \overset{\text{bad}}{\Rightarrow}$ iff $s \overset{a}{\Rightarrow}$, for every state s. The formula $[a]\mathit{ff}$ is thus testable, in the sense of Definition 7.4.

The formula defined by the recursion equation

$$F \overset{\max}{=} [a]\mathit{ff} \wedge [b]F$$

is satisfied by those states that cannot perform any $\overset{a}{\Rightarrow}$-transition, no matter how they engage in a sequence of $\overset{b}{\Rightarrow}$-transitions. (Why?) A suitable test for such a property is

$$X \overset{\text{def}}{=} \bar{a}.\overline{\text{bad}}.\mathbf{0} + \bar{b}.X,$$

and the recursively defined formula F is thus testable.   ◆

Exercise 7.13 *Consider the following LTS:*

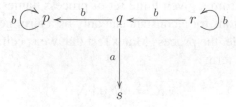

Compute the set of states in this LTS that satisfy the property

$$F \overset{\max}{=} [a]\mathit{ff} \wedge [b]F \ .$$

Which states in the LTS pass the test

$$X \overset{\text{def}}{=} \bar{a}.\overline{\text{bad}}.\mathbf{0} + \bar{b}.X?$$

Argue for your answers!   ◆

Exercise 7.14 *Prove the claims that we have made in the above example.*   ◆

In Example 7.1 we met two examples of testable formulae. But, can each formula in HML with recursion be tested in the sense introduced above? The following instructive result shows that even some very simple HML properties are *not* testable in the sense given in Definition 7.4.

Proposition 7.3 (Two negative results)

1. For every action a in $\mathcal{L}$, the formula $\langle a \rangle tt$ is not testable.
2. Let a and b be two distinct actions in $\mathcal{L}$. Then the formula $[a]\mathit{ff} \vee [b]\mathit{ff}$ is not testable.

Proof. We prove each statement in turn.

Proof of 1. Assume, towards a contradiction, that a test T tests for the formula $\langle a \rangle tt$. Since T tests for $\langle a \rangle tt$ and $\mathbf{0} \not\models \langle a \rangle tt$, we have that

$$(\mathbf{0} \mid \mathsf{root}(T)) \setminus \mathcal{L} \stackrel{\overline{\mathrm{bad}}}{\Rightarrow}.$$

Consider now the term $P = a.\mathbf{0} + \tau.\mathbf{0}$. As $P \stackrel{a}{\rightarrow} \mathbf{0}$, the process P satisfies the formula $\langle a \rangle tt$. However, P fails the test T because

$$(P \mid \mathsf{root}(T)) \setminus \mathcal{L} \stackrel{\tau}{\rightarrow} (\mathbf{0} \mid \mathsf{root}(T)) \setminus \mathcal{L} \stackrel{\overline{\mathrm{bad}}}{\Rightarrow}.$$

This contradicts our assumption that T tests for $\langle a \rangle tt$.

Proof of 2. Assume, towards a contradiction, that a test T tests for the formula $[a]\mathit{ff} \vee [b]\mathit{ff}$, with $a \neq b$. Since the state $a.\mathbf{0} + b.\mathbf{0}$ does not satisfy the formula $[a]\mathit{ff} \vee [b]\mathit{ff}$, it follows that

$$((a.\mathbf{0} + b.\mathbf{0}) \mid \mathsf{root}(T)) \setminus \mathcal{L} \stackrel{\overline{\mathrm{bad}}}{\Rightarrow}. \tag{7.2}$$

We now proceed to show that this implies that either the state $a.\mathbf{0}$ fails the test T or $b.\mathbf{0}$ does. This we do by examining the possible forms that transition (7.2) may take.

- $((a.\mathbf{0} + b.\mathbf{0}) \mid \mathsf{root}(T)) \setminus \mathcal{L} \stackrel{\overline{\mathrm{bad}}}{\Rightarrow}$ because $\mathsf{root}(T) \stackrel{\overline{\mathrm{bad}}}{\Rightarrow}$. In this case, every state of an LTS fails the test T, and we are done.
- $((a.\mathbf{0} + b.\mathbf{0}) \mid \mathsf{root}(T)) \setminus \mathcal{L} \stackrel{\tau}{\Rightarrow} (\mathbf{0} \mid t) \setminus \mathcal{L} \stackrel{\overline{\mathrm{bad}}}{\rightarrow}$ because $\mathsf{root}(T) \stackrel{\bar{a}}{\Rightarrow} t$ for some state t of T. In this case, we may infer that

$$(a.\mathbf{0} \mid \mathsf{root}(T)) \setminus \mathcal{L} \stackrel{\tau}{\Rightarrow} (\mathbf{0} \mid t) \setminus \mathcal{L} \stackrel{\overline{\mathrm{bad}}}{\rightarrow}$$

and thus that $a.\mathbf{0}$ fails the test T.

- $((a.\mathbf{0} + b.\mathbf{0}) \mid \mathsf{root}(T)) \setminus \mathcal{L} \overset{\tau}{\Rightarrow} (\mathbf{0} \mid t) \setminus \mathcal{L} \overset{\overline{\mathsf{bad}}}{\rightarrow}$ because $\mathsf{root}(T) \overset{\overline{b}}{\Rightarrow} t$ for some state t of T. In this case, reasoning as above, it is easy to see that $b.\mathbf{0}$ fails the test T.

Hence, as previously claimed, either $a.\mathbf{0}$ fails the test T or $b.\mathbf{0}$ does. Since both $a.\mathbf{0}$ and $b.\mathbf{0}$ satisfy the formula $[a]\mathit{ff} \vee [b]\mathit{ff}$, this contradicts our assumption that T tests for it.

The proof is now complete. $\square$

The collection of formulae in *safety HML* is the set of formulae in HML with recursion that do *not* contain occurrences of $\vee$, $\langle \alpha \rangle$ and variables defined using least-fixed-point recursion equations. For instance, the formula $\langle a \rangle X$ is not a legal formula in safety HML if X is defined thus:

$$X \overset{\min}{=} \langle b \rangle \mathit{tt} \vee \langle a \rangle X.$$

Exercise 7.15 (Strongly recommended) *Can you build a test (denoted by a process in the regular part of CCS) for each formula in safety HML without recursion? Hint: Use induction on the structure of formulae.*   ◆

It turns out that, with the addition of recursive formulae defined using largest fixed points, the collection of testable formulae in HML with recursion is precisely the one for which you built tests in the previous exercise! This is the import of the following result from Aceto and Ingolfsdottir (1999).

Theorem 7.1 The collection of formulae in safety HML is testable. Moreover, every testable property in HML with recursion can be expressed in safety HML.

Thus we can construct tests for safety properties expressible in HML with recursion. We refer the interested readers to Aceto and Ingolfsdottir (1999) for more details, further developments and references to the literature.

Part II

A Theory of Real-time Systems

8

Introduction

8.1 Real-time reactive systems

In the first part of this book, we motivated and developed a general-purpose theory that can be used to describe, and reason about, reactive systems. The key ingredients in our approach were:

- an algebraic language, namely Milner's CCS, for the syntactic description of reactive systems;
- automata, e.g. labelled transition systems (LTSs), for describing the dynamic behaviour of process terms;
- structural operational semantics allowing us to associate systematically an LTS with each process term in a syntax-directed fashion;
- notions of behavioural equivalence for the comparison of process behaviours; and
- modal and temporal logics to specify desired properties of reactive systems.

These ingredients gave the foundations for the formal modelling and verification of reactive systems and are the bedrock for the development of (semi-)automatic verification tools for reactive systems.

The theory that we have developed so far, however, does not allow us to describe naturally all the important aspects in reactive computation. Consider, for instance, some, by now ubiquitous, examples of reactive systems, namely embedded systems like the ABS and air bags in cars, cruise-control systems, digital watches, mobile phones, computer monitors, production lines and video-game consoles. These are all examples of *real-time systems*. A real-time system is a system whose

159

correct behaviour depends not only on the logical order in which events are performed but also on their timing. Think for a moment about the expected behaviour of an air-bag system in a car. Such a system is intended to inflate the air bags in the case of a car crash, but this behaviour is not just expected to occur 'eventually'. Rather, we should like to have some (hopefully small) hard bounds on the timing of its occurrence. A suitable correctness criterion for such a system might therefore be, say,

> if the car crashes, the airbag must be inflated within 50 milliseconds,

rather than a not-so-reassuring 'eventually the air bag will be inflated'.

Another instructive, and suggestive, example of a real-time system is that of a control program, which we met when introducing the general notion of a reactive system. Recall that, at a high level of abstraction, the behaviour of a control program can be seen to be governed by the following pseudocode algorithm skeleton:

loop
> read the sensors' values at regular intervals
> depending on the sensors' values trigger the relevant actuators
forever

In the above description, we have an implicit and qualitative description of the real-time behaviour of a control program. Such a program can be thought of as being in an 'idling mode' in between consecutive readings of the values of the sensors. When the 'idling interval' is over, the system polls the values of the sensors, triggers the relevant actions that interact with its environment, and then re-enters its 'idling mode'. Such a system is a typical example of a *hybrid system*, i.e. a discrete system that interacts with a continuously evolving one, namely its environment. (In the jargon of control theory, the environment is usually referred to as the *plant*.) As we shall see in what follows, the expected behaviour of the aforementioned control program will serve as a useful example for explaining some choices that researchers have made in designing appropriate modelling formalisms for the description of reactive real-time computation. In the next two chapters we shall give in-depth accounts of two such formalisms, namely TCCS, the timed extension of CCS developed by (Yi, 1990, 1991a, b) and the notion of timed automata introduced by Alur and Dill (1990, 1994).

9

CCS with time delays

In this chapter we will have a close look at the elegant timed process algebra TCCS introduced by Yi (1990, 1991a, b). Syntactically, TCCS extends CCS with just a single construct, a new prefix $\varepsilon(d).P$ that means 'delay d units of time and then behave as P'. As is the case for a number of other timed process algebras, TCCS takes the view that a real-time system has a two-phase behaviour, phases when the system idles while time passes and phases when the system performs atomic actions, assumed to be instantaneous in time. As we shall see, this separation of concerns – together with other design decisions (e.g. so-called time determinism and maximal progress) – makes for a very elegant TCCS semantics.

9.1 Intuition

All the types of reactive system mentioned in Chapter 8 should give us sufficient motivation to describe and analyze formally real-time reactive computations. In the first part of the book, we introduced a collection of languages and models based on the flexible and intuitive idea of communicating state machines, and we argued, by means of several examples, that the resulting formalisms can be used to describe and analyze non-trivial reactive systems. When real-time constraints become important to the proper functioning of reactive systems, we should like to continue building on the time-honoured formalisms we have introduced previously. But are those formalisms sufficiently powerful to describe timing constraints in computation? Can we use them to specify, for instance, features such as time-outs?

Consider, by way of example, a light switch that has the following behaviour.

If the switch is off, and is pressed once, then the light will turn on. If the switch is pressed again 'soon' after the light was turned on then the light

161

becomes brighter. Otherwise, the light is turned off by the next button press. The light is also turned off by a button press when it is bright.

A way of describing this behaviour using CCS is to construct a process with three states – say, Off, Light and Bright – describing the three possible states mentioned in the above English description of the behaviour of the system. Modelling the behaviour of the switch in the Off or Bright states is easy:

$$\text{Off} \stackrel{\text{def}}{=} \text{press.Light},$$
$$\text{Bright} \stackrel{\text{def}}{=} \text{press.Off}.$$

How can we describe the behaviour of the system in the Light state? One approach would be to write the following CCS term:

$$\text{Light} \stackrel{\text{def}}{=} \tau.\text{press.Off} + \text{press.Bright},$$

which describes the possible effects that pressing the button can have when the system is in the Light state. Note, however, that the above description does not capture the requirement that if the user presses the button 'quickly' after the light is on then the light will become brighter. (Rather, intuitively it states that the system may internally choose to switch off the light at the next button press.) This is a timing requirement on consecutive button presses, and CCS offers no facility for describing it. What kind of constructs can we add to CCS in order to describe systems, such as the light switch above, whose behaviour is time dependent?

One of the most important principles underlying the development of CCS, and of all the models and languages that we have met so far, is that of *parsimony*. These models are built on a small collection of operators that are sufficient to describe the computational phenomena under study. Using this principle, we should like to extend a language like CCS, and the model of LTSs, with the least amount of machinery that allows us to describe time-dependent behaviour. As we shall see, the lessons we learned in Chapter 8 from the behaviour in time of the skeleton control algorithm will help us a lot in deciding how to extend CCS and LTSs with timing.

Intuitively, we argued that one can view a real-time system such as the aforementioned skeleton of a control program as having a two-phase behaviour. In fact, that system alternates between phases in which the system is idle, i.e. it does not perform any action and time passes, and phases in which the system performs sequences of actions triggering the relevant actuators, and possibly chooses between different courses of action, before returning to its idling mode. As in CCS, it is a useful abstraction to consider the sequence of actions performed by the system as being instantaneous in time.

We already know how to describe syntactically action occurrences: by means of the action-prefixing operator of CCS. What is the minimum amount of machinery that we can add to our language to give a faithful description of the passage of time? A possible, conservative, answer is to view the passage of time as being some kind of 'action' that a system may perform. This action can be specified by means of a new prefixing operator that describes time delays – say $\varepsilon(d)$, where d is a non-negative real number that specifies the amount of time that needs to elapse before the 'idling time' is over. For example, using this new type of prefixing operator, the behaviour of the light switch in the state Light could be described by means of the equation

$$\text{Light} \stackrel{\text{def}}{=} \varepsilon(1.4).\tau.\text{press.Off} + \text{press.Bright}, \tag{9.1}$$

assuming that pressing the button 'quickly' means doing so within 1.4 seconds, say. The reason why we have included here the action τ might not be completely obvious at this moment and will be explained fully later on; intuitively, the reader should think of τ as an action that cannot be delayed and must be performed as soon as it becomes available. This introduces the notion of urgency, which is useful for describing features like time-outs.

The term on the right-hand side of the above equation, however, needs to be given a semantics in order for its behaviour to be understood. In particular, this involves giving the formal semantics of the delay operator and describing how it interacts with the other constructs of the language. Moreover, we need to choose a suitable semantic model that can be used to describe formally the behaviour of terms in a timed version of CCS. Last but not least, a choice has to be made of a structure to model time. In what follows, we shall use the set $\mathbb{R}_{\geq 0}$ of non-negative real numbers as our time domain. This appears as a natural choice, if we think of the flow of time as being continuous. However, some researchers prefer to work with a discrete notion of time, and this can be modelled by using the set of natural numbers $\mathbb{N}$ as the time domain.

9.2 Timed labelled transition systems

In the first part of this book, we used labelled transition systems to model the behaviour of reactive systems. Since this model of computation is very intuitive and flexible, we should like to use a variation on it to give semantics to real-time reactive systems. In the light of the above discussion, it is natural to assume that we can describe the passage of time by adding special 'delay' transitions to the model. Such transitions could, for instance, be used to give the formal semantics of the delay-prefixing operators $\varepsilon(d)$, with $d \in \mathbb{R}_{\geq 0}$, used in (9.1). The resulting structure is a timed version of the model of LTSs. This we now proceed to describe formally.

Definition 9.1 A *timed labelled transition system* (TLTS) is a triple

$$(\mathsf{Proc}, \mathsf{Lab}, \{\overset{\alpha}{\longrightarrow} \mid \alpha \in \mathsf{Lab}\}),$$

where

- Proc is a set of *states* (or processes),
- $\mathsf{Lab} = \mathsf{Act} \cup \mathbb{R}_{\geq 0}$ is a set of *labels* (consisting of *actions* and *time delays*), and
- $\overset{\alpha}{\longrightarrow} \subseteq \mathsf{Proc} \times \mathsf{Proc}$, for each $\alpha \in \mathsf{Lab}$, is a binary relation on states called the *transition relation*.

(It should be noted that TLTSs are also known, more briefly, as timed transition systems.)   ♦

As usual, we write

$s \overset{a}{\longrightarrow} s'$ if $a \in \mathsf{Act}$ and $(s, s') \in \overset{a}{\longrightarrow}$, and
$s \overset{d}{\longrightarrow} s'$ if $d \in \mathbb{R}_{\geq 0}$ and $(s, s') \in \overset{d}{\longrightarrow}$.

Transitions of the type $s \overset{a}{\longrightarrow} s'$ are ordinary transitions that are due to the performance of actions, and those of the form $s \overset{d}{\longrightarrow} s'$, with $d \in \mathbb{R}_{\geq 0}$, are time-elapsing transitions describing how a system evolves as time passes. A little reflection, however, leads us to conclude that not all structures of the above kind reflect our intuition about the passage of time. Assume, for instance, that a state s in a timed LTS affords a transition of the form $s \overset{1.4}{\longrightarrow} s'$. (Such a state could, for instance, describe the timing behaviour of the process Light in (9.1).) This transition tells us that a system in state s can wait for 1.4 units of time and thereby evolve into s'. However, if a system can wait for 1.4 seconds say, then it is natural to expect that it can delay for, say, 0.8 seconds and thereby reach a state that can then proceed to wait for 0.6 seconds and become s' in doing so. This expresses the idea that time is *additive*, and that the transition relation of a TLTS must satisfy the following *time-additivity requirement*:

$$\text{if } s \overset{d}{\longrightarrow} s' \text{ and } 0 \leq d' \leq d \text{ then } s \overset{d'}{\longrightarrow} s'' \overset{d-d'}{\longrightarrow} s' \text{ for some state } s''. \qquad (9.2)$$

Note that d' could be 0. Since it is reasonable to assume that a state can (only) reach itself without delay, we also postulate that

$$s \overset{0}{\longrightarrow} s \text{ for each state } s. \qquad (9.3)$$

A final requirement that is imposed on TLTSs captures the way in which a system can evolve just by idling as time passes. In order to motivate this requirement, consider the control program that we have already discussed. When in idling mode, that program is, intuitively, just updating the value of some timer that measures the amount of time that needs to elapse before the system next polls the values of its sensors. Each time delay therefore brings the system to a unique next state, in which intuitively the value of the timer has decreased by the amount of delay. This example indicates that delay transitions are *deterministic*, i.e. for all s, s', s'' and for each $d \in \mathbb{R}_{\geq 0}$

$$\text{if } s \xrightarrow{d} s' \text{ and } s \xrightarrow{d} s'' \text{ then } s' = s''. \tag{9.4}$$

In what follows, we shall restrict our attention to TLTSs that satisfy requirements (9.2)–(9.4).

Example 9.1 Consider the following timed transition system:

$$(\mathsf{Proc}, \mathsf{Lab}, \{\xrightarrow{\alpha} \mid \alpha \in \mathsf{Lab}\})$$

where $\mathsf{Proc} = \mathbb{R}_{\geq 0}$, $\mathsf{Lab} = \{a\} \cup \mathbb{R}_{\geq 0}$ such that $\xrightarrow{a} = \{(5, 0)\}$ and, for all $d \in \mathbb{R}_{\geq 0}$, we define $\xrightarrow{d} = \{(d', d'') \in \mathbb{R}_{\geq 0} \times \mathbb{R}_{\geq 0} \mid d' + d = d''\}$. The diagram below shows a small part of the timed transition system defined above. Note that we have included only very few timed transitions; in fact, infinitely (indeed uncountably) many transitions should be added to the picture.

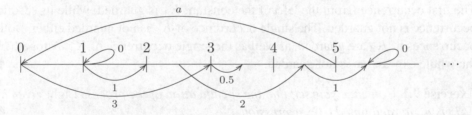

It is easy to verify that this transition system satisfies conditions (9.2)–(9.4). The only ordinary action is called a and, at time point 5, the system can move to its initial state by performing this action. ♦

9.3 Syntax and SOS rules of timed CCS

In the remainder of this section, we shall specify TLTSs using a timed version of the language CCS that is essentially Wang Yi's timed CCS (henceforth abbreviated to TCCS) Yi (1990, 1991a, b). As indicated in our discussion in Section 9.1, the only constructs that we shall add to the syntax of the language CCS presented in Definition 2.3 are the delay-prefixing operators $\varepsilon(d)$, with $d \in \mathbb{R}_{\geq 0}$.

Formally, the collection $\mathcal{P}$ of *timed CCS expressions* is given by the grammar for CCS expressions given in Definition 2.3, extended by the following formation rule:

if P is in $\mathcal{P}$ and $d \in \mathbb{R}_{\geq 0}$ then $\varepsilon(d).P$ is in $\mathcal{P}$.

In what follows, we shall not distinguish the terms P and $\varepsilon(0).P$.

As in the case of standard CCS, we assume that the behaviour of each process constant is given by a defining equation

$$K \stackrel{\text{def}}{=} P.$$

Definition 9.2 An occurrence of a constant K in an expression P is *guarded* if it occurs within a subexpression of P of the form $\alpha.Q$, for some action $\alpha \in \mathsf{Act}$ or delay prefixing $\alpha = \varepsilon(d)$ with $d > 0$. ◆

In what follows, we shall restrict ourselves to considering only processes involving constants whose defining equations contain only guarded occurrences of constants. These expressions are called *guarded*.

Example 9.2 Consider the following timed CCS expression:

$$\big(a.K_1 + (K_2 \mid b.K_3) + K_1\big) \mid \big(\varepsilon(4.2).(K_4 \mid \mathbf{0}) + \varepsilon(1.2).K_3\big).$$

The first occurrence (from the left) of the constant K_1 is guarded, while its second occurrence is not guarded. The single occurrence of K_2 is not guarded either. Both occurrences of K_3 are guarded, as well as the single occurrence of K_4. Altogether, the whole expression is not guarded. ◆

Exercise 9.1 *Convince yourself that the specification of the process* Light *given in (9.1) is a guarded timed CCS expression.* ◆

By analogy with standard CCS, we expect that the behaviour of the process Light given in (9.1) is determined by that of the right-hand side of its defining equation, namely the expression

$$\varepsilon(1.4).\tau.\text{press}.\text{Off} + \text{press}.\text{Bright}.$$

The action transitions of this expression are determined by the same SOS rules that we used for standard CCS. (See Table 2.2.) Moreover, since we are identifying P with $\varepsilon(0).P$, we have the following rule:

$$\frac{P \stackrel{\alpha}{\to} P'}{\varepsilon(0).P \stackrel{\alpha}{\to} P'}.$$

$$\frac{P \xrightarrow{d'} P'}{\varepsilon(d).P \xrightarrow{d+d'} P'} \qquad \frac{}{\varepsilon(d).P \xrightarrow{d'} \varepsilon(d-d').P} \text{ for } d' \leq d$$

$$\frac{P \xrightarrow{d} P'}{K \xrightarrow{d} P'} K \stackrel{\text{def}}{=} P \qquad \frac{}{\alpha.P \xrightarrow{d} \alpha.P} \text{ for } \alpha \neq \tau \qquad \frac{P_i \xrightarrow{d} P_i' \text{ for each } i \in I}{\sum_{i \in I} P_i \xrightarrow{d} \sum_{i \in I} P_i'}$$

$$\frac{P \xrightarrow{d} P'}{P[f] \xrightarrow{d} P'[f]} \qquad \frac{P \xrightarrow{d} P'}{P \setminus L \xrightarrow{d} P' \setminus L}$$

Table 9.1 SOS rules for TCCS ($d, d' \in \mathbb{R}_{\geq 0}$)

So, as you can easily check,

$$\varepsilon(1.4).\tau.\text{press.Off} + \text{press.Bright} \xrightarrow{\text{press}} \text{Bright}. \tag{9.5}$$

Since the other press-labelled transition is only available after 1.4 units of time have elapsed and an internal action has occurred, we expect that this is the only action transition that is initially possible for the term on the left-hand side of (9.5). However, this term can delay some amount of time $d \leq 1.4$ by virtue of the transition

$$\varepsilon(1.4).\tau.\text{press.Off} + \text{press.Bright} \xrightarrow{d} \varepsilon((1.4 - d)).\tau.\text{press.Off} + \text{press.Bright}.$$

Note that, unlike action transitions, delay transitions such as the one above do *not* resolve nondeterministic choices. This is in line with our intuition that delay transitions ought to be deterministic. In the above example, transition (9.5) is available immediately, and it remains available after d units of time have elapsed.

When d equals 1.4 we expect that, after the internal action has occurred, the press-labelled transition leading to the Off state becomes enabled and therefore that the transitions

$$\varepsilon(0).\tau.\text{press.Off} + \text{press.Bright} \xrightarrow{\tau} \text{press.Off} \xrightarrow{\text{press}} \text{Off}$$

are possible.

To capture formally our intuitive understanding of the effect of delay transitions on TCCS expressions, we introduce the collection of SOS rules in Table 9.1. (For the sake of clarity, we restrict ourselves for the moment to expressions that contain neither occurrences of the parallel composition operator nor τ-prefixes.) A transition $P \xrightarrow{d} Q$, with $d \in \mathbb{R}_{\geq 0}$, holds for TCCS expressions P, Q iff it can be proved using these rules.

The SOS rules for standard actions are the same as for CCS.

Exercise 9.2 *Prove the transition*

$$\text{Light} \xrightarrow{d} \varepsilon((1.4 - d)).\tau.\text{press.Off} + \text{press.Bright},$$

with $d \leq 1.4$, using the above rules.   ◆

Exercise 9.3 (Strongly recommended) *Prove the following determinacy property of delay transitions.*

For all processes P, P', P'' and delay d, if $P \xrightarrow{d} P'$ and $P \xrightarrow{d} P''$ then $P' = P''$.

Prove the following persistency property of action transitions.

For all processes P, Q, action a and delay d, if $P \xrightarrow{a}$ and $P \xrightarrow{d} Q$ then $Q \xrightarrow{a}$.

For simplicity, you may restrict yourself to considering process terms that do not contain constants.   ◆

Exercise 9.4 *An alarm timer is a process that can be set to time-out after a prescribed time period has elapsed. Model as a TCCS agent an alarm timer T that can be set to time-out after 5, 10 and 30 minutes by discrete actions set5, set10 and set30. After the prescribed time period, T signals the time-out by the action $\overline{\text{to}}$. The alarm timer can be reset with a new time-out period at any given moment, in particular before the previously set time period has elapsed.*   ◆

Consider a process expression of the form

$$\sum_{i \in I} \varepsilon(d_i).\alpha_i.P_i.$$

Intuitively, we may think of the operational rules in Table 9.1 as implementing the following idea of the expected behaviour of this process. The process has a stopwatch, or *clock*, that is used to measure the amount of time that has elapsed since it last embarked upon action. As time progresses and the process idles, the value of the stopwatch increases. When this value is greater than, or equal to, d_i for some $i \in I$ then action α_i becomes enabled and can be performed. If this happens, the process enters state P_i, the stopwatch is reset and the future behaviour is determined according to the same approach. Note that this intuitive description of the dynamics of processes is fully in line with our view that the behaviour of processes consists of two alternating phases, idling (when time passes) and action (when actions are performed instantaneously). Moreover, in the absence of parallel composition, the above approach to the description of the behaviour of processes can be 'implemented' by using only one clock.

However, parallel composition is fundamental for the description of interacting reactive systems, and we therefore now examine what happens when we consider real-time parallel systems.

9.4   Parallel composition

Assume now that we have a user of our light switch whose behaviour is described by the following expression:

$$\text{FastUser} \stackrel{\text{def}}{=} \overline{\text{press}}.\varepsilon(0.3).\overline{\text{press}}.\text{FastUser}.$$

We expect that FastUser will be able to synchronize with the switch in the Off state immediately, resulting in the transition

$$(\text{FastUser} \mid \text{Off}) \setminus \text{press} \stackrel{\tau}{\to} \left((\varepsilon(0.3).\overline{\text{press}}.\text{FastUser}) \mid \text{Light}\right) \setminus \text{press}.$$

In the target state of the above transition, the $\overline{\text{press}}$-transition of the left-hand expression is only available after a delay of 0.3 time units. As we have already seen in Exercise 9.2, the process Light can delay as much and reach the state

$$\varepsilon(1.1).\tau.\text{press}.\text{Off} + \text{press}.\text{Bright}.$$

It is natural to expect that the whole system can therefore perform the delay transition

$$\left((\varepsilon(0.3).\overline{\text{press}}.\text{FastUser}) \mid \text{Light}\right) \setminus \text{press}$$

$$\stackrel{0.3}{\to} \left((\overline{\text{press}}.\text{FastUser}) \mid (\varepsilon(1.1).\tau.\text{press}.\text{Off} + \text{press}.\text{Bright})\right) \setminus \text{press}.$$

(Recall that we identify an expression P with $\varepsilon(0).P$.) In the target state of the above transition, FastUser is eager to press the button once more, and the press-transition of the switch leading to the Bright state is enabled. This means that the two transitions can synchronize without further delay, yielding the τ-transition

$$\left((\overline{\text{press}}.\text{FastUser}) \mid (\varepsilon(1.1).\tau.\text{press}.\text{Off} + \text{press}.\text{Bright})\right) \setminus \text{press}$$

$$\stackrel{\tau}{\to} (\text{FastUser} \mid \text{Bright}) \setminus \text{press}. \tag{9.6}$$

This is nicely in agreement with our intuition.

Note, however, that both parallel components of the expression

$$(\overline{\text{press}}.\text{FastUser}) \mid (\varepsilon(1.1).\tau.\text{press}.\text{Off} + \text{press}.\text{Bright})$$

can delay indefinitely. How can we formally capture our intuition that the τ-transition (9.6) must occur immediately and therefore that the above term cannot delay even though both its parallel components can do so? The solution adopted by Wang Yi in the design of TCCS and by the researchers who developed other process calculi for real-time systems (see e.g. Hennessy and Regan (1995), Nicollin and Sifakis (1994) and Schneider (1995)) is to postulate that the evolution of processes obeys the so-called *maximal-progress assumption*. Intuitively, this means that if a process is ready to perform an action that is entirely under its control immediately then it will do so without further delay. In the setting of timed CCS, the only action that is entirely under the control of a process is the internal τ-action. Therefore the maximal-progress assumption for this calculus can be formalized as follows.

For each TCCS process P, if $P \xrightarrow{\tau}$ then $P \xnrightarrow{d}$ for any $d > 0$.

In particular, in the light of (9.6), this means that the expression

$$((\overline{\text{press}}.\text{FastUser}) \mid (\varepsilon(1.1).\tau.\text{press}.\text{Off} + \text{press}.\text{Bright})) \setminus \text{press}$$

cannot delay by any positive amount of time.

The maximal-progress assumption is expressed in the operational semantics of timed CCS by the following rules:

$$\frac{}{\tau.P \xrightarrow{0} \tau.P}, \qquad \frac{P \xrightarrow{d} P', \; Q \xrightarrow{d} Q' \text{ and NoSync}(P, Q, d)}{P \mid Q \xrightarrow{d} P' \mid Q'},$$

where the predicate NoSync(P, Q, d) intuitively expresses that no synchronization between P and Q becomes available by delaying less than d time units. Formally, NoSync(P, Q, d) holds if and only if the following holds.

For each $0 \le d' < d$ and expressions P', Q', if $P \xrightarrow{d'} P'$ and $Q \xrightarrow{d'} Q'$ then $P' \mid Q' \xnrightarrow{\tau}$.

Exercise 9.5 *Argue, using the SOS rules for timed CCS, that*

$$((\varepsilon(0.3).\overline{\text{press}}.\text{FastUser}) \mid \text{Light}) \setminus \text{press} \xnrightarrow{0.4}$$

and that the expression

$$((\overline{\text{press}}.\text{FastUser}) \mid (\varepsilon(1.1).\tau.\text{press}.\text{Off} + \text{press}.\text{Bright})) \setminus \text{press}$$

cannot delay by a positive amount of time.

How long can the expression $\varepsilon(\pi).\tau.\mathbf{0} + a.\mathbf{0}$ *delay?*   ♦

In order to familiarize ourselves better with the role played by the maximal-progress assumption in describing the dynamics of processes, let us consider the possible interplay between the switch and SlowUser, whose behaviour is described by the following expression

$$\text{SlowUser} \overset{\text{def}}{=} \overline{\text{press}}.\varepsilon(1.7).\overline{\text{press}}.\text{SlowUser}.$$

As before, SlowUser will be able to synchronize with the switch in the Off state immediately, resulting in the transition

$$(\text{SlowUser} \mid \text{Off}) \setminus \text{press} \overset{\tau}{\to} ((\varepsilon(1.7).\overline{\text{press}}.\text{SlowUser}) \mid \text{Light}) \setminus \text{press}.$$

In the target state of the above transition, the $\overline{\text{press}}$-transition of the left-hand expression is only available after a delay of 1.7 time units. However, because of the maximal-progress assumption, the process Light can delay by at most 1.4 units of time. (Why?) Delaying that much yields the transition

$$((\varepsilon(1.7).\overline{\text{press}}.\text{SlowUser}) \mid \text{Light}) \setminus \text{press}$$

$$\overset{1.4}{\to} ((\varepsilon(0.3).\overline{\text{press}}.\text{SlowUser}) \mid (\varepsilon(0).\tau.\text{press}.\text{Off} + \text{press}.\text{Bright})) \setminus \text{press}.$$

Since the right-hand process can perform a τ-transition, no further delay is possible and the slow user cannot press the button leading to the Bright state. The system can now internally reach the state

$$((\varepsilon(0.3).\overline{\text{press}}.\text{SlowUser}) \mid (\text{press}.\text{Off})) \setminus \text{press}.$$

You should now be able to argue that the next button press issued by the user will bring the switch into the Off state.

Exercise 9.6 *Consider the following four alternative definitions of TCCS agent* M.

$$M_1 \overset{\text{def}}{=} \varepsilon(3).(\varepsilon(2).a.M_1 + b.M_1),$$
$$M_2 \overset{\text{def}}{=} \varepsilon(5).a.M_2 + \varepsilon(3).b.M_2,$$
$$M_3 \overset{\text{def}}{=} \varepsilon(3).(\varepsilon(2).a.M_3 + \tau.M_3),$$
$$M_4 \overset{\text{def}}{=} \varepsilon(5).a.M_4 + \varepsilon(3).\tau.M_4.$$

For which of the above four definitions do we have $M_i \overset{4}{\to}$? *In the affirmative case(s) use the SOS rules for TCCS to prove the delay transition as well as identify the target process* P_i *such that* $M_i \overset{4}{\to} P_i$. *Discuss the general relationship between the process terms* $\varepsilon(d).(P + Q)$ *and* $\varepsilon(d).P + \varepsilon(d).Q$. ♦

Exercise 9.7 *Consider the agent M and the three variants of agent N defined below.*

$$M \stackrel{\text{def}}{=} \varepsilon(3).(\varepsilon(2).\bar{a}.M + \bar{b}.M),$$

$$N_1 \stackrel{\text{def}}{=} \varepsilon(5).b.N_1 + \varepsilon(3).a.N_1,$$

$$N_2 \stackrel{\text{def}}{=} \varepsilon(3).(\varepsilon(2).a.N_2 + \tau.N_2),$$

$$N_3 \stackrel{\text{def}}{=} \varepsilon(5).\tau.N_3 + \varepsilon(3).b.N_3.$$

Indicate the values of i for which (a) $M|N_i \stackrel{3}{\rightarrow}$, (b) $M|N_i \stackrel{5}{\rightarrow}$ and (c) $M|N_i \stackrel{8}{\rightarrow}$. In these affirmative case(s) give proper proofs using the SOS rules for TCCS.　◆

How many clocks?　Consider, by way of example, a process expression of the form

$$\left(\sum_{i \in I} \varepsilon(d_i).\alpha_i.P_i \right) \Bigg| \left(\sum_{j \in J} \varepsilon(e_j).\beta_j.Q_i \right).$$

We have already seen that, intuitively, the timing behaviour of each of the two parallel components can be described by using a single clock that is reset each time the relevant component performs an action. So, intuitively, the behaviour of the above parallel process can be described by using two local clocks, say x and y, as follows.

- The process can idle for d units of time, for some $d \in \mathbb{R}_{\geq 0}$, provided that the following conditions are all met.

  If d_i is smaller than the value of x plus d then $\alpha_i \neq \tau$, i.e. no τ-transition of the left-hand expression becomes enabled by delaying less than d units of time.
  If e_j is smaller than the value of y plus d then $\beta_j \neq \tau$, i.e. no τ-transition of the right-hand expression becomes enabled by delaying less than d units of time.
  If d_i is smaller than the value of x plus d, and e_j is smaller than the value of y plus d then α_i and β_j are not complementary, i.e. no synchronization becomes enabled as the processes delay less than d units of time.

- If the process has idled d units of time, then
  1. update the values of the clocks x and y by adding d to them,
  2. perform one of the actions that becomes enabled after this delay, if any, and
  3. reset the clocks of the processes that were involved in that action. In particular, if the action was a synchronization then both x and y are reset.

In fact, one clock is not sufficient to implement the above procedure. Moreover, as shown in Godskesen and Larsen (1992), in general the more parallel components we have in our system, the more clocks we need to 'implement' its behaviour. A formal proof of this fact is beyond the scope of this introductory text.

9.5 Other timed process algebras and discussion

Around the same time that Yi introduced TCCS, several other timed process algebras were proposed. We mention the following.

- The Temporal Process Algebra (TPA) (Hennessy and Regan, 1995) extends Milner's CCS with discrete time. This calculus is closely related to Yi's TCCS in being based on the assumptions of maximal progress and time determinism.
- The Temporal Calculus of Communicating Systems (also known as Temporal CCS) (Moller and Tofts, 1990) is also based on CCS. Similarly to TCCS, the semantics follows the two-phase principle, according to which action and delay transitions 'alternate' in the behaviour of processes. However, the maximal-progress and time-determinism assumptions are rejected.
- Several proposals to extend the Algebra of Communicating Processes (ACP) (Baeten and Weijland, 1990) with time have been made. We refer the reader to Baeten and Middelburg (2002) for a comprehensive account. Timed ACP (Baeten and Bergstra, 1991) takes the approach that time is absolute, and each action is associated with a time stamp. In particular the basic prefix operator, $a(t)$, indicates that the action a should be taken at exactly (global) time t. To express that an action is continuously enabled within a certain time interval, the integration operator (essentially an infinitary summation) is used. For example, the term $\int_{l \le t \le u} a(t) \cdot P$ expresses that the action a can take place at any moment v within the interval $[l, u]$, after which the behaviour will continue according to $P[t/v]$ (as P may be a process term that depends on t).
- The Algebra for Timed Processes (ATP) (Nicollin and Sifakis, 1994) follows the time-determinacy assumption but replaces the maximal-progress assumption with an explicit time-out operator and is based on a discrete interpretation of time.
- Various timed extensions of CSP have been given. Timed CSP (TCSP) (Reed and Roscoe, 1988, Davies and Schneider, 1989) extends standard CSP with a delay construct similar to the delay prefix $\varepsilon(e).P$ of TCCS. Also, the principle of maximal progress is applied in TCSP. We refer to Schneider (1999) for a full account of Timed CSP.

At least syntactically, Timed CCS is a simple extension of Milner's original CCS that, as we have seen, can be used to describe some aspects of time-dependent behaviour in the evolution of reactive systems. For instance, we have described how to specify time-outs in the calculus by means of a combination of urgent actions (the internal action τ, in the setting of TCCS) and the maximal-progress assumption. From an expressiveness viewpoint, however, the resulting calculus is not completely satisfactory. For example, the simple TLTS depicted in Example 9.1 cannot be described, up to isomorphism, using TCCS. To see this, recall that in Exercise 9.3 you showed that a subclass of TCCS process terms affords the following persistency property of action transitions.

For all processes P, Q, action a and delay d, if $P \xrightarrow{a}$ and $P \xrightarrow{d} Q$ then $Q \xrightarrow{a}$.

In fact, a slightly more elaborate argument shows that each TCCS process term affords the above property. However, the TLTS depicted in Example 9.1 does *not* have the above persistency property. In fact, state 5 in that TLTS has an outgoing a-labelled transition, but none of the states that it can reach by delaying a positive amount of time has that transition.

This lack of expressiveness of TCCS is somewhat unsatisfactory, since the above-mentioned TLTS can intuitively be captured by the following very informal, but hopefully natural and unambiguous, process description, which uses a stopwatch.

1. Set the stopwatch to 0.
2. Let time pass; the amount of elapsed time is recorded by the stopwatch.
3. If the value of the stopwatch is 5 then action a may be performed. In that case, go to step 1 above, and continue from there. If action a is not performed at time 5 then idle forever.

If our desideratum is to have a formalism for the specification of real-time systems in which this type of process can be described, then TCCS falls short of our expectations.

Moreover, one can argue that the use of urgent actions and of the maximal-progress assumption in the implementation of features like time-outs is somewhat artificial. It would be more intuitive to have a formalism in which such features can be described without recourse to assumptions like action urgency or maximal progress.

The above example and our previous discussions would seem to suggest that an automaton-based formalism with some explicit notion of clocks (or stopwatches) that can be used to determine when transitions are available and when they are disabled might be a natural and powerful specification formalism for real-time behaviours. In the following section, we shall introduce one such formalism, namely, that of timed automata. These were introduced by Alur and Dill in their seminal paper (1990); see also Alur and Dill (1994).

10

Timed automata

The model of timed automata, introduced by Alur and Dill (1990, 1994), has by now established itself as a classical formalism for modelling real-time systems with a dense representation of time. The development of the timed-automata formalism was carried out largely in parallel with – and independently of – the work on timed extensions of process algebras. Roughly speaking, whereas the development of timed process algebras was driven by their (relative) expressiveness, their revealing of new behavioural equivalences and their axiomatizations, the development of the timed-automata formalism was largely driven by the goal of obtaining decidability results for several important properties (Dill, 1989). By now, real-time model checking tools such UPPAAL (Behrmann, David and Larsen, 2004) and KRONOS (Bozga *et al.*, 1998) are based on the timed-automata formalism and on the substantial body of research on this model that has been targeted towards transforming the early decidability results into practically efficient algorithms.

10.1 Motivation

Timed automata are essentially nondeterministic finite automata equipped with a finite number of real-valued clocks, so that transitions can be conditioned on clock values and the performing of a particular transition can reset selected clocks. We shall now introduce the formalism intuitively, showing how the light switch from the start of the previous chapter can be described using the formalism of timed automata without recourse to assumptions such as the urgency of some actions or maximal progress. Graphically, we could model the light switch as in Figure 10.1.

Initially the switch is in the control location Off and, under certain circumstances, it can reach the other two locations, Light and Bright. From the initial location, performing the action 'press' will cause the clock x to be reset to zero.

175

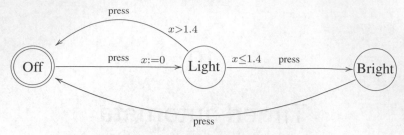

Figure 10.1 Light switch.

This means that the value of the clock x will be zero whenever we enter the location Light. Therefore, x represents the amount of time that has passed since we entered that location. The expressions $x > 1.4$ and $x \leq 1.4$ are called guards and they restrict the possibility of performing a transition. If the time that has elapsed since we entered the location Light is smaller than or equal to 1.4 then, after pressing the switch, we move to the location Bright. If the clock value is greater than 1.4 and the switch is pressed, we have to move to the location Off, because the guard labelling the edge from Light to Bright is not satisfied and that edge is therefore disabled.

In what follows, we shall formalize this simple and intuitive model and develop the basic theory of timed automata.

10.2 Syntax of timed automata

As we have seen above, the main ingredients that timed automata add to the standard model of nondeterministic finite automata are clocks, clock constraints (guards) and clock resets. These notions can be formally defined as follows.

Let us fix a finite set $C = \{x, y, \ldots\}$ whose elements represent the clock names that we can use in the automaton.

Definition 10.1 The set $\mathcal{B}(C)$ of *clock constraints* (or *guards*) over the set of clocks C is defined by the abstract syntax

$$g, g_1, g_2 ::= x \bowtie n \mid g_1 \wedge g_2$$

where $x \in C$ is a clock, $n \in \mathbb{N}$ and $\bowtie \in \{\leq, <, =, >, \geq\}$.   ♦

Example 10.1 The following expressions belong to $\mathcal{B}(C)$, where $C = \{x, y, z\}$:

$$x \leq 5,$$
$$x \geq 0 \wedge x < 5,$$
$$x > 3 \wedge y = 2.$$

We shall often write the constraints in a more usual mathematical notation. For example, $x \geq 0 \ \wedge \ x < 5$ can be written as $0 \leq x < 5$.   ◆

Exercise 10.1 *Is $x \leq 1.4$ a syntactically correct constraint?*   ◆

Each clock from the set C is assumed to store the amount of time elapsed from the last moment when the clock was reset. This can be expressed formally as a function $v : C \rightarrow \mathbb{R}_{\geq 0}$, which we shall call a *(clock) valuation*. The value of a particular clock x is denoted by $v(x)$. Assume, for example, that $C = \{x, y\}$ and consider a valuation v such that $v(x) = 1.34$ and $v(y) = 5.333$. We shall often denote the valuation v simply by $[x = 1.34, y = 5.333]$.

Note that the values of clocks can be arbitrary non-negative real numbers. So, for instance, $[x = \pi, y = \sqrt{2}]$ is a valuation.

In what follows, we will need two important operations, called *delay* and *reset*, which help us to manipulate clock valuations. Let v be a clock valuation. By $v + d$ we denote a clock valuation where the value of every clock is increased by a given non-negative real number d. For a given subset r of clocks, we use $v[r]$ to denote the clock valuation where the values of clocks from r are set to zero and the values of the other clocks are the same as in v. Formally:

- for each $d \in \mathbb{R}_{\geq 0}$, the valuation $v + d$ is defined by

$$(v + d)(x) = v(x) + d \text{ for each } x \in C;$$

- for each $r \subseteq C$, the valuation $v[r]$ is defined by

$$v[r](x) = \begin{cases} 0 & \text{if } x \in r, \\ v(x) & \text{otherwise.} \end{cases}$$

Remark 10.1 In the case where $r = \{x\}$ is a singleton set, we shall often use an alternative notation for reset such that instead of $v[\{x\}]$ we write $v[x \mapsto 0]$.   ◆

Now that we have in place the notions of clock constraints and clock valuations, we can define naturally when a clock constraint satisfies a given valuation or, alternatively, how the constraint evaluates under the valuation.

Definition 10.2 Let $g \in \mathcal{B}(C)$ be a clock constraint for a given set of clocks C and let $v : C \rightarrow \mathbb{R}_{\geq 0}$ be a clock valuation. The *evaluation* of clock constraints $(v \models g)$ is defined inductively on the structure of g by

$$v \models x \bowtie n \text{ iff } v(x) \bowtie n,$$
$$v \models g_1 \wedge g_2 \text{ iff } v \models g_1 \text{ and } v \models g_2,$$

where $x \in C$ is a clock, $n \in \mathbb{N}$, $g_1, g_2 \in \mathcal{B}(C)$ and $\bowtie \in \{\leq, <, =, >, \geq\}$. Note that the sign $\bowtie$ on the left-hand side of iff in the first statement is a purely syntactic symbol while $\bowtie$ on the right-hand side represents the standard corresponding arithmetic comparison on $\mathbb{R}_{\geq 0}$.

If $v \models g$ holds, we often write this as 'v satisfies g'. In the usual way, we write $v \not\models g$ when v does not satisfy the constraint g.   ◆

Example 10.2 Let $C = \{x, y\}$, and consider the valuation $v = [x = 1.2, y = 3.01]$. We can easily see that

$$v \models x > 1 \land x \leq 2,$$
$$v \models x > 0 \land y \geq 3,$$
$$v \not\models y \leq 3 \land x \geq 1.$$

◆

Exercise 10.2 *Can you give an example of a clock constraint that is satisfied by every valuation? What about one that is satisfied by no valuation?*   ◆

Definition 10.3 Two clock constraints g_1 and g_2 are *equivalent* iff they are satisfied by the same valuations, that is, for each valuation v,

$$v \models g_1 \Leftrightarrow v \models g_2.$$

◆

Example 10.3 The clock constraints $x \leq 5 \land x \geq 5$ and $x = 5$ are equivalent, and so are $y \geq 5 \land y \geq 0$ and $y \geq 5$. (Why?)   ◆

Exercise 10.3 (Strongly recommended)
1. *A constraint g is interval closed if, for each valuation v and non-negative real number d, it holds that $v \models g$ and $v + d \models g$ imply $v + d' \models g$ for each $0 \leq d' \leq d$.*

   Prove that each constraint in $\mathcal{B}(C)$ is interval closed.
2. *Show that there is no constraint in $\mathcal{B}(C)$ expressing that x is not equal to 2.*
3. *Let us define the relation $\leq$ over the collection of valuations as*

   $$v \leq v' \text{ iff } v(x) \leq v'(x) \text{ for each } x \in C.$$

   Prove that the relation so defined is a partial order.
4. *A constraint g is downward closed if $v' \models g$ and $v \leq v'$ imply $v \models g$ for all valuations v, v'.*

   Give examples of constraints that are downward closed. Are there constraints that are not downward closed?
5. *Show that constraints of the form $x < n$ are not definable in terms of the other guards in $\mathcal{B}(C)$. That is, argue that a constraint of the form $x < n$ is not*

equivalent to any constraint generated by the following grammar:

$$g, g_1, g_2 ::= x \bowtie n \mid g_1 \wedge g_2,$$

where $x \in C$ is a clock, $n \in \mathbb{N}$ and $\bowtie \in \{\leq, =, >, \geq\}$.

♦

We are now ready to provide the formal definition of timed automata.

Definition 10.4 A *timed automaton* over a finite set of clocks C and a finite set of actions Act is a quadruple

$$(L, \ell_0, E, I),$$

where

- L is a finite set of *locations*, ranged over by ℓ,
- $\ell_0 \in L$ is the *initial location*,
- $E \subseteq L \times \mathcal{B}(C) \times \mathsf{Act} \times 2^C \times L$ is a finite set of *edges*, and
- $I : L \to \mathcal{B}(C)$ assigns *invariants* to locations.

We usually write $\ell \xrightarrow{g,a,r} \ell'$ instead of $(\ell, g, a, r, \ell') \in E$. For such an edge, ℓ is called the *source location*, g is the *guard*, a is the *action*, r is the set of clocks to be reset and ℓ' is the *target location*. ♦

Timed automata are often given in a graphical representation, as in Figure 10.1. Locations are drawn as nodes in the graph, and the initial location is usually marked with a double circle. Edges in the graph have attributes: the beginning of an edge is assigned a guard, in the middle of the edge there is an action name and resets are written at the end of the edge, using the notation $x := 0$ for each clock that should be reset. Invariants are placed next to their corresponding locations. (Their role in the behaviour of timed automata will become clear in what follows. For the moment, you may think of them as imposing restrictions on the values that the clocks may have in control locations.) Irrelevant guards and invariants, i.e. those that are always satisfied, are omitted from the picture.

Example 10.4 The light switch in Figure 10.1 can be described formally as follows (let $g_t = x \geq 0$ be a guard that is true in any valuation):

- $C = \{x\}$,
- $L = \{\mathsf{Off}, \mathsf{Light}, \mathsf{Bright}\}$,
- $\ell_0 = \mathsf{Off}$,
- $E = \{\mathsf{Off} \xrightarrow{g_t,\mathrm{press},\{x\}} \mathsf{Light}, \mathsf{Light} \xrightarrow{x>14,\mathrm{press},\emptyset} \mathsf{Off},$
  $\mathsf{Light} \xrightarrow{x\leq14,\mathrm{press},\emptyset} \mathsf{Bright}, \mathsf{Bright} \xrightarrow{g_t,\mathrm{press},\emptyset} \mathsf{Off}\}$,
- $I(\mathsf{Off}) = I(\mathsf{Light}) = I(\mathsf{Bright}) = g_t$.

♦

Remark 10.2 Note that in the example above we have replaced the time point 1.4 with 14, because of the requirement that the constants in the guards of a timed automaton must be natural numbers. This is not a real restriction, however. We can also consider guards where the constants are rational numbers (irrational numbers in guards would be impossible to write in a finite way). In this case, we can always multiply all the constants in the guards by an appropriate number in order to raise them to natural numbers. Such stretching of time does not have any significant influence on the behaviour of an automaton; it is essentially like saying that, instead of writing a clock value as 0.145 seconds, we write it as 145 milliseconds.   ♦

10.3   Semantics of timed automata

We shall now discuss the intended behaviour of timed automata. Intuitively, a timed automaton can be in exactly one of its control locations at each stage of its computation. However, knowing the present control location is not enough to determine which of the outgoing edges can be taken next, if any. A 'snapshot' of the current state of the computation should also remember the present clock values. Therefore, a suitable notion of the *state* of computation of a timed automaton consists of a pair (ℓ, v), ℓ being the control location the automaton is in and v being the valuation determined by the current clock values. The pair (ℓ, v) is a legal state of the timed automaton only if the valuation v satisfies the invariant of location ℓ. (Initially, the control location is ℓ_0 and the value of each clock is 0.) If there is an edge whose source location equals the current location ℓ, and whose guard is satisfied by the current valuation v, then we can follow that edge, thereby changing the current location to the target location of the edge and resetting the set of clocks labelling the edge. Another possibility is to delay in the current location by increasing simultaneously the value of all clocks by a given amount of time d, without changing the control location. This is possible only if the invariant of the current location is satisfied by the valuation $v + d$. (Since invariants are interval closed – see Exercise 10.3 – this also means that the invariant is satisfied by all the intermediate valuations $v + d'$ with $0 \leq d' \leq d$.) For example, if the current value of the clock x is 0 and the invariant of the present location is $x \leq 1$ then the timed automaton can delay 1 time unit but not 1.00001 time units.

The reader might have observed already that essentially we have intuitively defined a timed transition system generated by a given timed automaton. These ideas can be formalized as follows.

Definition 10.5 Let $A = (L, \ell_0, E, I)$ be a timed automaton over a set of clocks C and a set of actions Act. We define the timed transition system $T(A)$ generated by A as $T(A) = (\mathsf{Proc}, \mathsf{Lab}, \{\xrightarrow{\alpha} \mid \alpha \in \mathsf{Lab}\})$, where:

- $\mathsf{Proc} = \{(\ell, v) \mid (\ell, v) \in L \times (C \to \mathbb{R}_{\geq 0}) \text{ and } v \models I(\ell)\}$, i.e. *states* are of the form (ℓ, v), where ℓ is a location of the timed automaton and v is a valuation that satisfies the invariant of ℓ;
- $\mathsf{Lab} = \mathsf{Act} \cup \mathbb{R}_{\geq 0}$ is the set of labels; and
- the transition relation is defined by

  $(\ell, v) \xrightarrow{a} (\ell', v')$ if there is an edge $(\ell \xrightarrow{g,a,r} \ell') \in E$ such that $v \models g$, $v' = v[r]$ and $v' \models I(\ell')$,

  $(\ell, v) \xrightarrow{d} (\ell, v + d)$ for all $d \in \mathbb{R}_{\geq 0}$ such that $v \models I(\ell)$ and $v + d \models I(\ell)$.

Let v_0 denote the valuation such that $v_0(x) = 0$ for all $x \in C$. If v_0 satisfies the invariant of the initial location ℓ_0, we shall call (ℓ_0, v_0) the *initial state* (or *initial configuration*) of $T(A)$. ♦

Example 10.5 Consider the timed automaton A defined in the following picture (there is one edge, labelled by a, with a guard $x \leq 1$ that resets the clock x, and the invariant in the location ℓ_0 is $x \leq 2$):

$$x \leq 2 \; \ell_0 \quad \overset{x:=0}{\underset{x \leq 1}{\curvearrowright}} a$$

A small part of the transition system $T(A)$ is shown below (there are in fact uncountably many different reachable states for every x in the interval $[0, 2]$).

$$(\ell_0, [x = 0]) \xrightarrow{0.6} (\ell_0, [x = 0.6]) \xrightarrow{0.4} (\ell_0, [x = 1]) \xrightarrow{0.3} (\ell_0, [x = 1.3]) \xrightarrow{0.7} (\ell_0, [x = 2])$$

Note that from the state $(\ell_0, [x = 1.3])$ it is not possible to perform a transition under the action a, and the state $(\ell_0, [x = 2])$ is essentially stuck since the only available transition is a time-elapsing step with time delay 0. ♦

There is a fundamental difference between situations where a clock constraint is used in the guard and where it is used in the invariant. This can be demonstrated by means of the simple example in Figure 10.2. In the timed automaton (a) $x \leq 1$ is a guard. There is no restriction on time-elapsing steps and hence arbitrarily long delays are possible. This means that, as long as the value of the clock x is smaller

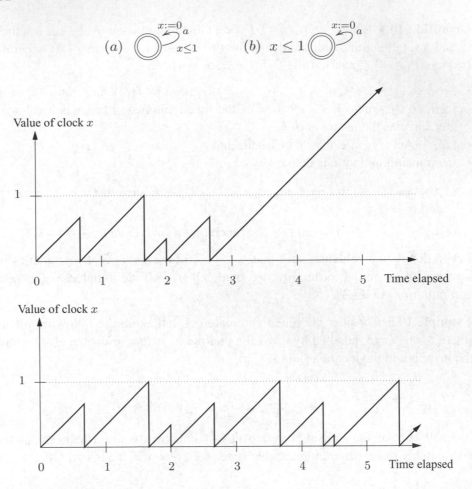

Figure 10.2 Clock constraint $(x \leq 1)$ (a) in the guard and (b) in the invariant. The upper graph shows the value of clock x for case (a) and the lower graph shows the value of clock x for case (b), as functions of the time elapsed.

than or equal to 1, we can perform the transition a and reset the clock x. However, if the total time delay after the last reset of the clock is strictly greater than 1 then it is not possible to enable the action a in the future and the only available transitions are the delay steps. In the timed automaton (b), $x \leq 1$ is used in the invariant. This means that it is never possible to delay more than 1 time unit and hence during each execution the action a is always available.

Exercise 10.4 *Let A be a timed automaton. Prove that $T(A)$ is a TLTS in the sense of Definition 9.1.*   ◆

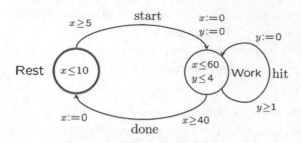

Figure 10.3 A small Jobshop.

Exercise 10.5 *Give a timed automaton A whose associated TLTS $T(A)$ is, modulo a renaming of the names of the states, precisely that in Example 9.1.* ◆

Exercise 10.6 *Is there a timed automaton whose associated TLTS has only one state? Argue for your answer.* ◆

Exercise 10.7 (For the keenest) *Show how to translate expressions of TCCS into timed automata in a syntax-directed fashion. Your translation should be such that the TLTSs determined by the source TCCS expression and the target timed automaton are isomorphic. Use your translation and your answer to Exercise 10.5 to argue that the formalism of timed automata is more expressive than TCCS.* ◆

Exercise 10.8 *In Exercise 10.3(2), you proved that there is no constraint in $\mathcal{B}(C)$ expressing that $x \neq 2$. Assume now that, using the formalism of timed automata, we wish to model a situation in which an action a is enabled in some location ℓ unless $x = 2$. Is this possible? If so, how would you do so?* ◆

Example 10.6 The timed automaton in Figure 10.3 describes the work in a small Jobshop where a Worker alternates between resting (in location **Rest**) and working (in location **Work**). Here the clock x is used for constraining the time spent by the Worker in these two modes, and the clock y is used to control the frequency with which the Worker is hitting nails while working. More precisely, the invariant $x \leq 60$ in the **Work** location guarantees that the Worker never works for more than 60 minutes without a rest, and the guard $x \geq 40$ on the 'done' transition forces the Worker to work for periods lasting at least 40 minutes. Similarly, the invariant $x \leq 10$ in the **Rest** location forces the Worker to work again after at most 10 minutes of rest, and the guard on the 'start' transition guarantees that the Worker is entitled to rest for periods of at least 5 minutes. While working, the invariant $y \leq 4$ in the **Work** location and the guard $y \geq 1$ on the 'hit' transition enforce that the time delays between consecutive hit-actions are in the range 1 to 4 minutes. ◆

Exercise 10.9 *Given that the Worker works for 70 minutes, what is the maximum and minimum number of hits if (s)he (a) starts with a rest (i.e. starts in state* (Rest, $[x = 0, y = 0]$)) *or (b) is immediately ready to work (i.e. starts in state* (Work, $[x = 0, y = 0]$)). *Provide valid transition sequences of the Worker that prove your claim.*   ◆

Exercise 10.10 *Reconsider the light controller in Figure 10.1. Modify the model so that the light cannot be switched off manually. Instead the light should be switched off automatically after 120 seconds without external action (i.e. by a press-action).*   ◆

Exercise 10.11 *Consider an autonomous elevator which operates between two floors. The required behaviour of the elevator is as follows.*

- *The elevator can stop either at the ground floor or the first floor.*
- *When the elevator arrives at a certain floor, its door automatically opens. This must not happen until at least 2 seconds from its arrival. However, the door must definitely open within 5 seconds.*
- *Whenever the elevator's door is open, passengers can enter. They enter one by one and we (optimistically) assume that the elevator has sufficient capacity to accommodate any number of passengers waiting outside.*
- *The door cannot close until 4 seconds after the last passenger enters.*
- *After the door closes, the elevator waits at least 2 seconds and then travels up or down to the other floor.*

Suggest a timed-automaton model of the elevator. Use the actions up *and* down *to model the movement of the elevator,* open *and* close *to describe the door operation and* enter *to indicate that a passenger is entering the elevator. Finally, provide two different timed traces of the system when it starts at the ground floor with the door open.*   ◆

Exercise 10.12 *We want to model an intelligent* interface *for a light control. The interface has to translate properly the* pressing *and* releasing *of a button into actions controlling the light and light intensity, based on their timing difference. In particular, the following requirements must be met.*

- *If the time difference between the* press *and the* release *is very short (no more than 0.5 seconds) then nothing happens (it was too fast to be noticed).*
- *If the time difference between the* press *and the* release *is between 0.5 seconds and 1 second, the light is toggled, i.e. it goes from on to off or from off to on.*
- *As soon as 1 second has elapsed from the* press *without the button having been* released, *the interface issues an instruction for letting the light intensity begin to dim. The dimming is stopped only when the button is* released.

Model the above Interface as a timed automaton with two input actions (press and release) and three output actions (toggle, dim and stop). ◆

10.4 Networks of timed automata

Many real-life systems consist of a number of independent components running in parallel and communicating whenever necessary. For example, a production line may consist of a number of independent sensors and actuators, for a single-purpose operation, that have to synchronize in order for the whole production task to be completed. Such a composed behaviour depends also on timing features, of course, and we should like to be able to model it by suitably combining descriptions of its components.

Process algebras such as CCS and its TCCS extension with timing features provide this possibility by means of the operation of parallel composition. The communication is implemented when one parallel component raises a synchronization request on a particular channel and another component accepts the request on the same channel. Both components can then simultaneously perform the communication transitions, and we assume that the duration of the synchronization action is zero time units – that is, communication is instantaneous. This form of communication is also called *hand-shake* synchronization. Furthermore, if we want to force communication on a particular channel, we can use the restriction operator on that channel, as demonstrated earlier in Section 2.2.

In the case of timed automata, our formalism so far enables us to model only a single component. Having in place our inspiration from CCS and TCCS, we shall develop a more general model consisting of a collection of timed automata running in parallel with one another. Such automata may also synchronize with each other. We shall call this kind of system a *network of timed automata*.

By way of an example, consider the two timed automata with initial locations A and B shown below:

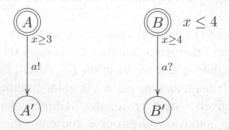

Note that the actions labelling the edges in these timed automata now take two forms. The action $a!$ means that, by performing the transition, process A wants to synchronize on channel a with some other process (in our case with process

B), offering the action a? in exchange. (By convention, we think of action a! as standing for an 'output on channel a', whereas a? stands for an 'input on channel a'.) The processes can then communicate using hand-shake synchronization. Moreover, all channels are implicitly assumed to be restricted at the highest level; hence the synchronization in networks of timed automata is always forced. In fact, we can describe the above behaviour in terms of TCCS as $(A \mid B) \setminus \{a\}$ where $A \stackrel{\text{def}}{=} \varepsilon(3).\bar{a}.A'$ and $B \stackrel{\text{def}}{=} \varepsilon(4).a.B'$.

Let us now consider another example, namely the light switch and the fast user from Section 9.4. The TCCS definition of the light switch can be directly rewritten into the timed automaton in the upper part of the following diagram. The fast user (in the lower part of the diagram) is performing the action 'press!' exactly every 3 time units.

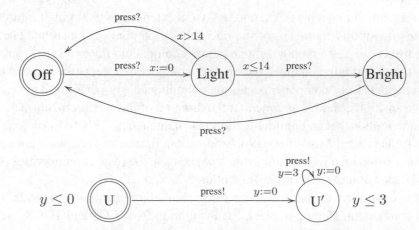

Note that we have 'stretched' the time by multiplying all constants by 10 in order to have only integer constants in our model (see Remark 10.2). We are also using a new clock y instead of x, in the automaton modelling the fast user. The reason is that we want to avoid a clash between the parallel components (should the user be using the same clock x, its reset would also influence the behaviour of the light switch).

The intended behaviour of the above network is as follows. The fast user presses the switch at time 0 and the upper automaton changes its location to Light. At the same moment the user enters the location U'. After another 3 time units the user presses the switch again and the automata enter simultaneously the locations Bright and U' respectively. After yet another 3 time units the user presses the switch again and both automata synchronize and enter the locations Off and U' respectively. The system behaviour then continues in a similar manner. Not surprisingly, the semantics of the network can be given via a TLTS. The structure of the states is now richer, as it contains pairs of locations of the respective timed automata together with information on the current value of the clocks in both automata, and, as in the case of CCS, the communication appears for an external observer as an action τ. A small part of the system looks as follows; we have omitted the values of the clocks for the sake of clarity.

$$(\text{Off}, U) \xrightarrow{\ \tau\ } (\text{Light}, U') \xrightarrow{\ 3\ } (\text{Light}, U') \xrightarrow{\ \tau\ } (\text{Bright}, U')$$

$$(\text{Off}, U') \xleftarrow{\ 3\ } (\text{Off}, U') \xleftarrow{\ \tau\ } (\text{Bright}, U')$$

with τ connecting (Off, U') up to (Light, U') and 3 connecting (Bright, U') down to (Bright, U').

Exercise 10.13 *Add the information on the clock values to the states in the fragment of the TLTS shown above.* ◆

We shall now proceed to formalize the notion of a network of timed automata. Assume that our set of actions consists of a finite set of channel names Chan (followed by one of the symbols '!' or '?', which respectively indicate that the action uses the channel for output or input) and a finite set N of ordinary action names including τ, formally

$$\text{Act} = \{c! \mid c \in \text{Chan}\} \cup \{c? \mid c \in \text{Chan}\} \cup N.$$

By analogy with CCS, we say that the actions $c!$ and $c?$ are *complementary*. We shall use α, β to range over Act.

Definition 10.6 Let n be a positive integer and, for each $i \in \{1, \ldots, n\}$, let

$$A_i = (L_i, \ell_0^i, E_i, I_i)$$

be timed automata over a set of clocks C and a set of actions Act. We call the composition $A = A_1 \mid A_2 \mid \cdots \mid A_n$ a *network of timed automata* with n parallel components. ◆

As already mentioned above, the semantics of the parallel composition $A = A_1 \mid A_2 \mid \cdots \mid A_n$ will be given by means of a TLTS. The following definition formalizes the behaviour of a network of timed automata.

Definition 10.7 Let $A = A_1 \mid A_2 \mid \cdots \mid A_n$, where $A_i = (L_i, \ell_0^i, E_i, I_i)$ for each $i \in \{1, \ldots, n\}$, be a network of timed automata over a set of clocks C and actions $\text{Act} = \{c! \mid c \in \text{Chan}\} \cup \{c? \mid c \in \text{Chan}\} \cup N$. We define the TLTS $T(A)$ generated by the network A as

$$T(A) = (\text{Proc}, \text{Lab}, \{\xrightarrow{\alpha} \mid \alpha \in \text{Lab}\}).$$

Here

- $\text{Proc} = \{(\ell_1, \ell_2, \ldots, \ell_n, v) \mid (\ell_1, \ell_2, \ldots, \ell_n, v) \in L_1 \times L_2 \times \cdots \times L_n \times (C \to \mathbb{R}_{\geq 0})$ and $v \models \bigwedge_{i \in \{1,\ldots,n\}} I_i(\ell_i)\}$ (i.e. *states* are of the form $(\ell_1, \ldots, \ell_n, v)$, where each ℓ_i is a location in the component timed automaton A_i and v is a valuation over the set of clocks C that satisfies the invariants of all locations ℓ_i present in the state),
- $\text{Lab} = N \cup \{\tau\} \cup \mathbb{R}_{\geq 0}$ is the set of labels, and
- the transition relation is defined as follows:

$(\ell_1, \ldots, \ell_i, \ldots, \ell_n, v) \xrightarrow{a} (\ell_1, \ldots, \ell_i', \ldots, \ell_n, v')$ if $a \in N$ and there is an edge
$(\ell_i \xrightarrow{g,a,r} \ell_i') \in E_i$ in the ith component automaton such that
$v \models g,\ v' = v[r]$ and
$v' \models I_i(\ell_i') \wedge \bigwedge_{k \neq i} I_k(\ell_k);$

$(\ell_1, \ldots, \ell_i, \ldots, \ell_j, \ldots, \ell_n, v) \xrightarrow{\tau} (\ell_1, \ldots, \ell_i', \ldots, \ell_j', \ldots, \ell_n, v')$ if $i \neq j$ and
there are edges $(\ell_i \xrightarrow{g_i,\alpha,r_i} \ell_i') \in E_i$ and $(\ell_j \xrightarrow{g_j,\beta,r_j} \ell_j') \in E_j$ such that
α and β are complementary,
$v \models g_i \wedge g_j,\ v' = v[r_i \cup r_j]$, and
$v' \models I_i(\ell_i') \wedge I_j(\ell_j') \wedge \bigwedge_{k \neq i,j} I_k(\ell_k);$

$(\ell_1, \ldots, \ell_n, v) \xrightarrow{d} (\ell_1, \ldots, \ell_n, v + d)$ for all $d \in \mathbb{R}_{\geq 0}$ such that

$$v + d' \models \bigwedge_{i \in \{1,\ldots,n\}} I_i(\ell_i)$$

for each real number d' in the interval $[0, d]$.

Let v_0 denote the valuation $v_0(x) = 0$ for all $x \in C$. If v_0 satisfies the invariants of all the initial locations ℓ_0^i, we shall call $(\ell_0^1, \ell_0^2, \ldots, \ell_0^n, v_0)$ the *initial state* (or *initial configuration*) of $T(A)$.   ♦

Even though this definition of the transition relation for networks of timed automata might look more technical than usual, the intuition behind it is easy to understand. The first part says that any component can make an independent move as long as it happens under an ordinary action from N, the move is enabled by the guard in the corresponding component, all clocks that are reset in the component are reset also in the composed state and we do not violate any invariant. The second part of the definition relates to the situation when two components are willing to perform respectively an input and an output action on a particular channel. The guards have to be satisfied as before, the collection of reset clocks is the union of the clocks that are reset in both automata and the invariants have to be satisfied as before. Moreover, in analogy with CCS and TCCS, this transition is supposed to be internal and is visible only under the silent action τ. Finally, the last part of the

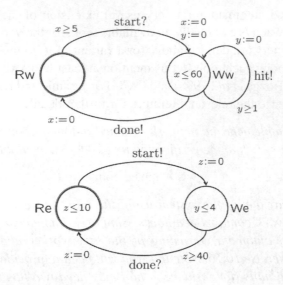

Figure 10.4 The lazy worker and his demanding employer.

definition allows arbitrary time delays as long as the invariants of all components are not violated as time progresses.

Exercise 10.14 (Mandatory) *Use the formal definition above to draw a small part of the TLTS for a network of timed automata consisting of the light switch and the fast user. Determine all the transitions in the TLTS for the network of timed automata given at the beginning of this section.* ♦

Exercise 10.15 *Let $A = A_1 \mid A_2 \mid \cdots \mid A_n$, where $A_i = (L_i, \ell_0^i, E_i, I_i)$ for each $i \in \{1, \ldots, n\}$, be a network of timed automata over a set of clocks C and actions* $\mathsf{Act} = \{c! \mid c \in \mathsf{Chan}\} \cup \{c? \mid c \in \mathsf{Chan}\} \cup N$. *Can you define a single timed automaton B such that $T(A)$ and $T(B)$ are isomorphic? How many locations does B have if each timed automaton A_i has, say, ten nodes?* ♦

Exercise 10.16 *Consider the pair of timed automata in Figure 10.4 consisting of a worker and his employer, where* hit *is the only ordinary action. Explain why it is fair to characterize the worker as being lazy and the employer as being demanding. Use your construction from Exercise 10.15 to provide a single timed automaton* Jobshop *having semantics (in terms of the induced TLTS) isomorphic to that of the network* (Worker | Employer). ♦

Networks of timed automata are a very useful extension of the model of timed automata, and nowadays essentially all available tools for the verification of timed automata use the network defined above (or a variant of it) to model real-life real-time systems. Among such tools, let us mention at least UPPAAL (Behrman *et al.*, 2004) KRONOS (Bozga *et al.*, 1998) and CMC Laroussinie and Larsen (1998), and we refer the reader to the relevant literature for further details.

Exercise 10.17 *Implement the network of timed automata consisting of the fast user and the light switch in the verification tool* UPPAAL *available at*

www.uppaal.com.

Simulate the behaviour of the system using the tool, and use the tool to check whether this network contains deadlocks. Similarly, implement and analyze the network of timed automata consisting of the lazy worker and the demanding employer from Exercise 10.16. Note that you will need to provide timed-automata models for hitting nails (for instance, a nail may need two hits before it is completely down) in order to have a closed system, as required by UPPAAL.   ◆

10.5 More on timed-automata formalisms

The behaviour of timed-automata models may show various types of anomaly. In particular, models may exhibit *timelocks* in different ways; a timed automaton may reach a state s that is time deadlocked, in the sense that no discrete transition is enabled and time cannot proceed. The timed automaton of Example 10.5 provides such an example. The passage of time is also essentially blocked in behaviours where infinitely many discrete transitions are performed in a finite amount of time (so-called Zeno behaviour). Ideally a timed automaton should be *non-Zeno* in the sense that from any of its states some time-divergent sequence of transitions can be followed. Tripakis (1999) provided a sound method for ensuring non-Zeno-ness from the syntactic structure of the loops in the automaton. The check simply requires that in any syntactic loop there exists a clock that is both reset in the loop and bounded from below in one of the guards of the loop. The loops of the timed automaton of Figure 10.3 clearly satisfy this requirement, and that automaton is thus non-Zeno.

Another important issue in modelling the timing behaviour of real-time systems is that of urgency – that is, mechanisms for ensuring that some discrete action is taken without any further delay or at least before some given deadline expires. The timed-automata formalism presented in this chapter uses invariants in locations for this purpose. Here an invariant imposes a *hard deadline* on the system by insisting that discrete transitions must be taken before the invariant of a given location ceases to hold. However, as already demonstrated, expressing urgency using invariants may result in unnecessary time deadlocks. On the basis of this observation, Bornot and Sifakis (2000) and Sifakis and Yovine (1996) advocated the use of so-called *deadlines*, which are additional predicates decorating the transitions of a timed automaton. These predicates specify when a transition becomes urgent (i.e. when it must be made). An advantage of the deadline approach is that, under some reasonable assumptions, it ensures the absence of time deadlocks.

The timed-automata model is at the very border of decidability, in the sense that even small additions to the formalism in terms of permissible operations for clock updates or clock constraints will soon led to the undecidability of reachability questions. In the timed-automata formalism the ability to update clocks is restricted to simple resets, and clock constraints are restricted to simple (lower or upper) bounds on individual clocks. However, a thorough study by Bouyer *et al.* (2004) showed that certain combinations of more general updates – including resets to values other than 0, resets to the value of another clock, increments and various nondeterministic updates – together with bounds on differences between the values of two clocks (so-called *diagonal constraints*) maintain the decidability of reachability analysis. However, extensions beyond these, say to using linear expressions in guards and resets or allowing different clocks to grow at different rates, will result in undecidability. This generalization of timed automata has led to another formalism known as linear hybrid automata (Alur *et al.*, 1995), for which the tool HyTech (Henzinger, Ho and Wong-Toi, 1997) provides a semi-decision procedure for model checking.

A recent extension of timed automata aimed at performance analysis is that of *priced or weighted timed automata* (Larsen *et al.*, 2001, Alur, La Torre and Pappas, 2001). Here the timed-automata formalism is extended with an additional continuous cost variable, which may grow at different rates in different locations. This cost variable models the consumption of a certain resource (e.g. energy or memory) during the behaviour of the underlying timed automaton. Surprisingly, a number of properties have been shown to be decidable for this formalism (Larsen *et al.*, 2001, Alur *et al.*, 2001, Bouyer, Brinksma and Larsen, 2004); the model checker UPPAAL CORA provides an efficient tool for solving cost-optimal reachability problems and has been applied successfully to a number of optimal scheduling problems.

The developments of timed automata and of timed process algebra were initially carried out independently and with different goals. However, translations between suitable timed process algebras and timed automata were given in Fokkink (1993), enabling the transfer of results and methods from one set of formalisms to the other.

Also, notions of timed Petri nets were proposed early on as timed extensions of Petri nets. The paper Bérard *et al.* (2005) shows that timed automata and bounded timed Petri nets are equally expressive formalisms with respect to timed-language acceptance, and Srba (2005) provides very tight mutual translations between the classes of 1-safe timed-arc Petri nets and networks of timed automata.

11

Timed behavioural equivalences

We shall now investigate behavioural aspects of timed models. In particular we will see how the behavioural equivalences from Chapter 3 can be generalized in various ways in order to take timing properties into account. Even though we shall often refer to timed automata, the notions are independent of the actual formalism used, as they will be defined purely in terms of timed labelled transition systems (TLTSs). Thus, for example, timed behavioural equivalences are valid for processes expressed in TCCS as well. We also give a detailed account of the so-called region-graph technique, which provides a universal tool for proving the decidability of several problems associated with timed models.

11.1 Timed and untimed trace equivalence

A natural way to begin is to define the timed traces of TLTSs; we define them in a similar way to traces for ordinary LTSs.

Let $A = (L, \ell_0, E, I)$ be a timed automaton over a set of clocks C and a set of actions Act.

Definition 11.1 A sequence $(t_1, a_1)(t_2, a_2)(t_3, a_3) \cdots$, where $t_i \in \mathbb{R}_{\geq 0}$ and $a_i \in$ Act, is called a finite or infinite *timed trace of A* iff there is a finite or infinite transition sequence

$$(\ell_0, v_0) \xrightarrow{d_1} (\ell_0, v_1) \xrightarrow{a_1} (\ell_1, v_2) \xrightarrow{d_2} (\ell_1, v_3) \xrightarrow{a_2} (\ell_2, v_4) \xrightarrow{d_3} (\ell_2, v_5) \xrightarrow{a_3} \cdots$$

in $T(A)$ such that $v_0(x) = 0$ for all $x \in C$, and, for each i,

$$t_i = t_{i-1} + d_i \text{ where } t_0 = 0.$$

◆

Intuitively, the real number t_i represents the absolute time (the *time-stamp*) at which a_i happens, measured from the start of the computation of automaton A. Note that the sequence of time-stamps $t_1, t_2, \ldots$ is non-decreasing.

Example 11.1 Consider the light switch from Figure 10.1. The following sequence can easily be seen to be a finite timed trace:

$$(2.3, \text{press})(2.5, \text{press})(2.51, \text{press})(5.6, \text{press})(5.6, \text{press})(7.0, \text{press}).$$

In fact, any non-decreasing sequence of time-stamps induces a timed trace of this timed automaton. (Why?)

If we consider the timed automata (a) and (b) from Figure 10.2 then for example the sequence

$$(0.2, a)(0.5, a)(1.5, a)(1.5, a)(2.0, a)$$

is a finite timed trace of both (a) and (b). In fact, it is not too hard to argue that these two timed automata afford the same timed traces. (Do so!)   ◆

We can now define the notion of timed-language equivalence.

Definition 11.2 The set of all finite timed traces of a timed automaton A is denoted by $L(A)$ and is called the *timed language of A*. Timed automata A_1 and A_2 are *timed-language equivalent* iff $L(A_1) = L(A_2)$.   ◆

As remarked above, the two timed automata in Figure 10.2 are timed-language equivalent.

Sometimes we would like to abstract from the particular time points when actions happen and consider only the action sequences that can be performed from the initial configuration of a given timed automaton. For this purpose, we shall define untimed traces and untimed-trace equivalence over timed automata.

Definition 11.3 We say that $a_1 a_2 a_3 \cdots$ is an *untimed trace of A* iff there exist $t_1, t_2, t_3, \ldots \in \mathbb{R}_{\geq 0}$ such that $(t_1, a_1)(t_2, a_2)(t_3, a_3) \cdots$ is a timed trace of A. ◆

Definition 11.4 The set of all the finite untimed traces of A is denoted by $L_u(A)$ and is called the *untimed language of A*. Timed automata A_1 and A_2 are *untimed-language equivalent* iff $L_u(A_1) = L_u(A_2)$.   ◆

The proof of the following theorem is straightforward and follows directly from the definitions.

Theorem 11.1 *Any two timed-language-equivalent automata are also untimed-language equivalent.*

Exercise 11.1 *Prove the above theorem.*   ◆

The converse of the above theorem does not hold, as demonstrated by the following example.

Example 11.2 Consider the following two timed automata:

$$
\text{(a)} \quad \overset{x:=0}{\underset{x\leq 1}{\circlearrowleft}} a \qquad\qquad \text{(b)} \quad \overset{x:=0}{\underset{x=1}{\circlearrowleft}} a
$$

We can easily observe that automaton (a) affords the timed trace $(0, a)$ but automaton (b) does not. Therefore the two automata are not timed-language equivalent. Note, however, that they are untimed-language equivalent. Moreover, each timed trace of automaton (b) is also a timed trace of automaton (a). ◆

Exercise 11.2 *Prove the claims made in the previous example.* ◆

As in the case of ordinary LTSs, language equivalence is not always the most suitable notion of behavioural equivalence to consider because, as argued in Section 3.2, it does not faithfully describe the deadlock behaviour of processes. Therefore we proceed to introduce the notions of timed and untimed strong bisimilarity.

11.2 Timed and untimed bisimilarity

From our discussion so far in this chapter, we know that the semantics of timed automata is given in terms of TLTSs, which can, in fact, be viewed as standard LTSs. Hence the first notion of bisimilarity over this model can be naturally defined as strong bisimilarity. In the timed case, we shall call it *timed bisimilarity*. This implies that in timed bisimilarity both visible actions and time-elapsing steps are considered as visible actions, which means that we can observe the precise duration of time delays.

Definition 11.5 (Timed bisimulation) A binary relation $\mathcal{R}$ over the set of states of a TLTS is a *timed bisimulation* iff whenever $s_1 \mathcal{R} s_2$, a is an action and d is a time delay:

if $s_1 \overset{a}{\to} s_1'$ then there is a transition $s_2 \overset{a}{\to} s_2'$ such that $s_1' \mathcal{R} s_2'$;

if $s_1 \overset{d}{\to} s_1'$ then there is a transition $s_2 \overset{d}{\to} s_2'$ such that $s_1' \mathcal{R} s_2'$;

if $s_2 \overset{a}{\to} s_2'$, then there is a transition $s_1 \overset{a}{\to} s_1'$ such that $s_1' \mathcal{R} s_2'$;

if $s_2 \overset{d}{\to} s_2'$ then there is a transition $s_1 \overset{d}{\to} s_1'$ such that $s_1' \mathcal{R} s_2'$.

Two states s and s' are *timed bisimilar*, written $s \sim s'$, iff there is a timed bisimulation that relates them. ◆

Definition 11.6 Timed automata A_1 and A_2 are *timed bisimilar* iff their initial states in the union of the timed transition systems $T(A_1)$ and $T(A_2)$ generated by A_1 and A_2 are timed bisimilar. (Here, and elsewhere in this section, we implicitly assume, without loss of generality, that the sets of locations of A_1 and A_2 are disjoint.)   ♦

In order to understand better the notion of timed bisimilarity, we will present a few examples.

Example 11.3 Consider the following timed automata with initial locations A and A' over the set of clocks $C = \{x\}$.

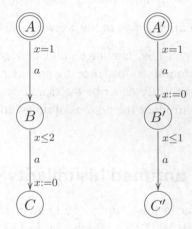

We shall argue that the given timed automata are timed bisimilar. In order to do so, we have to establish that their initial states (A, v_0) and (A', v_0) where $v_0(x) = 0$ are strongly bisimilar. This can be demonstrated, by e.g. defining a relation R of strong bisimulation as follows:

$$\{((A, [x = d]), (A', [x = d])) \mid d \in \mathbb{R}_{\geq 0}\}$$
$$\cup \{((B, [x = d + 1]), (B', [x = d])) \mid d \in \mathbb{R}_{\geq 0}\}$$
$$\cup \{((C, [x = d]), (C', [x = d'])) \mid d, d' \in \mathbb{R}_{\geq 0}\}.$$

One can easily see that $((A, v_0), (A', v_0)) \in R$, and we leave it to the reader to verify that R is indeed a strong bisimulation. (Do so!)   ♦

Exercise 11.3 *Reconsider the pair of timed automata in Figure 10.4 consisting of a worker and his employer, where* hit *is the only ordinary action. Construct a single timed automaton* Simple-Jobshop *with only two clocks that is timed bisimilar to the network* (Worker | Employer).   ♦

Example 11.4 Consider the following two timed automata:

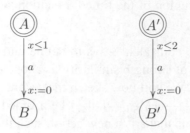

We will demonstrate that the initial states of these automata are not timed bisimilar, by finding a universal winning strategy for the attacker in the strong bisimulation game starting from the pair $(A, [x = 0])$ and $(A', [x = 0])$. In the first round the attacker plays the delay transition $(A, [x = 0]) \xrightarrow{1.7} (A, [x = 1.7])$ and the defender can only answer with $(A', [x = 0]) \xrightarrow{1.7} (A', [x = 1.7])$. The game continues in the second round from the pair $(A, [x = 1.7])$ and $(A', [x = 1.7])$. Now the attacker can switch sides and play $(A', [x = 1.7]) \xrightarrow{a} (B', [x = 0])$. The defender cannot answer this move from $(A, [x = 1.7])$. Hence the attacker has a universal winning strategy. This implies that $(A, [x = 0]) \not\sim (A', [x = 0])$, and so the given timed automata are not timed bisimilar. ◆

The reason why the two transition systems above are not timed bisimilar is that, in the case of timed bisimilarity, a specific time-elapsing step in one automaton has to be matched by a time-elapsing step of exactly the same duration in the other. This might sometimes be too strict a requirement, since delays can be arbitrary non-negative real numbers, and so one might try to relax this constraint. One possibility is to require that a time delay in one process has to be matched by a time delay in the other process, but this could be of a different duration. We shall call the resulting notion *untimed bisimilarity* and proceed to define it formally as follows.

Definition 11.7 (Untimed bisimulation) A binary relation $\mathcal{R}$ over the set of states of a TLTS is an *untimed bisimulation* iff whenever $s_1 \mathcal{R} s_2$, a is an action and d is a delay:

if $s_1 \xrightarrow{a} s_1'$ then there is a transition $s_2 \xrightarrow{a} s_2'$ such that $s_1' \mathcal{R} s_2'$;

if $s_1 \xrightarrow{d} s_1'$ then there is a transition $s_2 \xrightarrow{d'} s_2'$ for some d' such that $s_1' \mathcal{R} s_2'$;

if $s_2 \xrightarrow{a} s_2'$ then there is a transition $s_1 \xrightarrow{a} s_1'$ such that $s_1' \mathcal{R} s_2'$;

if $s_2 \xrightarrow{d} s_2'$ then there is a transition $s_1 \xrightarrow{d'} s_1'$ for some d' such that $s_1' \mathcal{R} s_2'$.

Two states s and s' are *untimed bisimilar*, written $s \sim_u s'$, iff there is an untimed bisimulation that relates them.

Two timed automata A_1 and A_2 are untimed bisimilar iff their initial states are untimed bisimilar in the union of the timed transition systems $T(A_1)$ and $T(A_2)$ generated by A_1 and A_2.   ◆

There are essentially two equivalent ways to define untimed bisimilarity: we can either modify the notion of strong bisimilarity as above or modify the underlying timed transition systems. We will now sketch the second possibility.

Let $T = (\mathsf{Proc}, \mathsf{Lab}, \{\xrightarrow{\alpha}_T \mid \alpha \in \mathsf{Lab}\})$ be a timed transition system where $\mathsf{Lab} = \mathsf{Act} \cup \mathbb{R}_{\geq 0}$. Assume that ε is a new action such that $\varepsilon \notin \mathsf{Lab}$. We construct the untimed LTS

$$T_\varepsilon = (\mathsf{Proc}, \mathsf{Act} \cup \{\varepsilon\}, \{\xrightarrow{a} \mid a \in \mathsf{Act} \cup \{\varepsilon\}\})$$

in the following way:

- for each transition $s \xrightarrow{a}_T s'$ in T, where $a \in \mathsf{Act}$, we add the transition $s \xrightarrow{a} s'$ to T_ε; and
- for each transition $s \xrightarrow{d}_T s'$ in T, where $d \in \mathbb{R}_{\geq 0}$, we add the transition $s \xrightarrow{\varepsilon} s'$ for the new action ε to T_ε.

(Note that $s \xrightarrow{\varepsilon} s$ holds for each state s. Can you see why?) This means that the label of each time-elapsing transition in T is replaced by ε and all the other standard transitions are preserved.

Lemma 11.1 Let $T = (\mathsf{Proc}, \mathsf{Lab}, \{\xrightarrow{\alpha}_T \mid \alpha \in \mathsf{Lab}\})$ be a timed transition system, where $\mathsf{Lab} = \mathsf{Act} \cup \mathbb{R}_{\geq 0}$. Two states s_1 and s_2 in Proc are untimed bisimilar iff they are strongly bisimilar, in the sense of Definition 3.2, in the untimed transition system T_ε.

Exercise 11.4 *Prove the above lemma.*   ◆

Example 11.5 We will demonstrate that the timed non-bisimilar automata from Example 11.4 are equivalent with respect to untimed bisimilarity. Consider the following relation R:

$$\{((A, [x = d]), (A', [x = d'])) \mid 0 \leq d \leq 1, \, 0 \leq d' \leq 2\}$$
$$\cup \{((A, [x = d]), (A', [x = d'])) \mid d > 1, \, d' > 2\}$$
$$\cup \{((B, [x = d]), (B', [x = d'])) \mid d, d' \in \mathbb{R}_{\geq 0}\}.$$

It remains to verify that R is a strong bisimulation over the corresponding untimed transition systems and that the initial states belong to R. We will examine one case of the analysis necessary to show that R is a strong bisimulation. Consider the pair $(A, [x = d])$ and $(A', [x = d'])$ for some d and d' such that $0 \leq d \leq 1$

and $0 \leq d' \leq 2$. There are three possible types of move from $(A, [x = d])$ (the situation from $(A', [x = d'])$ is symmetric).

- The move $(A, [x = d]) \xrightarrow{a} (B, [x = 0])$ can be matched by $(A', [x = d']) \xrightarrow{a}$ $(B', [x = 0])$ and the resulting pair belongs to R.
- The move $(A, [x = d]) \xrightarrow{d'} (A, [x = d + d'])$ such that $d + d' \leq 1$ can be matched by $(A', [x = d']) \xrightarrow{0} (A', [x = d'])$ and the resulting pair belongs to R. This answer is possible because all time-elapsing steps are observed only as the action ε.
- The move $(A, [x = d]) \xrightarrow{d'} (A, [x = d + d'])$ such that $d + d' > 1$ can be matched by e.g. $(A', [x = d']) \xrightarrow{3} (A', [x = d' + 3])$ for the same reasons as above, and the resulting pair of states belongs to R.

The reader is invited to finish the analysis of the remaining cases. ◆

Exercise 11.5 *Consider the four timed automata below. Determine for each pair of initial states $(A, [y = 0])$, $(X, [y = 0])$, $(U, [y - 0])$ and $(D, [y = 0])$ whether they are timed bisimilar, untimed bisimilar or neither.*

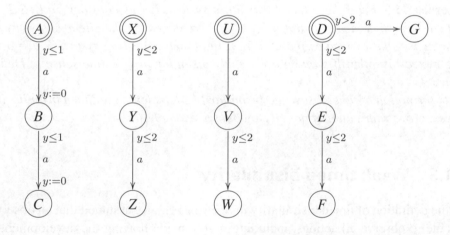

◆

As illustrated by the above example and exercise, there are untimed-bisimilar timed automata that are not timed bisimilar. However, one can observe the validity of the following theorem.

Theorem 11.2 *Any two timed bisimilar processes are also untimed bisimilar.*

Proof. Any relation that is a timed bisimulation is also an untimed bisimulation. One can easily argue for this fact, for example by using bisimulation games. Whenever the defender has an answer to an attack under a time-elapsing action d then the same defence is also valid when the time-elapsing label is replaced by ε.   □

Exercise 11.6 *Argue for each of the following claims in the positive case or give a counter-example in the negative case.*

- *If two timed automata are timed bisimilar then they are also timed trace equivalent.*
- *If two timed automata are timed bisimilar then they are also untimed trace equivalent.*
- *If two timed automata are untimed bisimilar then they are also untimed trace equivalent.*
- *If two timed automata are untimed bisimilar then they are also timed trace equivalent.*
- *If two timed automata are timed trace equivalent then they are also untimed bisimilar.*

♦

Exercise 11.7 *Let T be a timed transition system. Let us consider an LTS T' in which every time-delay action $d \in \mathbb{R}_{\geq 0}$ is replaced by the silent action τ. We now define that two states p and q from the timed transition system T are time-abstracted bisimilar iff p and q are weakly bisimilar in T' in the sense of Definition 3.4.*

Is the notion of time-abstracted bisimilarity equivalent to untimed bisimilarity? If yes, prove your claim. If no, give a counter-example.   ♦

11.3 Weak timed bisimilarity

In the definition of timed bisimilarity in Section 11.2, we assumed that an observer is able to observe all actions, including τ-actions. Following the development of weak bisimilarity for CCS, we wish to have a notion of *weak* timed bisimilarity that abstracts from τ-actions.

However, what does 'abstracting from τ-actions' mean in a timed setting? To obtain some intuition we may first consider some sample TCCS processes. For instance, we would expect $\tau.a.\tau.P$ to be weakly timed bisimilar to $a.P$, as is the case for untimed CCS. Similarly, we would expect $\varepsilon(4).\tau.\varepsilon(3).P$ to be equivalent to $\varepsilon(4).\varepsilon(3).P$, and – following the principle of time additivity for TLTSs – even to be equivalent to $\varepsilon(7).P$. This motivates the introduction of a new notion of transition relation for a TLTS.

Definition 11.8 Let $T = (\mathsf{Proc}, \mathsf{Lab}, \{\xrightarrow{\alpha} \mid \alpha \in \mathsf{Lab}\})$ be a timed transition system where $\mathsf{Lab} = \mathsf{Act} \cup \mathbb{R}_{\geq 0}$, and let s, t be states of T. For each action $\alpha \in \mathsf{Lab}$, we shall write $s \xRightarrow{\alpha} t$ iff

- $\alpha = \tau$ and $s(\xrightarrow{\tau})^* t$, or
- $\alpha = a \in \mathsf{Act}\backslash\{\tau\}$ and $s \xRightarrow{\tau} s_1 \xrightarrow{a} s_2 \xRightarrow{\tau} t$ for some states s_1 and s_2, or
- $\alpha = d \in \mathbb{R}_{\geq 0}$ and $s \xRightarrow{\tau} s_1 \xrightarrow{d_1} t_1 \cdots t_{n-1} \xRightarrow{\tau} s_n \xrightarrow{d_n} t_n \xRightarrow{\tau} t$ for some $n \geq 0$, states $s_1, \ldots, s_n, t_1, \ldots, t_n$ and delays $d_1, \ldots, d_n$ with $d = \sum_{i=1}^n d_i$. By convention, $d = 0$ when $n = 0$.

(Recall that $(\xrightarrow{\tau})^*$ denotes the reflexive and transitive closure of the relation $\xrightarrow{\tau}$.) ◆

Thus transitions $s \xRightarrow{a} t$, where $a \in \mathsf{Act}$, are defined as for ordinary LTSs. A transition $s \xRightarrow{d} t$, where $d \in \mathbb{R}_{\geq 0}$, represents a sequence of steps in the original timed transition system with no observable actions and whose total delay amounts to d. (Note that the relations $\xRightarrow{0}$ and $\xRightarrow{\tau}$ coincide.) For instance, a TCCS expression of the form $\varepsilon(4).\tau.\varepsilon(3).P$ affords the transition

$$\varepsilon(4).\tau.\varepsilon(3).P \xRightarrow{7} P.$$

Using the new transition relations $\xRightarrow{\alpha}$, weak timed bisimulation is defined as follows.

Definition 11.9 (Weak timed bisimulation) A binary relation $\mathcal{R}$ over the set of states of a TLTS is a *weak timed bisimulation* iff whenever $s_1 \mathcal{R} s_2$, a is an action (including τ) and d is a time delay:

if $s_1 \xrightarrow{a} s_1'$ then there is a transition $s_2 \xRightarrow{a} s_2'$ such that $s_1' \mathcal{R} s_2'$;

if $s_1 \xrightarrow{d} s_1'$ then there is a transition $s_2 \xRightarrow{d} s_2'$ such that $s_1' \mathcal{R} s_2'$;

if $s_2 \xrightarrow{a} s_2'$ then there is a transition $s_1 \xRightarrow{a} s_1'$ such that $s_1' \mathcal{R} s_2'$;

if $s_2 \xrightarrow{d} s_2'$ then there is a transition $s_1 \xRightarrow{d} s_1'$ such that $s_1' \mathcal{R} s_2'$.

Two states s and s' are *weakly timed bisimilar*, written $s \approx s'$, iff there is a weak timed bisimulation that relates them. ◆

Definition 11.10 Timed automata A_1 and A_2 are *weakly timed bisimilar* iff their initial states in the union of the timed transition systems $T(A_1)$ and $T(A_2)$ generated by A_1 and A_2 are weakly timed bisimilar. ◆

The relationship between timed bisimilarity and weak timed bisimilarity is as expected and left as the following exercise.

Exercise 11.8 *Let s, t be states of an arbitrary TLTS. Prove that $s \sim t$ implies $s \approx t$.*   ◆

To increase our understanding of the notion of weak timed bisimilarity we present a small example.

Example 11.6 Consider the following two TCCS processes P and Q:

- $P = (a.\varepsilon(3).\bar{b}.\mathbf{0} \mid b.\varepsilon(4).c.\mathbf{0}) \backslash b$, and
- $Q = a.\varepsilon(7).c.\mathbf{0}$.

We shall now argue that P and Q are weakly timed bisimilar. In order to do so, we need to exhibit a weak timed bisimulation R containing (P, Q). Let R be given as the following relation:

$$\{ ((\varepsilon(3 - d).\bar{b}.\mathbf{0} \mid b.\varepsilon(4).c.\mathbf{0}) \backslash b, \ \varepsilon(7 - d).c.\mathbf{0}) \mid 0 \leq d \leq 3 \}$$
$$\cup \{ ((\mathbf{0} \mid \varepsilon(4 - d).c.\mathbf{0}) \backslash b, \ \varepsilon(4 - d).c.\mathbf{0}) \mid 0 \leq d \leq 4) \} \cup \{ (P, Q) \}.$$

Obviously R contains (P, Q), and we leave it to the reader to prove that R is a weak timed bisimulation. (Do so!)   ◆

Exercise 11.9 *Consider the two timed automata below. Prove that $(A, [x = 0])$ and $(A', [x = 0])$ are not weakly timed bisimilar. Modify the guards and resets of the two automata A and A' in such a way that the resulting timed automata are weakly timed bisimilar.*

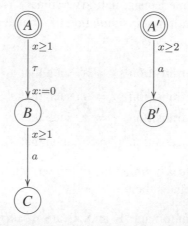

◆

Exercise 11.10 *Let T be the alarm timer from Exercise 9.4. In the present exercise we will show how to make use of T. We want to model a process which offers action a for 30 time units, after which a time-out will occur. We may express this* *behaviour directly in TCCS using the following definition:*

$$A \stackrel{\text{def}}{=} a.P + \varepsilon(30).\tau.Q\,,$$

where P is a term describing the behaviour after a and Q is a term describing the behaviour to be followed after the time-out. Now, using the alarm timer T we may express this behaviour alternatively as

$$B \stackrel{\text{def}}{=} \overline{\text{set30}}.(a.P + \text{to}.Q)\,.$$

Prove that this is an equivalent definition in the sense that the processes A and $(B\,|\,T)\backslash\{\text{set5},\text{set10},\text{set30},\text{to}\}$ are weakly timed bisimilar. ◆

11.4 Region graphs

Even the simplest timed automata generate timed transition systems with infinitely (even uncountably) many reachable states. This is due to the fact that states of timed automata contain not only the control location but also the particular valuations of clocks. In general we have uncountably many different valuations even in the situation when only one clock is considered (the value of this clock can be in general any number from $\mathbb{R}_{\geq 0}$).

Since good formalisms for the description of reactive systems should also support methods for their algorithmic analysis, a natural question the reader may ask at this point is the following.

Is algorithmic verification at all possible over timed automata?

Surprisingly, the answer to this question is positive, and in what follows we shall discuss a fundamental approach – due to Alur and Dill (1990, 1992, 1994) and called the *region-graph technique* – which will enable us to draw such a conclusion.

The key idea behind the region technique is very simple: even though the collection of valuations for a given timed automaton is uncountably infinite, it can be partitioned into finitely many equivalence classes in such a way that any two valuations from the same equivalence class will not create any 'significant difference' in the behaviour of the system.

Assume a given timed automaton A over a set of clocks C. Formally, our goal will be to define effectively an *equivalence relation* $\equiv$ over clock valuations, where $\equiv\, \subseteq (C \rightarrow \mathbb{R}_{\geq 0}) \times (C \rightarrow \mathbb{R}_{\geq 0})$ is such that

1. $v \equiv v'$ implies that the states (ℓ, v) and (ℓ, v') are untimed bisimilar for each location ℓ of the automaton A, and

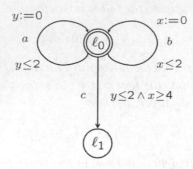

Figure 11.1 A simple timed automaton.

2. $\equiv$ has only finitely many equivalence classes, i.e. the set

$$\{[v]_\equiv \mid v \in (C \to \mathbb{R}_{\geq 0})\},$$

where $[v]_\equiv = \{v' \mid v' \equiv v\}$ is finite. We shall call $[v]_\equiv$ the equivalence class represented by v.

To get a first idea of the possible nature and existence of such a finite partitioning of the collection of clock valuations, let us consider a small example.

Example 11.7 Consider the small timed automaton in Figure 11.1, which has two locations $\{\ell_0, \ell_1\}$ and two clocks $\{x, y\}$. Each transition out of ℓ_0 partitions the set of clock valuations into two sets, those that satisfy the guard of the transition and those that do not. As an example, the state $(\ell_0, [x = 3.5, y = 1.5])$ satisfies the guard of the a-transition whereas the state $(\ell_0, [x = 3.5, y = 2.5])$ does not. Consequently, these two states cannot be untimed bisimilar, according to Definition 11.7.

As illustrated in the left-hand part of Figure 11.2, the guards of the three transitions out of ℓ_0 partition the set of clock valuations into eight classes; here clock valuations from different classes are distinguishable under untimed bisimilarity as they enable different sets of actions. As an example the state $(\ell_0, [x = 3.5, y = 1.5])$ enables only action a whereas the state $(\ell_0, [x = 1.5, y = 1.5])$ enables both a and b but not c.

Still, however, the left-hand part of Figure 11.2 does *not* constitute an untimed bisimulation, in the sense that whenever v and v' belong to the same partitioning then (ℓ_0, v) and (ℓ_0, v') are untimed bisimilar. To demonstrate this, we note that the two states $s_1 = (\ell_0, [x = 3, y = 0.25])$ and $s_2 = (\ell_0, [x = 3, y = 1.75])$ are in the same block P of the left-hand part of Figure 11.2, but whereas s_1 can

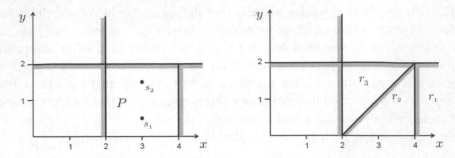

Figure 11.2 Partitioning of the valuations for the automaton in Figure 11.1.

do c (and reach ℓ_1) after a delay transition (e.g. by delaying 1) no delay transition from s_2 will ever enable c. (Check this!). Consequently, s_1 and s_2 are *not* untimed bisimilar. In fact, within the block P, the ability to enable a c-transition after some (arbitrary) delay is determined by the constraint $y \leq x - 2$. (Explain why!). Thus, as illustrated in the right-hand part of Figure 11.2, P must be divided into two smaller blocks, r_2 and r_3; r_2 comprises all clock valuations satisfying $(2 < x < 4)$ $\wedge (0 \leq y \leq x - 2)$ and r_3 comprises all clock valuations satisfying $(2 < x < 4)$ $\wedge (x - 2 < y \leq 2)$. Note that this partitioning of P is stable not only with respect to delay transitions but also with respect to discrete transitions: whenever an a-transition is made from states belonging to P, the resulting state will be in r_2 (as y is reset). We encourage the reader at this point to spend some effort in completing the partitioning in the right-hand part of Figure 11.2 to obtain equivalence classes with respect to untimed bisimilarity. ◆

Before embarking upon the definition of the equivalence relation $\equiv$, we first introduce some necessary notation.

Definition 11.11 Let $d \in \mathbb{R}_{\geq 0}$ be a real number. By $\lfloor d \rfloor$ we denote the integer part of d and by $frac(d)$ the fractional part of d. Any $d \in \mathbb{R}_{\geq 0}$ can be now written as $d = \lfloor d \rfloor + frac(d)$. ◆

Example 11.8 By the above definition, $\lfloor 2.345 \rfloor = 2$ and $frac(2.345) = 0.345$. ◆

We shall now proceed to motivate the definition of the relation $\equiv$ in stepwise fashion.

Let A be a timed automaton and let $x \in C$ be one of its clocks. We define $c_x \in \mathbb{N}$ as the largest constant against which the clock x is ever compared either in the guards or in the invariants present in A. For instance, c_x is 2 (respectively 1) for the timed automaton on the left (respectively on the right) in Example 11.4.

The first observation we can make is that the specific value of the clock x is irrelevant for the behaviour of the timed automaton, if that value is strictly greater than the constant c_x. In other words, for each clock constraint g in the automaton A, the satisfiability of g does *not* depend on the concrete value of the clock x as long as it is greater than c_x. For instance, in the timed automaton on the left in Example 11.4 a valuation that assigns a value greater than 1 to x satisfies none of the clock constraints in that timed automaton.

Hence, a first approximation of the relation $\equiv$ can be as follows:

$$v \equiv v' \text{ if, and only if } v(x) = v'(x),$$

$$\text{for each clock } x \in C \text{ such that } v(x) \le c_x \text{ or } v'(x) \le c_x. \qquad (11.1)$$

Equivalently, and perhaps more explicitly, we have that $v \equiv v'$ holds whenever, for each clock x, either $v(x) = v'(x)$ or both $v(x)$ and $v'(x)$ are greater than c_x.

The above argument, used to motivate the definition of $\equiv$, implies that if $v \equiv v'$ then for each location ℓ in the timed automaton the states (ℓ, v) and (ℓ, v') are indeed untimed bisimilar. (Prove this!) However, the equivalence relation $\equiv$ still has infinitely many equivalence classes and therefore does not satisfy the second requirement listed near the start of this section. (Why?)

In order to motivate further improvement upon the definition of $\equiv$, let us consider the following timed automaton A:

In this automaton $c_x = 2$. Consider the following two configurations of the timed automaton above: $(\ell_0, [x = 0.12])$ and $(\ell_0, [x = 0.97])$. A short reflection makes us realize that these configurations are untimed bisimilar. (Argue for this claim!) Similarly $(\ell_0, [x = 1.23])$ and $(\ell_0, [x = 1.467])$ are surely untimed bisimilar. This might motivate us to claim that the fractional parts of the clocks are irrelevant and to formulate the following refinement of condition (11.1):

$$v \equiv v' \text{ iff for each } x \in C,$$

$$\lfloor v(x) \rfloor = \lfloor v'(x) \rfloor, \text{ or both } v(x) \text{ and } v'(x) \text{ are greater than } c_x. \qquad (11.2)$$

We can now see that $\equiv$ has finitely many equivalence classes as required (only the integer parts of the clocks up to a given constant matter). The question is whether $v \equiv v'$ does indeed imply that, for each location ℓ, the states (ℓ, v) and (ℓ, v') are untimed bisimilar. The answer is, unfortunately, negative. For example, the valuations $[x = 1]$ and $[x = 1.4]$ should be equivalent according to our definition of $\equiv$, but in the timed automaton A the state $(\ell_0, [x = 1])$ can still perform the action a while $(\ell_0, [x = 1.4])$ cannot.

This leads us to the observation that if the fractional part of a clock is equal to 0, we should consider this as a 'special' situation because the guards can distinguish such a clock value from a clock value that has the same integer part but non-zero fractional part. Therefore we add the following requirement to condition (11.2):

$$v \equiv v' \text{ only if, for each } x \in C \text{ such that } v(x) \leq c_x,$$
$$(frac(v(x)) = 0 \Leftrightarrow frac(v'(x)) = 0). \tag{11.3}$$

Note that, in the presence of (11.2), we need only require that the above condition is met for each clock x with $v(x) \leq c_x$. Indeed, requirement (11.2) already ensures that whenever $v \equiv v'$ and $v(x) \leq c_x$, then $v'(x) \leq c_x$.

Exercise 11.11 *Prove the claim we have just made.* ◆

The number of equivalence classes of $\equiv$ still remains finite because we are refining an equivalence relation that already had finitely many equivalence classes. However, the equivalence relation $\equiv$ is still too coarse to achieve our aim as demonstrated by the following timed automaton.

Consider the valuations $v_1 = [x = 0.8, y = 0.3]$ and $v_2 = [x = 0.5, y = 0.9]$. You should be able to convince yourself that, by requirements (11.2) and (11.3), we have $v_1 \equiv v_2$. However, the states (ℓ_0, v_1) and (ℓ_0, v_2) are *not* untimed bisimilar. This can be easily seen since state (ℓ_0, v_1) can first delay 0.2 time units, perform the action a, delay a further 0.5 time units and finally perform the action b. However, the configuration (ℓ_0, v_2) cannot match this behaviour because in order to perform the action a we have to delay exactly 0.5 time units, which means that the value of the clock y necessarily grows to 1.4, disabling action b forever.

The reason why we have this problem is that $v_1(x) > v_1(y)$ while $v_2(x) < v_2(y)$. This indicates that the ordering between the fractional parts of two different clocks does in fact play an important role. This motivates us to add the following requirement on top of (11.2) and (11.3):

$$v \equiv v' \text{ only if, for all } x, y \in C \text{ with } v(x) \leq c_x \text{ and } v_y \leq c_y,$$
$$(frac(v(x)) \leq frac(v(y)) \Leftrightarrow frac(v'(x)) \leq frac(v'(y))). \tag{11.4}$$

In fact, this is all that we have to do to establish our goal that $\equiv$ has finitely many equivalence classes and yet preserves untimed bisimilarity. We now provide a summary of the final definition and also state the main theorem, to the effect that the equivalence relation $\equiv$ has the desired properties. The proof of this main theorem follows easily from the closure properties of the defined equivalence, which are given as exercises.

Definition 11.12 Let A be a timed automaton. We say that two clock valuations v and v' are equivalent, and write $v \equiv v'$, iff:

1. for each $x \in C$ we have that either both $v(x)$ and $v'(x)$ are greater than c_x or

$$\lfloor v(x) \rfloor = \lfloor v'(x) \rfloor;$$

2. for each $x \in C$ such that $v(x) \leq c_x$ we have

$$frac(v(x)) = 0 \text{ iff } frac(v'(x)) = 0;$$

    and

3. for all $x, y \in C$ such that $v(x) \leq c_x$ and $v(y) \leq c_y$ we have

$$frac(v(x)) \leq frac(v(y)) \text{ iff } frac(v'(x)) \leq frac(v'(y)).$$

$\blacklozenge$

Remark 11.1 Note that if $v \equiv v'$ then, for all $x, y \in C$ such that $v(x) \leq c_x$ and $v(y) \leq c_y$, we have that

$$v(x) = v(y) \text{ iff } v'(x) = v'(y).$$

Can you justify this claim? $\blacklozenge$

The equivalence $\equiv$ on clock valuations enjoys a number of closure properties, as we will see in the following three exercises.

Exercise 11.12 *Let A be a timed automaton and let g be one of its clock constraints. Assume that $v \equiv v'$. Show that constraint satisfaction is preserved by equivalence, in the sense that whenever $v \models g$ then we have $v' \models g$ also.*

    Would this property continue to hold if we allowed for clock constraints of the form $x - y \bowtie n$, where $x, y \in C$ are clocks, $n \in \mathbb{N}$ and $\bowtie \in \{\leq, <, =, >, \geq\}$? Argue for your answer. $\blacklozenge$

Exercise 11.13 *Let A be a timed automaton and let x be one of its clocks. Assume that $v \equiv v'$. Show that the resetting of a clock preserves equivalence, in the sense that $v[x \mapsto 0] \equiv v'[x \mapsto 0]$.* $\blacklozenge$

Exercise 11.14 (For the keenest) *Let A be a timed automaton and assume that $v \equiv v'$. Show that a delay preserves equivalence, in the sense that for any d there exists a d' such that $v + d \equiv v' + d'$. You may want to (first) prove this property in the simpler cases where C consists of one or two clocks.* $\blacklozenge$

Using the closure properties from Exercises 11.12–11.14 we are now able to conclude that the desired property of $\equiv$ is satisfied, as stated in the theorem below.

Theorem 11.3 *Let A be a timed automaton. The equivalence relation $\equiv$ partitions the clock valuations of A into finitely many equivalence classes. Moreover, whenever v and v' are in the same equivalence class (i.e. $v \equiv v'$ holds) then, for any location ℓ of A, the configurations (ℓ, v) and (ℓ, v') are untimed bisimilar.*

Exercise 11.15 *Prove Theorem 11.3.* ◆

We shall now define the notion of a region.

Definition 11.13 An $\equiv$-equivalence class $[v]_\equiv$ represented by some clock valuation v is called a *region*. ◆

Each region can be uniquely characterized by a finite collection of clock constraints that it satisfies. For instance, consider the valuation v over two clocks x, y such that $v(x) = \sqrt{2}$ and $v(y) = 1.3$. Assume that both c_x and c_y are equal to 2. Then, each valuation v' that is equivalent to v satisfies the constraint $1 < y < x < 2$, and we will use $[1 < y < x < 2]_\equiv$ to denote the region $[v]_\equiv$.

Exercise 11.16 *Check that each valuation v' that is equivalent to the valuation v introduced in the paragraph above does satisfy the constraint $1 < y < x < 2$, as claimed.* ◆

Example 11.9 Consider a timed automaton with only one clock x such that $c_x = 3$. There are exactly 8 regions, consisting of 4 corner points, 3 closed line segments and 1 open line segment:

- $[x = 0]_\equiv$, $[x = 1]_\equiv$, $[x = 2]_\equiv$, $[x = 3]_\equiv$,
- $[0 < x < 1]_\equiv$, $[1 < x < 2]_\equiv$, $[2 < x < 3]_\equiv$, and
- $[3 < x]_\equiv$.

We can illustrate the automaton as follows:

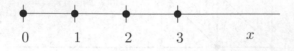

◆

Exercise 11.17 *Consider a timed automaton with only one clock x and whose constraints are $x > 0$ and $x \leq 2$. How many regions does this determine? What are they?* ◆

Example 11.10 Consider a timed automaton with two clocks x and y such that $c_x = 2$ and $c_y = 1$. There are exactly 28 regions consisting of 6 corner points, 9 closed line segments, 5 open line segments, 4 closed areas and 4 open areas:

- $[x = 0, y = 0]_\equiv$, $[x = 1, y = 0]_\equiv$, $[x = 2, y = 0]_\equiv$,
  $[x = 0, y = 1]_\equiv$, $[x = 1, y = 1]_\equiv$, $[x = 2, y = 1]_\equiv$,
- $[0 < x < 1, y = 0]_\equiv$, $[1 < x < 2, y = 0]_\equiv$,
  $[0 < x < 1, y = 1]_\equiv$, $[1 < x < 2, y = 1]_\equiv$,
  $[x = 0, 0 < y < 1]_\equiv$, $[x = 1, 0 < y < 1]_\equiv$, $[x = 2, 0 < y < 1]_\equiv$,
- $[0 < x < 1, 0 < y < 1, x = y]_\equiv$, $[1 < x < 2, 1 < y < 2, x = y]_\equiv$,
- $[2 < x, y = 0]_\equiv$, $[2 < x, y = 1]_\equiv$, $[x = 0, 1 < y]_\equiv$,
  $[x = 1, 1 < y]_\equiv$, $[x = 2, 1 < y]_\equiv$,
- $[0 < x < 1, 0 < y < 1, x > y]_\equiv$,
  $[0 < x < 1, 0 < y < 1, x < y]_\equiv$,
  $[1 < x < 2, 0 < y < 1, frac(x) > frac(y)]_\equiv$,
  $[1 < x < 2, 0 < y < 1, frac(x) < frac(y)]_\equiv$, and
- $[2 < x, 0 < y < 1]_\equiv$, $[0 < x < 1, 1 < y]_\equiv$,
  $[1 < x < 2, 1 < y]_\equiv$, $[2 < x, 1 < y]_\equiv$.

This can be depicted graphically as follows:

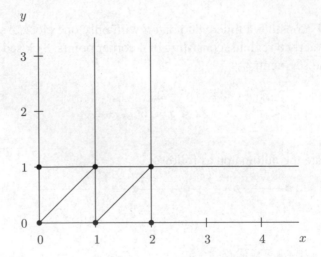

Exercise 11.18 *The regions for a timed automaton with two clocks x and y such that $c_x = 3$ and $c_y = 2$ are depicted as follows:*

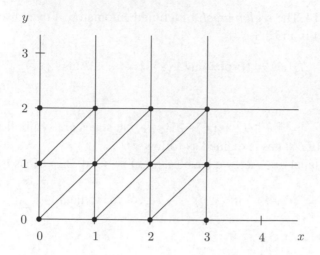

How many regions are there in the picture? ◆

As indicated by the above examples, each region of a timed automaton A can be uniquely represented by specifying the following items of information:

- for each clock x, one constraint from the set

$$\{x = n \mid n \in \{0, 1, \ldots, c_x\}\}$$
$$\cup \{n < x < n + 1 \mid n \in \{0, 1, \ldots, c_x - 1\}\} \cup \{c_x < x\};$$

- for each pair of distinct clocks x and y that, for some $n < c_x$ and $m < c_y$, satisfy constraints of the form $n < x < n + 1$ and $m < y < m + 1$, an indication of whether $frac(v(x))$ is smaller than or equal to $frac(v(y))$ or whether it is not, for each valuation v in that region.

Exercise 11.19 *Assume a timed automaton with a set of clocks $C = \{x, y\}$ and corresponding constants c_x and c_y. Find a general expression which describes the number of regions for the given constants c_x and c_y. (Hint: Count the number of possible combinations of constraints of the above form.)* ◆

We shall now define the fundamental concept of a *region graph*. The main idea is that every configuration of the form (ℓ, v) is replaced by a so-called *symbolic state* $(\ell, [v]_\equiv)$ in the region graph, where $[v]_\equiv$ is the region represented by v. Whenever we have a time-elapsing or standard transition between two configurations, we shall also have a transition between the corresponding symbolic states. This can be formally described as follows.

Definition 11.14 The *region graph* of a timed automaton A over a set of clocks C and actions Act is an LTS

$$T_r(A) = (\text{Proc}, \text{Act} \cup \{\varepsilon\}, \{\stackrel{a}{\Rightarrow} \mid a \in \text{Act} \cup \{\varepsilon\}),$$

where

- $\text{Proc} = \{(\ell, [v]_\equiv) \mid \ell \in L, \ v : C \to \mathbb{R}_{\geq 0}\}$, i.e. states are symbolic states, and
- $\Rightarrow$ on symbolic states is defined as follows:
  1. for each label $a \in \text{Act}$, we have $(\ell, [v]_\equiv) \stackrel{a}{\Rightarrow} (\ell', [v']_\equiv)$ iff $(\ell, v) \stackrel{a}{\longrightarrow} (\ell', v')$; and
  2. $(\ell, [v]_\equiv) \stackrel{\varepsilon}{\Rightarrow} (\ell, [v']_\equiv)$ iff $(\ell, v) \stackrel{d}{\longrightarrow} (\ell, v')$ for some $d \in \mathbb{R}_{\geq 0}$.

◆

Exercise 11.20 (Recommended) *Prove that the relation $\stackrel{\varepsilon}{\Rightarrow}$ in $T_r(A)$ is reflexive and transitive.*

◆

Example 11.11 Consider the following timed automaton A:

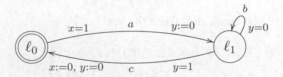

The regions with assigned numbers are depicted as follows:

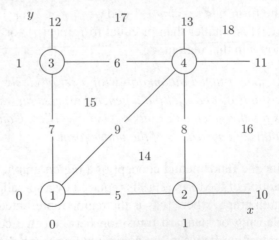

Part of the region graph reachable from the initial configuration $(\ell_0, 1) = (\ell_0, [x = y = 0]_\equiv)$ is depicted below:

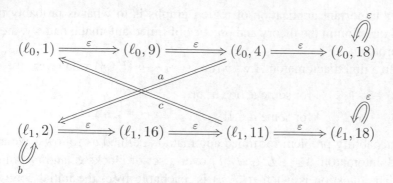

In order to make the picture simpler, the reflexive closure of the $\stackrel{\varepsilon}{\Rightarrow}$ transitions has been omitted. In particular, there are also the following ε-transitions, $(\ell_0, 1) \stackrel{\varepsilon}{\Rightarrow} (\ell_0, 4)$, $(\ell_0, 1) \stackrel{\varepsilon}{\Rightarrow} (\ell_0, 18)$, $(\ell_0, 9) \stackrel{\varepsilon}{\Rightarrow} (\ell_0, 18)$, $(\ell_1, 2) \stackrel{\varepsilon}{\Rightarrow} (\ell_1, 11)$, $(\ell_1, 2) \stackrel{\varepsilon}{\Rightarrow} (\ell_1, 18)$, $(\ell_1, 16) \stackrel{\varepsilon}{\Rightarrow} (\ell_1, 18)$, and ε-loops in every state. ◆

Exercise 11.21 *Construct the region graph of the following timed automaton:*

$$x:=0, y:=0 \quad \ell_0 \quad \substack{0 < x \le 1 \\ a \\ y:=0}$$
$$b \quad x=1 \wedge y=1$$

◆

Theorem 11.4 *The region graph $T_r(A)$ of any timed automaton A is finite and can be algorithmically constructed. Moreover, for each location ℓ and valuation v, it is the case that (ℓ, v) in the untimed transition system $T_u(A)$ is strongly bisimilar to $(\ell, [v]_\equiv)$ in the transition system $T_r(A)$.*

Proof. A proof to the effect that the region graph $T_r(A)$ of any timed automaton A is finite and can be algorithmically constructed may be found in the classic reference Alur and Dill (1994). That (ℓ, v) in the untimed transition system $T_u(A)$ is strongly bisimilar to $(\ell, [v]_\equiv)$ in the transition system $T_r(A)$ follows from Theorem 11.3 and from the fact that strong bisimilarity is an equivalence relation; see Theorem 3.1(1). □

Corollary 11.1 *Untimed bisimilarity between two timed automata is decidable.*

Proof. Theorem 11.4 shows that the problem of deciding untimed bisimilarity between two timed automata can be algorithmically reduced to that of checking whether their corresponding region graphs are strongly bisimilar. Since the region graph of an arbitrary timed automaton is finite, the claim follows. □

Another important application of region graphs is to what is probably the most studied question in the theory and practice of timed automata, namely, the reachability problem.

Given a timed automaton A we write $(\ell, v) \longrightarrow (\ell', v')$ whenever

- $(\ell, v) \xrightarrow{a} (\ell', v')$ for some action a, or
- $(\ell, v) \xrightarrow{d} (\ell', v')$ for some $d \in \mathbb{R}_{\geq 0}$.

The reachability problem for timed automata is defined as follows. We are given a timed automaton $A = (L, \ell_0, E, I)$ over a set of clocks C and a configuration (ℓ, v). The question is whether (ℓ, v) is reachable from the initial configuration, i.e. whether $(\ell_0, v_0) \longrightarrow^* (\ell, v)$ where $v_0(x) = 0$ for all $x \in C$.

Having the region-graph technique at hand, we can now see the validity of the following lemma.

Lemma 11.2 Let A be a timed automaton and (ℓ, v) a configuration. It holds that $(\ell_0, v_0) \longrightarrow^* (\ell, v)$ in A iff $(\ell_0, [v_0]_\equiv) \Rightarrow^* (\ell, [v]_\equiv)$ in its region graph $T_r(A)$.

A direct corollary of the above lemma is that, as first shown by Alur and Dill (1994), the reachability problem for timed automata is decidable.

Corollary 11.2 *The reachability problem for timed automata is decidable.*

Exercise 11.22 *Reconsider the simple timed automaton from Example 11.7. Construct the region graph for this timed automaton and use it to decide whether the location ℓ_1 is reachable from the initial state $(\ell_0, [x = 0, y = 0])$.* ◆

11.5   Zones and reachability graphs

On the one hand, region graphs provide a finite and elegant abstraction of infinite timed transition systems generated by timed automata, which enables us to prove the decidability of, for example, reachability, timed and untimed bisimilarity, untimed language equivalence and language emptiness (see the next section for references).

On the other hand, region graphs have very large state spaces. The state-space explosion is exponential in the number of clocks and in the maximal constants appearing in the guards. Indeed, as shown by Alur and Dill (1994), we have the following bound on the number of regions.

Proposition 11.1 Let A be a timed automaton with n clocks. Let C be the set of clocks in A. The number of regions of A is bounded by

$$2^n \cdot n! \cdot \Pi_{x \in C} (2c_x + 2).$$

It follows that the number of regions is exponential in the number of clocks in the automaton and in the constants mentioned in the clock constraints.

Researchers have therefore developed a more efficient representation of the state space for timed automata, using the notions of *zones* and *reachability graphs*; see, for instance, Bengtsson and Yi (2003). Zones are (convex) unions of regions and give a coarser and more compact representation of the state space, in practice.

In order to define the notion of a zone over a set of clocks C, we need to consider the set $\mathcal{B}^+(C)$ of *extended clock constraints*. This is the collection of clock constraints generated by the grammar

$$g ::= x \bowtie n \mid x - y \bowtie n \mid g_1 \wedge g_2,$$

where $\bowtie \in \{\leq, <, =, >, \geq\}$. (Compare with Definition 10.1. A guard of the form $x - y \bowtie n$ is called a *diagonal constraint*.) The notion of satisfaction of a clock constraint $g \in \mathcal{B}^+(C)$ by a valuation is given by extending Definition 10.2 by the clause

$$v \models x - y \bowtie n \text{ iff } v(x) - v(y) \bowtie n.$$

Formally, a zone Z is a set of clock valuations described by an *extended clock constraint* $g_Z \in \mathcal{B}^+(C)$:

$$Z = \{v \mid v \models g_Z\}.$$

In the reachability graph for a timed automaton A, a symbolic state is a pair (ℓ, Z), where ℓ is a location and Z is a zone. As we shall see, the reachability of (ℓ, Z) will witness that all states (ℓ, v), where $v \in Z$, are reachable.

Exercise 11.23 *Show that any zone Z is convex by showing that for any extended clock constraint g the set $\{v \mid v \models g\}$ is convex. That is, argue that, for all valuations v, v' that satisfy g and each real number $0 < \lambda < 1$, the valuation v' defined by*

$$v'(x) = \lambda v(x) + (1 - \lambda)v'(x), \text{ for each clock } x,$$

also satisfies g. ◆

First, let us introduce two useful operations on zones.

Definition 11.15 Let Z be a zone and r a set of clocks. Then

- $Z^\uparrow = \{v + d \mid v \in Z \wedge d \in \mathbb{R}_{\geq 0}\}$, and
- $Z[r] = \{v[r] \mid v \in Z\}$.

◆

It may be shown that zones are closed under the two operations above. That is, whenever Z is described by an extended clock constraint g then there are extended clock constraints g' and g'' describing $Z^\uparrow$ and $Z[r]$. Symbolic transitions between symbolic states describe sets of corresponding concrete transitions.

Definition 11.16 The symbolic transition relation $\rightsquigarrow$ over symbolic states is defined as follows:

- $(\ell, Z) \rightsquigarrow (\ell, Z^\uparrow \wedge I(\ell))$, and
- $(\ell, Z) \rightsquigarrow (\ell', (Z \wedge g)[r] \wedge I(\ell'))$ if $\ell \xrightarrow{g,a,r} \ell'$.

♦

In Definition 11.16, the first clause corresponds to (simultaneously) performing delay transitions from all concrete states corresponding to (ℓ, Z). The resulting target zone consists of all the valuations in the 'future' of Z that satisfy the invariant of location ℓ. Similarly, the second clause corresponds to (simultaneously) performing the discrete action corresponding to the edge $\ell \xrightarrow{g,a,r} \ell'$. The resulting target zone consists of all the valuations that satisfy the invariant of location ℓ', and it may be obtained by resetting the clocks in r in valuations in the zone Z that meet the guard g. The symbolic semantics corresponds closely to the concrete semantics for the timed automaton, as stated by the following theorem.

Theorem 11.5 The following properties hold for any timed automaton A.

- Whenever $(\ell, Z) \rightsquigarrow (\ell', Z')$ and $v' \in Z'$ then $(\ell, v) \xrightarrow{\alpha} (\ell', v')$ for some $v \in Z$ and $\alpha \in \text{Act} \cup \mathbb{R}_{\geq 0}$.
- Whenever $(\ell, v) \xrightarrow{\alpha} (\ell', v')$ with $v \in Z$ then $(\ell, Z) \rightsquigarrow (\ell', Z')$ with $v' \in Z'$.

It follows from the above theorem that the symbolic semantics is both sound and complete with respect to reachability. Here soundness means that whenever the initial symbolic state $(\ell_0, \{v_0\})$ may lead to a symbolic state (ℓ', Z') according to $\rightsquigarrow^*$ then all concrete states (ℓ', v') with $v' \in Z'$ are reachable from the initial state. Completeness means that if a concrete state is reachable from the initial state then this may also be concluded using the symbolic transition relation.

Example 11.12 Reconsider the simple timed automaton from Figure 11.1. The following sequence of symbolic transitions, illustrated in Figure 11.3, proves that

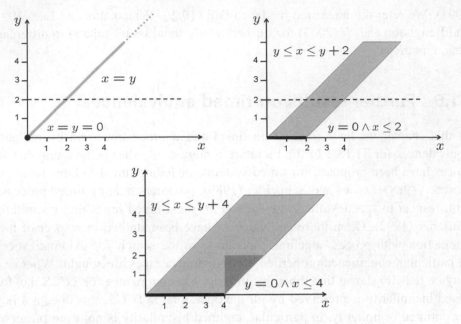

Figure 11.3 Symbolic exploration of the timed automaton in Figure 11.1.

the location ℓ_1 is indeed reachable:

$$
\begin{aligned}
(\ell_0, x = y = 0) &\rightsquigarrow (\ell_0, x = y) \\
&\rightsquigarrow (\ell_0, y = 0 \wedge x \leq 2) \\
&\rightsquigarrow (\ell_0, y \leq x \leq y + 2) \\
&\rightsquigarrow (\ell_0, y = 0 \wedge x \leq 4) \\
&\rightsquigarrow (\ell_0, y \leq x \leq y + 4) \\
&\rightsquigarrow (\ell_1, y \leq 2 \wedge 4 \leq x \leq y + 4).
\end{aligned}
$$

♦

Note that the shaded areas in the figure represent the 'futures' of the zones described by the solid lines. The darker grey area in the bottom figure describes the zone when location l_1 is reached.

Essentially, all tools that build on the theory of timed automata – for example, KRONOS (Bozga *et al.*, 1998) and UPPAAL (Behrmann *et al.*, 2004) – nowadays use zones as the basis of their verification engines, in combination with various strategies for searching the symbolic reachability graph. Let us conclude this section by mentioning that zones are often stored in memory in a data structure called *difference bound matrix* (Bellman, 1957, Dill, 1989, Yannakakis and Lee,

1993). We refer the interested reader to Dill (1989), Yannakakis and Lee (1993) and Bengtsson and Yi (2003) for further details about issues related to difference bound matrices.

11.6 Further results on timed equivalences

In this chapter we have focused on timed and untimed trace and bisimulation equivalences for TLTSs. In the literature a number of other behavioural equivalences have been proposed for timed systems, including timed failures Reed and Roscoe (1988), Davies and Schneider (1989), preorders relating timed processes with respect to speed Moller and Tofts (1991) and timed branching bisimilarity Klusener (1992). Often these equivalences have been studied in respect of their interaction with process-algebraic operators, in the search for axiomatizations. In particular, congruence properties of these equivalences are sought. Whereas it may be (easily) shown that timed bisimilarity is a congruence for TCCS, i.e. that timed bisimilarity is preserved by all the operators of TCCS, this does not hold for untimed bisimilarity. In particular, untimed bisimilarity is not even preserved by parallel composition. A surprising result is that timed bisimilarity is the largest congruence over TCCS included in untimed-bisimulation equivalence (Larsen and Yi, 1994).

The region-graph construction provides a universal tool for showing the decidability of a number of problems related to timed automata. In particular, it has been used for proving reachability and untimed-language equivalence for timed automata decidable in PSPACE (polynomial space) (Alur and Dill, 1994). Also, untimed bisimilarity for timed automata has been proved decidable in EXPTIME (deterministic exponential time) using regions (Larsen and Yi, 1997). A practically more efficient algorithm for untimed bisimilarity using zones is given in Alur *et al.*, (1992). Somewhat surprisingly, even timed bisimilarity for timed automata is decidable: using region graphs on a product construction, timed bisimilarity was shown to be decidable in EXPTIME Čerāns (1993).

Unfortunately, timed-language equivalence for timed automata is known to be undecidable (Alur and Dill, 1994). In fact, even the problem of universality testing – i.e. whether a given timed automaton generates *all* timed traces – is undecidable. Strongly related to these undecidability results are the facts that the class of timed languages described by timed automata is not closed under complement and that there are timed languages that are not describable by any *deterministic* timed automaton. To overcome these negative results, the notion of event-clock automata was proposed in Alur, Fix and Henzinger (1999) as a determinizable subclass of timed automata. Here for each action there is a unique clock recording the time elapsed since the last occurrence of that action.

The notions of timed and untimed bisimilarity as well as region graphs, zones and the reachability algorithms based on them can be directly transferred to network scenarios. The advantages of networks of timed automata for the modelling of systems are accompanied by a collection of pleasing theoretical results. For example, reachability problems for a single timed automaton as well as for a network are both PSPACE-complete (the reader is referred to Aceto and Laroussinie (2002) for further details on the complexity of verification problems for networks of timed automata), so – at least from the theoretical complexity point of view – the increase in the complexity of verification problems is not as dramatic as the reader might have thought at first glance. The theoretically minded reader might wish to compare this situation to that arising in the verification of untimed concurrent systems. In that setting, the modelling power that is gained in moving from single automata to networks of automata has a price: the complexity of verification problems increases dramatically over networks. You can find a discussion of this issue, and pointers to further reading, in the paper Aceto and Laroussinie (2002).

In order to understand the nature of the class of timed languages generated by timed automata, various extensions of regular expressions with time have been proposed (Asarin, Caspi and Maler, 2002; Dima, 2001; Bouyer and Petit, 2002). Also, the class of timed languages accepted by timed automata with ε-transitions has been studied (Bérard *et al.*, 1998)

For an overview of open questions and challenges in the area of timed languages and models we refer the interested reader to Asarin (2004).

12

Hennessy–Milner logic with time

Introduction

In Sections 11.1 and 11.2, we introduced some notions of behavioural equivalence over real-time systems specified by means of timed automata. These equivalences are based on various adaptations to the timed setting of the classic notions of trace equivalence and bisimilarity over LTSs – as presented in Sections 3.2 and 3.3 of this book – and may be used to perform implementation verification for real-time systems. This is useful because, at least in principle, a formalism like that of timed automata can be used to describe both actual systems and their specifications and, as we saw in Section 11.6, these notions of behavioural equivalence are decidable over (networks) of timed automata, with the notable exception of timed trace equivalence.

However, as we have already noted in the setting of modelling and verification for classic untimed reactive systems, when establishing the correctness of our system with respect to a specification using the methodology of implementation verification, we are forced to specify in some way the overall behaviour of the system under consideration. In a real-time setting, this often means that our specifications need to take into account many details pertaining to the timing behaviour of the implementation under analysis. This may lead to overly complex and subtle specifications. Moreover, sometimes we are interested only in specifying the expected behaviour of the system in certain specific circumstances.

Suppose, for instance, that all we want to specify for our system is that each a-labelled transition must be followed by a b-labelled transition within 2 time units. Expressing this requirement, and similar ones, in terms of observational equivalence is rather unnatural. In the setting of classic reactive systems, we saw in Chapter 5 that the so-called Hennessy–Milner logic (HML) is a suitable formalism

220

67 In Exercise 9: Section 3 $\longmapsto$ Sections 3 and 4

76 Line -5: 2(1) $\longmapsto$ 2(2)

80 Line -3: one-to one $\longmapsto$ one-to-one

97 Line 11: $Q - i \longmapsto Q_i$ Line 12: $P'_i = Q'_i[f_i] \longmapsto P'_i = Q'_i[f_i]$

98 Line 11: $P_2|Q' \overset{\alpha}{\leftrightarrows} P_2|Q' \longmapsto P_2|Q \overset{\alpha}{\leftrightarrows} P_2|Q'$

101 In Exercise 6: Proposition 14 $\longmapsto$ Proposition 12

102 Line -11: $E'_1|E'_2 \longmapsto E'_1|E'_2$

102 Lines -10, -8 (four times): $\{P/X\} \longmapsto \{\tilde{P}/\tilde{X}\}$

102 Line -2: X does not occur $\longmapsto$ no $X \in \tilde{X}$ occurs

104 Lines 11, 14, 17 (six times): $R \longmapsto \mathcal{R}$

108 Line -9: (Definition 7) $\longmapsto$ (Definition 5)

119 Line 9: $\backslash c \longmapsto \backslash c_i$

125 In rows (4), (8), (10) and (12) of table: $Mal \longmapsto Mal'$

126 Line -12: $Usem(j) \longmapsto Usetool(j)$

133 Line 9 (excluding diagram): Expansion $\longmapsto$ expansion

135 Line 25: basic the $\longmapsto$ basic

1

it took me a year to work out the courage to ...

Communication and Concurrency
ERRATA

This note lists some errata in my book **Communication and Concurrency** (Prentice Hall 1989). The first section is a list of minor errata; the second section deals with a rather more important correction to Definition 5.8. In the errata the symbol $\longmapsto$ is used to signify replacement, and 'Line -3' means the third line from bottom.

This is a good opportunity to point out that you can obtain a Solutions Manual, with solutions to all the exercises, if you write to Helen Martin at Prentice Hall International (UK) Ltd, 66 Wood Lane End, Hemel Hempstead, Hertfordshire HP2 4RG, UK.

Robin Milner, Edinburgh, November 1990

PAGE

9 Line 9: $\{f(l) : l \in L\} \longmapsto \{l : f(l) \in L\}$

9 Last line under Action Constructions: Product $\longmapsto$ product

52 Line -2: $1(2) \longmapsto 2(2)$ Line -1: $1(1) \longmapsto 2(1)$

56 Line 4: $E \longmapsto \mathcal{E}$ Line -11: $\sum_{v \in V} E_v \longmapsto \sum_{v \in V} \mathbf{in}_v.E_v$

for specifying properties of reactive systems. Indeed, not only does HML allow us to express natural requirements on the behaviour of reactive systems but, as originally shown by Hennessy and Milner in one of the most satisfying results in the theory of concurrent processes, it captures precisely all the behavioural properties of reactive systems that are relevant with respect to bisimilarity – recall Theorem 5.1.

Since HML is a convenient formalism for the description of behavioural properties of reactive systems modelled semantically as LTSs, and since the semantics of timed automata is given in terms of TLTSs (see Definition 9.1), it is natural to try to define a notion of HML for real-time systems. In what follows, our aim will be to motivate and introduce this variation on HML, argue by means of examples that it allows us to specify properties of real-time systems modelled as TLTSs or timed automata and investigate the use of regions introduced in Section 11.4 for the decidability of model checking. We will also study the relationship of this variation on HML to timed bisimilarity. As we shall see, the overall collection of results that we shall obtain mirrors, and is just as satisfying as, that presented in Chapter 5

12.1 Basic logic

As you might recall from our developments in Chapter 5, Hennessy–Milner logic is a modal logic obtained by adding to the syntax of boolean logic two modal operators that allow us to express properties of reactive systems (modelled as LTSs) which relate to the effect that the performing of actions has on the behaviour of these systems. More specifically, we recall, for the sake of clarity, that

- a process satisfies a formula of the form $\langle a \rangle F$ for some $a \in$ Act iff it affords an a-labelled transition leading to a state satisfying F, and
- a process satisfies a formula of the form $[a]F$ for some $a \in$ Act iff all its a-labelled transitions lead to a state satisfying F.

Formulae of the form $\langle a \rangle F$ express the 'possible behaviour' of processes, whereas formulae of the form $[a]F$ describe their 'necessary behaviour' – that is, properties that must hold for each of their a-derivatives.

Timed labelled transition systems, as presented in Definition 9.1, are just ordinary LTSs that have transitions whose labels can be also time delays. If we are to follow the lead of Hennessy and Milner in defining a modal logic for describing the properties of TLTSs, it seems therefore reasonable to augment the syntax of HML with two new modalities that can be used to express the possible and the necessary behaviour of systems as time progresses. Following the notation introduced in Laroussinie *et al.* (1995), these two new 'time modalities' will be denoted by $\exists$ and $\mathbb{W}$ respectively.

By analogy with the two classic action modalities, we expect that

- a process satisfies a formula of the form $\exists F$ iff it *can delay for some amount of time* thereby reaching a state satisfying F, and
- a process satisfies a formula of the form $\mathbb{W}F$ iff *no matter how long it delays* it will always reach a state satisfying F.

For instance, we would expect that the initial states of the following two timed automata (introduced in Example 11.4),

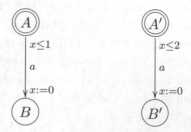

both satisfy the formula $\exists\langle a\rangle t\!t$ (as both these states can perform action a immediately) but that neither satisfies the formula $\mathbb{W}\langle a\rangle t\!t$ (since both can delay 2.1 time units, say, and reach a state where the a-action is no longer possible).

However, the mere addition of these two action modalities to HML does not suffice to express all the timing properties of systems that we should like to describe. For instance, we previously mentioned the property that

> each a-labelled transition is followed by a b-labelled transition within 2 time units

as an example of a property that we wish to express using our variant of HML. A brief examination of the behaviour of the two timed automata above leads us to expect that the automaton on the right enjoys the following property:

an a-labelled transition is possible after a delay of 2 time units.

However, the initial state of the automaton on the left should not afford this property.

Both of the aforementioned properties make explicit reference to time delays, and it seems therefore reasonable to extend our variant on HML with some way of expressing 'quantitative real-time constraints'. The design decisions taken by Alur and Dill in their development of timed automata provide us with suitable inspiration here. Timed automata use clock resets and guards to specify real-time constraints on the behaviour of real-time systems. For instance, we might specify that a b-action is to follow an a-action within 2 time units by resetting a clock x upon the performance of an a-labelled edge leading to a location ℓ and adjoining a guard such as $x \leq 2$ to b-labelled edges that emanate from ℓ. We shall therefore augment our variant on HML with clock constraints (whose syntax will take the form given in Definition 10.1) and clock resets. Intuitively, a formula of the form

$$x \text{ \underline{in} } F$$

says that a state in a TLTS will satisfy F after the value of x has been set to zero. For instance, the formula

$$y \text{ \underline{in} } \exists (y > 1 \wedge \langle a \rangle t\!t)$$

states intuitively that it is possible to delay more than 1 time unit and thereby to reach a state in which an a-labelled transition is possible. We shall assume for simplicity that the clocks used in the formulae are disjoint with the clocks that appear in timed automata (in the case where timed automata are used to generate the underlying timed transition systems).

We are now ready to present the syntax of Hennessy–Milner logic with time.

Definition 12.1 The set of Hennessy–Milner formulae with time (from now on referred to as $\mathcal{M}_t$) over a set of actions Act and a set of formula clocks D is given by the following abstract syntax:

$$F ::= t\!t \mid f\!f \mid F \wedge G \mid F \vee G \mid \langle a \rangle F \mid [a]F \mid \exists F \mid \forall F \mid x \text{ \underline{in} } F \mid g,$$

where $a \in$ Act, $x \in D$ and $g \in \mathcal{B}(D)$. (Recall that $\mathcal{B}(D)$ is the collection of guards over the set of clocks D; see Definition 10.1.) ◆

In writing formulae, we shall sometimes use the same abbreviations as those introduced in Definition 5.1. In particular we recall, for the sake of clarity, that, if $A = \{a_1, \dots, a_n\} \subseteq$ Act $(n \geq 0)$, we use the abbreviation $\langle A \rangle F$ for the formula $\langle a_1 \rangle F \vee \cdots \vee \langle a_n \rangle F$ and $[A]F$ for the formula $[a_1]F \wedge \cdots \wedge [a_n]F$. (If $A = \emptyset$ then $\langle A \rangle F = f\!f$ and $[A]F = t\!t$.)

We are interested in using the above logic to describe properties of states in a TLTS over the set of actions Act. The semantics of a formula in the language $\mathcal{M}_t$ is given by characterizing the collection of states that satisfy it. We have already presented the intuitive meaning of all the constructs in the logic; however, there is still a subtlety that needs to be dealt with before we can present the formal definition of the semantics of our variant on HML with time.

Clock constraints are first-class formulae in our language, and we wish to be able to determine whether a state in a TLTS satisfies a clock constraint. But when does a state satisfy the constraint $y > 1$, say? In our example formula

$$y \text{ \underline{in} } \exists (y > 1 \wedge \langle a \rangle t\!t),$$

we used this constraint as part of the formula to specify that we wish that a state from which an a-labelled transition is possible is reached after a delay of more than 1 time unit.

The answer to the question above is classic in logic: in order to determine whether a state satisfies a guard we need to make reference to a valuation for the clocks in the set D. The valuation will be used to check whether clock constraints are met.

The semantics of formulae is given with respect to a given TLTS

$$(\mathsf{Proc}, \mathsf{Lab}, \{\xrightarrow{\alpha} \mid \alpha \in \mathsf{Lab}\}).$$

An *extended state* over Proc is a pair (p, u), where p is a state in Proc and u is a time assignment for D, i.e. a mapping $D \to \mathbb{R}_{\geq 0}$. The set of extended states over Proc will be denoted by $\mathcal{ES}(\mathsf{Proc})$. We shall use $\llbracket F \rrbracket$, where F is a formula in $\mathcal{M}_{\mathsf{t}}$, to denote the set of extended states over Proc that satisfy F. This we now proceed to define formally.

Definition 12.2 We define $\llbracket F \rrbracket \subseteq \mathcal{ES}(\mathsf{Proc})$ for $F \in \mathcal{M}_{\mathsf{t}}$ by

$$\llbracket \mathit{tt} \rrbracket = \mathcal{ES}(\mathsf{Proc}), \qquad\qquad\qquad \llbracket F \vee G \rrbracket = \llbracket F \rrbracket \cup \llbracket G \rrbracket,$$

$$\llbracket \mathit{ff} \rrbracket = \emptyset, \qquad\qquad\qquad\qquad \llbracket \langle a \rangle F \rrbracket = \langle \cdot a \cdot \rangle \llbracket F \rrbracket,$$

$$\llbracket F \wedge G \rrbracket = \llbracket F \rrbracket \cap \llbracket G \rrbracket, \qquad\qquad \llbracket [a] F \rrbracket = [\cdot a \cdot] \llbracket F \rrbracket,$$

$$\llbracket \exists F \rrbracket = \langle \cdot \varepsilon \cdot \rangle \llbracket F \rrbracket, \qquad\qquad\qquad \llbracket \forall F \rrbracket = [\cdot \varepsilon \cdot] \llbracket F \rrbracket,$$

$$\llbracket x \underline{\mathrm{in}}\, F \rrbracket = \{(p, u) \mid (p, u[x \mapsto 0]) \in \llbracket F \rrbracket\}, \quad \llbracket g \rrbracket = \{(p, u) \mid p \in \mathsf{Proc}, u \models g\},$$

where we have used the set operators

$$\langle \cdot a \cdot \rangle, [\cdot a \cdot], \langle \cdot \varepsilon \cdot \rangle, [\cdot \varepsilon \cdot] : \mathcal{P}(\mathcal{ES}(\mathsf{Proc})) \to \mathcal{P}(\mathcal{ES}(\mathsf{Proc}))$$

defined by

$$\langle \cdot a \cdot \rangle S = \{(p, u) \in \mathcal{ES}(\mathsf{Proc}) \mid \exists p'.\ p \xrightarrow{a} p' \text{ and } (p', u) \in S\},$$

$$[\cdot a \cdot] S = \{(p, u) \in \mathcal{ES}(\mathsf{Proc}) \mid \forall p'.\ p \xrightarrow{a} p' \text{ implies } (p', u) \in S\},$$

$$\langle \cdot \varepsilon \cdot \rangle S = \{(p, u) \in \mathcal{ES}(\mathsf{Proc}) \mid \exists d \in \mathbb{R}_{\geq 0}.\ \exists p' \in \mathsf{Proc}.\ p \xrightarrow{d} p' \text{ and }$$
$$(p', u + d) \in S\},$$

$$[\cdot \varepsilon \cdot] S = \{(p, u) \in \mathcal{ES}(\mathsf{Proc}) \mid \forall d \in \mathbb{R}_{\geq 0}.\ \forall p' \in \mathsf{Proc}.\ p \xrightarrow{d} p' \text{ implies }$$
$$(p', u + d) \in S\}.$$

We write $(p, u) \models F$ iff $(p, u) \in \llbracket F \rrbracket$.

Two formulae are *equivalent* if, iff they are satisfied by the same extended states in every TLTS.   ♦

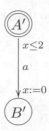

Figure 12.1 A simple timed automaton.

Definition 12.3 A state p in a TLTS satisfies a formula F (written $p \models F$) iff $(p, u_0) \models F$ where u_0 is the clock valuation mapping each formula clock to zero. ◆

Note that the above definitions apply equally well to the TLTS $T(A)$ generated from a timed automaton A. For this TLTS, however, extended states take the (notationally slightly unpleasant) form $((\ell, v), u)$, where v is a valuation for the set of clocks C in A and u is a valuation for the set of clocks D used in writing the formulae in $\mathcal{M}_t$. *From now on, we shall always tacitly assume that the set of clocks used in formulae is disjoint from that used in timed automata.* This means that reset operations on clocks from one of these sets will not have any effect on clocks in the other. So, when specialized over a TLTS of the form $T(A)$, the semantics of a formula of the form $x \underline{in} F$ becomes

$$[\![x \underline{in} F]\!] = \{((\ell, v), u) \mid ((\ell, v), u[x \mapsto 0]) \in [\![F]\!]\}. \tag{12.1}$$

Note how the reset operation only applies to clock x, whereas the values of each clock in the automaton A remain unchanged because we are requiring that

$$((\ell, v), u[x \mapsto 0]) \in [\![F]\!].$$

Definition 12.4 A timed automaton A satisfies a formula $F \in \mathcal{M}_t$ iff

$$((\ell_0, v_0), u_0) \models F,$$

where ℓ_0 is the initial location in A and v_0, u_0 are clock valuations respectively mapping each clock variable in the automaton and in the formula to zero. ◆

To understand better the above definition of the semantics of formulae in $\mathcal{M}_t$, it is instructive to use the formal definition of the semantics of $\mathcal{M}_t$ to establish that the initial state of the timed automaton of Figure 12.1 satisfies the formula

$$y \underline{in} \exists (3 \geq y > 1 \wedge \langle a \rangle t\!t).$$

To see that this holds, we use (12.1) to derive that

$$((A', [x = 0]), [y = 0]) \models y \underline{\text{in}}\ \exists(3 \geq y > 1 \wedge \langle a \rangle t\!t)$$
$$\text{iff } ((A', [x = 0]), [y = 0]) \models \exists(3 \geq y > 1 \wedge \langle a \rangle t\!t).$$

Now, observe that to establish that

$$((A', [x = 0]), [y = 0]) \models \exists(3 \geq y > 1 \wedge \langle a \rangle t\!t)$$

it suffices to find a $d \in \mathbb{R}_{\geq 0}$ such that

$$((A', [x = d]), [y = d]) \models 3 \geq y > 1 \wedge \langle a \rangle t\!t.$$

(Why?) It is easy to find such a d. In fact, each d in the interval $(1, 2]$ would do because if d lies in this interval then $[y = d] \models 3 \geq y > 1$ and $(A', [x = d]) \xrightarrow{a} (B', [x = 0])$ both hold.

As you might have noticed already, the above reasoning does in fact show that *any* extended state of the form $((A', [x = 0]), [y = d])$ satisfies the formula $y \underline{\text{in}}\ \exists(3 \geq y > 1 \wedge \langle a \rangle t\!t)$, regardless of the value of d. This is so because the use of the formula clock y in the clock constraint $3 \geq y > 1$ is within the scope of a $y \underline{\text{in}}$-construct. We call formulae in which each occurrence of a formula clock z in a clock constraint is within the scope of a $z \underline{\text{in}}$-construct *closed*. For example, the formula $y \underline{\text{in}}\ \exists y = 1$ is closed, whereas $y = 1$ and $(y \underline{\text{in}}\ \exists y = 1) \wedge (y \leq 2)$ are not.

If F is a closed formula then the collection of extended states satisfying F is independent of the valuation u for the formula clocks. This means that if F is closed then for each state p in a TLTS and valuations u, u' for the formula clocks we have that

$$(p, u) \models F \text{ iff } (p, u') \models F.$$

Therefore, when F is closed it makes sense to speak of a state p satisfying F, and we shall tacitly do so from hereon. For a timed automaton A and closed formula F, the suggestive shorthand $A \models F$ will be used in lieu of $((\ell_0, v_0), u_0) \models F$. *In what follows, whenever we say that a state in a TLTS satisfies a formula, we shall always assume that the formula is closed unless specified otherwise.*

Exercise 12.1 *Prove that, as claimed above, if F is a closed formula then the collection of extended states satisfying it is independent of the valuation u for the formula clocks. Does this hold for arbitrary formulae in $\mathcal{M}_t$?* ♦

Let us now try to use the logic $\mathcal{M}_t$ to express formally the following property of a state in a TLTS.

> Each a-labelled transition is followed by a b-labelled transition within 2 time units.

We can express that a b-labelled transition is available within 2 time units by means of the closed formula

$$y \; \underline{\text{in}} \; \exists (y \leq 2 \wedge \langle b \rangle t\!t).$$

Indeed, you should be able to convince yourself that a state s satisfies the above formula iff $s \xrightarrow{d} s' \xrightarrow{b}$ for some state s' and real number d in the interval $[0, 2]$. (Do so!) All we need to do now to express the desired property is to realize that the natural-language description 'each a-labelled transition' can be expressed in terms of the $[a]$-operator of HML. The resulting formula is therefore

$$[a](y \; \underline{\text{in}} \; \exists (y \leq 2 \wedge \langle b \rangle t\!t)).$$

As a further example, consider the following timed automaton:

We argued in Example 10.5 that this timed automaton can delay by 2 units of time, thereby reaching a state in which no a-labelled transition is possible. This can be expressed in the language $\mathcal{M}_t$ by means of the formula

$$y \; \underline{\text{in}} \; \exists (y = 2 \wedge [a] f\!f).$$

Moreover, you should be able to argue that this timed automaton also satisfies the formula $\exists [a] f\!f$. (Do so!) Furthermore, does it satisfy the formula

$$[a](y \; \underline{\text{in}} \; \exists (y = 1 \wedge \langle a \rangle t\!t))?$$

Exercise 12.2 *Use the logic $\mathcal{M}_t$ to formulate properties of the timed automata in Example 11.4, and argue that the two automata have (respectively do not have) those properties using the semantics of the logic $\mathcal{M}_t$. Can you give examples of properties that both timed automata afford?* ◆

Exercise 12.3
1. *Consider the formulae $y \; \underline{\text{in}} \; y = 0$ and $y \; \underline{\text{in}} \; y > 0$. Can you offer equivalent formulations of the properties described by these formulae?*
2. *Argue that the formulae $\exists \exists F$ and $\exists F$ are equivalent for each formula F. Are the formulae $\forall \forall F$ and $\forall F$ also equivalent?*
3. *Show that $[\cdot \varepsilon \cdot] \mathcal{ES}(\mathsf{Proc})$ and $\langle \cdot \varepsilon \cdot \rangle \mathcal{ES}(\mathsf{Proc})$ are both equal to $\mathcal{ES}(\mathsf{Proc})$. To what are the formulae $\forall t\!t$ and $[a] t\!t$ equivalent?*
4. *Argue that $(p, u) \models \forall \langle a \rangle t\!t$ iff $(p, u) \not\models \exists [a] f\!f$.*
5. *Prove that the formulae $x \; \underline{\text{in}} \; (y \; \underline{\text{in}} \; \exists F)$ and $y \; \underline{\text{in}} \; (x \; \underline{\text{in}} \; \exists F)$ are equivalent for any formula F. Are the two formulae $x \; \underline{\text{in}} \; \exists (y \; \underline{\text{in}} \; \exists F)$ and $y \; \underline{\text{in}} \; \exists (x \; \underline{\text{in}} \; \exists F)$ also equivalent? If yes, prove it, if not, give a counterexample.* ◆

As for standard Hennessy–Milner logic, it is sometimes useful to have an alternative characterization of the satisfaction relation $\models$ presented in Definition 12.2. This can be obtained by defining the binary relation $\models$ as relating extended states to formulae by structural induction on formulae, as follows.

$(p, u) \models \textit{tt}$ for each (p, u),

$(p, u) \models \textit{ff}$ for no (p, u),

$(p, u) \models F \wedge G$ iff $(p, u) \models F$ and $(p, u) \models G$,

$(p, u) \models F \vee G$ iff $(p, u) \models F$ or $(p, u) \models G$,

$(p, u) \models \langle a \rangle F$ iff $p \xrightarrow{a} p'$ for some p' such that $(p', u) \models F$,

$(p, u) \models [a]F$ iff whenever $p \xrightarrow{a} p'$ then $(p', u) \models F$,

$(p, u) \models \exists F$ iff $p \xrightarrow{d} p'$ for some p' and $d \in \mathbb{R}_{\geq 0}$ such that $(p', u + d) \models F$,

$(p, u) \models \mathbb{W}F$ iff $(p', u + d) \models F$ for each $d \in \mathbb{R}_{\geq 0}$ and p' such that $p \xrightarrow{d} p'$,

$(p, u) \models y \underline{\text{in}} F$ iff $(p, u[y \mapsto 0]) \models F$,

$(p, u) \models g$ iff $u \models g$.

Exercise 12.4 *Show that the above definition of the satisfaction relation is indeed equivalent to that given in Definition 12.2. Hint: Use induction on the structure of formulae.*   ♦

Note that, as was the case with classic Hennessy–Milner logic (see the discussion after Exercise 5.7), logical negation is *not* one of the constructs in the abstract syntax for $\mathcal{M}_t$. However, there we argued that the language $\mathcal{M}$ *is* closed under negation, in the sense that for each formula $F \in \mathcal{M}$ there is a formula $F^c \in \mathcal{M}$ that is equivalent to the negation of F. This result carries over to the setting of $\mathcal{M}_t$. The formula F^c is defined by structural induction on F by extending the clauses dealing with the constructs of classic Hennessy–Milner logic listed after Exercise 5.7, as follows:

$$(\exists F)^c = \mathbb{W}F^c,$$
$$(\mathbb{W}F)^c = \exists F^c,$$
$$(y \underline{\text{in}} F)^c = y \underline{\text{in}} F^c,$$
$$(y \leq n)^c = y > n,$$
$$(y < n)^c = y \geq n,$$
$$(y = n)^c = (y < n) \vee (y > n),$$
$$(y > n)^c = y \leq n,$$
$$(y \geq n)^c = y < n.$$

Note that the 'negation' of the clock constraint $y = n$ is *not* itself a clock constraint but rather a formula in $\mathcal{M}_t$. This is inevitable because, as we saw in Exercise 10.3, the negation of $y = n$ cannot be expressed as a clock constraint. (This is a good time for you to go back and solve that exercise if you have not done so already!)

Example 12.1 The negation of the formula $y \underline{\text{in}} \exists (y = 2 \wedge \langle a \rangle tt)$ is the formula $y \underline{\text{in}} \forall (y < 2 \vee y > 2 \vee [a] ff)$. ◆

Exercise 12.5 *Negate the formula* $\forall [a] ff \vee x \underline{\text{in}} \exists (x = 1 \wedge \langle a \rangle tt)$. ◆

Proposition 12.1 Let $(\mathsf{Proc}, \mathsf{Lab}, \{ \xrightarrow{\alpha} \mid \alpha \in \mathsf{Lab} \})$ be a TLTS. Then, for every formula $F \in \mathcal{M}_t$, it holds that $[\![F^c]\!] = \mathcal{ES}(\mathsf{Proc}) \setminus [\![F]\!]$.

Proof. The proposition can be proved by structural induction on F. The details are left as an exercise for the reader. □

Exercise 12.6
1. *Prove Proposition 12.1.*
2. *Prove, furthermore, that* $(F^c)^c = F$ *for every formula* $F \in \mathcal{M}_t$. *Hint: Use structural induction on* F.

◆

As a consequence of Proposition 12.1 we have that, for each extended state (p, u) and formula F, exactly one of $(p, u) \models F$ and $(p, u) \models F^c$ holds. In fact, each extended state is exclusively contained either in $[\![F]\!]$ or in $[\![F^c]\!]$.

Exercise 12.7 (Recommended) *Another natural way to introduce time-delay operators* $\exists$ *and* $\forall$ *that can specify particular time durations would be to decorate these operators with time intervals. For example, the formula* $\exists_{[3,5)} F$ *would mean that it is possible to perform a time delay, greater than or equal to 3 time units but strictly less than 5 time units, such that the formula* F *holds afterwards. Similarly,* $\forall_{(2,7)} F$ *stands for the fact that after all possible time delays, strictly between 2 and 7 time units, the formula* F *must hold.*

1. *Define formally the syntax and semantics of the above-mentioned variant of HML with time.*
2. *Prove that for any such formula one can construct an equivalent formula from* $\mathcal{M}_t$. *Hint: Use structural induction.*

◆

12.2 Hennessy–Milner logic with time and regions

In Section 11.4 we introduced the notions of regions and region graphs and used them to prove that reachability and untimed bisimilarity are decidable for timed automata. In this section we shall see that the notion of regions is also the key tool for proving the decidability of model-checking problems for timed automata in respect of Hennessy–Milner logic with time.

More precisely, we will show the decidability of (model-checking) problems of the form $((\ell, v), u) \models F$, where (ℓ, v) is a state of a given timed automaton A, ℓ being the location of A and v a valuation for the set of clocks C of A; F is a formula in $\mathcal{M}_t$ and u is a valuation for the set of formula clocks D. In order to achieve this aim we will consider *symbolic model-checking* problems of the form

$$[\ell, \gamma] \vdash F,$$

where γ is a region over $C \cup D$, i.e. a region over the *disjoint union* of the sets of formula clocks and automata clocks. In constructing such a region γ, the maximal constant associated with a formula clock is the largest integer with which that clock is compared in the formula F.

Before defining $\vdash$ formally, we introduce some notation for regions. According to Exercises 11.12–11.14, the notion of constraint satisfaction as well as the reset and delay operations for clock valuations may be lifted to regions. For a region γ and a constraint g we say that γ satisfies g, written $\gamma \models g$, if $v \models g$ for some (or, equivalently, all) $v \in \gamma$. Similarly, for two regions γ and γ' and a set of clocks r, we say that γ' is the reset of γ with respect to r, written $\gamma' = \gamma[r]$, if $v[r] \in \gamma'$ for some (or, equivalently, all) $v \in \gamma$. Finally, for two regions γ and γ', we say that γ' is a delay successor of γ, written $\gamma \rightsquigarrow \gamma'$, if for each $v \in \gamma$ there exists $d \in \mathbb{R}_{\geq 0}$ such that $v + d \in \gamma'$.

Definition 12.5 Let A be a timed automaton with clock set C, and consider formulae over $\mathcal{M}_t$ with a set of formula clocks D, where C and D are disjoint. If ℓ is a location of A, F is a formula and γ is a region over $C \cup D$ such that $\gamma \models I(\ell)$, we define symbolic satisfaction $[\ell, \gamma] \vdash F$ as follows:

$[\ell, \gamma] \vdash \mathit{tt}$ for each $[\ell, \gamma]$,

$[\ell, \gamma] \vdash \mathit{ff}$ for no $[\ell, \gamma]$,

$[\ell, \gamma] \vdash F \wedge G$ iff $[\ell, \gamma] \vdash F$ and $[\ell, \gamma] \vdash G$,

$[\ell, \gamma] \vdash F \vee G$ iff $[\ell, \gamma] \vdash F$ or $[\ell, \gamma] \vdash G$,

$[\ell, \gamma] \vdash \langle a \rangle F$ iff there is an edge $\ell \xrightarrow{g,a,r} \ell'$ in A with $\gamma \models g$ and $[\ell', \gamma[r]] \vdash F$,

$[\ell, \gamma] \vdash [a] F$ iff whenever $\ell \xrightarrow{g,a,r} \ell'$ is an edge in A such that $\gamma \models g$ then $[\ell', \gamma[r]] \vdash F$,

$[\ell, \gamma] \vdash \exists F$ iff $\gamma \rightsquigarrow \gamma'$ for some γ' such that $\gamma' \models I(\ell)$ and $[\ell, \gamma'] \vdash F$,

$[\ell, \gamma] \vdash \mathbb{W} F$ iff whenever $\gamma \rightsquigarrow \gamma'$ with $\gamma' \models I(\ell)$ then $[\ell, \gamma'] \vdash F$.

◆

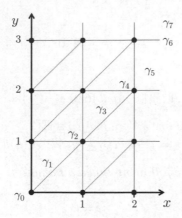

Figure 12.2 Regions for $c_x = 2$ and $c_y = 3$.

Importantly, symbolic model checking is in agreement with ordinary model checking, as stated in the following theorem and as discussed in more detail in Laroussinie *et al.* (1995).

Theorem 12.1 Let A be a timed automaton with clock set C and consider formulae over $\mathcal{M}_t$ with a set of formula clocks D, C and D being disjoint. Then

$$((\ell, v), u) \models F \text{ iff } [\ell, [vu]] \vdash F,$$

where v is a valuation over C, u is a valuation over D and vu is the valuation over $C \cup D$ such that $vu(z)$ equals $v(z)$ for $z \in C$ and $u(z)$ otherwise.

To illustrate the use of this theorem let us reconsider the timed automaton in Figure 12.1 and show that its initial state satisfies the formula

$$y \underline{\text{ in }} \exists (3 \geq y > 1 \wedge \langle a \rangle \mathit{tt}).$$

In this example, clearly $C = \{x\}$ and $D = \{y\}$. From the timed automaton and the given formula we see that the maximum constants are $c_x = 2$ and $c_y = 3$, and the relevant regions are thus the ones given in Figure 12.2. In this figure, for ease of reference we have named as $\gamma_0, \gamma_1, \ldots, \gamma_7$ the delay successors of the region γ_0. We note that $\gamma_i \rightsquigarrow \gamma_j$ whenever $i \leq j$. (Why?) Following Definition 12.5 we see that

$$[A', \gamma_0] \vdash y \underline{\text{ in }} \exists (3 \geq y > 1 \wedge \langle a \rangle \mathit{tt})$$
$$\text{iff } [A', \gamma_0] \vdash \exists (3 \geq y > 1 \wedge \langle a \rangle \mathit{tt})$$
$$\text{iff } [A', \gamma_i] \vdash (3 \geq y > 1) \wedge \langle a \rangle \mathit{tt} \text{ for some } 0 \leq i \leq 7.$$

Observe that

$$[A', \gamma_i] \vdash (3 \geq y > 1) \text{ for } 3 \leq i \leq 6$$

and

$$[A', \gamma_i] \vdash \langle a \rangle t\!t \text{ for } 0 \leq i \leq 4 .$$

We may therefore conclude that $[A', \gamma_0] \vdash y \ \underline{\text{in}} \ \exists (3 \geq y > 1 \wedge \langle a \rangle t\!t)$, and hence that $((A', [x = 0]), [y = 0]) \models y \ \underline{\text{in}} \ \exists (3 \geq y > 1 \wedge \langle a \rangle t\!t)$.

Exercise 12.8 *Consider the following timed automaton:*

$$x \leq 2 \ \textcircled{\small{ℓ_0}} \overset{x:=0 \quad a}{\underset{x \leq 1}{\curvearrowright}}$$

Show that $[\ell_0, \gamma_0] \vdash y \ \underline{\text{in}} \ \exists (y = 2 \wedge [a]f\!f)$. ◆

Exercise 12.9 (For the keenest) *Prove Theorem 12.1 using structural induction on the formula F.* ◆

Given the structural definition of symbolic model checking in Definition 12.5, and its agreement with ordinary model checking stated in Theorem 12.1, it follows immediately from the finiteness of the number of regions that model checking is decidable.

Theorem 12.2 The model-checking problem for timed automata with respect to Hennessy–Milner logic with time is decidable.

We refer the interested readers to Laroussinie *et al.* (1995) for further details and developments.

12.3 Timed bisimilarity versus HML with time

In Exercise 12.2 you were asked, amongst other things, to find properties distinguishing the two timed automata in Example 11.4. Those automata are not timed bisimilar.

Consider, as another example, the two timed automata

$$\textcircled{\small{\bigcirc}} \overset{x:=0 \quad a}{\underset{x \leq 1}{\curvearrowright}} \qquad x \leq 1 \ \textcircled{\small{\bigcirc}} \overset{x:=0 \quad a}{\underset{}{\curvearrowright}}$$

whose behaviour we analyzed in Figure 10.2. On the basis of that analysis, you should be able to convince yourself easily that these two timed automata are not timed bisimilar. A formula in the language $\mathcal{M}_t$ that distinguishes them is $y \ \underline{\text{in}} \ \exists(y > 1)$. In fact, the timed automaton on the left-hand side satisfies this formula, but the one on the right-hand side does not because it cannot delay for more than 1 time unit.

Exercise 12.10 *Prove the above claim formally using the semantics of formulae.* ◆

Again, faced with two timed automata that are not timed bisimilar, we have been able to find a formula in the logic $\mathcal{M}_t$ that distinguishes them, in the sense that one timed automaton satisfies it but the other does not. Is this true in general? And what can we say about two timed automata that satisfy precisely the same formulae in $\mathcal{M}_t$? Are they guaranteed to be timed bisimilar?

In Chapter 5, we saw that classic HML characterizes bisimilarity over image-finite processes; see Definition 5.3 for the formal definition of this class of processes. This is the import of an elegant characterization theorem due to Hennessy and Milner (Theorem 5.1). The acid test for our development of the language $\mathcal{M}_t$ $\mathcal{M}_t$ is whether a similar characterization theorem holds for timed bisimilarity. We shall now proceed to show that this is indeed the case, at least if we use timed automata as our model for real-time systems.

We first show that, in the technical sense stated in the following theorem, two timed bisimilar states in an arbitrary TLTS satisfy the same formulae in $\mathcal{M}_t$.

Theorem 12.3 Let $(\mathsf{Proc}, \mathsf{Lab}, \{\xrightarrow{\alpha} \mid \alpha \in \mathsf{Lab}\})$ be a TLTS. Assume that p, q are timed bisimilar states in Proc. Let u be a clock valuation for the formula clocks in D. Then the extended states (p, u) and (q, u) satisfy exactly the same formulae (both the closed and the open ones) in $\mathcal{M}_t$.

Proof. Assume that p, q are timed bisimilar states in Proc. Let u be a clock valuation for the formula clocks in D. Assume that $(p, u) \models F$ for some formula $F \in \mathcal{M}_t$. Using structural induction on F, we shall prove that $(q, u) \models F$. By symmetry, this is enough to establish that (p, u) and (q, u) satisfy the same formulae in $\mathcal{M}_t$.

The proof proceeds by a case analysis on the form of F. We present the details only for the case $F = \mathbb{W}G$ for some formula G. Our inductive hypothesis is that, for all states r and s, if r and s are timed bisimilar and $(r, u') \models G$ for some valuation u' of the formula clocks then $(s, u') \models G$. Using this hypothesis, we shall prove that $(q, u) \models \mathbb{W}G$. To this end, assume that $q \xrightarrow{d} q'$ for some state q' and $d \in \mathbb{R}_{\geq 0}$. We wish to show that $(q', u + d') \models G$. Now, since p and q are timed bisimilar and $q \xrightarrow{d} d'$, there is a process p' such that $p \xrightarrow{d} p'$ and p' is timed bisimilar to q'. (Why?) By our assumption that $(p, u) \models \mathbb{W}G$, we have that

$(p', u + d) \models G$. The inductive hypothesis yields that $(q', u + d) \models G$. Since q' and d were arbitrary we may conclude that $(q, u) \models \mathbb{W}G$, which was to be shown. □

By instantiating the above result to the TLTSs that give semantics to timed automata, we obtain the following result.

Corollary 12.1 *Let A and A' be timed bisimilar timed automata. Then A and A' satisfy exactly the same formulae in $\mathcal{M}_t$.*

Exercise 12.11 *Let p, q be timed bisimilar states in a TLTS. Suppose that each formula in $\mathcal{M}_t$ satisfied by p is also satisfied by q. Prove that p and q satisfy the same formulae in $\mathcal{M}_t$.* ◆

In the setting of image-finite LTSs, Theorem 5.1 tells us that two states that satisfy the same formulae in Hennessy–Milner logic are bisimilar. However, the converse of Theorem 12.3 does *not* hold over TLTSs, regardless of whether they are image-finite.

Intuitively, this lack of expressiveness of the logic $\mathcal{M}_t$ is due to the assumptions we have made about the syntax of clock constraints. Recall that this syntax allows us to compare the values of clocks with integer values. The delay transitions that are possible in a TLTS are, however, labelled by arbitrary non-negative real numbers. This means, for instance, that there is nothing that prevents us from specifying a TLTS as follows:

- the set of states of the TLTS is $\{(A, d), (B, d) \mid d \in \mathbb{R}_{\geq 0}\} \cup \{\text{End}\}$;
- for each $d < \sqrt{2}$ there are transitions $(A, d) \xrightarrow{a} \text{End}$ and $(B, d) \xrightarrow{a} \text{End}$;
- $(B, \sqrt{2}) \xrightarrow{a} \text{End}$ holds, and
- for each $d, d' \in \mathbb{R}_{\geq 0}$, we have that

$$(A, d) \xrightarrow{d'} (A, d + d'),$$
$$(B, d) \xrightarrow{d'} (B, d + d'),$$
$$\text{End} \xrightarrow{d'} \text{End}.$$

Observe, first of all, that the states $(A, 0)$ and $(B, 0)$ are not timed bisimilar. Indeed

$$(B, 0) \xrightarrow{\sqrt{2}} (B, \sqrt{2}) \xrightarrow{a} \text{End},$$

whereas, on delaying for $\sqrt{2}$ units of time the only state that $(A, 0)$ can reach is $(A, \sqrt{2})$, from which no a-labelled transition is possible. You should be able to convince yourself that this is the only difference in the behaviour of the two states $(A, 0)$ and $(B, 0)$. Therefore, we could logically distinguish the behaviour of these two states only if the logic $\mathcal{M}_t$ allowed us to express a property stating, informally, that

> on delaying by exactly $\sqrt{2}$ time units one can reach a state from which an
> a-labelled transition is possible.

Using the language $\mathcal{M}_t$ we are able to specify such properties for integer delays and, after an appropriate 'change in time scale', for rational delays (and you are encouraged to try and do so!) but not for irrational delays. Therefore our intuition suggests that the properties of the states $(A, 0)$ and $(B, 0)$ that are expressible in $\mathcal{M}_t$ are the same. Indeed, this intuition is confirmed by the following result.

Proposition 12.2 The states $(A, 0)$ and $(B, 0)$ satisfy the same properties expressible in $\mathcal{M}_t$.

Proof (sketch). The theorem follows from the following stronger claim.

> For each $d < \sqrt{2}$ and valuation u for the formula clocks, the extended states
> $((A, d), u)$ and $((B, d), u)$ satisfy the same formulae in $\mathcal{M}_t$.

The theorem follows immediately from the above claim by taking $d = 0$ and $u = u_0$. The proof of the claim is left as an exercise for the keenest readers. (See the next exercise)

Exercise 12.12 (For the keenest) *Show the claim made in the above proof. To this end, you might find it useful to begin by proving the claim by induction on the structure of formulae, assuming the following auxiliary statements:*

1. $(A, \sqrt{2})$ *and* (B, d) *are timed bisimilar for each* $d > \sqrt{2}$;
2. *for each* $d, e > \sqrt{2}$ *the states* (A, d) *and* (B, e) *are timed bisimilar; and*
3. *for each* $d < \sqrt{2}$, *for clock valuations* u, u' *and for each formula* F,
   $((A, \sqrt{2}), u) \models F$ *and* $((A, d), u') \models F$ *imply* $((B, \sqrt{2}), u) \models F$.

Next you should proceed to establish each of the above auxiliary statements. For the last statement, use structural induction on F.   ◆

To sum up what we have learned from the above discussion, we have no hope of achieving a characterization theorem for timed bisimilarity in terms of the logic $\mathcal{M}_t$ over arbitrary TLTSs. However, this is not as bad as it sounds! Indeed, TLTSs are a very expressive formalism for real-time systems and cannot in general be finitely described – for instance, by means of timed automata. Since timed automata provide a good formalism for the finite description of TLTSs and the syntactic restrictions that we have imposed on the clock constraints are exactly the same as those present in the syntax of the logic $\mathcal{M}_t$, we might expect that the converse of Theorem 12.3 holds over (states of) timed automata. The following result notes that this is indeed the case.

Theorem 12.4 Let A and B be two timed automata that satisfy the same formulae in the logic $\mathcal{M}_t$. Then A and B are timed bisimilar.

Proof. (sketch). A proof of this theorem may be obtained from the characteristic-property result for timed automata from Laroussinie *et al.* (1995) which is sketched in subsection 12.4.1. The details of the proof are beyond the scope of this introductory textbook. $\square$

As an immediate consequence of the above theorem and of Corollary 12.1, we can now obtain the following result, which offers a counterpart of the characterization theorem of Hennessy and Milner for timed automata.

Corollary 12.2 Two timed automata are timed bisimilar if, iff they satisfy the same formulae in the language $\mathcal{M}_t$.

An interesting, and useful, consequence of Theorem 12.4 above is that whenever two timed automata are *not* timed bisimilar then we can always find a formula in the language $\mathcal{M}_t$ that one automaton satisfies but the other does not. Such a formula, which is often referred to as a *distinguishing formula*, gives a reason why the two timed automata are not timed bisimilar, and can be algorithmically constructed. (The details of the algorithmic construction for the synthesis of a distinguishing formula are beyond the scope of this introductory textbook. We refer the interested readers to the paper Godskesen and Larsen (1995) for more information.)

   We have already seen examples of such distinguishing formulae in this section. These formulae play an important role in implementation verification. Indeed, if we use timed bisimilarity as our notion of equivalence between real-time systems, and the timed automaton describing an implementation of a system is *not* equivalent to the specification automaton, then a distinguishing formula offers a reason why the implementation is not correct with respect to the given specification. That formula can be used as debugging information to locate the source of the error in the implementation and correct it.

Exercise 12.13 *Would Theorem 12.3 hold if all we knew about the states p and q was that they are untimed bisimilar?* ◆

Exercise 12.14 *Find a sublanguage of $\mathcal{M}_t$ that characterizes untimed bisimilarity over TLTSs.* ◆

Exercise 12.15 *In Example 9.1, we saw how to view the set of non-negative real numbers as a TLTS. Using the same ideas, we can view the intervals $[0, \sqrt{2})$ and $[0, \sqrt{2}]$ as two TLTSs with the number 0 as their distinguished initial state.*

1. Are these two TLTSs timed bisimilar?
2. If your answer is no, can you find a formula in $\mathcal{M}_t$ that distinguishes them?

Explain your answers! ◆

12.4 Recursion in HML with time

In the previous developments on Hennessy–Milner logic we successfully extended the language to handle recursively defined formulae. In what follows we aim at introducing formulae with one recursively defined variable for Hennessy–Milner logic with time.

Consider the timed automaton below (this automaton will be our running example in this section):

Using the logic $\mathcal{M}_t$ we are able to express that, in its initial state, no matter how this automaton performs two a-actions in a row, the time delay between these action occurrences will be at most 1 time unit. A formula in the language $\mathcal{M}_t$ stating this property is

$$\text{TwoAs} \stackrel{\text{def}}{=} [a](y \underline{\text{ in }} \mathbb{W}[a](y \leq 1)). \tag{12.2}$$

(We encourage you to show that the initial state of the above timed automaton does satisfy this formula using the formal definition of the satisfaction relation for formulae in $\mathcal{M}_t$ over states of timed automata.) However, a little reflection should convince you that the above property does not just hold for the initial state of the timed automaton we are considering. Rather, it holds for all the states of the TLTS that gives semantics to that timed automaton. In other words, we expect that the automaton under consideration has the following property.

It is always the case that whenever two a-actions occur in a row, the time delay between them is at most 1 time unit.

This natural property, however, cannot be expressed in the language $\mathcal{M}_t$. In fact, even though the modal operators $\exists$ ('there is a delay') and $\mathbb{W}$ ('for each delay') allow us to examine the behaviour of a state of a timed automaton for arbitrarily long delays, an $\mathcal{M}_t$-formula can only describe a *finite* part of the overall behaviour of a process that is due to the performance of actions.

You might recall that we discussed a similar shortcoming for HML in Chapter 6. As was the case for HML, a single formula in the language $\mathcal{M}_t$ can only describe the properties of a fixed small part of the computations of a real-time system that are due to action occurrences. As we found out in Chapter 6, how much of the behaviour of a real-time system we can explore using a single formula is entirely determined by its so-called modal depth, i.e. by the maximum nesting of action modalities in it.

The formula that we stated informally above is an example of a *safety* or *invariant* property. In Chapter 6, we saw that a natural specification language in which one can express properties such as this is HML extended by a facility for the recursive definition of properties. Following the developments in that chapter, we shall now extend the language $\mathcal{M}_t$ using recursion in similar fashion. In order to keep our presentation as simple and intuitive as possible, we shall consider the language obtained by extending $\mathcal{M}_t$ with a single recursively defined formula, specified by the identifier X. As in the setting of HML with recursion, this identifier will denote a set of states (namely those that satisfy the property it expresses) and can be used in the definition of formulae using the abstract syntax of the language $\mathcal{M}_t$.

How can we specify a timing property recursively? Let us consider, by way of example, the formal description of the aforementioned property.

> It is always the case that whenever two a-actions occur in a row, the time delay between them is at most 1 time unit.

A state of a timed automaton satisfies this property if

- whenever it performs two a-actions in a row, the time delay between them is at most 1 time unit,
- each state that it can reach by delaying some amount of time has the property, and
- each state that it can reach by performing an action also has that property.

Assuming, for the sake of simplicity, that a is the only action performed by the timed automaton, this means that the property above should satisfy the following recursive equation:

$$X \equiv \text{TwoAs} \wedge \mathbb{W}X \wedge [a]X, \tag{12.3}$$

where the property TwoAs is given by (12.2). As claimed in our previous discussion, the first conjunct on the right-hand side of the recursive equation above states that if the present state performs two a-actions in a row then the time delay between them is at most 1 time unit. The second conjunct states the requirement that the property is preserved by arbitrary delays and the third that it still holds true after the performance of the action a.

As you might recall from our discussion in Chapter 6, the above recursive equation is meant to specify a set of states in a timed automaton, namely, the set of states satisfying the property that X is supposed to express. By analogy with our developments of the theory of HML with recursion, it is supposed that the formula X stands for a set S of states of a timed automaton such that

$$S = [\![\text{TwoAs}]\!] \cap [\cdot\varepsilon\cdot]S \cap [\cdot a\cdot]S, \tag{12.4}$$

where $[\![\text{TwoAs}]\!]$ stands for the set of states that satisfy the formula TwoAs in (12.2). Note that the empty set of states satisfies the above 'set equation'. This is due to the fact that $[\cdot\varepsilon\cdot]\emptyset = \emptyset$. However, this is certainly *not* the meaning we have in mind for the formula X!

Observe that the empty set is the least solution of the above set equation. By analogy with our developments in the context of HML with recursion, we expect instead that the solution we have in mind for the set equation corresponding to the recursive equation defining the property X is the *largest* one. This is so because the property that X is intended to formalize is a safety property. (See the discussion in Section 6.2.) In the TLTS that gives semantics to our running example, it turns out that the largest set of states that satisfies the set equation (12.4) is the set Proc of all states of that automaton. The reason is that $[\![\text{TwoAs}]\!]$ is equal to $\mathcal{ES}(\text{Proc})$ since, for each $d \in \mathbb{R}_{\geq 0}$,

$$(\ell, [x = d]) \xrightarrow{a} \text{ implies } d \leq 1.$$

As we shall see in what follows, the same techniques from standard fixed point theory, which turned out to be very useful in making sure that the set equations associated with recursively defined formulae in HML have least and largest solutions, can be applied here.

Formally, the syntax of Hennessy–Milner logic with time and one variable X is given by the following grammar:

$$F ::= X \mid t\!t \mid f\!f \mid F \wedge G \mid F \vee G \mid \langle a \rangle F \mid [a]F \mid \exists F \mid \forall F \mid x \underline{\text{ in }} F \mid g,$$

where $a \in \text{Act}$, $x \in D$ and $g \in \mathcal{B}(D)$.

In what follows, we shall interpret formulae in the above language over the collection of extended states associated with a given timed automaton A, for instance, the one in our running example. Let Proc denote the set of states of the timed automaton under consideration. Semantically, a formula F (which may contain the variable X) is interpreted as a function $\mathcal{O}_F : \mathcal{ES}(\text{Proc}) \rightarrow \mathcal{ES}(\text{Proc})$ that, given a set of extended states that are assumed to satisfy X, gives us the set of extended states that satisfy F. The function $\mathcal{O}_F$ may be defined as follows, along the lines of Definition 6.1.

Definition 12.6 For each $S \subseteq \mathcal{ES}(\mathsf{Proc})$ and formula F, we define $\mathcal{O}_F(S)$ inductively by

$$\mathcal{O}_X(S) = S,$$
$$\mathcal{O}_{t\!t}(S) = \mathcal{ES}(\mathsf{Proc}),$$
$$\mathcal{O}_{f\!f}(S) = \emptyset,$$
$$\mathcal{O}_{F_1 \wedge F_2}(S) = \mathcal{O}_{F_1}(S) \cap \mathcal{O}_{F_2}(S),$$
$$\mathcal{O}_{F_1 \vee F_2}(S) = \mathcal{O}_{F_1}(S) \cup \mathcal{O}_{F_2}(S),$$
$$\mathcal{O}_{\langle a \rangle F}(S) = \langle \cdot a \cdot \rangle \mathcal{O}_F(S),$$
$$\mathcal{O}_{[a]F}(S) = [\cdot a \cdot] \mathcal{O}_F(S),$$
$$\mathcal{O}_{\exists F}(S) = \langle \cdot \varepsilon \cdot \rangle \mathcal{O}_F(S),$$
$$\mathcal{O}_{\forall F}(S) = [\cdot \varepsilon \cdot] \mathcal{O}_F(S),$$
$$\mathcal{O}_{x \underline{\text{ in }} F}(S) = \{(p, u) \mid (p, u[x \mapsto 0]) \in \mathcal{O}_F(S)\},$$
$$\mathcal{O}_g(S) = \{(p, u) \mid u \models g\}.$$

$\blacklozenge$

Exercise 12.16 *Use the above definition to calculate*

$$\mathcal{O}_F\big(\{((\ell, [x = 0]), [y = 0])\}\big),$$

where F is the formula on the right-hand side of the defining equation for X, (12.3). $\blacklozenge$

Exercise 12.17 *Assume that S_1 and S_2 are subsets of $\mathcal{ES}(\mathsf{Proc})$ such that S_1 is included in S_2. Argue that*

$$\langle \cdot \varepsilon \cdot \rangle S_1 \subseteq \langle \cdot \varepsilon \cdot \rangle S_2,$$
$$[\cdot \varepsilon \cdot] S_1 \subseteq [\cdot \varepsilon \cdot] S_2,$$
$$\{(p, u) \mid (p, u[x \mapsto 0]) \in S_1\} \subseteq \{(p, u) \mid (p, u[x \mapsto 0]) \in S_2\}.$$

Use these observations, together with your answers to Exercise 6.5, to show that $\mathcal{O}_F$ is monotonic for each F. (In other words, for all subsets S_1, S_2 of $\mathcal{ES}(\mathsf{Proc})$, if $S_1 \subseteq S_2$ then $\mathcal{O}_F(S_1) \subseteq \mathcal{O}_F(S_2)$.) $\blacklozenge$

Exercise 12.18 *Show that $(\mathcal{P}(\mathcal{ES}(\mathsf{Proc})), \subseteq)$ is a complete lattice.* $\blacklozenge$

We now know that, for each F, the function $\mathcal{O}_F$ is *monotonic* over the complete lattice $(\mathcal{P}(\mathcal{ES}(\mathsf{Proc})), \subseteq)$. As mentioned above, and by analogy with our developments in Section 6.3, the idea underlying the definition of the function $\mathcal{O}_F$ is that if $[\![X]\!] \subseteq \mathcal{ES}(\mathsf{Proc})$ gives the set of extended states that satisfy X then $\mathcal{O}_F([\![X]\!])$ will be the set of extended states that satisfy F. As in the context of standard HML with recursion, syntactically we shall assume that the set of extended states $[\![X]\!]$ is implicitly given by a recursive equation for X of the form

$$X \stackrel{\text{min}}{=} F_X \quad \text{or} \quad X \stackrel{\text{max}}{=} F_X.$$

As argued by example above, such an equation can be interpreted semantically as the following set equation:

$$[\![X]\!] = \mathcal{O}_{F_X}([\![X]\!]). \tag{12.5}$$

As $\mathcal{O}_{F_X}$ is a monotonic function over a complete lattice we know that (12.5) has solutions – that is, that $\mathcal{O}_{F_X}$ has fixed points. In particular Tarski's fixed point theorem gives us that the *largest* fixed point and the *least* fixed point of $\mathcal{O}_{F_X}$ are given respectively by

$$\bigcup\{S \subseteq \mathcal{ES}(\mathsf{Proc}) \mid S \subseteq \mathcal{O}_{F_X}(S)\},$$
$$\bigcap\{S \subseteq \mathcal{ES}(\mathsf{Proc}) \mid \mathcal{O}_{F_X}(S) \subseteq S\}.$$

Let us use the former expression above to argue formally that the largest fixed point of the function $\mathcal{O}_F$, where F is the formula on the right-hand side of the defining equation (12.3) for X, over the set of extended states for our running example is indeed the whole collection of extended states, as claimed. To this end, it suffices to show that

$$\mathcal{ES}(\mathsf{Proc}) \subseteq \mathcal{O}_F(\mathcal{ES}(\mathsf{Proc})).$$

(Why?) We have already argued that $[\![\mathsf{TwoAs}]\!]$ is equal to $\mathcal{ES}(\mathsf{Proc})$ so, using Definition 12.6, you should be able to convince yourself that

$$\mathcal{O}_F(\mathcal{ES}(\mathsf{Proc})) = [\cdot\varepsilon\cdot]\mathcal{ES}(\mathsf{Proc}) \cap [\cdot a\cdot]\mathcal{ES}(\mathsf{Proc}).$$

Observe now that both $[\cdot\varepsilon\cdot]\mathcal{ES}(\mathsf{Proc})$ and $[\cdot a\cdot]\mathcal{ES}(\mathsf{Proc})$ are equal to $\mathcal{ES}(\mathsf{Proc})$ (Exercise 12.3). Therefore $\mathcal{O}_F(\mathcal{ES}(\mathsf{Proc}))$ is just $\mathcal{ES}(\mathsf{Proc})$, as claimed.

12.4.1 Characteristic properties for timed bisimilarity

In Section 6.7 we saw how to characterize the equivalence classes for strong bisimilarity with a *single* formula in HML with recursive definition. The formula that characterizes the bisimulation equivalence class for a state in a finite LTS was called its *characteristic formula*.

It is natural to ask whether the language $\mathcal{M}_t$ extended with recursively defined formulae is expressive enough to allow us to obtain a similar result for timed bisimilarity over timed automata. Indeed, achieving such a result would give us yet another indication that our design choices for the logic $\mathcal{M}_t$ are 'good', at least in that this language affords properties that are akin to those of classic Hennessy–Milner logic, with or without recursively defined formulae.

For the sake of simplicity, we shall focus in this section on timed automata without invariants – i.e. on timed automata whose location invariants are all tautologies – and over a single action a.

Consider again, by way of example, the timed automaton used as our running example in this section:

$$\ell \bigcirc \overset{x:=0 \;\; a}{\underset{x\leq 1}{\curvearrowleft}}$$

A formula characterizing node ℓ in this timed automaton up to timed bisimilarity should offer a description of

1. all the actions that are enabled in the node,
2. which node is entered on taking a given edge, together with the clock resets associated with it, and
3. the fact that arbitrary delays are allowed in the node.

The resulting characteristic formula is presented below, where we consider X_ℓ (the characteristic formula for node ℓ) to be our recursively defined variable. The formula consists of three conjuncts, each associated with one of the above properties:

$$X_\ell \overset{\max}{=} (y \leq 1 \Rightarrow (\langle a \rangle y \; \underline{\text{in}} \; X_\ell))$$
$$\wedge \, [a](y \leq 1 \wedge (y \; \underline{\text{in}} \; X_\ell))$$
$$\wedge \, \forall \!\!\! \forall X_\ell.$$

The above formula encodes the behaviour of the timed automaton as follows. The first conjunct in the formula on the right-hand side of the recursive equation states that if the value of the clock y is no larger than 1 then the timed automaton can perform an a-labelled transition and reach a state that satisfies the characteristic formula for node ℓ after resetting the clock y. (Note that this conjunct encodes the self-loop in the timed automaton, the formula clock y playing the role of the clock x in the timed automaton.) The second conjunct is intended to express that the self-loop edge is the only one in this timed automaton. This is done by saying that, no matter how an a-action is performed, it takes place within 1 time unit from the last time the clock y was reset and its performance will lead to a state that satisfies the characteristic formula for node ℓ after resetting clock y. The third and last conjunct expresses the fact that, no matter how long we delay, we should still satisfy the characteristic formula for node ℓ. (Recall that in this section we are assuming that we have no invariants in timed automata. Timed automata without invariants can delay arbitrarily long in each of their locations.)

The following theorem states that the above recursively defined formula is characteristic for our running example, modulo timed bisimilarity.

Theorem 12.5 Let A be a timed automaton without invariants whose set of clocks does not include y. Let ℓ' be a node of A. Assume that $d \in \mathbb{R}_{\geq 0}$ and u is a valuation for the clocks of A. Then $(\ell, [x = d])$ is timed bisimilar to (ℓ', u) iff the extended state $((\ell', u), [y = d])$ satisfies X_ℓ.

Proof. We first show that the extended state $((\ell', u), [y = d])$ satisfies X_ℓ whenever $(\ell, [x = d])$ is timed bisimilar to (ℓ', u). To this end, it suffices only to argue that

$$S \subseteq \mathcal{O}_F(S),$$

where F is the formula on the right-hand side of the recursive definition for X_ℓ and the set S is defined as

$$S = \{((\ell', u'), [y = d']) \mid (\ell, [x = d']) \text{ is timed bisimilar to } (\ell', u')\}.$$

(Convince yourself of this claim!)

Assume that $((\ell', u'), [y = d']) \in S$. We shall prove that $((\ell', u'), [y = d'])$ is also contained in $\mathcal{O}_F(S)$. By the definition of the function $\mathcal{O}_F$, this amounts to arguing that

1. $((\ell', u'), [y = d']) \in \mathcal{O}_{y \leq 1 \Rightarrow (\langle a \rangle y \text{ in } X_\ell)}(S)$,
2. $((\ell', u'), [y = d']) \in \mathcal{O}_{[a](y \leq 1 \wedge (y \text{ in } X_\ell))}(S)$, and
3. $((\ell', u'), [y = d']) \in \mathcal{O}_{\forall X_\ell}(S)$.

We shall limit ourselves to presenting verification details for the first of these claims. (You are invited to fill in the details of the proof of the latter two claims yourself.)

Observe, first of all, that $((\ell', u'), [y = d']) \in \mathcal{O}_{y \leq 1 \Rightarrow (\langle a \rangle y \text{ in } X_\ell)}(S)$ holds trivially if $d' > 1$. (Why?) Assume therefore that $d' \leq 1$. In this case, we wish to argue that

$$((\ell', u'), [y = d']) \in \mathcal{O}_{\langle a \rangle y \text{ in } X_\ell}(S).$$

By the definition of the function $\mathcal{O}$, this holds precisely when, for some state (ℓ', u') of the timed automaton A,

$$(\ell', u') \xrightarrow{a} (\ell', u') \text{ and } ((\ell', u'), [y = 0]) \in S.$$

(Check this claim!) To see that the above criterion is met by the state (ℓ', u'), we argue as follows. Since $d' \leq 1$, we have that

$$(\ell, [x = d']) \xrightarrow{a} (\ell, [x = 0]).$$

By the definition of S, the states (ℓ', u') and $(\ell, [x = d'])$ are timed bisimilar. Therefore, there exists a state (ℓ', u') of the timed automaton A such that

$$(\ell', u') \xrightarrow{a} (\ell', u') \text{ and } (\ell', u') \text{ is timed bisimilar to } (\ell, [x = 0]).$$

Again by the definition of S, we may conclude that

$$((\ell', u'), [y = 0]) \in S,$$

as required.

Our order of business now will be to show that if the extended state

$$((\ell', u), [y = d])$$

satisfies X_ℓ then $(\ell, [x = d])$ is timed bisimilar to (ℓ', u). To this end, it suffices only to prove that the relation

$$R = \big\{ ((\ell, [x = d]), (\ell', u) \,|\, ((\ell', u), [y = d]) \models X_\ell \big\}$$

is a timed bisimulation. The proof is left as a strongly recommended exercise for the reader.   □

Exercise 12.19 (Strongly recommended) *Complete the proof of the above theorem. Recall that A is a timed automaton without invariants.*   ♦

This theorem and the construction of the characteristic formula for our running example are specific instances of the general construction of a characteristic formula, and of the theorem showing its correctness, presented in Aceto *et al.* (2000). Related results may be found in Aceto *et al.* (2003) and Laroussinie *et al.* (1995) – the latter reference offers, to the best of our knowledge, the first construction of characteristic formulae for timed automata, modulo timed bisimilarity, presented in the literature.

Exercise 12.20 *Give characteristic formulae for the timed automata in Example 11.4 and prove a version of Theorem 12.5 for them. (You might find it useful to define a characteristic formula for each location in the timed automata. You will not need recursion!)*   ♦

Exercise 12.21 (Characteristic formulae for timed similarity) *A timed simulation over the set of states of a TLTS is a relation R such that, whenever $s_1 \mathrel{R} s_2$ and $\alpha \in$ Lab :*

if $s_1 \xrightarrow{\alpha} s_1'$ then $s_2 \xrightarrow{\alpha} s_2'$ for some s_2' such that s_1' R s_2'.

State s_1 is simulated by s_2 iff the pair (s_1, s_2) is contained in a timed simulation.

For timed automata A_1 and A_2, we say that A_1 is simulated by A_2 iff the initial state of A_1 is simulated by that of A_2.

Give a characteristic formula for our running example modulo timed simulation and prove a version of Theorem 12.5 for it. ◆

12.4.2 Examples of real-time temporal properties

The basic constructs of the logic $\mathcal{M}_t$ extended with recursive definitions can be used to define high-level temporal operators, which may be helpful in simplifying the writing of logical specifications. Here we confine ourselves to showing how to define the temporal operators *until*, *before* and *Inv* (in the following formulae, t is a non-negative integer):

$$F \ until \ G \stackrel{\mathrm{max}}{=} G \vee (F \wedge [\mathsf{Act}](F \ until \ G) \wedge \mathbb{W}(F \ until \ G)),$$
$$F \ until_{\leq t} \ G = x \ \underline{\mathrm{in}} \ ((F \wedge x \leq t) \ until \ G),$$
$$before_t \ F = t\!t \ until_{\leq t} \ F,$$
$$Inv(F) \stackrel{\mathrm{max}}{=} F \wedge [\mathsf{Act}]Inv(F) \wedge \mathbb{W}Inv(F).$$

The intuitive meaning of the above temporal operators is as follows.

- $F \ until \ G$ is true iff, no matter how long the system delays or what action transitions it takes, F is satisfied at least until G becomes true. Since we are specifying this property using a largest fixed point, the formula F may be satisfied forever and G might never become true. The above formula is therefore an example of a so-called *weak until*. (See the discussion in Section 6.1.)

  In fact, as shown in Bouyer, Cassez and Laroussinie (2005), the above recursive definition of $F \ until \ G$ does not exactly capture the property that F holds until G in all runs. The recursive property we have specified above is in general a bit stronger, insisting that if G does not hold in a particular state then $F \ until \ G$ must hold after any delay d, even if G were to hold already after some delay $d' < d$. In Bouyer *et al.* (2005) a new modality is introduced based on which an exact recursive specification of $F \ until \ G$ may be given. Alternatively, the above recursive specification is correct if the formula G is required to be *time invariant* – this means that once G holds then it continues to hold after any value of the delay.

- $F \ until_{\leq t} \ G$ is the time-bounded version of the above property. Here we are stating that F is satisfied at least until G holds, and moreover G is guaranteed to hold within t time units.

- The formula $before_t \, F$ states that F will hold within t time units. This is an example of a time-bounded eventuality property.
- Finally, $Inv(F)$ states that the formula F holds invariantly. (This is just a real-time version of the invariance property that we met in Chapter 6.)

The second and third properties introduced above are examples of so-called *bounded liveness* properties. This kind of property often arises when we try to describe the expected behaviours of real-time systems. Recall that a typical liveness property states intuitively that 'something good will eventually happen'. For instance, a liveness property could specify that each request to access some resource is eventually granted. In a real-time setting, however, often we are not just interested in knowing that our requests will be granted at some unspecified time in the future. Rather, we are expecting to be granted access to whatever service we need within a specified time bound! As a concrete example, consider again the behaviour of an airbag system in a car described by the following property.

If the car crashes, the airbag must be inflated within 50 milliseconds.

This property is an example of a bounded liveness property and can be described using the formula

$$Inv\big([\mathrm{crash}](before_{50} \, \langle\mathrm{inflate}\rangle t\!t)\big).$$

Indeed, the above formula states that no matter how the system evolves – i.e. in all reachable states – each crash action is followed by an inflate action within 50 time units.

12.5 More on timed logics

There has been extensive research on extending temporal logic to the setting of real time. Similarly to the way in which timed automata extend finite automata with time, temporal logic has also been extended by adding quantitative timing information. Timed propositional temporal logic (TPTL) (Alur and Henzinger, 1994) and metric temporal logic (MTL) (Koymans, 1990) are the two main timed extensions of so-called linear-time temporal logic (Manna and Pnueli, 1992; Lamport, 1983). Interested readers may refer to Maler, Nickovic and Pnueli (2005) and Henzinger (1998) for general surveys on timed temporal logic. More recently Bouyer, Chevalier and Markey (2005) compared the relative expressiveness of MTL and TPTL. A timed version of the branching-time temporal logic CTL (Clarke and Emerson, 1981), known as TCTL, appeared in Alur, Courcoubetis and Dill (1993) together with model-checking algorithms.

In this chapter we have studied Hennessy–Milner logic extended with time and recursion, as originally introduced in Laroussinie *et al.* (1995). In that paper, model checking as well as the more difficult problem of satisfiability checking (for given bounds on the number of clocks and the maximal constants) were shown to be decidable over timed automata. In Aceto and Laroussinie (2002) model checking with respect to Hennessy–Milner logic with time and a largest-fixed-point construction is proved to be EXPTIME-complete (complete for deterministic exponential time) in contrast with CTL and the alternation-free modal μ-calculus (Kozen, 1983), for which model checking is 'only' PSPACE-complete (complete for deterministic polynomial space).

We conclude by remarking that, as shown in Aceto and Laroussinie (2002), the model-checking problem for the logic $\mathcal{M}_t$ over timed automata is PSPACE-complete.

13

Modelling and analysis of Fischer's algorithm

Introduction

Mutual exclusion algorithms, like those we discussed in Chapter 7, have an abstract behaviour described by the following pseudocode:

while true do
begin
      remainder region
      trying region
      critical section
      exit region
end

It is supposed that such algorithms satisfy the following two properties.

* *Mutual exclusion* No two processes are in their critical sections at the same time.
* *Deadlock freedom* If some process is in its trying region then eventually some process is in its critical section. (Note that the process in the critical section might be different from the one initially in its trying region.) Moreover, if a process is in its exit region then that process will eventually enter its remainder region.

As stated in Lynch and Shavit (1992), the known asynchronous mutual exclusion algorithms for n processes require $O(n)$ read and write registers and $O(n)$ operations to access the critical section. These bounds make them rather impractical for large-scale applications, where the number of processes could be very large. This raises the question whether it is possible to achieve mutual exclusion in asynchronous systems consisting of n processes by using a smaller number of shared registers and/or fewer than $O(n)$ operations to access the critical section. Unfortunately, this is impossible for 'classic reactive systems' in an asynchronous setting. In fact, Burns and Lynch (1980, 1993) showed the following theorem.

Theorem 13.1 (Burns and Lynch) There is no asynchronous algorithm providing mutual exclusion with deadlock freedom for $n \geq 2$ processes that uses fewer than n shared read and write registers.

This theorem is a classic example of an *impossibility result* – a type of result that Nancy Lynch has contributed in abundance to the literature on distributed computation. (See, for instance, the impossibility results mentioned in her encyclopaedic book Lynch (1996).) Despite their apparently negative nature, such results play a fundamental role in the theory and practice of computing science because they set precise limits to what it is possible to achieve using some computational paradigm – thus preventing futile efforts to overcome computational barriers that cannot, in fact, be broken within a given computational model. For example, Theorem 13.1 above tells us that there is no point in trying to come up with asynchronous deadlock-free mutual exclusion algorithms that use fewer than n shared read and write registers because such algorithms do not exist!

However, as repeatedly stated by Richard Hamming in his general writings on science and engineering – see, for instance, Hamming (1997, p. 305) – all impossibility proofs must rest on a number of assumptions, and these assumptions may or may not apply in the particular situation under analysis or in the chosen computational model. For instance, the above result by Burns and Lynch applies to 'deadlock-free' algorithms. If we remove this, admittedly very reasonable, assumption, then we can find a mutual exclusion algorithm that uses no shared register at all. It suffices only to make the execution of all the processes enter a livelock at the start of the protocol and then none will access its critical section! This 'solution' to the mutual exclusion problem is, however, completely unacceptable – so much so that nobody would actually consider it a proper solution anyway. We can, however, ask the following natural question.

> Can the lower bound in Theorem 13.1 for deadlock-free mutual exclusion be overcome by considering computational models other than the one underlying the above-mentioned result of Burns and Lynch?

This is a typical question that arises from impossibility and lower-bound theorems and is another example of how apparently negative results can help stimulate the search for new computational paradigms and the exploration of their computing power.

13.1   Mutual exclusion using timing

According to Lynch and Shavit (1992), Michael Fischer seems to have been the first researcher who overcame the lower bound of n registers for deadlock-free mutual exclusion by assuming timing constraints. His, by now classic, algorithm uses just one shared multiwriter register 'id', whose initial value is 0. In order to ensure mutual exclusion, each process P_i, $i \in \{1, \ldots, n\}$, executes the following algorithm, Fischer's algorithm, where we use 'delay' to stand for a positive integer constant:

> **while true do**
> **begin**
>   'noncritical section';
>   L: **if** id $\neq 0$ **then goto** L;
>   1: id := i;
>   2: **pause**(delay);
>   3: **if** id $\neq i$ **then goto** L;
>   'critical section';
>   id := 0;
> **end**

In the above pseudocode algorithm the statement **pause**(delay) makes the process wait for the amount of time specified by the constant 'delay'. But what should be the value of such a constant? Since Fischer's algorithm is a real-time one, we might expect that its behaviour depends crucially on an appropriate choice for this timing parameter.

In order to find a suitable value for the constant 'delay', we assume an upper bound c, where c is a positive integer, for the time between successive steps of the execution of a process while it is trying to access its critical section. Intuitively, a process that takes steps every c time units is executing slowly. In Fischer's algorithm, we choose the value of 'delay' to be larger than c, the longest time that a process may take to perform a step while trying to enter its critical section. The key idea behind this choice for the parameter 'delay' is that by the time that process i has reached line 3 in the pseudocode algorithm, each process j that has passed the test in line L and might write j in the variable 'id' has already done so, since delay $> c$ and c is the longest time that such a step may take. Therefore, whenever process i finds that id $= i$ in line 3 then it can safely

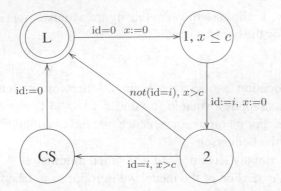

Figure 13.1 The timed automaton A_i for process i.

enter its critical section because all the other processes are either before line L or after line 1 with their index overwritten by process i, so they will fail the test at line 3.

The algorithm that we have just presented is conceptually very simple. However, as you will see later on, Fischer's algorithm has the drawback that it fails to guarantee mutual exclusion if the timing constraints on which its workings are predicated are not met.

It is well known that Fischer's algorithm is deadlock free and ensures mutual exclusion provided that its timing assumptions are met. Moreover, as shown by Lynch and Shavit (1992, Theorem 4.6), its timing behaviour is nearly optimal. Our order of business here is to model Fischer's algorithm using networks of timed automata, as supported by the verification tool UPPAAL, and to hint at the automatic verification of its behaviour using that tool.

13.2 Modelling Fischer's algorithm

Fischer's mutual exclusion algorithm for n processes can be modelled as a network of timed automata; see Section 10.4. Each of the n timed automata in the network describes the behaviour of one of the processes running Fischer's algorithm, given above in pseudocode. The timed automaton A_i modelling the code for process i in Fischer's algorithm will use a local clock x to guarantee that the upper bound between successive steps of the process, while it is trying to enter its critical section, is c; A_i will have access to the shared integer variable id. The timed automaton A_i is depicted in Figure 13.1.

The label applying to all edges is immaterial for this algorithm and is therefore omitted from Figure 13.1; for consistency with previous notation, you can assume that this label is τ. In the automaton in this figure, we use '*not* (id $= i$), $x > c$' as an abbreviation for the boolean condition

$$(\text{id} < i \lor \text{id} > i) \land x > c.$$

The edge from location 2 to location L should therefore be read as standing for two edges, one that applies when id $< i$ and $x > c$ and one that is enabled when id $> i$ and $x > c$. For pictorial convenience, we have written the invariant $x \leq c$ of node 1 within the node itself.

As you might already have noticed, the timed automaton A_i in Figure 13.1 is based on a slight extension of the model we introduced in Chapter 10. In fact, A_i uses an integer variable id as well as one clock x. The integer variable id can be updated when the automaton follows an edge, and its current value can be tested to determine whether an edge from the present location is enabled. This slightly extended model of timed automata is supported by the verification tool UPPAAL and makes it easier to model algorithms, like Fischer's mutual exclusion algorithm, that rely on the use of shared variables.

Nodes L, 1 and 2 in the timed automaton in Figure 13.1 model the similarly numbered steps in the pseudocode for Fischer's algorithm, and the timed automaton A_i begins its execution in location L. (Location L has no outgoing edge that is enabled when id has a value different from 0. The 'busy waiting' loop in the behaviour of the pseudocode algorithm is modelled by delaying in location L of automaton A_i.) The invariant $x \leq c$ in node 1 is used to model the upper bound on the time that a step of the process can take while it is trying to enter the critical section. Such an invariant ensures that process i can be in location 2 for at most c time units. Location 2 in the automaton A_i describes steps 2 and 3 in the pseudocode for Fischer's algorithm. In fact, since the private clock x of automaton A_i is reset upon entering location 2, the guard $x > c$ on the outgoing edges from that location ensures that the process delays for more than c units of time before it tests the value of the shared variable id. If, after that amount of time, the value of id is i then the process can safely enter its critical section – abstractly modelled here by the location CS – by following its edge from location 2 to location CS. The edge from location CS back to location L implements the exit from the critical section and the resetting of the shared variable id.

Fischer's algorithm for n processes is modelled as the network of timed automata

$$A_1 \mid A_2 \mid \cdots \mid A_n.$$

We recall that states of this network consist of an n-tuple of locations $(\ell_1, \ldots, \ell_n)$, where ℓ_i is a location of automaton A_i, $i \in \{1, \ldots, n\}$, and a valuation for the set of clocks $\{x_1, \ldots, x_n\}$; x_i stands for the local clock of automaton A_i. However, unlike for the networks of classic timed automata introduced in Section 10.4, this is not enough to give a complete picture of the behaviour of this system. In fact, since the value of the shared variable id determines whether certain edges are enabled in the component automata, a state of the network must record, in addition, the current value of the shared variable id. In what follows, we shall write a state of the network $A_1 \mid A_2 \mid \cdots \mid A_n$ thus:

$$(\ell_1, \ldots, \ell_n, x_1 = c_1, \ldots, x_n = c_n, \mathrm{id} = i),$$

where $c_1, \ldots, c_n$ are non-negative real numbers and $i \in \{1, \ldots, n\}$. The initial state of the network is

$$(L, \ldots, L, x_1 = 0, \ldots, x_n = 0, \mathrm{id} = 0),$$

because the initial value of each clock and of the variable id is 0.

13.2.1 Proving mutual exclusion using UPPAAL

Now that we have a model of Fischer's algorithm as a UPPAAL network of timed automata, our order of business will be to analyze the behaviour of this model in order to verify that it indeed affords the mutual exclusion property. Before doing so, however, we need to specify precisely what it means for our network of timed automata to guarantee mutual exclusion.

As we saw in Chapter 7, temporal logics such as Hennessy–Milner logic with recursive definitions provide a natural language in which one can specify properties of reactive systems such as mutual exclusion. In fact, everything we said there applies, making the necessary changes, to the setting of real-time systems described as networks of timed automata. It would therefore be tempting, and most natural, to describe the mutual exclusion property for our model of Fischer's algorithm using the real-time version of Hennessy–Milner logic with largest fixed points that we presented in Chapter 12.

Note, however, that on the one hand the network of timed automata describing Fischer's algorithm for n processes is a *closed system*. This means that the network is not willing to communicate with its environment. Moreover, interaction between the automata in the network takes place via the shared variable id.

On the other hand, Hennessy–Milner logic and its variants are *action-based* temporal logics, at least in our textbook presentation. This means that formulae in variants of Hennessy–Milner logic describe properties pertaining to the communication potential of processes via the labelled modalities $\langle a \rangle$ and $[a]$. At first sight, this makes these logics unsuitable for describing properties of systems that, like our model of Fischer's algorithm, exhibit no observable communication behaviour.

What we should like to express for Fischer's algorithm is an invariant property which states the following.

No matter how the network evolves, at no point of its computation will two different component automata each be in its location CS at the same time.

We have seen already how to express invariance properties in Hennessy–Milner logic with time (see Section 12.4), but how do we express the following requirement?

Two different component automata cannot each be in its location CS at the same time.

One possibility would be to modify our model by adding self-loop edges to location CS in timed automaton A_i. These edges could be labelled with some observable synchronization action, say $\text{in}_i!$, to signal to the environment that automaton A_i is in its critical section. One could then express mutual exclusion using the property

$$Inv \left(\bigwedge_{1 \leq i < j \leq n} ([\text{in}_i!]\mathit{ff} \vee [\text{in}_j!]\mathit{ff}) \right).$$

(You should try to convince yourself that the above property would indeed state that at most one automaton is in its critical section in each state of the computation of Fischer's algorithm.)

However, if we aim at verifying the correctness of Fischer's mutual exclusion algorithm using an automatic verification tool such as UPPAAL, we are forced to use a specification language, for the properties being model checked, that is accepted by the tool itself. Unfortunately, UPPAAL models can only be closed systems and the language supported by that tool for the writing of specifications does not allow us to write formulae such as the invariance property above.

The specification language of the tool UPPAAL, however, permits the use of *atomic predicates* whose truth value over states can be determined locally. An example of such a predicate is $A_i.\text{CS}$, $i \in \{1, \ldots, n\}$, stating that the ith automaton in the network is presently in location CS. Formally, a state

$$(\ell_1, \ldots, \ell_n, x_1 = c_1, \ldots, x_n = c_n, \text{id} = i)$$

of our network satisfies the atomic predicate $A_i.\text{CS}$ if, and only if, $\ell_i = \text{CS}$.

Using boolean combinations of these atomic predicates, we can therefore state that at most one of the component automata is currently in its critical section, by means of the formula

$$\text{MutexNow} = \bigwedge_{1 \le i < j \le n} (\neg A_i.\text{CS} \vee \neg A_j.\text{CS}),$$

where the symbol $\neg$ stands for logical negation.

One can therefore express mutual exclusion using the property

$$Inv(\text{MutexNow}).$$

Since the specification language for queries supported by the tool UPPAAL follows the syntax of timed computation tree logic (or TCTL) – see the reference Alur *et al.* (1993) – the above property is actually written thus:

$$A\Box\text{MutexNow}.$$

In the above formula, the initial A states that the formula $\Box$MutexNow must be satisfied in *all* the computation paths of the network. The truth value of the property $\Box$MutexNow is therefore evaluated over a single path. The $\Box$ modality here indicates that the property MutexNow should be true in *all* the states along the path. Following this informal explanation, you should be able to convince yourself that the above formula states the following property.

In all computation paths, and in each state along each path, at most one process is in its critical section.

This is precisely what 'ensuring mutual exclusion' means. Further information on the actual syntax of the specification language for queries used by UPPAAL may be found in the tutorial paper Behrmann *et al.* (2004).

Exercise 13.1 *Read the above-mentioned tutorial paper, Behrmann et al. (2004), carefully. Install the UPPAAL tool and experiment with the demonstration examples that come with the tool.* ◆

Exercise 13.2
1. *Create an UPPAAL model for Fischer's algorithm based on the one we have proposed. In your model you may assume that the network consists of four processes and that the value of the constant c is 2.*
2. *Upload the predefined collection of queries about Fischer's algorithm that comes with the UPPAAL tool. Check whether your model of Fischer's algorithm affords all the stated properties.*

◆

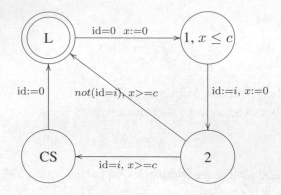

Figure 13.2 Erroneous timed automaton A_i^w for process i.

13.2.2 An erroneous version of Fischer's algorithm

We have mentioned already that timing plays a crucial role in the workings of Fischer's mutual exclusion algorithm. Indeed, this algorithm fails to ensure mutual exclusion if its timing assumptions are not satisfied. In particular, it is crucial that, on line 2 of the pseudocode algorithm, process i be delayed by some amount of time that is strictly larger than the constant c, the longest time that it takes for a process to execute a step while it is trying to enter its critical section. To see this, consider an erroneous version of Fischer's protocol, modelled by the timed automaton A_i^w in Figure 13.2. Note that the only difference between this timed automaton and that in Figure 13.1 is in the guards labelling the edges that stem from node 2. In particular, the process may now check whether the shared variable id has the value i after a delay of *exactly* c units of time.

We shall now exhibit a sequence of transitions for our model of this erroneous version of Fischer's algorithm that does *not* preserve mutual exclusion.

Assume, for the sake of simplicity, that there are only two processes running this version of Fischer's algorithm. The overall network of timed automata is therefore $A_1^w \mid A_2^w$, and its initial state is given by

$$(L, L, x_1 = 0, x_2 = 0, \mathrm{id} = 0),$$

where, for $i \in \{1, 2\}$, we write x_i for the local clock x of automaton A_i^w. Since the value of id is 0, and the edge from location L to location 1 does not change it, the network $A_1^w \mid A_2^w$ can perform the following two transitions:

$$(L, L, x_1 = 0, x_2 = 0, \mathrm{id} = 0) \rightarrow (1, L, x_1 = 0, x_2 = 0, \mathrm{id} = 0)$$
$$\rightarrow (1, 1, x_1 = 0, x_2 = 0, \mathrm{id} = 0).$$

In the state $(1, 1, x_1 = 0, x_2 = 0, \text{id} = 0)$, automaton A_1^w may follow the edge from location 1 to location 2, and thereafter the system may delay for c time units. Thus the network $A_1^w \mid A_2^w$ can perform the following two transitions:

$$(1, 1, x_1 = 0, x_2 = 0, \text{id} = 0) \rightarrow (2, 1, x_1 = 0, x_2 = 0, \text{id} = 1)$$
$$\xrightarrow{c} (2, 1, x_1 = c, x_2 = c, \text{id} = 1).$$

Since the value of x_1 is c and that of id is 1, automaton A_1^w may now enter its critical section:

$$(2, 1, x_1 = c, x_2 = c, \text{id} = 1) \rightarrow (\text{CS}, 1, x_1 = c, x_2 = c, \text{id} = 1).$$

At this point of the computation, automaton A_2^w may decide to follow the edge from location 1 to location 2, and thereafter the system may delay for c time units. Thus the network $A_1^w \mid A_2^w$ can perform the following two transitions:

$$(\text{CS}, 1, x_1 = c, x_2 = c, \text{id} = 1) \rightarrow (\text{CS}, 2, x_1 = c, x_2 = 0, \text{id} = 2)$$
$$\xrightarrow{c} (\text{CS}, 2, x_1 = 2c, x_2 = c, \text{id} = 2).$$

Note now that automaton A_2^w can also enter its critical section because the value of x_2 is c and that of id is 2:

$$(\text{CS}, 2, x_1 = 2c, x_2 = c, \text{id} = 2) \rightarrow (\text{CS}, \text{CS}, x_1 = 2c, x_2 = c, \text{id} = 2).$$

In the target state of the above transition, both A_1^w and A_2^w are in their critical sections, leading to the claimed failure of mutual exclusion.

We may therefore conclude that, as claimed previously, the correctness of Fischer's mutual exclusion algorithm depends crucially on its timing assumptions. In the following section, you will be working with, amongst others, a modification of this algorithm proposed by Lynch and Shavit that guarantees mutual exclusion regardless of whether the timing assumptions on the speed of the processes are met.

Exercise 13.3 *Implement the erroneous version of Fischer's algorithm for $n = 4$ and $c = 2$ in* UPPAAL. *Use the tool to determine that the system does not afford mutual exclusion and to find a shortest and fastest trace leading to a state where at least two processes are in their critical section at the same time.* ◆

13.3   Further exercises on timing-based mutual exclusion algorithms

In the previous sections, we have seen how to use timing information to ensure mutual exclusion in an asynchronous setting by means of a truly simple and beautiful algorithm due to Michael Fischer. In Fischer's solution, before it can enter the critical section a process accesses the single shared variable id thrice and delays by some amount of time larger than the upper bound on the time that processes need to execute a step. Note that, in Fischer's algorithm, a process delays itself even if it is the only one that is currently trying to enter the critical section.

Another elegant timing-based mutual exclusion algorithm was proposed by Alur and Taubenfeld (1992, 1996). The solution to the mutual exclusion problem proposed by these authors assumes that there is an upper bound Δ on the time required for reading or writing a variable in the shared memory. Furthermore, Alur and Taubenfeld supposed that this bound Δ is known to all the processes in the system. Access to the shared memory takes a non-zero time, and there is no lower bound on the time needed to execute a step. As in the pseudocode for Fischer's algorithm, processes can delay themselves by performing an explicit **delay**(d) statement, where d is a positive integer.

Alur and Taubenfeld's mutual exclusion algorithm uses three shared registers: the registers x, y hold integers, y having initially the value 0, and register z holds a boolean value that is initially the value *false*. In order to ensure mutual exclusion, each process P_i, $i \in \{1, \ldots, n\}$, executes the pseudocode algorithm shown below.

```
while true do
begin
        start: x := i;
        await (y = 0);
        y := i;
        if x ≠ i then  delay(2 · Δ);
                       if y ≠ i then goto  start;
                       await (¬z)
        else  z := true;
        'critical section';
        z := false;
        if y = i then  y := 0;
end
```

Note that, unlike in Fischer's algorithm, in the absence of competing processes that want to enter their critical section, in the algorithm by Alur and Taubenfeld a process can always enter and exit its critical section without having to delay itself. In fact, in this case, the process writes x, reads y, writes y, reads x (finding it equal to i because no other process started the protocol to enter the critical section), writes z and enters its critical section.

Alur and Taubenfeld (1992, 1996) proved that the above algorithm ensures mutual exclusion and is deadlock free. Moreover, they reported a mechanical verification of their proof for $n = 3$ processes using the verification tool COSPAN (Alur *et al.* 1995).

Exercise 13.4 *Model the algorithm of Alur and Taubenfeld given above in* UPPAAL *for* $n = 3$ *processes and* $\Delta = 2$*. Verify that it preserves mutual exclusion. Increase the number of processes to four and five, and repeat the verification.* ◆

Exercise 13.5 *Take the model you produced in your solution to the previous exercise and modify it so that at least one of the memory accesses of the processes takes at most 1 time unit. Does the resulting algorithm still preserve mutual exclusion? Experiment with different choices of 'fast steps'. Do your conclusions depend on the steps that are chosen to be 'fast'?* ◆

Exercise 13.6 *Consider the variation on the algorithm of Alur and Taubenfeld offered below. Model it using* UPPAAL *for* $n = 3$ *processes and* $\Delta = 2$*. Verify that it preserves mutual exclusion. Increase the number of processes to four and five, and repeat the verification.* ◆

```
while true do
begin
      start: x := i;
      await (y = 0);
      y := i;
      if x ≠ i then  delay(Δ);
                      if y ≠ i then goto  start;
                      delay(Δ);
                      await (¬z)
      else  z := true;
      'critical section';
      z := false;
      if y = i then  y := 0;
end
```

Despite being very elegant and fast, the algorithms by Fischer and Alur and Taubenfeld suffer from an important drawback: they fail to guarantee mutual exclusion if the timing constraints upon which their workings are predicated are not satisfied. (Indeed, the solutions you found for Exercises 13.3 and 13.5 should have already convinced you of this fact!)

According to Lynch and Shavit, a timing-based mutual exclusion algorithm should guarantee mutual exclusion regardless of the timing constraints. In Lynch and Shavit (1992), they offered a simple and efficient timing-based mutual exclusion algorithm that guarantees mutual exclusion regardless of the timing constraints. Their algorithm uses two shared integer registers x, y, whose value is initially 0. Moreover, as in Fischer's algorithm, 'delay' stands for a positive integer constant. The pseudocode for process i in their algorithm is as follows.

> **while true do**
> **begin**
>   'noncritical section';
>   L: **if** $x \neq 0$ **then goto** L;
>   1: $x := i$;
>   2: **pause**(delay);
>   3: **if** $x \neq i$ **then goto** L;
>   4: **if** $y \neq 0$ **then goto** L;
>   5: $y := 1$;
>   6: **if** $x \neq i$ **then goto** L;
>   7: 'critical section';
>   8: $y := 0$;
>   9: $x := 0$;
> **end**

Exercise 13.7 *Model the algorithm by Lynch and Shavit in* UPPAAL *for* $n = 3$ *processes and a delay equal to 2. Verify that it preserves mutual exclusion for different upper bounds on the time that it takes for processes to execute steps in their entry to the critical section. Increase the number of processes to four and five, and repeat the verification.*   ♦

Appendix A   Suggestions for student projects

This appendix describes three selected student projects. All these projects involve
the use of software tools for verification and validation. In our lecture courses we
have usually introduced the students to the Concurrency Workbench (CWB)[1] and
to UPPAAL,[2] but other tools could be used just as well. Further information on the
following projects and more suggestions for student projects are available from the
web page for the book at www.cs.aau.dk/rsbook/.

A.1   Alternating-bit protocol

In this project you are asked to model the alternating-bit protocol in the CCS language and verify your model using the CWB. The alternating-bit protocol is a
simple yet effective protocol for managing the retransmission of lost messages.
Consider a sender S and a receiver R, and assume that the communication medium
from S to R is initialized, so that there are no messages in transit. The alternating-
bit protocol works as follows.

- Each message sent by S contains an additional protocol bit, 0 or 1.
- When S sends a message, it does so repeatedly (with its corresponding bit) until
  it receives an acknowledgment (ACK) from R that contains the same protocol
  bit as the message being sent.
- When R receives a message, it sends an acknowledgment ACK to S and
  includes the protocol bit of the received message. When a message is received
  for the first time, the receiver delivers it for processing, while subsequent messages with the same bit are simply acknowledged.

---

[1]homepages.inf.ed.ac.uk/perdita/cwb/
[2]www.uppaal.com/

- When S receives an acknowledgment containing the same bit as the message it is currently transmitting, it stops transmitting that message, flips the protocol bit and repeats the protocol for the next message.

There is no direct communication between the sender and the receiver; all messages must travel through the medium.

Your tasks are as follows.

1. Implement the alternating-bit protocol in the CWB. You can ignore the content of the messages and focus only on the additional control bit. To model the decision whether the sender retransmits the message, use either nondeterminism or, even better, a special process called Timer. The process Timer will communicate with the sender on a channel called 'timeout' and will signal when a message should be retransmitted.
2. Suggest a specification of the expected behaviour of the protocol, and check whether it is equivalent to your implementation, using a suitable notion of equivalence available in the CWB. In particular, consider the following degrees of reliability of the communication medium, and answer the question in the previous sentence for each of these choices:
   (a) perfect channels (all received messages are delivered);
   (b) lossy channels (received messages may be lost without any warning); or
   (c) lossy and duplicating channels (in addition to (b) the received message may be delivered several times).
3. Check for possible deadlocks (stuck configurations) and livelocks (the possibility of an infinite sequence of τ-labelled transitions) in your model of the protocol, by formulating the properties as recursive formulae in Hennessy–Milner logic and by verifying whether the implementation satisfies these formulae.

A.2 Gossiping girls

In this project you are asked to model and analyze the following 'gossiping girls problem' in UPPAAL.

Problem description A number of girls, say $G_1, G_2, \ldots, G_n$, $n \geq 2$, initially know one distinct secret each. You can assume that the secrets are elements of $\{1, \ldots, n\}$ and that initially girl G_i knows only secret i, for each $i \in \{1, \ldots, n\}$. The current state of knowledge of a girl is represented by the set of secrets that she presently knows. So, for instance, the current knowledge of girl G_i is $\{i\}$, for each $i \in \{1, \ldots, n\}$. Each girl has access to a phone that can be used to call another girl to share their secrets. Every time two girls talk to each other, they always exchange all the secrets they know. Thus, after the phone call they both know all the secrets they knew separately before the phone call. The girls can communicate only in pairs (no conference calls are allowed), but it is possible that different pairs of girls talk concurrently.

Your tasks are as follows.

- Model the problem as a network of timed automata in UPPAAL, and use UPPAAL to find the smallest number of phone calls needed for four girls to know all the secrets.
- Refine your model so that each phone call lasts exactly 60 seconds. (For simplicity, the duration of a call is independent of the number of exchanged secrets.) Find the minimum time needed for four girls to know all the secrets.
- Experiment with the search options offered by UPPAAL, namely breadth-first or depth-first search, and with the diagnostic trace settings, namely fastest and shortest. Try to solve the problem for five girls.

A.3 Implementation of regions

In this project you are asked to develop and implement a data structure in a functional language (e.g. SML, Haskell or Lisp). The data structure allows one to represent and manipulate regions, as required when constructing the region graph of a timed automaton. In dealing with the exercise, you may find it useful to consult Section 11.4. Figure A.1 illustrates the 18 equivalence classes resulting when the region construction is applied in the presence of two clocks whose maximal constant is one. In this figure, we use γ_i to range over equivalence classes.

We recall from Definition 11.12 that equivalent clock valuations must (essentially):

- have the same integral part or exceed the maximal constant c_x, for each clock x;
- agree on the values of the clocks whose fractional part is 0; and
- agree on the ordering of clocks determined by the size of the fractional part.

Owing to the agreement mentioned in the second and third list items above, we may lift the information on the integral and fractional parts from clock valuations to their regions (equivalence classes of clock valuations). In particular, we write:

$\gamma(x) > c_x$ when $v(x) > c_x$ for all $v \in \gamma$; and
$\gamma(x) \leq c_x$ when $v(x) \leq c_x$ for all $v \in \gamma$.

For clocks x and y satisfying the latter condition, we have in addition:

$\lfloor \gamma(x) \rfloor = k$ when $\lfloor v(x) \rfloor = k$ for all $v \in \gamma$;
$frac(\gamma(x)) = 0$ when $frac(v(x)) = 0$ for all $v \in \gamma$; and
$frac(\gamma(x)) \leq frac(\gamma(y))$ when $frac(v(x)) \leq frac(v(y))$ for all $v \in \gamma$.

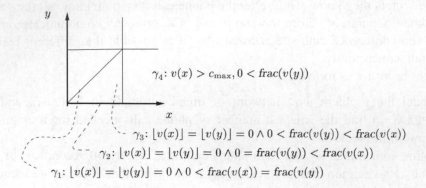

$$\gamma_4\colon v(x) > c_{\max}, 0 < \mathrm{frac}(v(y))$$

$$\gamma_3\colon \lfloor v(x)\rfloor = \lfloor v(y)\rfloor = 0 \wedge 0 < \mathrm{frac}(v(y)) < \mathrm{frac}(v(x))$$

$$\gamma_2\colon \lfloor v(x)\rfloor = \lfloor v(y)\rfloor = 0 \wedge 0 = \mathrm{frac}(v(y)) < \mathrm{frac}(v(x))$$

$$\gamma_1\colon \lfloor v(x)\rfloor = \lfloor v(y)\rfloor = 0 \wedge 0 < \mathrm{frac}(v(x)) = \mathrm{frac}(v(y))$$

Figure A.1 Some of the 18 regions when $C = \{x, y\}$ and $c_x = c_y = 1$.

According to Exercises 11.13 and 11.14, the reset and delay operations on clock valuations may also be lifted to regions. Thus, for two regions γ and γ' and a clock x, we say that γ' is the reset of γ with respect to x, written $\gamma' = \gamma[x \mapsto 0]$, if $v[x \mapsto 0] \in \gamma'$ for some $v \in \gamma$. For two distinct regions γ and γ' (i.e. $\gamma \neq \gamma'$), we say that γ' is the *immediate delay successor* of γ, written $\gamma' = delaysucc(\gamma)$, if for each $v \in \gamma$ there exists $d \in \mathbb{R}_{\geq 0}$ such that

$v + d \in \gamma'$, and
$v + d' \in \gamma \cup \gamma'$ whenever $0 \leq d' < d$.

List representation of regions   We suggest a list-based representation of regions. For a set A, we denote by $\mathsf{List}(A)$ the set of all lists over A. For a list L over A and an element a of A, we misuse notation slightly and use $a \in L$ to mean that a occurs as an element in L. A region γ is represented by a triple $\mathcal{C}_\gamma = (\mathcal{M}_\gamma, \mathcal{I}_\gamma, \mathcal{F}_\gamma)$, where

$\mathcal{M}_\gamma$ is in $\mathsf{List}(C)$,
$\mathcal{I}_\gamma$ is in $\mathsf{List}(C \times \mathbb{N})$, and
$\mathcal{F}_\gamma$ is in $\mathsf{List}(\mathsf{List}(C))$.

The three lists for $\mathcal{C}_\gamma$ represent a region γ in the following way.

- $\mathcal{M}_\gamma$ contains all clocks $x \in C$ for which $\gamma(x) > c_x$.
- $\mathcal{I}_\gamma$ gives information on the integral parts of the remaining clocks; we have that $(x, k) \in \mathcal{I}_\gamma$ iff $\lfloor \gamma(x) \rfloor = k$.
- $\mathcal{F}_\gamma$ has the form $\mathcal{F}_\gamma = [L_0, L_1, \ldots, L_k]$, where $L_0, L_1, \ldots, L_k$ constitutes a partitioning of the clocks for which $\gamma(x) \leq c_x$, i.e. each such clock belongs to precisely one list L_i. Only L_0 is allowed to be empty. Now, $\mathcal{F}_\gamma$ gives information

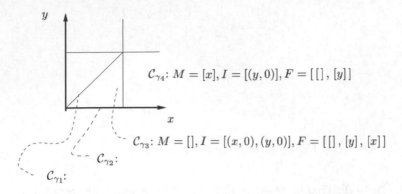

Figure A.2 List representation of some of the regions in Figure A.1.

on the relative ordering of fractional parts of clocks in a rather obvious way: L_0 contains all clocks with fractional part equal to 0; clocks belonging to the same list L_i have identical fractional parts; and the fractional parts of clocks increase according to the index of the list L_i to which they belong. That is,

$frac(\gamma(x)) = 0$ iff $x \in L_0$,
$frac(\gamma(x)) \leq frac(\gamma(y))$ iff $x \in L_i$ and $y \in L_j$ with $i \leq j$.

Fill in the list representation of the regions γ_1 and γ_2 in Figure A.2.

Implementation of region operations In what follows you are asked to define a number of useful operations on regions, on the basis of the list representation suggested in the previous subsection. Also, you are requested to implement the various operations as list-processing functions in a functional language.

Let $\mathcal{C}_\gamma = (M_\gamma, I_\gamma, F_\gamma)$ be the list representation of some region γ over a set of clocks C and a collection of maximal constants $\{c_x \mid x \in C\}$.

Guards Define and implement a boolean function $\mathsf{sat}_\leq$ that, given a clock x, a non-negative integer k and a list representation $\mathcal{C}_\gamma$ will test whether γ satisfies the guard $x \leq k$. That is,

$$\mathsf{sat}_\leq(x, k, \mathcal{C}_\gamma) = \text{true}$$

if and only if γ satisfies the guard $x \leq k$ (i.e. v satisfies $x \leq k$ for each $v \in \gamma$). Define in a similar way functions $\mathsf{sat}_\geq$, $\mathsf{sat}_<$ and $\mathsf{sat}_>$. As an example, $\mathsf{sat}_\leq(x, 1, \mathcal{C}_{\gamma_3}) = \text{true}$, in Figure A.2.

Reset Define and implement a function reset that, given a clock x and a list representation of a region γ, returns the list representation of the region

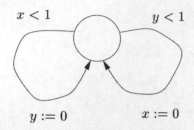

Figure A.3 A simple timed automaton.

$\beta = \gamma[x \mapsto 0]$. That is, $\mathsf{reset}(x, \mathcal{C}_\gamma) = \mathcal{C}_\beta$. As an example, $\mathsf{reset}(x, \mathcal{C}_{\gamma_3}) = \mathcal{C}_{\gamma_2}$ in Figure A.2.

Delay successor Define and implement a function succ that, given a list representation $\mathcal{C}_\gamma$, returns a list representation $\mathcal{C}_\delta$ of the immediate delay-successor region $\delta = delaysucc(\gamma)$. As an example, $\mathsf{succ}(\mathcal{C}_{\gamma_2}) = \mathcal{C}_{\gamma_3}$ in Figure A.2.

Application   Now consider the very simple timed automaton in Figure A.3. You are asked to use the implementation of the functions from the previous section to explore the corresponding region graph. Which of the following guards is or are satisfied by some region that is reachable from the initial region (i.e. $[x = y = 0]$)?

$$x = 0 \wedge y < 1,$$
$$x = 1 \wedge y = 0,$$
$$y < 1 \wedge x > 1,$$
$$x > 1 \wedge y = 0.$$

In the affirmative case(s), provide a sequence of regions (preferably a shortest such sequence) that will bring the automaton from the initial region to a region satisfying the property.

Using your implementation, give a diagram showing the part of the region graph that is reachable from the initial region. Each reachable region should be described in terms of its list representation.

References

Aceto, L., Bouyer, P., Burgueño, A. and Larsen, K. G. (2003). The power of reachability testing for timed automata, *Theoretical Computer Science* **300**(1–3): 411–475.

Aceto, L. and Ingolfsdottir, A. (1999). Testing Hennessy–Milner logic with recursion, in W. Thomas (ed.), *Foundations of Software Science and Computation Structure, Proc. Second International Conference, FoSSaCS'99*, Held as Part of the European Joint Conferences on the Theory and Practice of Software, ETAPS'99, Amsterdam, The Netherlands, March 22–28, 1999. Volume 1578 of *Lecture Notes in Computer Science*, Springer-Verlag, pp. 41–55.

Aceto, L., Ingolfsdottir, A., Pedersen, M. L. and Poulsen, J. (2000). Characteristic formulae for timed automata, *RAIRO, Theoretical Informatics and Applications* **34**(6): 565–584.

Aceto, L. and Laroussinie, F. (2002). Is your model checker on time? On the complexity of model checking for timed modal logics, *Journal of Logic and Algebraic Programming* **52–53**: 7–51.

Alur, R., Courcoubetis, C. and Dill, D. L. (1993). Model-checking in dense real-time, *Information and Computation* **104**(1): 2–34.

Alur, R., Courcoubetis, C., Halbwachs, N., Dill, D. L. and Wong-Toi, H. (1992). Minimization of timed transition systems, in Cleaveland (1992), pp. 340–354.

Alur, R., Courcoubetis, C., Halbwachs, N., *et al.* (1995). The algorithmic analysis of hybrid systems, *Theoretical Computer Science* **138**(1): 3–34.

Alur, R. and Dill, D. L. (1990). Automata for modeling real-time systems, in M. Paterson (ed.), *Proc. 17th ICALP*, Warwick. Volume 443 of *Lecture Notes in Computer Science*, Springer-Verlag, pp. 322–335.

Alur, R. and Dill, D. L. (1992). The theory of timed automata, in J. de Bakker, C. Huizing, W. d. Roever and G. Rozenberg (eds.), *Proc. REX Workshop on*

Real-Time: Theory in Practice, Mook, The Netherlands, June 1991. Volume 600 of *Lecture Notes in Computer Science*, Springer-Verlag, pp. 45–73.

Alur, R. and Dill, D. L. (1994). A theory of timed automata, *Theoretical Computer Science* **126**(2): 183–235. Fundamental study.

Alur, R., Fix, L. and Henzinger, T. A. (1999). Event-clock automata: a determinizable class of timed automata, *Theoretical Computer Science* **211**(1–2): 253–273.

Alur, R. and Henzinger, T. A. (1994). A really temporal logic, *Journal of the ACM* **41**(1): 181–204.

Alur, R., Itai, A., Kurshan, R. P. and Yannakakis, M. (1995). Timing verification by successive approximation, *Information and Computation* **118**(1): 142–157.

Alur, R., La Torre, S. and Pappas, G. J. (2001). Optimal paths in weighted timed automata, in *Proc. 4th Intl Workshop on Hybrid Systems: Computation and Control*, HSCC 01. Volume 2034 of *Lecture Notes in Computer Science*, Springer-Verlag, pp. 49–62.

Alur, R. and Taubenfeld, G. (1992). Results about fast mutual exclusion, *IEEE Real-Time Systems Symposium*. IEEE Computer Society Press, pp. 12–22.

Alur, R. and Taubenfeld, G. (1996). Fast timing-based algorithms, *Distributed Computing* **10**(1): 1–10.

Andersen, H. R. (1998). An introduction to binary decision diagrams. Version of October 1997 with minor revisions April 1998. 36 pp. Available at www.itu.dk/people/hra/notes-index.html.

Asarin, E. (2004). Challenges in timed languages: from applied theory to basic theory, *Bulletin of the European Association for Theoretical Computer Science* **83**: 106–120.

Asarin, E., Caspi, P. and Maler, O. (2002). Timed regular expressions, *Journal of the ACM* **49**(2): 172–206.

Baeten, J. C. (2005). A brief history of process algebra, *Theoretical Computer Science* **335**(2–3): 131–146.

Baeten, J. C., Bergstra, J. and Klop, J. W. (1987). On the consistency of Koomen's fair abstraction rule, *Theoretical Computer Science* **51**(1/2): 129–176.

Baeten, J. C., Bergstra, J. and Klop, J. W. (1993). Decidability of bisimulation equivalence for processes generating context-free languages, *Journal of the ACM* **40**(3): 653–682.

Baeten, J. C. and Klop, J. W. (eds.) (1990). *Proceedings CONCUR 90*, Amsterdam. Volume 458 of *Lecture Notes in Computer Science*, Springer-Verlag.

Baeten, J. C. and Bergstra, J. (1991). Real time process algebra, *Journal of Formal Aspects of Computing Science* **3**(2): 142–188.

Baeten, J. C. and Middelburg, C. A. (2002). *Process Algebra with Timing*. Monographs in Theoretical Computer Science, an EATCS Series, Springer-Verlag.

Baeten, J. C. and Weijland, P. (1990). *Process Algebra*. Cambridge Tracts in Theoretical Computer Science, Volume 18, Cambridge University Press.

Balcázar, J. L., Gabarró, J. and Santha, M. (1992). Deciding bisimilarity is P-complete, *Journal of Formal Aspects of Computing Science* **4**(6A): 638–648.

Bar-Hillel, Y., Perles, M. and Shamir, E. (1961). On formal properties of simple phrase structure grammars, *Zeitschrift für Phonetik, Sprachwissenschaft, und Kommunikationsforschung* **14**: 143–177.

Basten, T. (1996). Branching bisimilarity is an equivalence indeed!, *Information Processing Letters* **58**(3): 141–147.

Behrmann, G., David, A. and Larsen, K. G. (2004). A tutorial on UPPAAL, in M. Bernardo and F. Corradini (eds.), *Formal Methods for the Design of Real-Time Systems, International School on Formal Methods for the Design of Computer, Communication and Software Systems, SFM-RT 2004*, Bertinoro, Italy, September 13-18, 2004. Revised Lectures, Volume 3185 of *Lecture Notes in Computer Science*, Springer-Verlag, pp. 200–236.

Bellman, R. (1957). *Dynamic Programming*. Princeton University Press.

Bengtsson, J. and Yi, W. (2003). Timed automata: semantics, algorithms and tools, in J. Desel, W. Reisig and G. Rozenberg (eds.), *Lectures on Concurrency and Petri Nets*. Volume 3098 of *Lecture Notes in Computer Science*, Springer-Verlag, pp. 87–124.

Bérard, B., Cassez, F., Haddad, S., Lime, D. and Roux, O. H. (2005). Comparison of the expressiveness of timed automata and timed Petri nets, in Pettersson and Yi (2005), pp. 211–225.

Bérard, B., Diekert, V., Gastin, P. and Petit, A. (1998). Characterization of the expressive power of silent transitions in timed automata, *Fundamenta Informaticae* **36**(2): 145–182.

Bergstra, J. and Klop, J. W. (1982). Fixed point semantics in process algebras, Report IW 206, Mathematisch Centrum, Amsterdam.

Bergstra, J., Ponse, A. and Smolka, S. A. (eds) (2001). *Handbook of Process Algebra*. Elsevier.

Best, E. (ed.) (1993). *Proceedings CONCUR 93*, Hildesheim, Germany. Volume 715 of *Lecture Notes in Computer Science*, Springer-Verlag.

Bornot, S. and Sifakis, J. (2000). An algebraic framework for urgency, *Information and Computation* **163**: 172–202.

Boudol, G. and Larsen, K. G. (1992). Graphical versus logical specifications, *Theoretical Computer Science* **106**(1): 3–20.

Bouyer, P., Brinksma, E. and Larsen, K. G. (2004). Staying alive as cheaply as possible, in *Proc. 7th Intl Workshop on Hybrid Systems: Computation and Control, HSCC'04*. Volume 2993 of *Lecture Notes in Computer Science*, Springer-Verlag, pp. 203–218.

Bouyer, P., Cassez, F. and Laroussinie, F. (2005). Modal logics for timed control, in M. Abadi and L. de Alfaro (eds.), *Proc. CONCUR 2005 – Concurrency Theory, 16th Intl Conf.*, San Francisco CA, USA, August 23–6, 2005. Volume 3653 of *Lecture Notes in Computer Science*, Springer-Verlag, pp. 81–94.

Bouyer, P., Chevalier, F. and Markey, N. (2005). On the expressiveness of TPTL and MTL, in R. Ramanujam and S. Sen (eds), *Proc. FSTTCS 2005: Foundations of Software Technology and Theoretical Computer Science, 25th Intl Conf.*, Hyderabad, India, December 15–18, 2005. Volume 3821 of *Lecture Notes in Computer Science*, Springer-Verlag, pp. 432–443.

Bouyer, P., Dufourd, C., Fleury, E. and Petit, A. (2004). Updatable timed automata, *Theoretical Computer Science* **321**(2–3): 291–345.

Bouyer, P. and Petit, A. (2002). A Kleene/Büchi-like theorem for clock languages, *Journal of Automata, Languages and Combinatorics* **7**(2): 167–186.

Bozga, M., Daws, C., Maler, O., Olivero, A., Tripakis, S. and Yovine, S. (1998). Kronos: a model-checking tool for real-time systems, in A. J. Hu and M. Y. Vardi (eds.), *Proc. Computer Aided Verification, 10th Intl Conf., CAV 98*, Vancouver BC, Canada, 28 June – 2 July, 1998. Volume 1427 of *Lecture Notes in Computer Science*, Springer-Verlag, pp. 546–550.

Bryant, R. E. (1992). Symbolic boolean manipulation with ordered binary-decision diagrams, *ACM Computing Surveys* **24**(3): 293–318.

Burkart, O., Caucal, D., Moller, F. and Steffen, B. (2001). Verification on infinite structures, in Bergstra, Ponse and Smolka (2001), pp. 545–623.

Burkart, O., Caucal, D. and Steffen, B. (1995). An elementary decision procedure for arbitrary context-free processes, in *Proc. 20th Intl Symp. on Mathematical Foundations of Computer Science, MFCS 95*. Volume 969 of *Lecture Notes in Computer Science*, Springer-Verlag, pp. 423–433.

Burkart, O. and Esparza, J. (1997). More infinite results, *Bulletin of the European Association for Theoretical Computer Science* **62**: 138–159. Columns: Concurrency.

Burkart, O. and Steffen, B. (1997). Model checking the full modal mu-calculus for infinite sequential processes, in *Proc. 24th Intl Colloq. on Automata, Languages and Programming, ICALP 97*. Volume 1256 of *Lecture Notes in Computer Science*, Springer-Verlag, pp. 419–429.

Burns, J. E. and Lynch, N. A. (1980). Mutual exclusion using indivisible reads and writes, in *Proc. 18th Annual Allerton Conf. on Communications, Control and Computing*, Monticello IL, University of Illinois, pp. 833–842.

Burns, J. E. and Lynch, N. A. (1993). Bounds on shared memory for mutual exclusion, *Information and Computation* **107**(2): 171–184.

Caucal, D. (1996). On infinite transition graphs having a decidable monadic theory, in *Proc. 23th Intl Colloq. on Automata, Languages and Programming*,

ICALP 96. Volume 1099 *of Lecture Notes in Computer Science*, Springer-Verlag, pp. 194–205.

Čerāns, K. (1993). Decidability of bisimulation equivalences for parallel timer processes, in G. von Bochmann and D. K. Probst (eds.), *Computer Aided Verification, 4th Intl Workshop, CAV 92*, Montreal, Canada, 29 June – 1 July, 1992. Volume 663 of *Lecture Notes in Computer Science*, Springer-Verlag, pp. 302–315.

Christensen, S. (1993). *Decidability and Decomposition in Process Algebras*. Ph.D. thesis, University of Edinburgh.

Christensen, S., Hirshfeld, Y. and Moller, F. (1993). Bisimulation is decidable for basic parallel processes, in *Proc. 4th Intl Conf. on Concurrency Theory, CONCUR 93*. Volume 715 of *Lecture Notes in Computer Science*, Springer-Verlag, pp. 143–157.

Christensen, S., Hüttel, H. and Stirling, C. (1995). Bisimulation equivalence is decidable for all context-free processes, *Information and Computation* **121**(2): 143–148.

Clarke, E. and Emerson, E. (1981). Design and synthesis of synchronization skeletons using branching time temporal logic, in D. Kozen (ed.), *Proc. Workshop on Logics of Programs*. Volume 131 of *Lecture Notes in Computer Science*, Springer-Verlag, pp. 52–71.

Clarke, E., Emerson, E. and Sistla, A. P. (1986). Automatic verification of finite-state concurrent systems using temporal logic specifications, *ACM Transactions on Programming Languages and Systems* **8**(2): 244–263.

Clarke, E., Gruemberg, O. and Peled, D. (1999). *Model Checking*. MIT Press.

Cleaveland, R. (ed.) (1992). *Proceeding CONCUR 92*, Stony Brook NY, USA. Volume 630 of *Lecture Notes in Computer Science*, Springer-Verlag.

Cleaveland, R., Parrow, J. and Steffen, B. (1993). The concurrency workbench: a semantics-based tool for the verification of concurrent systems, *ACM Transactions on Programming Languages and Systems* **15**(1): 36–72.

Cleaveland, R. and Steffen, B. (1992). A linear-time model-checking algorithm for the alternation-free modal mu-calculus, in K. Larsen and A. Skou (eds.), *Proc. 3rd Workshop on Computer Aided Verification*, Aalborg, Denmark, July 1991. Volume 575 of *Lecture Notes in Computer Science*, Springer-Verlag, pp. 48–58.

Courcoubetis, C. (ed.) (1993). *Proc. 5th Intl Conf. on Computer Aided Verification*, Elounda, Greece, July 1993. Volume 697 of *Lecture Notes in Computer Science*, Springer-Verlag.

Davey, B. A. and Priestley, H. A. (2002). *Introduction to Lattices and Order*, second edn. Cambridge University Press.

Davies, J. and Schneider, S. (1989). An introduction to Timed CSP. Technical Monograph PRG-75, Oxford University Computing Laboratory, Programming Research Group.

De Nicola, R. and Hennessy, M. (1984). Testing equivalences for processes, *Theoretical Computer Science* **34**: 83–133.

Dijkstra, E. W. (1965). Solutions of a problem in concurrent programming control, *Communications of the ACM* **8**(9): 569.

Dijkstra, E. W. (1971). Hierarchical ordering of sequential processes, *Acta Informatica* **1**(2): 115–138.

Dill, D. L. (1989). Timing assumptions and verification of finite-state concurrent systems, in J. Sifakis (ed.), *Automatic Verification Methods for Finite State Systems*, Volume 407 of *Lecture Notes in Computer Science*, Springer-Verlag, pp. 197–212.

Dima, C. (2001). *An Algebraic Theory of Real-time Formal Languages*. Ph.D. thesis, Université Joseph Fourier, Grenoble, France.

Esparza, J. (1994). On the decidability of model checking for several μ-calculi and Petri nets, in S. Tison (ed.), *Trees in Algebra and Programming, Proc. 19th Intl Colloq., CAAP 94, Edinburgh, April 11–13, 1994*. Volume 787 of *Lecture Notes in Computer Science*, Springer-Verlag, pp. 115–129.

Esparza, J. (1997). Decidability of model-checking for infinite-state concurrent systems, *Acta Informatica* **34**: 85–107.

Esparza, J. and Kiehn, A. (1995). On the model checking problem for branching time logics and basic parallel processes, in Courcoubetis (1993), pp. 353–366.

FOC (1977). *Proc. 18th Annual Symp. on Foundations of Computer Science*. IEEE.

Fokkink, W. (1993). An elimination theorem for regular behaviours with integration, in Best (1993), pp. 432–446.

Fokkink, W. (2000). *Introduction to Process Algebra*. Texts in Theoretical Computer Science, an EATCS Series, Springer-Verlag.

Gelernter, D. (1985). Generative communication in Linda, *ACM Transactions on Programming Languages and Systems* **7**(1): 80–112.

Glabbeek, R. v. (1990). The linear time–branching time spectrum, in Baeten and Klop (1990), pp. 278–297.

Glabbeek, R. v. (1993). The linear time–branching time spectrum II: the semantics of sequential processes with silent moves, in Best (1993), pp. 66–81.

Glabbeek, R. v. (2001). The linear time–branching time spectrum. I. The semantics of concrete, sequential processes, in Bergstra *et al.* (2001), pp. 3–99.

Glabbeek, R. v. (2005). A characterisation of weak bisimulation congruence, in A. Middeldorp, V. van Oostrom, F. van Raamsdonk and R. C. de Vrijer (eds.),

Processes, Terms and Cycles. Volume 3838 of *Lecture Notes in Computer Science*, Springer-Verlag, pp. 26–39.

Glabbeek, R. v. and Weijland, W. (1996). Branching time and abstraction in bisimulation semantics, *Journal of the ACM* **43**(3): 555–600.

Godskesen, J. C. and Larsen, K. G. (1992). Real-time calculi and expansion theorems, in *Proc. Conf. on Foundations of Software Technology and Theoretical Computer Science,* New Delhi, 1992. Volume 652 of *Lecture Notes in Computer Science*, Springer-Verlag, pp. 302–315.

Godskesen, J. C. and Larsen, K. G. (1995). Synthesizing distinguishing formulae for real time systems, *Nordic Journal of Computing* **2**(3): 338–357.

Graf, S. and Sifakis, J. (1986). A modal characterization of observational congruence on finite terms of CCS, *Information and Control* **68**(1–3): 125–145.

Greenlaw, R., Hoover, H. J. and Ruzzo, W. R. (1995). *Limits to Parallel Computation: P-Completeness Theory.* Oxford University Press.

Groote, J. and Hüttel, H. (1994). Undecidable equivalences for basic process algebra, *Information and Computation* **115**(2): 353–371.

Hamming, R. W. (1997). *The Art of Doing Science and Engineering (Learning to Learn).* Gordon and Breach Science Publishers.

Harel, D. and Pnueli, A. (1985). On the development of reactive systems, in *Proc. Conf. on Logics and Models of Concurrent Systems,* La Colle-sur-Loup, 1984. Volume 13 of *NATO Adv. Sci. Inst. Ser. F Comput. Systems Sci.*, Springer-Verlag, pp. 477–498.

Har'El, Z. and Kurshan, R. P. (1987). Cospan user's guide. Technical report, AT&T Bell Laboratories, Murray Hill NJ.

Harju, T. (2006). Ordered sets. Collection of lecture notes available from http://users.utu.fi/harju/orderedsets/Mainorder.pdf. 77 pages.

Hennessy, M. (1988). *Algebraic Theory of Processes.* MIT Press.

Hennessy, M. and Milner, R. (1985). Algebraic laws for nondeterminism and concurrency, *Journal of the ACM* **32**(1): 137–161.

Hennessy, M. and Regan, T. (1995). A process algebra for timed systems, *Information and Computation* **117**(2): 221–239.

Henzinger, T. A. (1998). It's about time: real-time logics reviewed, in D. Sangiorgi and R. de Simone (eds.), *Proc. 9th Intl Conf. on Concurrency Theory, CONCUR 98,* Nice, France, September 8–11, 1998. Volume 1466 of *Lecture Notes in Computer Science*, Springer-Verlag, pp. 439–454.

Henzinger, T. A., Ho, P.-H. and Wong-Toi, H. (1997). Hytech: a model checker for hybrid systems, in O. Grumberg (ed.), *Proc. 9th Intl Conf. on Computer Aided Verification, CAV 97,* Haifa, Israel, June 22–25, 1997. Volume 1254 of *Lecture Notes in Computer Science*, Springer-Verlag, pp. 460–463.

Hirshfeld, Y. (1994). Petri nets and the equivalence problem, in *Proc. 7th Workshop on Computer Science Logic, CSL 93*. Volume 832 of *Lecture Notes in Computer Science*, Springer-Verlag, pp. 165–174.

Hirshfeld, Y., Jerrum, M. and Moller, F. (1996a). A polynomial algorithm for deciding bisimilarity of normed context-free processes, *Theoretical Computer Science* **158**: 143–159.

Hirshfeld, Y., Jerrum, M. and Moller, F. (1996b). A polynomial algorithm for deciding bisimulation equivalence of normed basic parallel processes, *Mathematical Structures in Computer Science* **6**: 251–259.

Hoare, C. (1978). Communicating sequential processes, *Communications of the ACM* **21**(8): 666–677.

Hoare, C. (1985). *Communicating Sequential Processes*. Prentice-Hall International.

Holzmann, G. J. (2003). *The SPIN Model Checker*. Addison-Wesley.

Hunt, H. B., Rosenkrantz, D. J. and Szymanski, T. G. (1976). On the equivalence, containment, and covering problems for the regular and context-free languages, *Journal of Computer and System Sciences* **12**: 222–268.

Hüttel, H. (1994). Undecidable equivalences for basic parallel processes, in *Proc. 2nd Intl Symp. on Theoretical Aspects of Computer Software, TACS 94*. Volume 789 of *Lecture Notes in Computer Science*, Springer-Verlag, pp. 454–464.

Huynh, D. and Tian, L. (1995). On deciding readiness and failure equivalences for processes in Σ_2^P, *Information and Computation* **117**(2): 193–205.

Hyman, H. (1966). Comments on a problem in concurrent programming control, *Communications of the ACM* **9**(1): 45.

Ingolfsdottir, A., Godskesen, J. C. and Zeeberg, M. (1987). Fra Hennessy–Milner logik til CCS-processer. Master's thesis, Department of Computer Science, Aalborg University. In Danish.

Jančar, P. (1995). Undecidability of bisimilarity for Petri nets and some related problems, *Theoretical Computer Science* **148**(2): 281–301.

Jančar, P. (2003). Strong bisimilarity on basic parallel processes is PSPACE-complete, in *Proc. 18th Annual IEEE Symp. on Logic in Computer Science, LICS 03*. IEEE Computer Society Press, pp. 218–227.

Jurdziński, M. (1998). Deciding the winner in parity games is in UP ∩ co-UP, *Information Processing Letters* **68**(3): 119–124.

Kanellakis, P. C. and Smolka, S. A. (1990). CCS expressions, finite state processes, and three problems of equivalence, *Information and Computation* **86**(1): 43–68.

Keller, R. (1976). Formal verification of parallel programs, *Communications of the ACM* **19**(7): 371–384.

Klusener, A. (1992). The silent step in time, in Cleaveland (1992), pp. 421–435.

Knaster, B. (1928). Un théorème sur les fonctions d'ensembles, *Annales Societatis Mathematicae Polonae* **6**: 133–134. In French.

Knuth, D. E. (1966). Additional comments on a problem in concurrent programming control, *Communications of the ACM* **9**(5): 321–322.

Koymans, R. (1990). Specifying real-time properties with metric temporal logic, *Real-Time Systems* **2**(4): 255–299.

Kozen, D. (1977). Lower bounds for natural proof systems, *in* FOC (1977), pp. 254–266.

Kozen, D. (1983). Results on the propositional mu-calculus, *Theoretical Computer Science* **27**: 333–354.

Kupferman, O., Vardi, M. Y. and Wolper, P. (2000). An automata-theoretic approach to branching-time model checking, *Journal of the ACM* **47**(2): 312–360.

Lamport, L. (1983). What good is temporal logic?, *in* R. Mason (ed.), *Proc. IFIP 9th World Congress, Information Processing 83*. North-Holland, pp. 657–668.

Lamport, L. (1986). The mutual exclusion problem: Part II – statement and solutions, *Journal of the ACM* **33**(2): 327–348.

Laroussinie, F. and Larsen, K. G. (1998). CMC: a tool for compositional model-checking of real-time systems, *in* S. Budkowski, A. R. Cavalli and E. Najm (eds.), *Formal Description Techniques and Protocol Specification, Testing and Verification, Proc. Joint Intl Conf. on Formal Description Techniques for Distributed Systems and Communication Protocols (FORTE XI) and Protocol Specification, Testing and Verification (PSTV XVIII)*, 3–6 November 1998, Paris. Volume 135 of *IFIP Conference Proceedings*, Kluwer, pp. 439–456.

Laroussinie, F., Larsen, K. G. and Weise, C. (1995). From timed automata to logic – and back, *in* J. Wiedermann and P. Hájek (eds.), *Proc. 20th Intl Symp. on Mathematical Foundations of Computer Science, 1995*. Volume 969 of *Lecture Notes in Computer Science*, Springer-Verlag, pp. 529–539.

Laroussinie, F. and Schnoebelen, P. (2000). The state-explosion problem from trace to bisimulation equivalence, in *Proc. 3rd Intl Conf. on Foundations of Software Science and Computation Structures, FoSSaCS 2000*, Berlin, March 2000. Volume 1784 of *Lecture Notes in Computer Science*, Springer-Verlag, pp. 192–207.

Larsen, K. G. (1990). Proof systems for satisfiability in Hennessy–Milner logic with recursion, *Theoretical Computer Science* **72**(2–3): 265–288.

Larsen, K. G., Behrmann, G., Brinksma, E. *et al.* (2001). As cheap as possible: efficient cost-optimal reachability for priced timed automata, in G. Berry, H. Comon and A. Finkel (eds.), *Proc. 13th Intl Conf. on Computer Aided Verification, CAV 2001*, Paris, July 18–22, 2001. Volume 2102 of *Lecture Notes in Computer Science*, Springer-Verlag, pp. 493–505.

Larsen, K. G. and Yi, W. (1994). Time abstracted bisimulation: implicit specifications and decidability, in S. D. Brookes, M. G. Main, A. Melton, M. W. Mislove and D. A. Schmidt (eds.), *Proc. 9th Intl Conf. on the Mathematical Foundations of Programming Semantics*, New Orleans LA, April 7–10, 1993. Volume 802 of *Lecture Notes in Computer Science*, Springer-Verlag, pp. 160–176.

Larsen, K. G. and Yi, W. (1997). Time-abstracted bisimulation: implicit specifications and decidability, *Information and Computation* **134**(2): 75–101.

Libkin, L. (2004). *Elements of Finite Model Theory*. Texts in Theoretical Computer Science, an EATCS series, Springer-Verlag.

Lions, J. L. (1996). ARIANE 5 flight 501 failure: report by the inquiry board. Available on-line at the URL www.cs.aau.dk/~luca/SV/ariane.pdf.

Luttik, B. (2006). What is algebraic in process theory?, *Bulletin of the European Association for Theoretical Computer Science* **88**: 66–83.

Lynch, N. A. (1996). *Distributed Algorithms*. Series in Data Management Systems, Morgan Kaufmann.

Lynch, N. A. and Shavit, N. (1992). Timing-based mutual exclusion, in *Proc. 13th IEEE Real-Time Systems Symposium*, Phoenix AZ, 1992, pp. 2–11.

Magee, J. and Kramer, J. (1999). *Concurrency: State Models and Java Programs*. John Wiley.

Maler, O., Nickovic, D. and Pnueli, A. (2005). Real time temporal logic: past, present, future, in Pettersson and Yi (2005), pp. 2–16.

Manna, Z. and Pnueli, A. (1992). *The Temporal Logic of Reactive and Concurrent Systems (Specification)*. Springer-Verlag, New York.

Mayr, R. (1998). Strict lower bounds for model checking BPA, *Electronic Notes in Theoretical Computer Science* **18**. 12 pp.

Mayr, R. (2000). Process rewrite systems, *Information and Computation* **156**(1): 264–286.

Milner, R. (1989). *Communication and Concurrency*. Prentice-Hall International.

Moller, F. and Tofts, C. (1990). A temporal calculus of communicating systems, in Baeten and Klop (1990), pp. 401–415.

Moller, F. and Tofts, C. (1991). Relating processes with respect to speed, in J. Baeten and J. F. Groote (eds.), *Proc. CONCUR 91*, Amsterdam. Volume 527 of *Lecture Notes in Computer Science*, Springer-Verlag, pp. 424–438.

Muller, D. and Schupp, P. (1985). The theory of ends, pushdown automata, and second order logic, *Theoretical Computer Science* **37**(1): 51–75.

Nicollin, X. and Sifakis, J. (1994). The algebra of timed processes, **ATP**: theory and application, *Information and Computation* **114**(1): 131–178.

Nielson, H. and Nielson, F. (1992). *Semantics with Applications: A Formal Introduction*. Wiley Professional Computing, John Wiley & Sons.

Paige, R. and Tarjan, R. E. (1987). Three partition refinement algorithms, *SIAM Journal of Computing* **16**(6): 973–989.

Park, D. (1981). Concurrency and automata on infinite sequences, in P. Deussen (ed.), *Proc. 5th GI Conf.*, Karlsruhe, Germany. Volume 104 of *Lecture Notes in Computer Science*, Springer-Verlag, pp. 167–183.

Patterson, D. A. (2005). 20th century vs. 21st century C&C: the SPUR manifesto, *Communications of the ACM* **48**(3): 15–16.

Peterson, J. and Silberschatz, A. (1985). *Operating Systems Concepts*, 2nd edition. Addison Wesley.

Petri, C. (1962). *Kommunikation mit Automaten*. Volume 2 of *Schriften des IIM*, Institut für Instrumentelle Mathematik, Bonn.

Pettersson, P. and Yi, W. (eds.) (2005). *Proc. 3rd Intl Conf. on Formal Modeling and Analysis of Timed Systems, FORMATS 2005*, Uppsala, Sweden, September 26–28, 2005. Volume 3829 of *Lecture Notes in Computer Science*, Springer-Verlag.

Plotkin, G. D. (1981). A structural approach to operational semantics, Report DAIMI FN-19, Computer Science Department, Aarhus University.

Plotkin, G. D. (2004a). The origins of structural operational semantics, *Journal of Logic and Algebraic Programming* **60–61**: 3–15. The paper is available from www.dcs.ed.ac.uk/home/gdp/publications/.

Plotkin, G. D. (2004b). A structural approach to operational semantics, *Journal of Logic and Algebraic Programming* **60–61**: 17–139. This is a revised version of the original DAIMI memo Plotkin (1981).

Pnueli, A. (1977). The temporal logic of programs, in FOC (1977), pp. 46–57.

Pratt, V. R. (1995). Anatomy of the Pentium bug, in P. D. Mosses, M. Nielsen and M. I. Schwartzbach (eds.), *Proc. 6th Intl Joint Conf. on the Theory and Practice of Software Development, TAPSOFT 95, Aarhus, Denmark, May 22–26, 1995*. Volume 915 of *Lecture Notes in Computer Science*, Springer-Verlag, pp. 97–107.

Reed, G. and Roscoe, A. (1988). A timed model for communicating sequential processes, *Theoretical Computer Science* **58**: 249–261.

Reisig, W. (1985). *Petri Nets: An Introduction*. EATCS Monographs on Theoretical Computer Science, Volume 4, Springer-Verlag.

Roscoe, B. (1999). *The Theory and Practice of Concurrency*. Prentice-Hall International.

Schneider, S. (1995). An operational semantics for timed CSP, *Information and Computation* **116**(2): 193–213.

Schneider, S. (1999). *Concurrent and Real-time Systems: The CSP Approach*. John Wiley.

Sénizergues, G. (1998). Decidability of bisimulation equivalence for equational graphs of finite out-degree, in *Proc. 39th Annual IEEE Symp. on Foundations of Computer Science*. IEEE, pp. 120–129.

Sifakis, J. and Yovine, S. (1996). Compositional specification of timed systems (extended abstract), in C. Puech and R. Reischuk (eds.), *Proc. 13th Annual Symp. on Theoretical Aspects of Computer Science, STACS 96*, Grenoble, France, February 22–24, 1996. Volume 1046 of *Lecture Notes in Computer Science*, Springer-Verlag, pp. 347–359.

Sipser, M. (2005). *Introduction to the Theory of Computation*, second edition, Course Technology.

Sistla, A. P. and Clarke, E. M. (1985). The complexity of propositional linear temporal logics, *Journal of the ACM* **32**(3): 733–749.

Srba, J. (2002a). Strong bisimilarity and regularity of basic parallel processes is PSPACE-hard, in *Proc. 19th Intl Symp. on Theoretical Aspects of Computer Science, STACS 02*. Volume 2285 of *Lecture Notes in Computer Science*, Springer-Verlag, pp. 535–546.

Srba, J. (2002b). Strong bisimilarity and regularity of Basic Process Algebra is PSPACE-hard, in *Proc. 29th Intl Colloq. on Automata, Languages and Programming, ICALP 02*. Volume 2380 of *Lecture Notes in Computer Science*, Springer-Verlag, pp. 716–727.

Srba, J. (2002c). Undecidability of weak bisimilarity for pushdown processes, in *Proc. 13th Intl Conf. on Concurrency Theory, CONCUR 02*. Volume 2421 of *Lecture Notes in Computer Science*, Springer-Verlag, pp. 579–593.

Srba, J. (2004). *Roadmap of Infinite results, Volume 2: Formal Models and Semantics*. World Scientific Publishing Co. An online up-to-date version is available at www.brics.dk/ srba/roadmap/.

Srba, J. (2005). Timed-arc Petri nets vs. networks of timed automata, in *Proc. 26th Intl Conf. on Application and Theory of Petri Nets, ICATPN 2005*. Volume 3536 of *Lecture Notes in Computer Science*, Springer-Verlag, pp. 385–402.

Steffen, B. and Ingolfsdottir, A. (1994). Characteristic formulae for processes with divergence, *Information and Computation* **110**(1): 149–163.

Stirling, C. (1995). Local model checking games, in *Proc. 6th Intl Conf. on Concurrency Theory, CONCUR 95*. Volume 962 of *Lecture Notes in Computer Science*, Springer-Verlag, pp. 1–11.

Stirling, C. (2000). Decidability of bisimulation equivalence for pushdown processes. Research Report EDI-INF-RR-0005, School of Informatics, Edinburgh University.

Stirling, C. (2001). *Modal and Temporal Properties of Processes*. Springer-Verlag.

Tarski, A. (1955). A lattice-theoretical fixpoint theorem and its applications, *Pacific Journal of Mathematics* **5**: 285–309.

Thomas, W. (1993). On the Ehrenfeucht–Fraïssé game in theoretical computer science (extended abstract), in *Proc. 4th Intl Joint Conf. on Theory and Practice of Software Development, TAPSOFT 93*. Volume 668 of *Lecture Notes in Computer Science*, Springer-Verlag, pp. 559–568.

Tripakis, S. (1999). Verifying progress in timed systems, in *Proc. 5th Intl AMAST Workshop on Formal Methods for Real-Time and Probabilistic Systems, ARTS 99*. Volume 1601 of *Lecture Notes in Computer Science*, Springer-Verlag, pp. 299–314.

Vardi, M. Y. (1991). Verification of concurrent programs: the automata-theoretic framework, *Annals of Pure and Applied Logic* **51**(1–2): 79–98.

Vardi, M. Y. (1995). An automata-theoretic approach to linear temporal logic, in F. Moller and G. M. Birtwistle (eds.), *Proc. of the Banff Higher Order Workshop*. Volume 1043 of *Lecture Notes in Computer Science*, Springer, pp. 238–266.

Vardi, M. Y. (2001). Branching vs. linear time: final showdown, in T. Margaria and W. Yi (eds.), *Proc. TACAS*. Volume 2031 of *Lecture Notes in Computer Science*, Springer, pp. 1–22.

Vardi, M. Y. and Wolper, P. (1994). Reasoning about infinite computations, *Information and Computation* **115**(1): 1–37.

Walukiewicz, I. (2001). Pushdown processes: games and model-checking, *Information and Computation* **164**(2): 234–263.

Yannakakis, M. and Lee, D. (1993). An efficient algorithm for minimizing real-time transition systems, in Courcoubetis (1993), pp. 210–224.

Yi, W. (1990). Real-time behaviour of asynchronous agents, in Baeten and Klop (1990), pp. 502–520.

Yi, W. (1991a). *A Calculus of Real Time Systems*. Ph.D. thesis, Chalmers University of Technology, Göteborg, Sweden.

Yi, W. (1991b). CCS + time = an interleaving model for real time systems, in J. Leach Albert, B. Monien and M. Rodríguez (eds.), *Proc. 18th ICALP*, Madrid. Volume 510 of *Lecture Notes in Computer Science*, Springer-Verlag, pp. 217–228.

Index